The Putney School

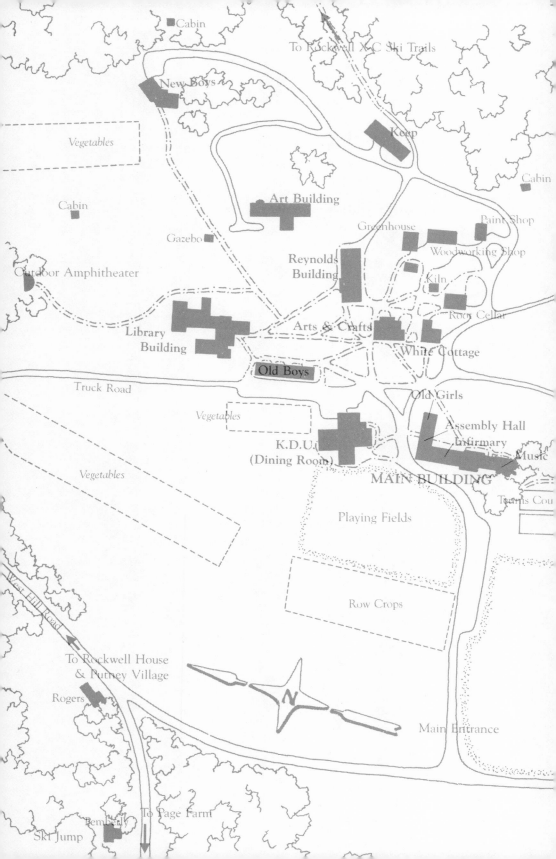

Cabin

To Rockwell X-C Ski Trails

New Boys

Keep

Vegetables

Cabin

Cabin

Art Building

Paint Shop

Greenhouse

Woodworking Shop

Gazebo

Reynolds
Building

Kiln

Outdoor Amphitheater

Root Cellar

Library
Building

Arts & Crafts

White Cottage

Old Boys

Old Girls

Truck Road

Vegetables

Assembly Hall

Infirmary

K.D.U.
(Dining Room)

Music

Vegetables

MAIN BUILDING

Tennis Cou

Playing Fields

West Hill Road

Row Crops

To Rockwell House
& Putney Village

N

Rogers

Main Entrance

Pemberly

To Page Farm

Ski Jump

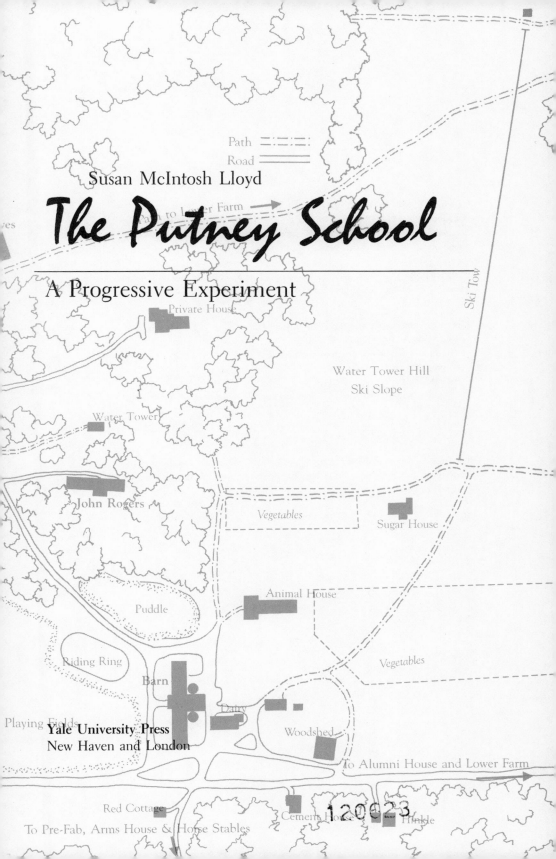

Path
Road

Susan McIntosh Lloyd

The Putney School

A Progressive Experiment

To Lower Farm

Private House

Ski Tow

Water Tower Hill
Ski Slope

Water Tower

John Rogers

Vegetables

Sugar House

Animal House

Puddle

Vegetables

Riding Ring

Barn

Dairy

Playing Fields

Woodshed

Yale University Press
New Haven and London

To Alumni House and Lower Farm

Red Cottage

Cement House

Hinkle

120023

To Pre-Fab, Arms House & Horse Stables

Designed by Nancy Ovedovitz and set in Electra type by The Composing Room of Michigan. Printed in the United States of America by Halliday Lithograph, West Hanover, Mass.

Library of Congress Cataloging-in-Publication Data
Lloyd, Susan McIntosh, 1935–
  The Putney School : a progressive experiment.
  Bibliography: p.
  Includes index.
  1. Putney School—History.   2. Boarding schools—Vermont—Putney—History.   I. Title.
LD7501.P96L56 1987   373.743'9   86-24638
ISBN 0-300-03742-2

The paper in this book meets the guidelines for permanence and durability of the Committee on Production Guidelines for Book Longevity of the Council on Library Resources.

10   9   8   7   6   5   4   3   2   1

For Bob

Contents

120623

Theodore R. Sizer

Foreword: An Outrageous School

The idea was irresponsible, even outrageous. Start a private school from scratch during a national economic depression? A boarding school too, thus especially complicated and expensive, in remote rural Vermont? And more, a *coeducational* school? (What will the boys and girls do with each other?) Furthermore, a school that expected parents to pay precious money so that their children could raise pigs, shovel manure, and wash dishes? Is *this* education? And atop this extraordinary edifice is a woman as headmaster (though she *will* call herself director, like some factory foreman . . . or forewoman). Good grief.

From such outrageousness did Putney School spring. It was a piece of the last, great flowering of progressive school building, and its founder, Carmelita Hinton, was friendly with many of the key figures in that movement. Putney reflected some, but not all, of the progressive impulses in education. It was child-centered to a fault, often at the expense of the faculty. It was utopian; the community on the Vermont hilltop was to be a microcosm of a better, more democratic world, and the lines between schooling, education, and life were to be erased. And it was deeply impaled on the paradox that has riven all progressive education, that a good school must impose and channel its adult definition of freedom; that utopia is delivered, not fashioned; that ultimate free and decent will must be autocratically educed. Putney—which, in the early days, meant Carmelita Hinton—took progressive ideas seriously. They were not mere catalogue copy. The school had the integrity to insist on them, sometimes with spectacular unanticipated consequences (such as a CIO-affiliated teachers' union and a strike). These incidents make the story of this school especially lively. Putney in its early years was not a typical school but an extreme school, a place where ideas that many merely discussed were vigorously pursued. Its very distinctiveness makes it important and gives us a glimpse of the practical playing out of ideas of wide importance in the progressive movement.

Susan McIntosh Lloyd's "biography" of Putney's first thirty years adds richness and detail to the history of education and of women, fields either neglected or pursued largely through the statements of purported leaders. The stories of Putney School and of Carmelita Hinton add an important dimension to our understanding of mid-twentieth-century American life, of the practical realization of influential ideas about schooling, of the ethos of the world of a restless, thoughtful woman, of the strains of institution building.

Putney was a little, "outrageous" school, and the determined optimism of its leader and her colleagues properly chides us, followers living in a more tentative, cautious, regulated, and unadventuresome day.

Acknowledgments

A school's history makes a lens through which past lives can be seen: young people marching or muddling their way toward maturity, adults defining the meaning of adulthood, and communities searching for exemplary mutuality. Putney School held an unusually interesting collection of lives during its first thirty years. With a confidence so large it bordered on hubris, it also dealt itself a world-reforming mission, a mission addressed to the unprecedented national and international stresses of the years 1935–65. Putney's fiftieth anniversary in 1985 was the occasion for beginning an exploration of the lives and the mission that created the school.

Many people helped to write this book. The first was a Putney School student, A. Katie Geer, '79. Her senior history project, written with Sven Huseby's guidance, involved extensive research on "The Progressive Origins of the Putney School." Katie's long paper under that title, later published by the Putney School, was based on more than twenty-five interviews with people who had launched the school. Assisted by Sue Mulcahy, who collected many archival materials for the broader history project, Katie began a dialogue by questionnaire and letter with early alumni and founding teachers, a complex interchange that Sue and I greatly extended later on. When Katie Geer died in a fire in 1982, the project lost a co-author.

A small group of alumni continued the hunt for a principal author. I took on the job when it became clear that all those who had begun the research were ready to allow me entire freedom to complete it, wherever truth might lead. With the freedom came access to a wealth of materials and historical informants, many of them contradictory: the stuff of which schools are made. Ninety-six further interviews were conducted, most of these by the author, about a third of them by the History Project Committee and others, including Margot Sproul Shaw, Ted and Elena Dodd, Laura Heller, Anne Lamont Jafferis, Judy Gregory, Peggy Squibb Stevens, Jock Glidden, and

Sue Mulcahy. Several alumni and former teachers taped their own reminiscences for me; others contributed journals, Putney letters, and notebooks. Over 380 letters and questionnaires came in from people connected with the school. The Putney alumni office helped alumni in the Boston and New York areas to organize four "history taping sessions," to which ninety-four more people came.

As the source material from willing Putney people piled up, I worked to find key teachers and alumni long out of touch with the school, whether from disillusionment or from a "putting away of childish things." Comments on school life from these, as from virtually all others, were remarkably raw and frank. When in this history one reads, "Alumni say . . ." or "Teachers say . . . ," what was said reflects themes and events mentioned over and over again. Most quotations from individuals are also confirmed by many others. I have cited individual or controversial perceptions in the endnotes. Thus, the notes include a few names of the hundreds of people who contributed to the story of the early Putney School.

The notes also mention the principal written sources for this book. Since Putney's founder did her thinking on her feet, and wrote nothing of any length, it has been especially useful to read the books that impressed her: books and essays by Friedrich Froebel, John and Evelyn Dewey, William James, and Jane Addams; Thorstein Veblen's *Theory of the Leisure Class.* Also helpful in understanding Putney adults' assumptions about youth and schooling have been works of education and social history such as Joseph Kett's *Rites of Passage: Adolescence in America from 1790 to the Present,* Lawrence Cremin's classic history of progressive education, *The Transformation of the School,* and *Public Schools in Hard Times,* by David Tyack, Robert Lowe, and Elisabeth Hansot. Novels, history books, and science texts frequently assigned by Putney teachers have also been helpful, as have walks in the woods and fields surrounding Elm Lea Farm—the setting for much local contemplation of learning and of life from 1935 on.

Four people kept track over three decades of the events and the people who make a school. Jane Arms, one of Putney's founding teachers, began writing things down in 1954. Ruth Hodgdon, the school's bookkeeper, and Nancy West, its long-time alumni secretary, know the corners and crannies of school life as no one else does. Jean Hinton Rosner has been extraordinarily generous in sharing both her perceptions of her mother's career and many of Carmelita Hinton's personal papers. The last three people have read the manuscript through, making scores of helpful suggestions. Other critics of the full book both perceptive and kind have been John Moyer, Dorothy

Tyack, Edward H. Dodd, Jr., Barbara Breasted Whitesides, Edward Yeomans, Jr., Janet Thompson Keep, Robert Lloyd, and Rustin and Millicent McIntosh. Warren Leonard and John and Anne Holden read and commented on parts I–III, filling in details that only they could have known. Finally, several thoughtful educator-historians have reviewed near-final drafts and held invaluable çonversations by letter or marginal note: Arthur Powell, of the NAIS Commission on Educational Issues, David Tyack and John Wirth of Stanford University, Kathleen Dalton of Phillips Academy, Andover, and Theodore Sizer of Brown University.

The Trustees of Putney School, Thomas Jones, Putney's director from 1974 to 1984, and its present director, Barbara Barnes, helped me by refusing to interfere, no matter what my conclusions. They also arranged for essential assistance from the alumni office staff and others. Alfred Hudson volunteered many hours of time to make the index. Clare Sullivan and Alice Persichetti prepared the manuscript with patience and skill.

The Putney School

Part I

Beginnings
1890–1936

"David! I've decided to do it!" said Carmelita Hinton to David Barnes at 6:30 one spring morning in 1934. When the phone rang, Barnes had not even had his coffee, much less recovered from the trip just completed the night before. Together the two friends had driven from Boston to Putney, Vermont, and back. "Mrs. H." wanted to look over the hilltop estate one more time before deciding to found her school there; Mr. Barnes, her architectural advisor, hoped to talk her out of it. The place was inaccessible; the scheme was impractical—no, impossible, he had told her on their way home. It was "her wildest dream yet." And here was this tireless, relentless woman who needed no coffee, telling him that she was ignoring his advice and that the Putney School would open in one short year.[1]

It did. Planted through the vision and obstinacy of one person, Putney's hardy growth would become the concern of well over a hundred—David Barnes included—by June 1936, the end of its first year.

Chapter 1

A Passion for Adventure

Carmelita Hinton had been drawn to Elm Lea Farm as like to like. The main house was outsized, the elm trees huge. The whole place looked larger than life by comparison with the smaller farms around. As one looked west over the wooded valley, Putney Mountain seemed only a little higher than the estate on West Hill; twenty-five miles to the east, Mt. Monadnock appeared to stand level with Elm Lea Farm. The whole site matched its proprietor-to-be, whose vivid energy made her look taller than she was. Her wide shoulders and face, her large smile and equally impressive frown, her long, muscular strides around her prospective school added to the illusion. And now that she had explored her new place and found it good, she could name her school for the township in which it would be rooted: the Putney School.

Mrs. H. had already drafted a letter, "Castles in the Air," to hundreds of friends and fellow-teachers describing her vision of a school, the castle in the air she had been building of late. Now it would come to earth at Elm Lea Farm. The dreamer could turn her mind to the ways in which adolescents might grow to their full strength in her school and "pattern their lives on their own convictions" in the complex world beyond.

Mrs. Hinton had cast her plan in a utopian mold, for she envisioned more than just a new school. She hoped for a new society. "What kind of human beings will be needed in the generation to come?" she asked in her prospectus, "A New Secondary School."

> If we face facts and do not dodge them to think only along comfortable lines, we must perceive that we are probably leaving behind us the kind of existence to which we and our parents and grandparents were accustomed. The need becomes increasingly imperative for people who can think straight and wish to do so, who do not want to live on the surface of the times, but have the desire, courage and moral strength to grapple with complex problems; who want to lead and not be led— living up to ideals which demand scaling difficult peaks, not down to the paths of least resistance, [those] easy imitations of what everyone else is doing.

To become such people, children—both boys and girls, since "life is coeducational"[1]—must have the chance to tackle real problems. They could assume responsibility for themselves and others in a setting where help is always needed: a working farm which puts to use humans' basic impulses to be "attached to the soil, to care for animals, to be an integral part of the cycle of the seasons." Children might build and maintain their own small houses; they would certainly help build the school. They would learn to enrich their own lives through the arts and through study of the conventional academic disciplines (Mrs. H. felt no need to describe these). Outdoor sports would abound when work was done, and families would be invited "to join in the labor and fun" during vacations. Thus may today's children lead a "very good life" while tomorrow's adults prepare to lead humanity out of the man-made plagues of economic depression and war.

Impractical. Impossibly out of line with traditional boarding schools and with nearly all the best public schools of the day. But the dream became reality. It led both the dreamer and all those she brought with her to places beyond their farthest imaginings, dark places as well as bright ones. The Putney School opened in the spring of 1935. Its first thirty years gathered an ever-increasing crowd of young people on a hilltop farm. They moved from there into lives that will ultimately tell the full story of Putney School. The story can be begun, however. Who was this woman who took dreams for plans, and how did the dreams arise?

Carmelita Chase Hinton was born in Omaha, Nebraska, in April 1890, the second child and first daughter in a family of four children. Her parents had "come from two directions," as she used to say; her mother, Lula Bell Edwards, from an old Kentucky family transplanted to California, and her father, Clement Chase, from a New England family which had arrived in Omaha in 1866. Grandfather Champion Chase had been paymaster general of the Union Army, and was looking for a new life. By the mid-1870s, the Chase family was well established in Omaha. Champion Chase was mayor of the expanding city, and his young son Clement would soon begin printing the *Excelsior*, a "society" weekly of local affairs, which he continued to publish for most of his adult life. Clement Chase worked as Washington secretary to a Nebraska senator for a few years after his graduation from the University of Nebraska, but he returned to Omaha to take up his weekly once more, to open a stationery and bookstore, and to establish himself as editor of two financial papers. And a rising young man must marry. One evening, while on a business trip in California, Chase sat down and "made a list of all the young women he would consider marrying." Forthwith he proposed to Lula Bell Edwards, the beauty at the top of the list, telling her he had, by reason and reflection, come to the conclusion that she would make the best wife a man could find.[2]

The marriage brought four healthy children to life. Carmelita remembered growing up in a house full of love, certain of her father's civic importance, admiring her mother's social gifts and philanthropic works, and constantly aware of her parents' respect for her abilities. It was a recipe for self-confidence. Clement Chase believed in equal rights for women and equal access for his sons and daughters to the responsibilities and joys of life. For Carmelita, there were plenty of joys: all-day family hikes and picnics; sleeping out on the bluffs above the Missouri River, first with her father, then with her brothers alone; learning to make pancakes in the rain. She and Clement, her older brother, rode their ponies into the surrounding countryside and struck up an acquaintance with a group of Indians, who made them blood brother and sister.[3]

Mr. Chase often traveled on railroad passes, and whenever he could, he would take one of his children along. "I have to go to Chicago tomorrow," he might say as he came in the door at night. "Is there any little girl around here who would like to go to Chicago?"[4] For eleven years, the only little girl was Carmelita, adored by her father. When baby Helena was born, Carmelita was allowed a great deal of responsibility for her. She loved children. Wherever she went as an older child or adult, babies seemed to find their way to her lap. She felt that her teaching career began during her high school years, when each afternoon she would walk away from the grinding routine of Omaha's Episcopal preparatory school to a neighbor's house and invent games or other delights for the six small children who lived there.

Public elementary school had been dull for Carmelita, its teaching by rote relieved only by occasional artwork or part-music singing. Her most vital education she gave herself (reading, by age nine, the entire works of Dickens—and many other books besides—on the floor of her father's bookstore when she went with him to "help") or received at home, listening to her father read aloud to the family every evening. She joined the Campfire Girls, whose activities at least partly matched her energy. At midnight she still had plenty of strength left to practice the piano for an hour or so. But in high school, even the relief provided by music was gone. "We were preparing for college or some kind of undefined 'life,' and I always wondered why."[5] She and her classmates were expected to concentrate their emotions on the prospect of coming out in society. Carmelita, busy with her six child-friends and her tennis matches (she was on her way to the Omaha women's championship), was not interested—but her mother was. As her unwanted debut neared, Carmelita realized that her mother's high-society, high-church values could never be hers; she could not even argue with her, as she did cheerfully with her father. "Mother always got upset at my ideas," she has ruefully said.

Yet mother and father together urged Carmelita into her choice of a college: she should go to Bryn Mawr—academically demanding and socially unquestionable. She went briefly to tutoring school to prepare for the Bryn Mawr entrance exams, which exactly and intentionally duplicated Harvard's; she entered in the fall of 1908.

Bryn Mawr was then a small, intense community of scholars and women pioneers led by President M. Carey Thomas, an uncompromising feminist whose intellectual ambitions for her students were as large as they had been for herself. Carmelita so disliked esoteric courses such as Anglo-Saxon that she decided against the English major, which required them. "I'm no scholar," she said later. Already she cared far more for the future than the past. Instead, she plunged into a French/German major, and into a heady student life which offered a multitude of opportunities for plain fun as well as leadership. She acted in class plays, she sang in the college choir. She was captain of several hockey teams in succession and became the college's champion shotputter in 1912. She consistently defeated her tennis opponents—not so much by superior skill as by wearing them out—and in her senior year was elected president of the College Athletic Association. All this she did with an exuberance none of her classmates ever forgot. She herself remembered that *"Laughing* became one of my favorite pastimes."[6]

She was also searching for commitments. To become a teacher seemed the most obvious one, especially at Bryn Mawr, whose Quaker founder had intended his college to "fit young women to be teachers of a high order." Carmelita Chase tried to imagine herself as the "heroic" teacher William James envisioned.[7] Yet teaching seemed impossible, because schools were impossibly dull. Marking time, she "adopted" an orphan in Philadelphia and acted as a kind of big sister to the girl; she began to search the college catalogue for courses that might help her in some career with children. Finally, she embarked on Bryn Mawr's one-year education program. This involved a series of challenging psychology courses, including Dr. James Leuba's elective "The Psychology of Instinct, Emotion, and the Will," three powerful elements in Carmelita's own personality. For the first time, through Friedrich Froebel, an early founder of the kindergarten movement, through Rousseau, Pestalozzi, John Dewey, and—most important—William James, she realized how much more there could be to education than schools as she had known them. As Santayana wrote, "James felt the call of the future, and the assurance that it could be made far better, totally other, than the past."[8] One of James's precepts particularly impressed Carmelita. "If you find yourself deeply stirred by what you read and see," she recalled James writing, "it is harmful for you to let this emotion dissipate itself without resultant action. Do something."[9]

Doing something came naturally to Carmelita Chase. That year, she made a new kind of alliance with her generous, ever-optimistic mother: together they brought the Philadelphia orphan girl and her sister to Omaha and found a wealthy family to adopt them. Within a few years, she would make doing something habitual, as, brick by brick, she began to build the foundation for her own unprecedented work with young people.

Also strengthened by Bryn Mawr was Carmelita's love of festivals, since the college year was measured in candlelight processions, class days, field days, and May days. She learned (and loved) speechmaking at special athletic assemblies, during one of which she "got so excited [while telling fellow students] how to have the best possible health that I said 'If you keep eating just any old thing and go to bed at any old time, some morning—*some morning*—you will wake up dead.' This brought down the house."[10] In a sense, a crusading women's college was the ideal haven from the pressures Carmelita had tried to face in Omaha, providing as it did a rich social life amid women of purpose and enthusiasm. Few of her contemporaries there had "dates" or allowed themselves even to think about sex. If anything, Bryn Mawr and other women's colleges tended to foster the notion that women were *superior* to men because of their capacity to control the "lower impulses" and to devote their finer feelings to the service of society. Throughout Carmelita's college years, this myth was driving the woman suffrage movement toward its final triumph in 1919.

Fervent spirits at Bryn Mawr attached themselves to causes of every stripe on the progressive spectrum. Though Carmelita was not a political person, her father was a Roosevelt Republican. T.R. was the president of her adolescence, the eloquent, rigidly idealistic Wilson the president of her young adulthood. More than one U.S. history buff has found a match for Carmelita Hinton's ebullience and optimism in Teddy Roosevelt, whose style of speech and action may well have reinforced hers. These were the hopeful years before World War I and the Russian Revolution, years when all problems seemed soluble by the enlightened application of human creativity and organizational skill. And who could be more fit for such a task than the heroic teacher? "The problem of the twentieth century is to make education an engine for social betterment," wrote Frank Tracy Carlton, an eminent sociologist. Progressive politics made fertile soil for the work of statesmen and schoolmen alike. Progressives envisioned the profound improvement of society as educated individuals at all social levels gradually transformed their political and economic environment.[11] Even Bryn Mawr, with its rigorous traditional curriculum, was instilling the skills that many of its graduates—including Carmelita Chase Hinton—would use to transform traditional schools.

College had been fine, but Bryn Mawr's "Miss Chase" was glad to return in the summer of 1912 to the Midwest. President Thomas, for all her grand accomplishments, Carmelita thought "too much in love with England and English ways."[12] To join her father as a writer on *The Excelsior* and to help him in his many efforts to bring the arts and culture to Omaha seemed for a while a welcome change. It took her a year to decide that her father was too easy an employer, that she must move out on her own to reach adulthood.

Carmelita chose Chicago, for she was eager somehow to enter the world of childhood education that Francis Parker, John Dewey, and their followers had been building there since the 1890s. But how? She tossed aside the Chicago University people's advice to take five further years of nurse's training and study of kindergarten teaching, knowing from experience how much more she could learn from experience. "What would I actually know about children after five *more* years of school?" she asked herself. She had heard much of Hull House, Jane Addams' renowned settlement house in the middle of Chicago's west-side immigrant section. When she learned that Miss Addams might need secretarial help, she went to see her in the summer of 1913 and arranged to work two days every week in return for room and board, first as a substitute secretary, then as a Hull House volunteer. She would stay for two-and-a-half years.

Hull House had been founded in 1889, wrote Jane Addams, "to provide a center for a high civic and social life," to "test the value of human knowledge by action," and to "express . . . in terms of [such] action the spirit of Christ."

> It is an experimental effort to aid in the solution of the social and industrial problems which are engendered by the modern conditions of life in a great city. . . . It is an attempt to relieve, at the same time, the over-accumulation at one end of society and the destitution at the other.

Men had largely failed to address these issues. It was time for women to try. [13] Although Jane Addams herself was usually preoccupied—with any problem from world peace to city garbage collection—Carmelita came to know her quite well. "She had a way of drawing people out"; she would stop by Carmelita's bedroom almost every evening on the way to her own to ask how the day had gone. Also admirable were the other experienced, devoted women social workers, the neophyte labor organizers of both sexes, and the aspiring political reformers lately sprung from elite colleges.

Carmelita found Hull House and its founder enormously inspiring. Jane Addams convinced her that "you can't just bathe babies. You've got to go deep down and really change things whether people like it or not." [14] She took to herself Miss Addams' educational philosophy, which brought to life the readings of the Bryn Mawr education course. The Hull House programs for children emphasized the "social value" of each child's experience and the child's complementary need to understand his place both in the immediate community and in "the industrial organization as a whole." [15] Carmelita volunteered her help to the collegiate placement office in the mornings, and to play groups in the afternoon. Watching her groups and the older children's clubs, she saw how powerful music and drama could be in bringing together people of diverse ethnic traditions. Daily her experience confirmed Froebel's concept of the arts as a means for both shaping and expressing the inmost self. [16]

At supper, the residents were often joined by youth workers who lived in the flats nearby, or by former Hull House residents. One of the latter was Edward Yeomans, an intense young engineer with small children of his own. Yeomans had become deeply involved in bringing the ideas of progressive education to the public schools in Winnetka, where he lived. An Andover graduate, he was determined there would be no more Andovers like the tradition-bound academy he had known. Before long he would become chairman of the school board that brought Carlton Washburne to the Winnetka superintendency. He was already outlining in his own mind the ideas on progressive teaching that he later celebrated in his "ringing critique of the academic lockstep," *Shackled Youth*. [17] They were the very ideas he would cheer on at the Putney School.

In such dinner-table conversations such as those with Yeomans and in Carmelita's work at Hull House, the principles of progressive education converged. What could make more sense than to "respect the child," as Dewey enjoined teachers—to search out each child's needs or particular strengths, to allow all learning to be powered by the human desire to understand the world and to engage in the life of an ever-widening community? Carmelita embraced these progressive ideas as her own because they *were* her own. It was easy enough to respect the child when you had loved children ever since you could remember. It was equally natural for her to stay clear of the pseudo-Freudian branch of progressive education, which blithely advocated clearing away all repressive adult demands so that children might grow like flowers toward their natural goodness and competence. Love in Carmelita's family had been expressed in the high expectations her parents and her older brother, Clement, held for her, as well as in the joys of adventurous play. At its best, the Victorian family challenged the individual to perfect herself. Now technological and economic changes demanded that individuals join to create a new social order and a democratic politics capable of managing the vast and complex urban-industrial economic system. It was not a job for grown "flowers," but for resourceful, scientifically trained adults, who could use new knowledge of human development and social organization along with the new technology to create a humane future for all.

And women must be equal partners in this grand enterprise. Carmelita's association with the powerful women of Hull House brought this home to her as no Bryn Mawr chapel talk could do. Ready for life as she was, these women offered her a rich induction into the adult world. "The desire for action, the wish to right wrong haunts them daily," wrote Jane Addams of the settlement house residents.[18] Their example confounded the popularized psychology that many progressives had embraced—Victorian concepts of woman enshrined in scientific terms by such as G. Stanley Hall, founder of the child-study movement and author of the 2000-page best-seller, *Adolescence*. "Woman's body and soul are made for maternity," Hall told his eager audience. She works not "by consciousness [but] by intuition and feeling. . . . Her sympathetic and ganglionic system is relatively to the cerebrospinal more dominant."[19] Through their daily work, Jane Addams and her colleagues made nonsense of such "scientific" conclusions.

In these years from 1913 to 1915, Hull House resounded with talk of education. Scattered through the Midwest, experimental schools were demonstrating the strength of progressive ideas in the face of what Yeomans called the "oceanic inertia" of traditional education both public and private. In Chicago, the University's Laboratory School (founded by John and Evelyn Dewey) and the Francis Parker School both went back two decades or more, as did the Menomonie, Wisconsin, public schools, which were demonstrating that schools and their agricultural workshops could be centers for the effective teaching of scientific skills vital to rural progress. The Gary, Indiana, and Winnetka public schools were subjects of daily conversation around the dinner tables in Hull House, where Dewey, Ella Flagg Young, and other progressives had often been welcome guests. Almost certainly Carmelita Chase heard how the new Gary Plan involved students in shop work, kitchen and garden work, art, and music; how it brought them together for assemblies and scattered them abroad for individual projects or for field trips through the industrialized city.[20] Central aspects of the Gary Plan would be reproduced in miniature at the Putney School.

Though Chicago had lost Dewey to Columbia's Teachers College in New York, the Midwest remained a center of innovation, especially for the play-school and kindergarten movements now finding a foothold in America. It was the prospect of joining these movements that finally impelled Carmelita to return to school herself. In the fall of 1914, her second year at Hull House, she enrolled in the playground course under Neva Boyd at the new Chicago School of Civics and Philanthropy.

What she learned there "fed [her] like a thirsty plant."[21] "This year made the real beginning of my constant work in the education of children," she said.

> At the school I took two different courses. The morning course was the active one; we learned carpentry, how to use hand saws and planes, and the things that we would let the children use. . . . We'd find a song, we'd have to learn it by heart, sing it, know the music and be able to take a class ourselves and teach them. . . . We treated ourselves as children, then we treated ourselves as teachers. . . .
>
> In the afternoon course, people came in to lecture—people who worked in the city doing all different things. They'd be working in the newspapers, working in the courts; working where there were problems to be solved. . . . They knew their stuff. They didn't just lecture in an academic way. . . . They taught courses in sociology and economics, but when they came to our school they were coming from everyday jobs: social welfare, hospitals, public works of all kinds.

From these talks, from her Hull House companions, and from her many trips through the city, she also learned much of Chicago itself, its dangers as well as its exciting cultural life. "Man is a stranger in the modern world," wrote Joseph Lee that same year in his influential book *Play and Education*, his inner life is "defeated" by urban conditions. City youth precociously enter a social world littered with snares for the weak. Carmelita Chase recalled all the more fondly the hikes and camping trips of her Nebraska childhood, and began to think of leaving Chicago.[22]

Carmelita did not quite finish the two-year playground course because one evening Yeomans brought a friend of his to Hull House, a brilliant young patent lawyer[23] named Sebastian Hinton. "Ted" Hinton had been born into a distinguished, intellectual English family, and his interests were as broad as Carmelita's, though more political. Between heady discussions of Thorstein Veblen's *Theory of the Leisure Class*, Ted proposed marriage to her. Their wedding took place in April 1916. The couple found an apartment near the Francis Parker School that looked out on a park ideal for a nursery play class. Carmelita began one immediately and continued it through most of her first pregnancy. After their daugher Jean was born, the Hintons bought a house outside the city in Winnetka, and within a year, the new baby was listening from her carriage to the joyful clamor of the first school founded by Carmelita Hinton.

For Mrs. Hinton "had been fired with enthusiasm about the new nursery schools. . . . With William James's admonition not the least bit faded in my memory, I started such a school in my own backyard in our carpentry shop, with my own and my neighbors' children for pupils."[24] There were twelve children the first year, twenty-four the second (when Billy Hinton was born), and thirty-six the third, with two more teachers and visiting artists for the children's delight. Mrs. Hinton was now putting into action all she had learned of children in the previous half-dozen years. Her pupils knew nothing of the elementary school routine that their teacher had found so dreary as a schoolgirl, of the punishments for petty offenses by which she had been humiliated, of the traditional school's emphasis on classical learning, which John Dewey found so class-bound and so contrary to democratic culture.[25]

Yet her reaction against her own rigid schooling had nothing to do with permissiveness. Her resistance to this post-Dewey strain of the progressive education movement was now strengthened by her experience as a parent. She saw that her children needed discipline as well as room for growth. As Jean joined her nursery classes, and later Billy and Joan Hinton came to Putney School, it was as though she had arranged both schools above all for them.

She taught all the nursery children through shop work and through play. "The play group is society epitomized," Neva Boyd had written: "When the child attempts to take more than his share of 'turns,' the protest is immediate and expressed in terms he understands."[26] Thus did Mrs. Hinton's nursery pupils satisfy Dewey's conviction that "Democracy is more than a form of government; it is primarily a mode of associated living [in which each] individual has to refer his own action to that of others." In Ted Hinton's shop, the children began to make those connections with the world of adult technology that Dewey considered essential to the well-socialized child of an industrial age. Moreover, they had a wonderful time. Mrs. Dorothea Smith Ingersoll, sent to the nursery school as a small child by her educator father, Perry Dunlap Smith, vividly recalls the excitement her teacher engendered.

> I remember her with a great deal of warmth. I remember her almost boisterously. She would come into a room and it was an explosion. But it was a happy occasion. She could sweep people up and carry them off to Mars. You'd believe anything she told you. I can see her in the room, in the house where the kindergarten was held, talking to people, talking to children, and the children all looking at her, spellbound. She was a dynamic person who never came on quietly. Noise, I associate with her, joyful noise.

Ted Hinton found some of his happiest moments working with his wife on nursery school carpentry projects. Jean and Billy Hinton also joined in the fun, embarking on their multifaceted childhood roles as their mother's pupils, advisors, and inspiration. "She was an energetic, enthusiastic person," Mrs. Ingersoll continues. "She went after her own children energetically and enthusiastically, just as she went after the challenge of setting up a nursery school."[27] The last Hinton baby, Joan, was the youngest child enrolled. Mrs. Hinton's circle of loyal parents and admirers grew ever wider. Before long she was having to turn away as many children as she gathered in.

In 1923, Ted Hinton, whose tendency to depression seemed to have been intensified by a series of minor illnesses, traveled to the Riggs Psychiatric Clinic in Stockbridge, Massachusetts, hoping for relief. While he was there he hanged himself.[28]

It was a terrible tragedy for his young family. No explanation could ever really make the act comprehensible for Carmelita, nor could she bring herself to share the pain of her husband's suicide with her friends or her children. Friends remembered him as "a wonderful man." His children thought of him as a warmhearted teacher, the parent most responsible for their appreciation of craftsmanship and their love of animals. Jean says her chief recollection of her father is his almost weekly gift to her of some animal, wild or tame, and his patient teaching of its care. She also remembers the morning family bathroom scene—her father shaving and talking, her mother sweeping the children through those daily cold-water baths required by the most modern physicians.[29]

According to Mrs. Ingersoll, her parents saw Ted Hinton as "a genius who never found his location." His death, however, seemed to impel his widow to locate herself all the more firmly in her chosen work. Mrs. Hinton gave up the nursery school and found a position teaching kindergarten at the North Shore Country Day School in Winnetka, a private elementary school begun by parents for whom even the Winnetka public schools were too conservative, and directed by Mrs. Ingersoll's father, Perry Dunlap Smith, who had lived progressive reform since early childhood. Smith's grandmother Lucy Flowers had helped to found Hull House, and he himself had attended the Francis Parker School. As near neighbor to the Hintons, Perry Smith had worked with Ted Hinton to design and build the original jungle gym in the Hinton backyard, a step away from the bamboo model Ted's mathematician father had once made in order to demonstrate the fourth dimension to some of his students. The Hinton and Smith children had hours of fun climbing around it. (Though Ted Hinton's company didn't keep the patent on the later metal version, sales of the wooden jungle gym and savings invested in the Wrigley Chewing Gum Company provided a continuing, if modest, income for Mrs. Hinton over many years.) Smith did all he could to close a little the gap that Ted's death had left, becoming Mrs. Hinton's close friend and advisor as well as her employer.

It was a good job and an active, healing two years for Mrs. Hinton, but she decided not to stay on. "Winnetka was becoming a society suburb," she remembered.[30] If she couldn't bring up her children in real country, she might do best to move back to a city for a while. She had heard much of the new Shady Hill School in Cambridge, Massachusetts, another parent-founded elementary school whose faculty and principal combined progressive methods with the educated New Englander's passion for high culture. The arts flourished there; so did a cheerful Puritanism that relished intellectual challenge, preferably in frigid temperatures (early students brought sleeping bags to the open-air classrooms in winter time). Shady Hill needed a second-grade teacher. Mrs. Hinton applied and was accepted sight unseen.

In the late summer of 1925, the Hintons "hit Cambridge like a cyclone," says one old family friend.[31] They found and settled into a large Victorian house on Avon Street, with a barn that soon filled up with animals. Every school morning after 1927, all three children rode their ponies to the new Shady Hill Campus near the Charles River, with a valiant collie loping behind. Watching them with awe as they negotiated traffic and trolley tracks, the neighbors dubbed them "the Suicide Club"—"but we never had even one accident," Mrs. Hinton said. In the winter, the children made shafts out of garden rakes for their flexibile flyers and sleighed to school behind their ponies, while their mother drove Whiz-Bang, a vigorous pinto gelding.

In Shady Hill's second-grade classroom, Mrs. Hinton was Whiz-Bang herself. John Coolidge had the luck to be there that first year, and he has never forgotten it. Every day there was a new plan: a Hinton family sheep to be sheared, then its wool washed and dried, carded and spun, then looms constructed so the wool could be woven into cloth by small hands, guided, if necessary, by large, kindly ones.[32] The class visited a sugar refinery and came back to draw up an exhibit of sugar production, from cane field to dinner table. These were not original teaching methods. Mrs. Hinton knew they had been used in many progressive schools, beginning with those organized by Francis Parker and the Deweys in the 1890s. But the commanding energy that she brought to her work made it new for all those around her.

Certainly the Shady Hill second graders experienced "the creative power of integrated group functioning" that Neva Boyd celebrated so often in her writing and her teaching of teachers.[33] By spring, the sheep must have been tired of all the attention he was getting; he escaped down Kirkland Street, running all the way to Brattle Street with Carmelita Hinton and a dozen second graders following behind. An alert policeman captured the sheep, and a construction worker lent a wheelbarrow on which he was loaded and wheeled back to the school—the sheep truculent, the children triumphant. In short order Mrs. Hinton and her pupils had made a song about the whole adventure; to this day it is remembered word for word by several alumni.[34]

When Shady Hill moved the following year to its Coolidge Hill campus off Mt. Auburn Street, the second-grade projects expanded to fill the new space. In the winter of 1927, children began bringing home measured carpenter's drawings they had made themselves—plans for real child-sized two-story houses. They and their teacher were going to build a town all their own! And the parents had better like it, because a little help would be needed. A few, like architect David Barnes, must have given more than a little help, for the Barnes children's houses always displayed a panache lacking in humbler structures. However, by far the bulk of the plan making and building was done by the children under their teacher's guidance, so that no one had failed to learn multidigit addition and subtraction by the end of second grade. Many had simple geometry, multiplication, and division under their belts as well by the time the town was laid out, the houses completed, and the post office and railroad station built. The top of the year was the spring night spent in the houses, now furnished with sheep's-wool rugs and fired clay dishes, with parents bringing breakfast to their sleepless, exhilarated children in the morning. "How we looked forward to second grade!" says an alumna who remembers her desperate envy of an older brother.

Carmelita settled in to stay at Shady Hill, flourishing as teacher under principal Katharine Taylor (a graduate of Francis Parker School and Vassar) and enjoying the friendship and support of an extraordinary group of colleagues. Back on Avon Street, the Hinton family began to grow, boarding children of faraway families who wanted their daughters and sons to go to Shady Hill. On weekends the whole gang might pile into Mrs. Hinton's 1923 Franklin touring car and drive to the beach or the mountains. In the summer, the Hintons took off, traveling to Mexico, to the Isle of Skye, and other points west and north. On a sea voyage off the Mexican coast in 1928, Mrs. Hinton found that John and Evelyn Dewey were fellow passengers. They had six days to talk over education and schools and the differences between the two. [35]

Liebe Coolidge Winship remembers how she learned that the Hinton crowd was about to arrive at the Coolidge summer home in Northern Vermont. Her mother

> picked up the phone, and heard it over the party line. 'Well, Elvira, I'll tell you how to make them mustard pickles. You just take . . . LAND! Did you see what just went by? One of them tourin' cars with a lady driving' and ten or twelve, no— thu'teen children, and a dog. And a goat! Yes, there's a goat hangin' out the back seat. Must be some kind of gypsies!'

Another summer the four Hintons made the Coolidges' farm one stop on a horseback trip from the Hinton summer house at the arts colony in Woodstock, N.Y. to the Hudson River, down the Hudson on the night boat to Manhattan, where they and the horses caught the ferry to Maine to stay with friends. They mounted again after a week and traveled by train and dirt road to the Coolidges'. Another week and they were off for the two-hundred-mile ride back to Cambridge. "Your adventures make my youth look like kindergarten," wrote Edward Yeomans (whose youth had been more adventurous than most) to the Hinton family some years later. "You should write a book about yourselves, and call it 'The Indestructible Hintons' or 'The All-Weather, Heavy-Duty, Uncollapsible Hintons.'"

As the indestructible Hinton children grew, the Cambridge house seemed to shrink; in 1931, Mrs. Hinton found a burnt-out house on a little farm in Weston, fifteen miles west of Shady Hill, hired David Barnes to supervise its rebuilding, and moved the family there. Now there were a tennis court and a pond. There was barn space for chickens, a pig, and two cows as well as for ten horses—and a rider for each horse, six boarders having come along with the family. A couple had been hired to cook and to run the farm. Carmelita's mother, "a beautiful grandmother," had come to join her.[36] The Hintons went on long weekend expeditions to the Catskills and the White Mountains. "It was action, action, action," says Liebe's older brother John, who went to board at the Weston house and ride his horse with Jean and Bill each weekday for two years to the Cambridge School nearby. Both boarders and Hinton children cared for their horses, helped the resident farmer with chores, and shared the weekend fun. "My God! The things we did!" says Coolidge. Much later, Carmelita Hinton told her Putney School colleague Jane Arms that after her husband's death, she had put her faith in the power of vigorous activity to generate trust in life and to dispel the depression toward which every adolescent tended at times.[37]

It could be wearing. Liebe Coolidge went along on a hundred-mile horse-back ride from Weston to Westport to spend spring vacation on the beach. "It was great fun for us," Liebe says; "I was fascinated by her, but a little afraid, too. She always made me feel that I was Okay, but a little lazy. If I really tried, I could do ever so much better." Jean, Bill, and Joan Hinton tended to be held up as models for the boarders to emulate. This was sometimes annoying to both parties, but it could be amusing, too. John Coolidge and the other boarders relished a life so adventurous that it verged at times on an entire denial of danger. At the same time, Coolidge recalls, Mrs. Hinton was "repressively Victorian" toward their barely repressible sexuality. At least some of the fervent activity of the household seemed designed to dilute and replace undesirable urges. One who is really noble doesn't even feel such urges. Boys especially are "*that way*. Now when my Billy feels *that way* he goes and chops down a tree."

"Her Billy" has different memories. He recalls only his mother's entire trust in him, and her success at communicating the beauty of loving, romantic relationships such as the one he remembers his parents having had. It was natural, however, for Mrs. Hinton to be more anxious about the boarders' behavior and to instruct them accordingly. This small coeducational experiment would have been ruined by a single pregnancy. She preached against outward snares as well: liquor, coffee, cigarettes. John remembers the thrill of sneaking into the kitchen and talking in whispers with the farmer while they sat around the table with him, reveling in the cups of coffee he poured for each one. The boarders felt two ways about Mrs. Hinton's strategies for household reform. On the one hand they grumbled, resenting her efforts to change them whether they liked it or not; on the other, they admired their energetic guardian, loved living with her, and "were jealous as hell of her kids, who really *were* virtuous."[38]

It was during the Weston years that Mrs. Hinton learned about the Experiment in International Living, a year-old venture that exactly suited the internationalist idealism she had brought with her from Hull House. Donald Watt took her on as an Experiment leader for a trip to Austria and Germany in 1933. This was merely a further expansion of her family: of the fifteen Experimenters in Mrs. Hinton's charge, eight were related to her. The following summer she led a trip through France to Nazi Germany. In their travels, the group visited the Collège Cevenol and other European progressive high schools. In Germany, to Mrs. Hinton's disappointment, Hitler had already rooted out the Oldenwaldschule and other schools she had learned to admire. But the young people got to live with German families, then, with their German "brothers" and "sisters," join a German leader to go bicycling. They watched—and briefly helped out on—an outdoor construction project at a youth camp.

For an enthusiast and her children, it was a heady introduction to the German youth movement. Her political self-education having taken second place to other concerns, Mrs. Hinton entirely missed the connection between the Nazis' military preparations and the rugged, uniformed outdoor youth-camp life with its songs and its drills. What excited her was the young people's genuinely fervent participation in making a society work, pulling it out of the ruinous Depression of the pre-Hitler years. Much of the fun and German-American camaraderie Mrs. Hinton created herself. The American students were soon in rebellion against the German coleader, who demanded that the whole group line up two abreast for bicycling and stop and go by his whistle. "Why?" they wanted to know. They all piled into each other several times to show what they thought of this regimentation. Finally, they came to their first real hill, writes Jean Hinton Rosner. "The leader slowed down. The teenagers, full of energy, simply passed him. He blew his whistle. The Americans ignored the whistle and kept on to the top and soon the German youth followed suit. They disappeared ahead." The German leader departed in disgust, "taking the first train back to the city," and leaving his restive troops in Mrs. Hinton's charge. "The German kids had never had such freedom, and they were delighted," said Mrs. Hinton.[39]

The large German and American group proceeded by bicycle from youth hostel to youth hostel, paddled faltboats down the Mosel, and had a wonder-

ful holiday. At one hostel they heard that Adolf Hitler would be speaking in a
field nearby, and all walked over to listen. Two thousand throats opened and
roared when *der Führer* appeared; Hitler roared his speech as well in his
usual style. Mrs. Hinton, ordinarily fearless, found herself horrified, although she was no more aware than most Germans or Americans "what
Nazism would become."[40] Uppermost in her mind was the major purpose of
all Experiment trips: "to create better understanding among young people in
order to avoid future wars," in the words of a refugee from Nazism who first
met Mrs. Hinton on one of the German Experiment trips. When the group
got off the boat in New York a month later, four boys wore swastika arm-
bands given them by German friends, and Bill and Joan Hinton raised their
arms in the Nazi salute.[41]

The year 1934 promised change. Throughout the last academic year,
Shady Hill colleagues remember Mrs. Hinton talking about her disappointment with the Cambridge School in Weston—her sense that even in this
"progressive" secondary school, with its "Dalton Plan" of projects and unit
study, learning for Jean and Billy had been reduced to college preparation.[42]
Elementary school had been for them "a delight, an enchanted land . . . full
of singing, playing of instruments, carpentering, acting . . . learning to think
scientifically, to figure with intelligence, to read with avidity . . . and that was
not an easy diet, but a hard one." Why now should "the shadows of the old
pedagogy" fall between the young person and the real world, obscuring both
his responsibilities toward that world and the joy of learning? Why should play
be organized in the "fierce, competitive spirit" that dominated high schools
outside the classroom?[43] While Mrs. Hinton's Shady Hill pupils—now the
third graders—found their teacher as inventive and ebullient as ever (their
projects included the building of a Viking village on the playfield and an
elaborate concrete relief map of Boston Harbor), her mind was often on a
puzzle: Why were there so few secondary schools as good for growing children
as Shady Hill and the other truly progressive elementary schools?

One day in early spring she was driving from Weston to Woodstock alone,
the pieces of the puzzle shifting in her mind, and quite suddenly she knew
her solution. She would begin a school herself, a school without shadows. It
must be "coeducational, in real country, a school on a farm, with plenty of
room." To make real the early progressives' image of the "educational village," it must be a boarding school, integrating academic learning with an
active, purposeful community life. As the car sped along, she realized how
much suspicion such a school would raise in an age when the fully coeduca-

tional boarding school was almost unknown in the United States. Most of those few that existed were tiny and impermanent, or were small boarding departments within much larger day schools like the Cambridge School. A few Quaker institutions such as the George School offered coeducation "under guarded home conditions," separating the sexes outside adult-supervised activities. Only Marietta Johnson's Edgewood School and small Cherry Lawn approached Mrs. Hinton's vision, and these two had suffered constant financial difficulty.[44]

None of these concerns cast doubt on her new dream. She returned to Weston the same evening and, she wrote, "gathered my children around me and unfolded my plan."[45] She enlarged eagerly on the work that would be required, and finally, since it would be a family project, asked their permission to go ahead. There were no dissents.

Evidence indicates that Mrs. Hinton's compelling inspiration was not so sudden as she suggests. The 1920s saw a proliferation of experimental private schools, some of which she knew about and admired. In the files lies a single letter, written but never mailed.

> Dear Mrs. [no name given]:
> I remember when I met you two summers ago on my sister's, Helena Johnson's, porch in Winnetka that you said you longed to have a school for boys and girls preparing for college out on a ranch, that you were sure they could lead a free life and a life that at the same time would not unfit them for that bugbear, college entrance. Has anything ever come of your dream? I have a child who is entering the last year of Shady Hill School this year, the ninth grade, and, as I look about me here, there does not seem to be any next school that is ideal.

The last sentence suggests a date as early as 1929, when Jean Hinton was nearing high school age; so does the next part of the letter, which describes an inspiring speech Mrs. Hinton had just heard: Francis Froelicher of Avon-Old-Farms School describing his plan for the Fountain Valley boys' school near Colorado Springs, a school he founded in 1930. She was "fired with enthusiasm" for his ideas on arts and academics and education for democracy. "Young people go often to Europe but seldom West." Don't you think we might work out a similar scheme for both boys and girls, who will actually take part in ranch life, "grow up together and learn to know each other . . . through working together?" I want, she finishes, "to *do* something as you see and not dream."

By 1934, Carmelita Hinton was ready to push ahead on her own. She immediately began drafting her prospectus and trying out her idea on Cambridge friends, realizing that if she moved fast enough, Billy and Joan could be students at her school. Much later, she would say to a friend, "I decided that if I was going to struggle with my own three children, I might as well struggle with fifty."[46]

Mrs. H. asked her Shady Hill colleague, Isabel Stephens, to design a curriculum and schedule that would allow for much more than mere college preparation, both inside the classroom and out. And she asked Katharine Taylor for a year's leave to try to bring her dream to fruition, a request quickly granted. Her nine years at Shady Hill had been wonderful ones—she felt she had learned more there than at Bryn Mawr—but she realized that she badly needed a break from teaching,[47] and that the new task she had set herself was enormous.

Now to find a *place*. On weekends, Mrs. Hinton drove all over New England, sometimes with David Barnes in tow, looking at farms for sale. There were many in those hard days, and not all had been bought up by corporation lawyers hoping for a hedge against disaster, but none seemed just right. Some time that spring, however, Edward Yeomans heard of her plans, and wrote to her. He thought he might have found the place she needed: Elm Lea Farm in Putney, Vermont, which had just been offered to him as the ideal site for a school.

In the twenty years since Edward Yeomans and Carmelita Chase had met at Hull House, Yeomans had become increasingly involved in progressive education. He had retired from his business and engineering work in Chicago and founded the Ojai Valley elementary school in California at the urging of local parents, staying in Ojai long enough to make certain that his great love for carpentry, for nature in all its intricacies, for literature, and for the singing and playing of music could be shared by the children as a central aspect of their education. He had also been consultant to the founders of Antioch, Bennington, and Black Mountain Colleges.

In that spring of 1934, the Misses Mary and Sarah Andrews, owners of Elm Lea Farm, who had read Yeomans' latest design for "A Small Rural Private School," invited him to realize his plan at their family estate, a working farm with twenty-five pure-bred cows. The large central house and attached dormitory and assembly hall had been in active use as a summer theater school. The directors of the theater school, Katherine Everts and Elizabeth Whitney, had tried to extend the reach of their highly successful Camp Arden to a year-long drama school at Elm Lea, but the Depression had stifled all plans. Yeomans answered no to the four ladies' proposal; one school-founding was enough. But he knew a woman named Carmelita Hinton. . . . Within the month, Mrs. H. and her son Billy had driven up to Elm Lea to see for themselves that the place promised fair.

In June, Miss Everts and Miss Whitney invited Mrs. Hinton to visit them at Camp Arden and Elm Lea Farm, bringing her two Shady Hill friends and fellow-planners Isabel Stephens and Betty Frothingham. There were a few odd moments: the ladies offering breakfast coffee specially made, the stalwart Cambridge women refusing; the ladies, dressed in "ground-sweeping gowns," sitting down in their formal garden to begin negotiations with a woman far more at home in riding breeches; an aging actor, also visiting, dashing through in white tie and tails, loudly declaiming, "Now is the winter of our discontent. . . ." But Mrs. Hinton was delighted with Elm Lea. She already saw in the elegant drawing rooms of the main house a serviceable pair of classrooms. The coach house, the farmer's house (the White Cottage) with the huge barn in back—all proclaimed Elm Lea a farm, and that was what she wanted. She took one look at the carriage shed and had the boys' dorm planned. She met Clyde Hulett, the teamster, and Edwin and Mabel Gray, the young couple who kept farms and grounds and household in order for the Drama School. It would more than do. It was the ideal place for Putney School, if the four ladies would let her have it.

They would. They were willing to pass on the place to Mrs. Hinton on a one-year trial, renewable for two years at a $1.00 rent, before final sale for about $20,000, and would continue to pay tax and insurance bills throughout the three-year trial period. When the new school was incorporated not-for-profit, Miss Everts and Miss Whitney would be included on the board of directors. Mrs. H., fearing that the two women wished to run her school for her, traded the last provision for a charter that gave her "very great powers" as principal.[48] The ladies also specified that Yeomans (who soon purchased a house in East Putney) be the school's educational advisor.

It was an extraordinarily generous offer. Miss Everts and Miss Whitney had invested over $40,000 in Elm Lea since the Andrewses had turned it over to them. Nearly all furnishings would go to the new school, including a hundred place settings of silver plate and linen, dormitory beds, elegant polished Victorian end tables, and chairs. It took enormous imagination and trust for the Elm Lea owners to be so willing to give over the place to the rough-and-tumble Hinton crowd, and to envision there a successful secondary school.

There remained for the rest of the family to visit and delightedly agree on Elm Lea Farm, then for architect David Barnes to disapprove both site and buildings—and be roundly, exuberantly countermanded by this adventurer too much in motion to turn back, Carmelita Hinton.

Chapter 2

One to Get Ready

Within a week, Mrs. Hinton was standing at the Shady Hill mimeograph machine, grinding out her finished prospectus. She paused before the mailbox to realize that this act would commit her irrevocably to a course more hazardous than any she had taken before, then mailed the letters to educators, friends, and friends of friends all over the United States.[1]

"Carmelita Hinton's life has a mythic quality," a journalist has written, "a singleness of purpose, a constancy of major themes."[2] The seven-page prospectus carries forward the major themes that Mrs. Hinton had been composing in her mind and playing out in her experience ever since she had first read James and Dewey in college. She had written the progressive philosophers' theories into her prospectus to introduce Putney School to others, but as always her confidence in their ideas derived from her confidence in her own. "I never really doubted that the school would succeed," she has said. "There was no time to be afraid."[3] So certain was she of her approach that she would be able to resist every diversion and, for better or worse, to slough off most criticisms as though they had not been made at all. As Mrs. Ingersoll has said, "She would fly in the face of any convention. . . . She'd fight anyone to the death if she believed in the principle."[4] Until her own death she always spoke of the Putney School as *"my* school." While she had an extraordinary gift of recognition that discovered kindred spirits in friends and prospective teachers outwardly unlike her, she could never cope with fundamental disagreement or even give it sympathetic consideration. Ultimately it was the authority of her own experience that guided her. "Stubborn?" said her close friend Jane Arms. "You might as well call the root stubborn for holding up the tree."[5] Even while it sowed problems for almost everyone around her, Mrs. Hinton's obstinate self-confidence was a priceless asset to the new Putney School.

Arguments and revisions came back in the mail throughout summer and

23

early fall from those who had received the prospectus. Several friendly critics agreed: the less said about the virtually unprecedented plan for full coeducation in a New England boarding school, the better.[6] Mrs. Hinton did not need to assure parents (or warn prospective students) that "romances . . . died in the daily contact of one sex with another" when they had surfaced in her extended household and on the Experiment trips abroad. At least one correspondent commended her assertion that adolescence is the time when young people "first wake up to the meaning of the mature world, wish to become a part of it—to test their powers," appreciating that they would be able to do so through the farm and construction work of the Putney School community. However, this same critic did *not* think it wise for Mrs. Hinton to add that "it is this . . . impulse to work hard for a cause—for something bigger than themselves—that the Germans and Italians have so capitalized in their youth organizations."[7] Mrs. Hinton, never in love with her own phraseology, welcomed the suggestions and deleted the questionable sentences in the final printed brochure for parents, prospective students, and teachers.

Many arguments came from friends incredulous at Mrs. Hinton's timing. The Depression was near its deepest trough; private schools were closing on every hand. Free enterprise seemed to be on the barricades, yet Carmelita Hinton proposed to open a new private school for which no sure market existed. However, the Depression worked two ways. It "helped us, as well as hindering us at every turn," Isabel Stephens says. For example, neither Elm Lea Farm, nor the 900-acre neighboring Houghton Farm soon added to it, would have been available in flush times. Furthermore, extraordinary teachers were looking for jobs. So were some young professionals willing to try anything that would put bread on the table.

Most profoundly for an innovative enterprise like Putney School, the Crash had called into question every social and economic assumption on which industrial America had been building since the Civil War. Progressive education had originally arisen out of a broad movement for democratic reform. Now it appeared that the reforms had been woefully incomplete. The failure of thousands of banks and the disappearance of millions of jobs, the terrible suffering of particular groups such as blacks, textile and coal workers, sharecroppers and Southwestern farmers, made it clear that the 1920s boom had been hollow all along for many Americans. Even before Franklin Roosevelt took office in 1933, progressive thinkers were finding an audience once more.

As historian David Tyack and his colleagues have written, school people in 1932 felt that wicked men in high places had destroyed prosperity. They saw themselves as the keepers of a dream that selfish capitalists had betrayed.[8] The 1932 convention of the Progressive Education Association was a revival meeting. "Dare we build a new social order?" Teachers College professor George Counts asked both the PEA group and, two days later, a turbulent crowd of delegates at the 1932 convention of the National Education Association. His speech so electrified the social reconstructionists in the PEA that they pushed through an on-the-spot revision of the agenda to begin answering Counts's question. Many teachers saw every day the desperate poverty of children in their charge. Stung by the efforts of business-oriented school boards to cut bare-bones school budgets even while school enrollments climbed, they were willing to consider radical solutions. There had to be some way of redressing the balance of power between the common people and the business leaders responsible for this "Saturnalia of Ruin."[9]

Thus the progressive educators' mission to improve society, largely eclipsed during the self-centered twenties, now energized the movement anew. Dewey's and Parker's emphasis on cooperation and community suddenly looked relevant again in an economy that appeared to have been brought to its knees by the excesses of individualism. "A new age of collectivism is emerging," wrote the Social Studies Commission of the American Historical Association.[10] Historian Charles Beard was perhaps the most erudite of all critics of laissez-faire economics, and FDR's U.S. Office of Education invited him to compile for high school libraries all over the nation a list of books about "this new world we are entering."[11] A spirit of invention was abroad in the land. "The New Deal itself became a great schoolhouse," writes Arthur Schlesinger, with a preaching president bent on teaching the nation to change its ways.[12] The huge New Deal youth agencies, the CCC and the NYA, took on a reformist educational role as, by their example, they pointed up the rigidities of most local public school systems: their disgraceful regional and racial inequalities and their inability, despite increasing enrollments, to meet a national emergency head on. WPA workers—preschool teachers, remedial, arts, and vocational teachers—introduced public schools to a range of new responsibilities. The TVA, said one prominent educator, was a "social laboratory" of massive dimensions.[13] Education's public was ready for new ideas.

Free of public school constraints and buoyed up by the grand designs of mid-thirties reformers, small Putney School might develop its own strategies to "pull civilization up" within a world community, as eighteen years of early Putney catalogues put it.[14] And the Depression was steering toward

Putney some teachers peculiarly suited to such strategies. Soon after Mrs. Hinton returned from Germany in late summer, she began receiving letters from Edward Yeomans about teachers worth interviewing. The first described Hugh MacDougall, a young research engineer whose MIT laboratory had lost its grants, and who had—with his wife, Ursula—been teaching at a private school. Mrs. Hinton wrote to Vannevar Bush and to another MIT professor under whom MacDougall had worked, asking, "Is he forceful and interesting in his thinking?" Yes, all answers said. Bush had tried to hire him back, but MacDougall was a busy science teacher by then. Ursula Mac-Dougall, a poet and an experienced, committed English teacher, was equally well recommended.

Mrs. Hinton said that the MacDougalls fell in love with the Putney ideas and with Elm Lea Farm at once and had signed on by early November. Hugh MacDougall himself agrees that they were negotiating throughout the fall with Mrs. Hinton ("I'm fond of music," wrote Hugh, "but can't play or sing, I can't folk dance but would like to learn; . . . I like all kinds of hand craft and carpentry, and out-of-doors sports;" and Ursula: "I'd like to give a poetry course *beginning* with the modern poets and working back"). However, a February visit to a dismal Elm Lea decided them against the job. The snow was plowed only halfway up West Hill and they had to get out and walk—not Ursula's style. Besides, even before its opening, Putney School was obnoxious to some skeptics. "A coed boarding school in *New England?*" they asked the MacDougalls. Not until May, when Mrs. Hinton organized another weekend stay for teachers, at apple-blossom time, did the couple change their minds. [15]

Jane Arms, a friend of Ursula's and a fellow poet, did say yes as soon as she was invited in January; so did Daniel Morris, recommended by Yeomans as a brilliant research chemist of wide enthusiasms, even though he had never taught school before. His wife, Carol, while an invalid, was also a sculptor and a musician, exactly what Putney required.

Another source of teacher-pioneers was the Hinton household in Weston. During the 1934 Experiment summer, Mrs. Hinton had invited Ewald Schnitzer, a young German teacher, to cross the Atlantic and live with the Hinton family. Schnitzer held a "freshly baked" doctorate in modern European history from the University of Leipzig. [16] A real scholar and a sensitive pianist, Schnitzer, with Dan Morris and several other early teachers, seemed amply to match Mrs. Hinton's respect for intellect. [17] She knew she was no intellectual herself, nor had she ever taught beyond the third grade. She realized how crucial it was to the school's success that she engage a superior faculty oriented toward older students. Indeed, in the first three years, she welcomed five classroom teachers (out of a total of nine) whose preparation or experience or both had been in college teaching.

Also living at Weston was Arthur Green, B.S., Massachusetts State College, and farmhand-chauffeur. He had majored in English, but had noticed while still a junior that only the animal husbandry and poultry graduates were finding jobs. He signed up for three poultry courses as a senior, and sure enough, on his graduation he was offered a job building up a poultry farm for $15 a month. He rejected it for a $20-a-month haying job, which was fortunate, because there he learned to milk a cow. When he sought to rise in the world to the $30-a-month Weston job, Mrs. Hinton had already turned down six Harvard students in a row because none of them could milk a cow. Green greatly enjoyed the crowded Weston life. "There was lots going on in that family, believe me," he writes.[18] Mrs. Hinton kept "rushing off to New York, Philadelphia, etc." in her search for teachers, for financial backing, and for parents of likely children. On Columbus Day weekend, they all drove to Elm Lea Farm, the Franklin touring car "crammed with children and camping gear."[19] Those who slept out opened their tents the first morning and found three inches of snow, says Green.[20] He would stay as poultry farmer, dormitory head, and youth hostel supervisor until he left in 1940 to travel and to join the army.

To visit Elm Lea Farm was, for most prospective faculty, the final push toward Putney School. Deciding that the same might be true for students, Mrs. Hinton arranged a ten-day Christmas vacation house party there, and invited twenty-five young people and teaching candidates to join her. The four Hintons arrived early at the caretakers' house. Ed Gray had just finished milking the cows, and Mabel was putting the couple's Christmas dinner on the table. Somehow, she expanded the feast to feed four more. Three days later, twenty-eight people were sitting down around dining tables in the main house, and Minnie Wood of Putney Village was hired to cook for the rollicking, ravenous crowd. The holidaymakers made the somber dining room ring with song and laughter. They introduced the assembly hall to square dancing in what would soon become the leaping, stomping Putney School style.

Mrs. Hinton brought along a movie camera to take footage for a film to use for recruiting students: shots of sledding, of snowball fights and other romps underneath bare elms. The mayhem inside the main house and the dormitory was, perhaps mercifully, unrecorded, except by Ed and Mabel Gray, who cleaned up after the crowd had left. They were aghast at the scratches left by hobnailed boots on polished floors. Before the Misses Everts and Whitney could get over to Elm Lea to discover the mess (and possibly, the Grays feared, to change their minds about giving over Elm Lea to Putney School), they worked for hours scrubbing, waxing, and polishing to return the buildings to their original state of spotless decorum.[21] This was the beginning of a long, problematical partnership between Carmelita Hinton and the Grays, whom many students and teachers place together at the center of the Putney School. Highly intelligent and observant, Mabel had a sharp tongue to go with her abounding kindness. Ed was a stubbornly honest critic as well as a staunch supporter of Mrs. H.'s enterprises, and he refused to accept that shortcuts might be used to reach the goals the three shared. It was a fortunate but volatile combination.

Back in Weston, Mrs. H. prepared for a round of trips west and southeast, armed with her Elm Lea movie and a growing list of committed faculty. The first student did not actually commit herself until February: Liebe Coolidge, oldest daughter of Sprague Coolidge of Cambridge and Margaret Coolidge, Mrs. H.'s Shady Hill friend. Two other Shady Hill teachers' daughters applied next. "An unusually fine lot of girls" signed up in Chicago, Mrs. Hinton wrote her Bryn Mawr friend Margaret Thompson, "but only a few boys. Can't you find me a fine youth?" Mrs. Thompson had only her daughter Janet to offer.[22]

Male applicants would be a problem that year and for many years to come. John Coolidge, who wanted very much to transfer to Putney, was reasonably told by his parents that he should finish his last year at the Cambridge School, but many parents refused even to consider Putney for their sons. It was a man's world; boys must prepare for it at Andover and Exeter and St. Paul's, where they would no longer be addled and coddled by females. Anticipating the difficulty, Mrs. H. determined from the beginning that male faculty and students should always be in the majority, no matter how small the pool of male applicants. Only by giving in at this one point to the man's-world myth could Putney School become truly coeducational. The result for the first year, says one pioneer, was that "we had a few weird boys at Putney" including one "who always wore an Indian headband and walked around on tiptoe."[23]

Yet slowly more and more parents were persuaded. Again Mrs. H. traveled to hospitable elementary schools[24] and to the large living rooms of her admirers in Winnetka, Chicago, New York, and Philadelphia. She showed the house party movie and announced that three, then ten, then fifteen students had applied and been accepted. All applicants had to describe in detail their reasons for wanting to come and to demonstrate in some way that they were the "superior" young people Mrs. Hinton considered essential to the school's success. Few were actually rejected that first year, but self-selection was a major means of screening. Mrs. H. may not have realized how challenging she herself was to prospective students. "At least one strapping boy refused to attend the school because he was physically afraid of its foundress-director," remembers an alumna, still amused.[25]

Parents, too, were selecting themselves. Almost to a man and woman, they were college-educated, internationalist liberals who had caught the spirit of the New Deal or even helped to design it: "professors, lawyers, architects, doctors, government workers, musicians," wrote Mrs. H. for *The Vermonter* magazine—"and businessmen," she added at the end of the list.[26] A not-so-different crowd was paying tuition for daughters and sons at the new Bennington and Black Mountain colleges. Bennington's president had signed his two sons up for Putney, and Jean Hinton was a sophomore at Bennington. There was a mere handful of Republican parents, among them George Aiken, who would be Vermont's governor from 1936 to 1940 and one of its Senators for over thirty years more. Aiken was a local nurseryman and thus a major employer in Putney village as well as moderator of Town Meeting, and his support in these early days was crucial. Three other town families sent their children as endorsement of the experiment on West Hill, along with whatever they could pay of the day-student tuition (about half the $1400 boarding tuition). The town, having no high school of its own, contributed the $80 it would have cost for a year of Brattleboro High. "We tried to take everyone from the Town who applied," Mrs. Hinton said. For these and other families, scholarships were negotiated wherever necessary. In effect, the wealthier two-thirds of parents paid for the needier children, a tradition that would go on for over three decades.

In spite of the intent that students should do much of the work needed to maintain and feed the school, the tuition was about $300 above the average for independent boarding schools in the Depression years. It originally included, for four-year students, two optional summer Experiment trips for intensive practice of French or German, whichever the student was taking. Putney's financial pattern was set: a relatively high tuition; an extraordinarily high teacher-pupil ratio and proportion of scholarship students, both benefits made possible by simple living, student work, and the willingness of most faculty and staff to live on Depression-level salaries throughout the school's first fifteen years. Only the summer language study offering was dropped (and with it the tuition), a casualty of World War II.

Barely twenty of the fifty students planned for had committed themselves by May first, most of them children of Mrs. H.'s friends or of Putney School teachers-to-be, or classmates of Bill's and Joan's who couldn't bear to be left behind. But there could be no turning back. It was seed time on the farm, the anchor of the school, and thus the Putney School had already begun. With much encouragement from Edward Yeomans, Mrs. Hinton had decided that a school on a farm would be the best way to replicate the older agrarian society whose educational force John Dewey had so admired. Through the "meaningful work" of the farm, Dewey wrote, the "entire industrial process stood revealed to the child." While Dewey, Parker, and other progressive pioneers had sought ways to integrate schooling with the new urban, industrial life, Carmelita Hinton planned to reproduce the "old-time social integrations" in a place apart from urban confusions—a place where farming still made economic sense.[27]

Fortunately, Mrs. H. had found a farm manager. An intriguing letter from C. Hutchins Maynard, teacher-farmer at a women's reformatory, arrived in January in response to her ads; it described the career of a farmer, writer of poetry and plays, cow expert, and traveler to Alaska. Mrs. H. replied immediately, asking to meet Mr. Maynard forthwith. Mr. Maynard wrote back to apologize that she was not a man. Mrs. H. had badly wanted a man ("I was certainly upset to find that you were a woman," she wrote), but "Hutch" was irresistible. Already in her forties, small and spry though not unusually strong, she had great confidence in the methods of teaching through farmwork that she had developed over many years. Her broad experience and love of the land won Mrs. H. over. Hutch was offered $900 and a living with promise of more "if the pupils pour in."[28] It was as much as the average faculty salary that year.

Hutch opened the farm in April, buying from the Misses Everts and Whitney all the horse-powered equipment a 1930s hill farm could use (threshing machine, $65, binder and walking plows, $20 each). She engaged county agents to help her test the soils and look for the reasons that a herd of twenty Guernseys should have run a deficit in 1934 as big as her salary. Once the soils were proved excellent and the cows had been culled and cleared for TB and Bangs disease, she went to work with Clyde Hulett, his horses, and the hired man. They plowed and planted and set out fruit trees for an all-purpose farm that would grow nearly all its own animal feed and—with much help from the garden Ed Gray managed—about half the food for eighty to ninety people.

It was soon clear to Hutch that more land was needed to support the cows. Since Mrs. H. had long had in mind at least six or seven acres for each energetic adolescent, she was as excited as Hutch to learn that the nine-hundred-acre Houghton and Shaw lots on the south and east borders of Elm Lea might be for sale. But by this time, her working funds were virtually exhausted. Two summer houses in Woodstock, the Wrigley and jungle gym stock, and the Weston house remained. The Weston house went, mortgaged for $10,000, one-third the cost of buying and building it, and later was sold. The Houghton farm, with its beautiful old farmhouse and sturdy barns and sheds became Putney School's Lower Farm. Its pastures, ski hills, and sugar bush, inn for parents, youth hostel and store, and eventually its blacksmith shop, theater, and lower school for faculty children completed the "village" Carmelita Hinton had dreamed of as the ideal site for a progressive secondary school.

Now came the final push to get Elm Lea ready for the first "summer labor camp" of school-builders. Beginning on April 19, 1935, weekend work parties cleaned the bullpen and helped with the planting. In early June, every stick of furniture in the Weston house was moved to Elm Lea Farm, and silver tea sets were put away. On June 15, the labor camp opened to seventy campers and twenty adults, most of them future teachers. A favored few (some not so pleased to be favored) moved into the dormitory rooms and the main house or Houghton House; four teachers joined the Grays in the White Cottage, and everyone else set up tents on Water Tower Hill above the Lower Farm. Monica Owen of Shady Hill was director of this first summer work camp for school-age boys and girls in the United States. The young people, including about half the students already enrolled for September, were paying $10 a week for the privilege of helping the staff and faculty revive a farm and build a boarding school; the faculty exchanged work for board.

How they worked! "Buildings . . . matter practically not at all compared with teachers," Mrs. H. had written in her prospectus, but somehow teachers and students had to be housed. Hugh MacDougall had drawn plans to make over the large carriage shed into a dormitory for twenty boys and the smaller carriage shed into a science and art building, not such difficult feats for a builder of suspension bridges. He and Ed Gray took charge of the construction work. This was the first chance for Ed and the students to work together. He had taken his first job in a textile mill at age 14, and it surprised him how quickly the soft "city kids" learned; they in turn thrived on his precise and kindly direction. Mabel too, was a tireless marvel. Her title was dietitian, but she fell to as boss-housekeeper, seamstress, pastry cook, barber, and peerless scolder, comforter, and inspiration for the students, talking, talking all the time. It was she who made the cream puffs, a feature of Mabel's wonderful career that Mrs. H. still could taste in her imagination at ninety-one; and Mabel introduced the "Putney Special" (stewed tomatoes on peanut buttered toast) to the hungry laborers of 1935. It is doubtful that Putney could have opened in September without the Grays.

Hutch, too, had crews spending whole mornings pulling out weeds, for the corn and the witch grass had come up together on the newly plowed Houghton land. "She kept us at it four hours at a time, and she made us understand *why*," says one weeder.[29] The two teams worked twelve and more hours each day at cultivating, haying, and hauling lumber, Clyde driving his own horses and young John Holden driving Bob, a sway-backed bay, and Jerry, twenty-eight years old.

As a senior English major at Bowdoin, Holden had seen a copy of Mrs. H.'s brochure and "was so excited by the Putney idea that (he) called the Dean and got permission to go, right then, for an interview."[30] "All my life led to Putney," Holden has said. Prep school had left him dissatisfied, but he longed to teach. He had helped to found the Bowdoin Outing Club, he was both captain and coach of the ski team; he had worked as a farmhand for six summers in Montana and Vermont. It was terribly disappointing to learn that no more English teachers were needed—that not a penny more of salary could be allocated. But "Can you drive a team?" Mrs. H. asked. He certainly could, and he was signed on for the 1935 labor camp as teamster for $5 a month. Always the optimist, Mrs. H. hoped to keep him on in the fall as an English tutor.

In the afternoons most of the student work crews dispersed for play: a swim at Garland's Pond, a horseback ride, or three hours' canoeing on the Connecticut River. Just before supper the men came in from the fields for their baths in the pond. (They never wore suits of course, and of course they caught at least one girl hiding in the bushes, watching.) Someone had an Irish Water Spaniel that would dive off the high tower into the pond.

At supper, the laughter heard from Jane Arms's table often signaled a favorite intellectual game: giving Jane a topic and five minutes to turn it into a sonnet.[31] Between courses there were German hiking songs, and yodeling or spirituals and part-songs for dessert. Evening and weekend recreation was homemade too: camping trips up Putney Mountain or along the West River, rock climbing on the cliffs above the Connecticut River, (using the haymow hoisting ropes for safety). Though a professional square-dance caller came every other Saturday, young and old made their own dances many other evenings or traveled to nearby towns. Writes Jean Hinton Rosner, "A square dance could be found for every night of the week" in these Vermont towns still rich in folk culture. [32]

It was a frantic summer, a grand summer. For some of the campers who were supposed to leave for Exeter or Brearley School that fall, the combination of serious work and jubilant play had become irresistible; they began working on their parents to let them stay on at Putney School. This was heartening news for Isabel Stephens, Mrs. H.'s energetic Shady Hill friend, who continued through the summer heat searching for students to fill the school. Isabel also joined many informal conversations with teachers planning for this still-mythical student body. Some hot arguments arose over the issues of grades and examinations, Jane Arms advancing her long campaign to do away with both, and others equally certain that the fledgling school would collapse if colleges saw its academic program as lax in any respect. Mrs. H., to whom the bright, inventive Arms was quickly becoming first lieutenant, [33] took her side. Though other faculty refused to give up examinations, a compromise on grades was reached: students should receive comments on papers and tests, effort marks, and detailed reports four times a year, but grades would be recorded only in the office, to help with college applications. [34] Regardless of pressures to change, Mrs. H. remained adamant about this strategy for focusing students' minds on learning and trying, rather than on "ornamental pots," as Virginia Woolf had called academia's outward rewards. [35] Many other plans laid and traditions seeded in the first months would become equally sacrosanct, setting patterns for over thirty years of Putney School's existence.

In the meantime, the builders were racing toward September 9, the day school was to open. The early starting date further set Putney off from its private school peers, but the harvest does not wait, and late summer is one of Vermont's loveliest seasons. Vacation time would be made up in December and January with a five-week holiday. Though one camper decided it made no sense to pay to work so hard and went home, ten campers signed on as Putney School students, including a German boy, and two Austrian children whose mother agreed to teach German in exchange for their tuition. Parents had paid or pledged $34,000 in tuition monies. By opening day, the corn was in—acres of it having been cut by hand and fed to the ensilage chopper just hours before—and fifty-four students were expected.

Chapter 3
Shaping Time: The First Year

It poured rain. The boys' dorm was not yet closed in; mothers in high heels and fathers in business suits opened the front doors and looked through the back wall to the trees beyond. They could see the puddles on the floors and the ladders that still served as stairways to the second floor. One grandmother was far from pleased to see the *principal* climbing up and down the ladders, settling boys in. The boys' bathrooms were not yet in working order, nor would they be for three weeks. Girls moving into their rooms off the Assembly Hall discovered that finished dormitories at Putney sheltered vegetables in their cellars and that the celery was rotting. [1] But no child was taken home again, to the principal's great joy.

"It depends on us whether this school goes or not," Ewald Schnitzer remembers thinking. Nearly everyone thought the same, and those who did not heard Mrs. H.'s almost daily exhortations in the same key. There was no doubt that Putney School would ask as much as it offered. The daily and weekly schedules went into effect as Isabel Stephens had written them, except that the students voted to work outdoors three afternoons a week instead of two. Three evening activities a week, plus one reading night and Friday night singing were retained, though Isabel had thought two evening activities were plenty for a college preparatory school. There would be one eighty-minute class on Saturday, with makeup for those requiring it before lunch. Through the schedule, Carmelita Hinton built into her secondary school abundant scope for Froebel's "instinctive activities" of the child: "for play, for producing, for shaping, for knowledge, for society, and for cultivating the ground." [2] Scheduled hours were rung out twenty times a day on the great locomotive tire that Ed Gray and "Pop" Sage had hung from a tree near the center of the school.

Most courses met for three periods a week, except for beginning language

SCHEDULE

Weekdays

6:15 a.m.	Chores
7:05 a.m.	Rising bell
7:30 a.m.	Breakfast; cleaning rooms, etc., follows immediately
8:35 a.m.	First period begins
11:20 a.m.	Fifteen-minute recess—milk lunch
11:30–12:55	class
1:00 p.m.	Lunch
2:00–3:20	p.m. class spring and fall; 4:30–5:50 winter
	Classroom clean-up follows immediately after afternoon class.
3:30–5:00 p.m.	spring and fall, outdoor work jobs or recreation
2:00–3:30 p.m.	winter, outdoor work jobs or recreation
5:00–6:00	p.m. spring and fall; 3:30–4:30 winter
	Make-up study period for those who need it; leisure for others.
6:25 p.m.	Dinner
7:15–7:30 p.m.	Evening Meeting
	Evening activities follow immediately on Monday, Tuesday and Thursday. (Later, the Wednesday "reading" evening would become Thursday "study" night.)
9:00 p.m.	bed for students under 15
	10:00 p.m. bed for older students

Weekends

8:25–9:45 a.m.	Saturday morning class
	Saturday assembly follows immediately after class.
	Make-up period right after assembly.
9:00 a.m.	Sunday breakfast
	Bible group, late afternoon, for those interested.
7:15 p.m.	Sunday evening meeting

classes, which usually met for five half periods. About half of each regular class period was for study or individual conferences, but if a lab was scheduled, or all of *Macbeth* was to be read aloud, or discussion was getting hot, the full eighty minutes (later seventy-five) were available. Thus study could be concentrated during the week, reasoned Mrs. H., and weekends left free for outdoor fun, for trips, for impromptu music and optional Saturday evening dances, lectures, or (occasionally) movies. If students had caught up with their work, they were reluctantly allowed to leave for visits home.[3] (Parents more often visited their children at Putney in the early days, some staying at the school's Winter Sports Inn for $3 a night.) Student adventurers were supposed to sign out when they took off for the hills, whether on foot, horseback, or bicycle. Almost no one paid any attention to this, however. It was a spatial freedom unthinkable in other boarding schools, whose rules— for girls' schools especially—commonly required participation or attendance at Saturday athletic contests and chaperons for any trip off campus unless it appeared on the map as an "Approved Walk." (Girls at Abbot Academy in Andover were given demerits for speaking with boys on the sidewalk; even through the mid-sixties, such dangerous dialogue was allowed for only five minutes, and Abbot teachers were required to time conversations whenever they observed them.[4]) Putney opened with virtually no rules except those implied by the demanding daily schedule.

6:15 A.M.: Chores

All students helping with the farm animals had to join Hutch in the barn by 6:15 A.M. More than half the cows had been bred to freshen in the fall; parents got used to receiving postcards announcing, "A new calf was born this morning." Each calf was quickly claimed by a student on the waiting list, until ten students "owned" both a calf and a schedule for feeding, watering, weighing, and training to halter, as well as a nine-month record book fashioned after 4-H club forms. If the calf was late, the student might be assigned to care for the mother-to-be and perhaps to bring her through postpartum troubles, massaging a swollen udder, keeping compresses hot in the early-morning chill. One boy's hard-born calf became one of a pair of bull calves named Thor and Loki, whose "owners" began within two weeks of their birth to train them together. By spring the boy was using much of his morning chore time to accustom the two small oxen to the yoke he'd carved himself, and Hutch had entered the $42.79 expense of raising the pair as inventory on the capital side of her ledger.

Those who noticed the rush on calves too late to join it wrote in the 4-H reports or letters home, "I had to be content with one of the four pigs," or, "I'm taking care of fifty chickens."[5] Those late for chores were apt to miss breakfast. Peter Ringland, the youngest and sleepiest boy in the school, soon found that Hutch, impatient with his continued late arrivals to the pigsty, had transferred his pig to another student. A handful of sheep were placed in one girl's charge; a valuable cow was assigned to another. Several alumni describe the thrill of learning how to care safely for an animal "five times as big as you are." A good deal of prestige attached to the boy in charge of the bull and to the girl who drove the second team, knowing herself (she wrote) "a king" as she did so. She also loved "the feeling of going into the barn for morning chores, calling the horses names and having them answer."[6] One younger girl traded prestige for the affection of her small flock of goats, who were as likely as not to escort her to breakfast after chores.

Breakfast at 7:30; cleaning rooms, etc. follows immediately

The food was good. Over a third of it came up the hill from the farm to Minnie's kitchen and was served in the two main building dining rooms by a student table-waiting crew. Mrs. H., no respecter of age over talent, named Janet Thompson, not quite fourteen, headwaitress midway through the fall, making her responsible for all five waiters, for dining-room cleanliness, and for the dishwashing afterwards. Teachers went to work on student decorum. After Ewald and others complained of the stink of barn clothes at breakfast, all were required to change their clothes for breakfast as well as for class (slacks or dresses), then sports or work, then supper (fresh dresses, with lisle stockings in winter, coats and ties), then sometimes again for a blacksmithing or woodworking evening activity. Students protested that they were *always* changing their clothes, but several also say they appreciated Mrs. H.'s explanation that "Coming to the dining room in work clothes was not respectful to the people in the kitchen who had worked hard to prepare a nice meal."[7]

Once breakfast was over, students were supposed to clean up their rooms and dorms. John Holden and carpenter-painter Henry Webb together contended with everyday dirt in the made-over carriage shed. Slow to anger but quick to act once riled, Holden dealt with one boy-barbarian absent during cleanup by picking up a week's worth of clothes and bedclothes from the floor and throwing them out the window. For years faculty fought to civilize the feckless young. Setting punishments for infractions was always a problem. Work could never be a punishment, because work was everyone's responsibility and privilege. Rewards were tried, as announced by this sheet of paper which appeared on school bulletin boards early the first fall.

The school has worked out the amount of money saved by having the children clean their own rooms and the class rooms. This saving will be divided in this way: one half of the money will be given to the scholarship fund, one fourth to the foreign travel fund, and one fourth to the students to defray expenses on trips, or for pocket money. This money is considered earned only if the condition of the rooms is satisfactory.

Sometimes this was successful.

8:35: First period begins

On the surface Putney's course of study looked conventional: a new, untried school had no alternative in an educational world that still counted college credits in the terms laid out by Harvard president Charles W. Eliot and the Committee of Ten in the 1890s. Though Mrs. H. had hoped that intensive college preparation could be confined to the senior year, the faculty aimed to win certification by the New England College Entrance Certificate Board as soon as possible; thus preparation for College Board exams could not be left until the last minute.

It was not unusual to require (as Putney did) that students take four years of correlated history and English courses. However, Putney's mandatory year of music, drama, or art was rare even among private schools. Nor did many school catalogues tell parents that Latin was "too remote to be given a large share of the average student's consideration" and promise not to push mathematics beyond minimum college requirements for the inept or uninterested, as did Putney's prospectus. (Later catalogues would speak of math more positively: "In Mathematics one may go as far as one pleases."[8])

College boards prescribe, and catalogues describe, but teachers pursue their art and craft in the privacy of their classrooms—especially at Putney, whose principal both believed in teachers' freedom and felt unqualified to interfere. Jane Arms's English grammar lessons were as perfunctory as her final exams, but she urged Latin (whose grammar she taught superbly) on all her English students and kept track of college requirements for the whole school. Ewald Schnitzer's passion was European culture, and most early students willingly took his combined American-European history course for three years running.

The surprising variety of this small school's course offerings could only be achieved by teachers of renaissance talents. Almost every one of the nine full-time teachers taught in at least two different academic disciplines, and part-time teachers like Arthur Green gave their skills as well. A bright and sensitive young Smith graduate taught art history and flute and served as head of girls' athletics. Ewald taught German, music, history, skiing, and rock-climbing. Carol Morris, though not strong enough to teach full time, taught both violin and mathematics. In addition to his heavy teaching load and the work of building equipment for the science laboratories, Hugh MacDougall was on call whenever anything went wrong with the plumbing, the heating, or the electricity. Otti Hirt and another Austrian Experimenter were learning English and earning their keep by peeling vegetables for ninety eaters in the kitchen (Minnie Wood loved their help and jolly company, and says she learned more German than they did English). These two also set up housekeeping in the little red cottage on Mrs. H.'s Shaw Lot, opened it up for eight girls taking German as the "German House" dormitory, and conducted a lively German Evening Activity there. Within a month, "everybody" (well, "all 25 girls, at least") was wearing dirndl skirts. This may have mitigated Otti's and Friedl's homesickness, which often, says Otti, brought them to the Grays' tiny apartment for kindly comfort.[9]

Otti and Friedl presided over German tables several times a week, while the first school nurse, an aristocratic French woman, brought her charm to a French table. Mrs. H. centered Putney's advanced-language program in these informal conversations and in the promised summer trips to Europe. The first year's French literature class met only one period a week, however, and few of its students ever did travel to France. Too soon, all European travel would become impossible.

Teachers had to be versatile enough to deal with different age groups, for as Mrs. H. had searched farther for prospective pupils, they came in younger: there were enough seventh- and eighth-grade students for John Holden to move from the farm to the academic staff in the fall, his salary rocketing from $5 to $50 a month. There was even one sixth grader who hung on surprisingly well. Until John took her youngest pupils, Ursula MacDougall taught six levels of English, and a history class, too.

Some teachers tended to focus attention on (and to remember) the many students of "very high intellectual caliber" and were as excited as most of their students by the level of discussion;[10] but Mrs. H., always wanting her school to stress much more than academic learning, had deliberately enrolled several youngsters with limp academic records whom she considered strong, vital persons and *potentially* able students. "We were giving individual instruction" to many of these, says Hugh MacDougall, speaking of the perplexing disparity in mathematics training that he encountered in his first physics and senior math classes. Meanwhile, two twelve-year-olds sped to the end of eighth grade in one year's time. As Janet Thompson happily wrote her mother, "Nobody pays any attention to age."

Effort ratings counted most. "No child was ever put down for not being a

good scholar," says Hugh MacDougall. The academic faculty met once a
week to discuss each child's progress, to work out strategies for "putting the
lazy, smart students under pressure" and jogging weaker youngsters awake.
Hugh MacDougall managed to catch one lagging chemistry student's attention by persuading her to make lipstick and face creams in the laboratory, a
complex and intriguing procedure.[11]

A few of these first-year students never noticed the faculty's efforts on their
behalf or joined in the constant talk with peers, which often meant far more
than classroom discussion. One alumnus (not chosen for his reading skill)
still remembers a Putney filled with "snotty little spoiled kids who were
cliquey, cruel and arrogant."[12] Another, who loved the school for its freedom and for her calf and horse, wishes she had had "more help in class
work." She recalls that Mrs. H. "told my mother I was not college material,
which destroyed any future educational possibilities for me—even a post-
graduate course." A third, in a complaint that would be made repeatedly
about the particular brand of "lemon" teacher in which Putney specialized,
remembers chemistry as a disaster. A "research man" appeared from Yale in
September, then as abruptly returned to Yale in June. ("Carmelita," wrote a
friend, "now I know you will run a good school, because you are willing to
fire people.")[13]

However, most students found most classes exciting. "Six really great
teachers were enough," says one alumnus. Some of those who most appreciated the academic program had entered Putney from other progressive
schools. "I've done seven Physics experiments, written eight history papers
and eight English themes since the opening of school," Janet Thompson
wrote her mother on November 1, 1935—more English papers than she had
submitted through the entire year at Spring Hill School. Another Spring Hill
graduate, who had thought herself a mediocre student, nevertheless found
"every (Putney) class an adventure—a slightly dangerous one." McGregor
Gray, who had skipped four years in public school, then been pulled back at
the Cambridge School in Weston "to be with my age group—a horrible
mistake," finally met exactly the challenges he needed at Putney, including
the discipline he had missed in Cambridge School classrooms.

"Up here," continued Janet, "we work ahead just as far as we want to in
everything . . . and there's always someone to compete with."[14] Work
weeks, Putney's version of the Dalton plan, allowed those already steeped in
books to speed ahead without leaving others behind. "The training in long-
term projects . . . the nourishing of intellectual curiosity, the acknowledge-

ment of students as people with opinions of their own"—all these were new to most students. New even to a "bookworm" who knew how to learn was the help he got adjusting to other students. McGregor Gray desperately needed his peers' acceptance, but did not find it at first.

> At one moment of depression (and the flu) I was in the infirmary feeling sorry for myself. Maria Phaneuf, the new nurse, must have told Mrs. Hinton for [Mrs. H.] came to visit me and talked to me at length, not in a motherly way, but as an outsider—a fully understanding outsider. She suggested things I could do to better my relations with others and gently pointed out why I was having problems. (Intellectual intolerance was first on my list of bad traits.) It helped! And then she retreated into her aloof position and never again alluded to my moment of panic and fear, for which I was totally grateful.

This "smallest, weakest boy in [his] class" began to enjoy first farm and hand work, then skiing, and with them, the companionship he had refused in his classes. Before long, intellectual discussion with friends came easily. "The sky's the limit," Putney School seemed to say, both to the students in their classrooms and far beyond.[15]

3:30–5:00: Outdoor work jobs and recreation

Carmelita Hinton had always believed that the most important education took place outdoors. There were no gymnasiums in the early Putney School; a gym was eventually built, but it would rarely be used. Nowhere in Putney's landscape did the metaphor of institutional growth more fully shape individual growth than on the school farm. For a hearty minority, Putney was a farm school; for everyone, the farm was home, and three afternoons a week, crews fanned out over this home ground to do the work required. Animals were all about in these early days, and the garden, fruit plantation, and poultry work went on in the school's front yard.

The farm had a double purpose. Much as it had been for the rural school children of the Country Life Movement twenty years earlier, the farm was Putney students' textbook. "Cities are *parasites*," Carmelita Hinton wrote that first year.[16] She, like Francis Parker, "cherished all (her) life the education which the farm gave," the "physical strength, self-control, resourcefulness and kind helpfulness" engendered by rural life.[17] Hutch the poet shared this philosophy. On the other hand, Hutch the farm manager wanted the farm to pay. The two purposes converged in students' perceptions of the farm as a place of real work, as a common ground shared with adults where

GENERAL FACTS

Name of Animal __Adis Abaha__ ____ __(Bamba)__
Date of Birth __Oct. 3__ __1935__ ___ Date Starting Record __Oct. 3 1935__
Breed __Guernsey__ _____ Sex __Female__
Pure-Bred _____ Reg.No. _____
Weight at Beginning __56 lbs__ Weight at Finish __?__

FEED RECORDS

Month	Silage Milk Lbs.	Cost	Hay Lbs.	Cost	Grain Lbs.	Cost	Pasture Costs	Total Cost
October	460 lb	1.15	186 lb	1.36				$2.51
November	450	1.25	180	1.35				2.60
December	496	1.25	186	1.36				2.61
January	460	1.15	186	1.36				2.61
February	420	1.05	168	1.28				2.33
March	9.32	2.32	186	1.36				3.68
April	1050	2.27	180	1.35				3.62
May	600	1.50	93	75				2.25
June							1.00	1.00
July							50	50
August							50	50
September			63	34			50	50
Total	4868	11.94	305	10.17			2.50	24.61

SUMMARY

Income

    Value of animal at Finish .... $ 50.00
    Prizes Won 1.00
    Other Income   51.00
            Total Value $ 56.10

Expenses

    Value animal at start .... $ 5.00
    Cost of Feed 49.10
    Misc. Expenditures
            Total Expenses $ 54.10

        Total Profit (loss)   - $ 3.10 30 (av

their own developing skills could advance an enterprise integral to the regional economy. Foremost in a boy's feelings might be his sweet, contrary little calf.

A baby face looked queerly up at me,
Its eyes were filled with mischief.
I gave it two small specks of grain.
It raised one small black hoof,
And pawed the ground, oh, how gently.
I led it forth. . . .
It flipped its little tail . . .
And frisked in all the cool fresh air,
This tiny active spot, all mine.[18]

The calf's life, however, depended on its usefulness, as defined in the columns of the record book its caretaker had to submit to Hutch once a term. The same was true of the hogs, of the lovely sugar bush and the blueberry bushes, of the too-thin hay in the Elm Lea fields, of the corn thickening in the rich Houghton farm soil—of all living things. Hutch listed each item of expense and all income gained by wholesales to the school of milk, meat,

Silage Corn and Mangel Beets: 2½ Acres

25 tons silage @ 5.00	$125.00
seed	$1.63
fertilizer	9.73
tractor labor	2.25
fertilizer for beets	6.03
193 man hours	48.25
241 horse hours	39.28
241 equip. hours	7.23
straw for silo	4.00
balance to Bunker (exchange of work) filling silo	2.70
	121.10
gain	3.90
	125.00

The yield was higher than indicated—nearer 35 tons, but many tons were lost by spoilage in the 18-ft. silo (adequate for a herd of 75–100 cows). The spoiled silage went out as humus to the fields.

eggs, and vegetables. In this first year of experiments and adjustments, nearly every farm account revealed the disjointed nature of a new enterprise (see tables, above).

Nearly every account turned a small gain: $44.20 for the field corn, $101.54 for potatoes, $10.01 for pastures, etc., offsetting losses incurred by the too-small flock of sheep (−$7.52), the hogs (−$14.68), which were too few to be more than "garbage incinerators," and the poultry (−$54.30). Though the reorganized dairy showed a surplus of $222.59, twenty cows were too few to pay all of Hutch's salary. Hutch hoped that her culling and selective breeding of the herd would bring future returns.[19]

The sugar bush and wood lot were the most productive sectors of the farm. Together they helped to accomplish one of the farm's major tasks: support of the several part-time and two full-time adult hands who were central to Putney's curriculum. John Dewey would have applauded these outdoor teachers' concentration on essential skills, those "experience[s] in which the widest groups share."[20]

Clyde Hulett, the Putney School teamster, earned 25¢ an hour plus board for his horses, himself, and his wife, Ruby (who helped with the cleaning), but Ed Gray and Carmelita Hinton both considered him priceless. For Mrs. H.—and all others who came to know him—he personified the "kind helpfulness" Francis Parker celebrated. He was "a real, practicing Christian," with no need for a church, wrote Arthur Green, the poultryman.[21] For Ed Gray, Clyde was the craftsman who cared about details. Students counted themselves fortunate to be standing next to him on a September afternoon, learning how to swing a scythe against the bushy overgrowth in the corners of the hayfield.[22] Clyde could forecast the weather by looking and feeling, his gentleness allowing him a purchase on nature's moods that is denied all those noisier than he.

In that first fall, student-adult work crews harvested fall crops, fenced sheep pasture, mended rotting pigsties and bull pens. They set out the fruit plantation, one future Vermont Secretary of Agriculture working alone (and with the barest sufficiency of energy, scolded Hutch), to protect the new apple orchard against invading sheep and goats. A crew sorted out rotten celery in the girls' dorm cellar. Liebe Coolidge was sent alone to shovel pig manure from under the barn. She discovered that an old sow protected her piglets against creatures like her, and that after being chased round a wheelbarrow a few times one quickly learned the defensive uses to which a wheelbarrow could be put. Some have argued that Putney School pushed its luck on student safety. Though the school instructed its student drivers and ski teachers at length and warned the uninitiated at every turn, it refused to coddle youngsters with continual protection against the daily hazards that accompany responsibility for animals and equipment.. "And somehow, none of us every really got hurt!" says one incredulous alumna, marveling at a record unsurprising to others who see safety as largely a function of experience.[23]

Late in September, Hutch decided that something should be done to celebrate all the farmwork done since April and the wonderful harvest it had earned. Mrs. H., the faculty, and the students quickly agreed to hold Putney's first harvest festival. They sent invitations to 4-H clubs, church groups, and town and village people all through Windham County. Hutch wrote poetry, floats were built, songs and dances practiced, horses, calves, and teams given last-minute groomings. October 12, the day of the festival, dawned clear. About 180 people came to the pageant and the fair that followed. A whole year's farmwork in dance and music was brought before those gathered on the main building lawn: the "Sugar Harvest Song," plowing, planting, and hoeing songs, summer pasture songs, the "Tune the Old Cow Died On" (William Hinton, soloist), and nine haying and corn-harvesting songs. For the fair Hutch had written a cow-judging song, sung to the winning Guernsey. There were horse races, a midway—all that anyone could wish for. It was a banner day. Even the Brattleboro *Reformer*, whose editors had first viewed the Putney experiment with suspicion, was pleased: "The type of entertainment presented by the Putney School is different from anything seen locally. Throughout the whole program the ideals of rural life figure prominently in a manner which dignifies and idealizes, rather than ridicules, as so often happens in rural dramatics."[24] After cleanup was done, weary revelers took up their Monday-morning chores and their afternoon farm jobs with a new pride in their enterprise and a fresh sense of its place among their neighbors.

Farm and grounds work spilled over into student-faculty free time over the weekends. Mrs. H. had promised in her first prospectus that "the playing fields need only to have the grass cut short and goal posts erected," but many Saturdays found teams of brush cutters on the fields instead of the soccer players other schools boasted. Work crews were still leveling the playing fields in 1939.

Students played anyway over the lumps and bumps: coed field hockey two afternoons a week in the fall, baseball and softball in the spring. Visiting teams had not developed their superior technique practicing on pastures, so the scruffy Putney players began a long tradition of winning home games and losing games away. It was always the fun of the game that mattered to Mrs. H.; early alumni remember her just returned and glowing with pleasure from yet another lost game with the Bennington hockey team. Most of Putney's energy for play went into individual sports that could be continued through adulthood: hiking, biking, riding, skating, and especially skiing. The horse stalls finally having been built, twelve horses and their riders roamed farm and hills, their movements interrupted by the occasional accidents ("Liebe fell off Allan and got a concussion of the brain"[25]) against which—Mrs. H. was convinced—only more and freer riding experience could protect.

On winter afternoons, students thought of classes "only as a means to an end," wrote Janet Thompson as Putney's first January drew to a close, "that end being the time when we can go out to skate or ski."[26] Seven skiers competed in meets all over New England, finally winning the Boys' Vermont State Championship meet. Two of the "boys" were Joan Hinton and Marjorie Hollister, who tucked their hair under stocking caps so they could join the competitions.

The first winter began without any change in the class schedule, and dusk always came too soon. Liebe Coolidge describes how the first winter schedule seems to have come about.

> I had a fine Morgan horse and a fine boyfriend. One winter afternoon we were out in my sleigh, getting our fresh air. Coming home about 5 o'clock, it was pitch dark. We were snuggled cosily under the rug, when Mrs. H. overtook us in a car. "What are you two doing out here in the dark?" she demanded, with some feeling. "Getting our outdoor exercise," we piped in unison.
>
> She had no come-back for that. But the next day she announced at milk lunch that the school would change to the winter schedule. Afternoon class would now be held at 5. Right after lunch the outdoor activities would begin, so everyone would have plenty of light and good healthy sunshine![27]

5:00–6:00 P.M.: Make-up study period for those who need it; leisure for others

Hal Sproul, "a genius of a conductor" by many reports, arrived from Cambridge every Friday in time to direct the 5:00 rehearsal of the Putney Orchestra.[28] This leisure activity swept almost everyone in the school into the assembly hall to make music, or at least to try. "Carmelita has taken up the clarinet!" wrote Janet Thompson to her mother near the end of October. "What a woman!" Janet and her coeditors had been reading manuscripts for the *Putney Magazine* in their main building workroom, when they heard a noise like "a dog caught in a door." They looked for the dog and found Mrs.

H., face brick-red from her first practice session—"and she intends to play in orchestra this coming Friday!!!"

Three days a week, however, and for much of the weekend, there really was some leisure time. "I had never known such freedom," writes one alumna for many. Most thrived on it; some used it to sample forbidden fruits; some did both. Mrs. H. had powerful ideas about every human indulgence known to her. ("Very fussy about health and neatness in everything," wrote Janet Thompson, anxious to reassure a worried aunt that the dearth of "real rules" needn't matter.) Rules or no rules, alcohol was anathema, and Putney was puritanical about smoking ("Never let it start," Yeomans had warned Mrs. H.), allowing only eighteen-year-old boys their pipes that first year and limiting teachers' smoking to the small coffee room. Coffee and tea were simply not served in the dining room. Mrs. H. tried to understand others' weaknesses for nefarious beverages by reflecting on her passion for ginger ale, but she never really succeeded.[29] Both her upbringing in a region permeated by the enthusiasms of the WCTU and the clean living imposed on all Bryn Mawr and Hull House boarders made it impossible for her to believe that moderation is possible in such matters. But her own abundant health and her passionate abstention from all things that adolescents desire won many over. "We laughed at her" says one alumnus, "but we usually did as she wished." "It took a forceful person to make one rebel thoughtfully," recalls another.

Nor was music spared her scrutiny. One radio was allowed per dorm, to be tuned to "good programs" and monitored by adult dorm heads; common rooms would be kept clear of objectionable records and sheet music. Jazz was not forbidden at first, "for fear of giving it a lure," but this soon changed to complete prohibition.

In such ways, rules gradually evolved against the temptations of leisure time. Those who felt unable to bear these limitations on the freedom they had expected from a progressive school often found themselves in long conversations with Mrs. H. around her kitchen table, one of the few private places in her life. Four boys demonstrated their disenchantment in several ways before Mrs. H. "sat down and talked with them one last time." "She said that she had certain ideas about the school, and she gathered from their behavior that they had different ideas. She pointed out that if Putney School was to succeed, she could not bend to their wishes or desires. Whereupon they agreed to leave the school."[30]

Though basic expectations were fixed by Mrs. H. and the faculty, students joined in community decisionmaking through all-school discussions, many of these scheduled in leisure time. After the first year, there was a Community Council of seven (later nine) students and six (later eight) teachers and staff members, chaired by a student. In early years Mrs. H. appointed the students, but this practice became a rallying point for the local democrats, and in time all students and most faculty were elected by the entire school community. From the beginning, however, the students' ideas really counted, and they knew it. "Our decisions made a difference in school rules and even curriculum," writes one graduate. Earnest indeed were the all-school discussions that first year. The pioneers were setting precedents for years to come.

6:25 P.M.: Dinner
7:15–7:30, Evening Meeting

Young and old shook off their barnyard demeanor and dressed for dinner. Table manners were a sensitive subject for the faculty, who knew how quick critics were to condemn progressive schools on this score. For years, students rose when adults appeared at dinner table and waited for all to finish before leaving. Waiters stood by to refill serving dishes; dishes were scraped and washed out of sight. Mrs. H. always tried to break up the cliques and couples constantly forming and re-forming, urging every student to "sit with children you don't yet know." A majority obeyed her wishes, for "her approval lay behind one's thinking whenever a choice came up," no matter how small the matter for decision.[31]

No dinner decorum could interfere with the fun of between-course singing, however, or the occasional special dinner. Late one rainy afternoon, Mrs. H. went the rounds of every dorm and music room announcing a costume party for that evening's meal. Jane Arms and Charles Hapgood came dressed as each other, "each knowing the other's motions perfectly." Five small students diapered themselves up as the Dionne quintuplets, with a larger doctor and nurse in tow.[32] When Edward Yeomans brought his college-age son, the meal might end with a round of dancing, to Ed Jr.'s accordion. Even the dishwashing crew could make a festival of its job. "For some reason, dishwashing was a lot of fun," Liebe Coolidge remembers.

> Perhaps it was our substitute for competitive sports. We did it at first by hand, and later got a great Rube Goldberg-sort-of dishwasher, with immense trays and splashing and lots of steam. The assembly line was hectic and erratic. We broke things constantly, and were supposed to pay something like 50¢ a dish. But we discovered a hole in the wall, under the counter, and simply filed broken crockery in there.
>
> Later on this wall was torn down, and it was discovered that the whole side of the building was practically supported by bits of china and glass. The school leveled a general fine on all the students. We thought it seemed perfectly fair.

After dinner came all-school Assembly, where students or teachers could describe a special project in progress, Mrs. H. give one of her exhortations, a school trip be planned, or a community decision be made. Sometimes guests appeared: a famous Vermont fiddler, who held his fiddle under his ribs and made sounds student violinists only long for; a poet who lived nearby came to read his poems.[33]

Evening activities follow immediately

A host of activities, each longer than a daytime class, added choices for the students and further work for the multitalented faculty and staff. Some directly enriched classroom work. An evening discussion group gave one girl her first chance to like the history teacher who ran it ("Lucky, as I had him in history for three years"). Mrs. H. wrote this original evening schedule and turned it out on the school mimeograph machine.

Mrs. H. had, against much advice to the contrary, reduced study time to a minimum unprecedented in the world of college preparatory education. "Happy, well-rounded youngsters will study more efficiently," she said.[34] Thirty years of college entrance statistics seem to prove her right. If faculty had doubts, or longings for evening time all their own, they hid them for the present, putting aside their own unfinished poems or paintings to make the program work.

9:00 P.M.: Bed for students under 15
10:00 P.M.: Bed for older students

Some collapsed. Others unwound with hours of talk in darkened rooms, or finally—reading by flashlight under the covers, or sitting on the toilet where no dorm head could question the need for light—found time for themselves. Coeducational night life was minimal in Putney's early years, however often "we made out in the barn" by day.[35] Without actually mentioning the word, Mrs. H. had successfully gotten across the point that a single student *pregnancy* could destroy a small public's fragile trust in boarding-school coeducation, and with it, the Putney School itself.

In spring, sleeping time was most likely to be pared off at sunrise. Several riders would make their silent ways to the barn long before the approved 6:00 A.M. rising time to bridle their horses and be off into the morning mist. More than once they got caught, too—but kindly caught, for who at Putney School could blame the adventurous? The entire school plan invited adventure. A broken routine showed that the plan was working.

Evening activities

Monday	Tuesday	Wednesday	Thursday	Friday	Saturday
Magazine / Miss Arms	Magazine / Miss Arms		Play Reading / Mr. Hapgood	Singing 7:30–8:45	Dramatics / Spontaneous Entertainment (Students in charge)
Sketching / Miss Campbell	Domestic Science / Mrs. Gray		Reading / Mr. Holden		
Modeling / Mrs. Morris	Photography / (Alan Winkelstein)	Reading	Dramatics / Mrs. MacDougall	Folk and Square Dancing (every other week)	
Shop (Wood-carving) / Mr. MacDougall	The 4H Club / Meets once a month on this night.	for	Domestic Science / Mrs. Gray	Outside Speakers	
Laboratory (Chemistry Experiments) / Mr. Morris	Shop (carpentry) / Mr. Gray / Mr. Holden	Everyone	Sketching / Miss Campbell	Current Events / Mr. Hapgood	
Mechanics	Laboratory (Physics Experiments) / Mr. Sage		Photography / Mr. Morris		
Dramatics / Mrs. MacDougall	Mechanics		Modeling (Sculpture) / Mrs. Morris		
			Shop (carpentry) / Mr. Gray		
			Laboratory (Scientific Experiments) / Mr. MacDougall		
			Mechanics		

Groups to be formed:
ASTRONOMY, AERONAUTICS
What Would You Like?

Weekends

Weekends opened the countryside to all. Students did not even have to show up at Saturday lunch but could join the rush to the kitchen the split second Saturday morning Assembly was dismissed and make a pile of sandwiches to last them over the mountain to Newfane and back. In winter there was skiing. Two boys spent their Saturdays enlarging a hollow they had dug into an enormous snowdrift and enjoying their candle-lit retreat. Several others disappeared into the woods to work on the private sleeping cabins Mrs. H. had imagined so excitedly in her first dreams of a new secondary school— and (perhaps to settle the score as to whose dreams were whose) often got in some time to smoke in peace or enjoy applejack carefully nursed to potency in a bedroom closet.

Other weekend activities included rehearsing plays or working on the long job of wiring the Lower Farm barn and constructing stage and backstage for a theatre. As though Friday evening's music making powered a spigot not readily turned off, there was much practicing over weekends, a dozen pian-ists competing for time on the two school pianos. Usually, Ewald would have already invited anyone who cared to listen to sit by his own piano after Friday night singing; on Saturday, the Morrises' love of chamber music often over-came their desire for adult privacy, and privileged student instrumentalists joined them for string or piano quartets. To the deep joy of both the musical and the tone-deaf, record listening crept in, too. Mrs. H. didn't approve any nonparticipatory activity, but she only scolded a bit—and asked Hal Sproul to begin building a library of classical recordings. In November and May, adults and students made early soundings of each others' interests in anticipa-tion of the project week that capped the fall and spring terms.

Saturday night entertainment was often a homegrown play or skit, but at least once a month a square-dance band came up from Putney village. The new Putney students quickly discovered "the jollity and bracing exercise of the peasant dance," which Jane Addams had often praised in comparison with the lugubrious allurements of modern social dancing.[36]

Putney's boundaries were probably wider and vaguer than those of any boarding school in the nation, but now and then freedom propelled a student beyond them and smack into a roar of community indignation. The first year's most dramatic instance was plain to see one bright breakfast-time: a Nazi swastika flapping in the breeze where the school's American flag should have been. The culprit was Peter Ringland, who had thought it hilarious to be living on a Vermont farm in the midst of lederhosen, dirndl skirts, German Youth camp songs and a souvenir Nazi flag kept by Joan Hinton out of loyalty to summer friends. He planned his flag "borrowing" and flag-raising as a practical joke. A group of townsfolk, more aware of Hitler's latest power grabs, took it otherwise. "I'm taking Jimmy right out of that school!" said one mother. At noon, a group of angry townsmen, selectmen included, were gathering on Mr. Darrow's porch to demand that Peter Ringland· be expelled, when Carmelita Hinton drove up to talk with them. "Honestly, we do not support Hitler—just the opposite," she told them, and her tears may have convinced some where words could not. "Peter is only the littlest boy in the school!" The furor died down and both Peter and Jimmy stayed on, but local suspicision of Putney School's political connections would flare up from time to time for decades to come.[37]

Adult-organized adventures could be both safer and more daring. "Who's for Ascutney Mountain? I'm driving the red truck!" Mrs. H. asked on a Sunday morning after breakfast, and a whole gang raced to gather hiking boots and sweaters for the particular adventure of climbing—and of driving—with Mrs. H. Alumni of the first year remember the Ascutney trip because the party took a shortcut down a ravine, and Mrs. H. got stuck in a crack of the mountain; the students pulled and pushed, and suddenly she popped out again. "There were several Putney School excursions over the weekend," reported the Brattleboro *Reformer* one Spring Monday. "Mr. Hapgood and three students" went to Mr. Monadnock "to look for the steepest rocks." Two students "suffered falls." Jay Cooke "fell about fifty feet but sustained only slight injuries."[38]

Memorable also were trips down the Connecticut and cliff climbs above it, an all-school ski trip to Mt. Washington, trips to Boston and New York City to present plays or concerts at friendly schools, 4-H Club trips to county fairs and calf-judging contents—or simply trips to pick up a pig or cow, or a load of sawdust and the chance to talk alone with Hutch or Ed Gray. Everyone from seventh graders to secretaries was welcome to go.

7:15 P.M.: Sunday evening meeting

The entire Putney School gathered in the Assembly Hall after supper, bringing to a close the weekend's dispersals, each person bending attention to the relationship between self and community and all creation. Putney imposed no prayers, except in the sense that music is prayer. Mrs. Hinton chose readings that offered those confused by her everyday pace and power an orderly access to her thought. Olive Shriner's *Story of an African Farm* was a favorite, though alumni remember little of the plot and much of her dirndl skirt, of the chair she sat in, and of a voice that conveyed loving absorption in the details of a world far beyond West Hill. The best-rehearsed music was performed. Parents often spoke on Sunday nights. Two students' letters home describe the excitement of hearing a scientist who came to describe molecular structure to an audience made ready to revere science. Yeomans was the most frequent and welcome outside speaker, the one who always stayed afterward the longest and provoked the most intense talk through nights supposedly reserved for sleep. Somehow the intensity with which he spoke his philosophy was taken not as a command but as a release. "Mr. Yeomans gave us the most thrilling speech we ever heard," wrote Janet Thompson to her aunt in the fall of 1935. Afterward "He and I had a long discussion on chickens and a short one on God."

So ended the day and the week; so began the next measured round of Putney's wheel. It was the school's genius to send its students into each Sunday night, each season, each year, each life under a juxtaposition of chickens and ultimate concerns.

Part II
"Utopia Was at Hand"
1936–1948 and Beyond

So wrote Carmelita Hinton in recalling the school's opening year and the intense philosophical planning for Putney's future undertaken by teachers and students alike.[1] It would be a utopia recognized as successful even by its most ruthless critics, because it endured.[2] The school met each of the four criteria for endurance proposed by Schlesinger in his discussion of the sixty-odd communitarian experiments that flourished or (much more often) blossomed and died in the middle decades of the nineteenth century:

> The *work* of the community was organized in such a way as to insure its economic viability in the larger world, and to evoke each member's wholehearted contributions to the communal economy;
>
> the communitarians were held together by some *religious* faith, or by a powerful ethical consensus that had the force of a spiritual bond and filled individuals' spiritual needs;
>
> the community offered some outlet for *sexual drives*, or accomplished an acceptable repression of such drives, or both.
>
> The community had some means of *screening* all new candidates to insure their sincerity and competence.[3]

Finally, it should be added that all viable utopian experiments managed to relate themselves, whether in harmony or cranky opposition, to their *times*. The Perfectionists thrived because many antebellum Americans, unmoored from traditional faiths, believed in and longed for human perfection, and because their potent saint, John Humphrey Noyes, was willing to move his flock from his own hometown of Putney, Vermont (which by 1847 had reached toleration's limit), to the still wilder pastures of Oneida, New York.[4] Some Shaker communities survived for over 150 years. Their farming and craftsmanship served both their own and the larger community, and they lived their religion (and reproduced themselves) by offering a secure family to the lonely or the orphaned. Sexuality was subsumed in the ecstasies of their dancing and in the urgencies of Christian love. These and other successful communities "drew on powerful ideas and structures available in the broader culture," writes one scholar, instead of walling themselves off entirely from the world outside.[5]

Carmelita Hinton saw no contradiction between her desire for broad social change and her conception of a utopian school isolated on a Vermont hill. Ever since Johann Pestalozzi's invention of the Swiss boarding school in the early nineteenth century, educators had found promise in the maximum control over the growing person that a residential school afforded, especially one far from urban distractions. It is no coincidence that Robert Dale Owen, son of the utopian socialist, attended one of the Swiss schools established on Pestalozzi's design. Founders of the Round Hill school for boys in rural Massachusetts consciously built a humane community of learners after Pestalozzi's ideas, establishing it in 1823 "on the brow of a beautiful hill" above the Connecticut River. At Round Hill, boys would be "govern[ed] by persuasion" and could learn from desire, not fear.[6] Round Hill and female academies like Mt. Holyoke Seminary were helping to invent adolescence as a stage of life with needs and potentialities of its own. The Victorians carried the definition further: charged with dangerous energies and peculiarly vulnerable to the new urban temptations, adolescents needed a place apart, such as the many new boarding schools for gentlemen's sons founded in New England between 1856 (St. Paul's) and 1903 (Deerfield).[7]

Strengthened in isolation, adolescents could reenter the urban world ready to apply their full powers to adult concerns. Beginning with Erik H. Erikson, twentieth-century psychoanalytic thinkers added their endorsement of a "psycho-social moratorium" within which adolescents could experiment "with inner and outer dangers, including those emanating from the adult world." Adults could count on the young to gather in "presocieties" of their own;[8] a boarding school, however, could amplify the adolescent's opportunity for safe experiment, especially a school like Putney, whose laboratory was so wide and so richly furnished. Whatever one thinks of adult utopias, the boarding schools have been among the most enduring utopian communities the United States has known—the more so, perhaps, because they hold their younger members' participation to four or five years at most. They also live daily with the perils and possibilities that pervaded the nineteenth-century utopias: questions of privacy, of power, of rights, of community ethos, of financial survival.

Chapter 4

Work I

Putney's work had many dimensions. Any new secondary school must produce college-ready graduates to survive, but Putney's founding director and teachers wanted much more: classroom and studio work that was its own reward as well as preparation; physical work that would both materially support a complex educational "village" and connect adolescent strivings with adult realities. Over the years, the academic program, whatever its bumps and omissions, grew itself a "high reputation for intellectual honesty"[1] among parents seeking good schooling for their children.

By the early 1940s, the school enrolled 150 students, the full-time academic and arts staff had increased to 20, (13 men and 7 women in 1941), and the course of study for the pre-1950s period was complete.

Science (1 yr. required)	*History* (4 yrs.)	*Languages* (3 yrs.)
General Science	Ancient	General Language
Biology	Mediaeval	Latin
Chemistry	Renaissance to 1815	French
Physics	Modern European	German
	American Civilization	Spanish
	(2 yr. course)	(Russian added in 1946)
Mathematics (3–4 yrs.)	*English* (4 yrs.)	*Arts* (1–4 yrs.)
Arithmetic		Music (theory, advanced
Algebra		theory, literature)
Plane Geometry		Art (graphic, plastic)
Solid Geometry		Drama
Trigonometry		Shop
Calculus		

The average class had twelve students, though a few advanced music and language classes held but two or three or were tutorials.

"We had to work hard to prove that we were more than a 'farm school,'" says Hugh MacDougall. "We had to get them into Harvard—and we did."

These imperatives distanced Putney's academic curriculum from its thoroughly progressive center, though Mrs. H. and her teachers kept in touch with other progressive educators' projects, including the Eight Year Study, begun in 1932. Participating colleges—including several Ivy League universities—had set aside College Board examination requirements for entering students recommended by the study's thirty secondary schools. The study proved that 1475 students prepared through a progressive curriculum could do as well in college as 1475 controls traditionally taught. Indeed, the more daring the curriculum attempted by the schools under scrutiny, the better they did.[2] Yet Mrs. H. found herself "a rebel against schools of education," whatever their original role in the progressive movement. She had become involved in schooling by way of her two passionate interests: children and social reform. For progressive education to become the captive of the professional "educationists" was to reduce it to an academic exercise. Carmelita Hinton had always been repelled by academic exercises.[3]

Secondary schools in general were still seeking their place in progressive education, powered as it had been by the kindergarten and child-study movements. Infighting within the P.E.A. was draining energy from broader issues of educational reform. The only thing high school progressives could agree on was the importance of manual training, the arts, and occasional projects that demanded individual planning and execution. For all their appreciation of the educative power of choice and the joy of learning by doing, few Putney adults believed that "the prolonging of childhood is the hope of the race," as Marietta Johnson put it. Johnson, founder of the Organic School and "the guiding spirit of the progressive education movement"[4] repudiated examinations, but nearly all Putney teachers gave final exams in one form or another until at least halfway through the war. Before 1942, seniors took three-hour practice examinations in preparation for College Boards, many of which required long essays on specific topics. Even those dangerous talismans, grades and class rank, were not shrouded from seniors being counseled toward college entrance. "Tests were given frequently," wrote Dan Morris of his physics course, "and were not easy. In every case they were used as study material afterwards. . . . It happens that 'easy' approaches to Physics are often basically wrong."

Carmelita Hinton no more believed in unbridled freedom than did John Dewey. With Dewey she also felt that true discipline is built by "engaging the mind in activities worthwhile for their own sake."[5] Putney adults energetically arranged such engagements of the mind, even while they acknowledged that discipline ultimately comes from within. Rejecting the romantic Freudian progressive philosophies that had come to the fore during the

1920s, teachers took attendance in classes, in study halls, in work crews, everywhere. Jane Arms and, later, Gerry Biddle worked out intricate schedules for each student.[6] Only seniors were automatically placed on the independent study list. All others—seniors too, as soon as they faltered—had to study under supervision until they had proved to every teacher and to all student members of the council their conscientiousness in every area of school life. As Joan Strong wrote of her life off the independent study list,

> "I learned to study after I had spent study-hall time reading O. Henry stories when I should have been preparing for a history class. Consequently I wrote a paper in which I hopelessly confused the Pyramid Age and the Federal Age of ancient Egypt. The truth dawned only when my paper was read in class and supplied more laughing matter than information."[7]

College counselors Warren Leonard and James K. Angell orchestrated students' academic programs through seventeen of the school's first twenty years, both men deeply involving themselves in the life of the school as a whole. In spite of democratic forms, authority over long-term school decisions tended to fall to these men and, most of all, to Carmelita Hinton. As the school grew larger, it was only the "strange ducks" whose records were scrutinized in faculty meetings.[8] Increasingly, tough decisions on individuals were made during August. ("_____ should not return," wrote Mrs. H. to Warren Leonard. "I'm not sure it's *safe* to have him at school. Kids say he's cruel to animals . . . keeps guns.") Putney was not a school for everyone.

Progressive educators, ever watchful for science's contributions to their art, embraced psychological testing in the 1930s and 1940s.[9] While test scores were never taken as definitive at Putney, they were frequently used as guides. Given the school's initial struggles to find a full complement of able boys, it is interesting to add up the group IQ scores for one prewar student body. One-fifth of the entire tested group scored over 130 points, but girls' IQ's averaged 116, and boys', 124, with five girls scoring below 100.[10] Remedial English testing and teaching became one of Anne Holden's multiple duties soon after her arrival in 1936 as John Holden's wife and teacher in the "Little School" for faculty children. Then in 1941 remedial work and all standardized testing, including IQ and vocational testing, was taken over by an expert who came from Boston's Children's Hospital two days a week in return for her son's tuition.

Even this progressive psychologist saw tests as single tools in a shopful of teaching techniques. So did her successors later on.[11] Other educationist science was similarly modified. Many students still marvel at the power of such teachers as Eric Rogers, who had read the literature of progressive educationists' experiments disproving the transfer theory of skill learning but had become convinced by his own scholarly experience that "*delight* in scientific accuracy" would enrich all learning, even where the effects of specific training exercises were limited.[12] Students knew Rogers as the Englishman who so delighted in physics that he regularly drove all the way to Brattleboro in second gear while pondering a problem in motion or causality. The many-dimensioned Putney community could not have reduced education to tidy formulae even if it had wished to do so.

In addition to their classroom teachers, all students also had faculty counselors who watched and prodded—but who, just as often (perhaps pursuing their own small rebellions against Putney's exacting pace) gave their counselees balm of acceptance and simple appreciation, usually accompanied by *tea* or *coffee*, or both. After all, the school was too small, the "children's . . . eagerness and enthusiasm"[13] too great, the total indoor and outdoor curriculum too rich in varieties of learning and social interaction for any individual student to be mistaken for his or her scores, grades or reputation among the classroom faculty.

It is not possible to give a coherent description of Putney's pre-fifties academic curriculum, because the curriculum was often incoherent. This was particularly the case after the early forties, when the College Board abandoned its three-hour essay exams, and English and history teachers no longer felt so tightly bound by CEEB requirements. Like many progressive educators, Mrs. H. feared that strong departments would set the "whole child" aside in favor of their own fiefdoms. Some teachers made academic freedom an excuse for disdaining useful cooperation. Though courses always ran in close sequence in two-person departments like music and art, sequence in the larger departments came to depend largely on whether those teaching within them liked each other or not. For a single year, history students learned economics from Charles Hapgood, who was in the flush of his Marxist young-manhood, but after that economics was not taught again in concentrated fashion until Edwin Smith brought his experience in the labor movement to Putney after the war.[14] Some disjointedness was inevitable in a school where teachers came and went so rapidly. During Carmelita Hinton's twenty-year tenure as Putney's director, classroom teachers, 140 of them altogether, stayed an average of three years. Subtract the four longest tenured, full-time teachers—the Holdens, Norwood Hinkle, and Warren Leonard—and the average falls to 2 1/4 years.

Yet no alumni have been heard to complain of the dazzling unpredictability of Putney's course offerings, engendered by teacher freedom and high turnover. On the contrary, the curriculum seemed to cohere inside students' heads, if they were interested in academic work at all, its cacophonies tumbling toward harmony in the personalities of a few key teachers whom students saw all day in many roles. On the whole, it worked.[15]

To think scientifically was to master "the machine age,"[16] Mrs. H. had written in her 1934 prospectus. Her original conviction, shared by many progressives, had been strengthened by years of introducing wondering elementary school children to the natural world. For adolescents searching out a future, science would provide the essential map, history of science a perspective on present reality. Though Putney School required only one year of science, Mrs. H. expected students to elect three or four years, and many did. Three powerful science teachers stayed five years or more before 1949; Dan Morris, Hugh MacDougall, and Olwen Williams. Biology was anything but a "soft science" in Olwen's hands. Two alumni trace their start in medical careers to her rigorous training; many more were first warmed by her enthusiasm for botanical study, then gradually initiated into precise skills of observation and analysis that have helped them in a variety of vocations.

Each June, all teachers were required to describe and evaluate the courses they had taught through the year, a practice Mrs. H. had learned at Shady Hill. These detailed reports helped Mrs. H., Warren Leonard, and Jim Angell to keep track of teachers' work and provided a record useful to new teachers. For science courses, they reveal particular problems as well as teachers' efforts to solve them. Maximum and minimum assignments were used by the science faculty (as they were by virtually all Putney teachers) to accommodate different levels of competence, for even though applicants began pounding on Putney's doors in the early forties, Mrs. H. still believed more in character than intelligence and still sought special talents rather than admitting the capable-but-dull.[17] Thus one 1940s physics teacher labored to teach a single class of students whose science aptitude scores ran from the fifth to the ninety-fifth percentile.

That physical science students had to build or improve equipment was not entirely a hardship: building a balance meant beginning to learn its function, and it was exciting to watch Eric Rogers grab the fire extinguisher off the wall and shoot its contents across the room to demonstrate a parabola. Rogers taught equations by using a student to represent the equal sign ($=$); others stood as symbols on either side and moved back and forth according to mathematical rules. Dan Morris, always unsatisfied with others' texts and lab manuals, insisted that students "write out their own (physics) lab notes rather than filling in blanks. This makes for much more intelligent experimentation, or shows up lack of intelligence." His successors might add ("21 films and a unit on nuclear physics") or subtract from the syllabus, but the best continued to reinvent the science courses every year.[18]

Putney's farm and forest land made an ideal laboratory for those life-science teachers with the energy and imagination to use it. It also provided grist for work weeks. Once students had mastered some basics, Putney's teachers would periodically turn them loose on small research projects of their own and expect them to teach what they had learned to the class in the ensuing week. A census of local birds or wildflowers for a work week (or for the twice-yearly project weeks), a nutrition experiment in the henhouse, the botanical mapping of a ten-yard square of forest floor—these made for intensive learning experiences.

The project method could also be sadly misused by the unprepared teacher or the youngster whose "charming laziness" deflected criticism. "None of my 10th grade teachers seemed to even care what I did on work weeks," recalls a '44 alumnus who didn't care much either. Though no one could label her irresponsible, Jane Arms sometimes excused eleventh graders from English classes for weeks at a time.[19] Werner Heider, a sensitive scholar of Latin and history who was pressed into chemistry teaching during the war, promised still more work weeks and chapter reports "if I do have to teach this course again." To his great relief, he did not. In her chemistry section, on the other hand, Olwen Williams eschewed the contemporary currents that some students found "a revelation", and concentrated instead on "supervised study of the fundamental ideas" of chemistry. There was little departmental continuity in the sciences.[20]

A four-year mathematics course of study was recommended for college entrance; thus there was more continuity in math at Putney—but the quality of the teaching was also more erratic. Alumni and colleagues describe as "brilliant" those physical science teachers who also taught math. During his nine years at Putney, Dan Morris made his mathematics teaching one vehicle for his own continual exploration of the mystery of life, putting aside set texts altogether in geometry, where he simply presented students with the theorems, each to be proved. Eric Rogers did much the same for his classes, with equal success,[21] and the energetic Warren Leonard soon added strength to the mathematics curriculum. In other hands, some upper-level students floundered. Hans Hollstein's ebullience, so attractive outside class, could not by itself teach logarithms. Several alumni remember what a letdown it was to move from Hollstein's exciting geometry class or Anne Holden's algebra into the advanced courses once Morris and Rogers had left. Some girls may have picked up Mrs. H.'s opinion that mathematics was too far from real life to matter very much and used it to bolster their conviction that advanced math was a "Mt. Everest" that girls were not really expected to climb. Now, though grateful for generally "splendid college preparation," a few alumnae wish that "better math had been forced on us."[22]

"Along with Hugh MacDougall's General Science, Jane Arms' Ancient History set my life's course and work," writes a '40 alumnus, now a physician. Jane Arms was primarily an English and Latin teacher, superlatively a teacher of poetry writing. In her wide enthusiasms, she represented Mrs. H's "zest for correlations," as did Ewald Schnitzer.[23] While this passion could become dilettantism in both teachers and students, all in all it made for a stimulating English and history curriculum. One English teacher worked out her tenth-grade assignments with the ancient history teacher. Both kept an eye on the plays in rehearsal at the Lower Farm theater: "*Due Tuesday*: Learn at least 75 lines of an Iknaton poem. 28th Week: Hand in vocabulary lists, library books, etc. Finish reading *Iphigenia in Tauris* aloud." Students taking Music I gave special reports in medieval and Renaissance history classes. One year, two of them reported to both their music and their general science classes on the physics of musical tones.[24]

For seven years, Ursula MacDougall's craftsmanlike teaching balanced Jane Arms's dash and energy. Alumni still think of Ursula "with awe and fondness." Ursula took on the role of basic skills developer among the English teachers, urging on them her system of evaluating students every four weeks on precisely defined tasks.

Of Jane Arms, Judy Gregory says, "She seemed to live entirely from within, regardless of how she might be seen by anyone else—which, I of course gathered, was precisely what no woman might do without great and nameless risk." When the students weren't running the *Putney Magazine* alone, either Ursula or Jane, each one a writer herself, was usually the *Magazine* advisor. Mrs. Hinton had originally planned that the *Magazine* should appear every month at the least and publish articles of interest to "young people all over the world." It would cast an international net in its solicitation of artistic and literary contributions; it would become a world "trading post for student thought on economics and politics."[25]

Though this plan proved overambitious, the *Magazine* ranged unusually wide for a student publication. For six years, there were indeed several "outside" articles in every term's issue: by Edward Yeomans ("Observations on Spiders"); by Chinese students at Shansi-Oberlin Memorial College describing life under pressure of war; by a Spanish Experimenter, on the Spanish revolution, excoriating "The Reds" and finishing "Hurray General

Name	Spelling	Writing	Gen'l Appear.	First Draft	Sent. Struct.	Grammar	Para-g'phs	Punct.	Progress
	Poor –	Fair	Good	Good	Good	Good	Fair	Fair	Fair –
	Good	Good	Good	Good	Good	Good	Good	Good	Good
	Poor	Fair	Fair	Fair	Poor+	Poor	Poor	Poor –	Fair
	Good+	Good	Good	Good	Good+	Fair+	Good	Good	Good
	Poor	Poor	Poor	Poor	Poor–	Poor+	Fair	Poor	Fair
	Fair+	Fair	Good	Good	Poor	Poor	Fair	Poor	Fair
	Good–	Good	Good	Good	Good	Good	Good	Good	Good
	Fair	Fair	Poor	Fair	Fair	Fair	Poor	Fair	Poor
	Poor	Fair	Fair	Fair	Fair–	Fair	Fair	Poor	Fair
	Poor	Fair	Fair	Fair	Fair	Fair	Fair	Fair	Fair
	Fair+	Fair	Fair	Poor	Good	Fair	Poor	Fair+	Fair
	Excellent	Excellent	Excellent	Excellent	Good+	Excellent	Good	Excellent	Good
	Good+	Good	Excellent	Good	Fair+	Good	Fair	Good	Good
	Fair	Fair–	Poor	Poor	Fair+	Fair	Fair	Fair	Fair
	Good+	Fair+	Fair	Fair	Good+	Excellent	Good	Excellent	Good

Franco!" and by a Putney School Experimenter shuddering for both sides in Spain's civil war; by college deans or Putney alumni all over the country describing their colleges. Young editors pored over articles on the WPA and the approaching war, often correcting their elders' prose. They sprinkled the best student 4-H reports on milking and pigraising among the overdone blank verse that usually overwhelms the adult reader of student magazines and the portraits of poor but noble Negro sharecroppers. This poem, written in Jane Arms' style by a girl who would soon be a professional journalist, represents the poetry all too well:

> There is a power in me
> Lying deep.
> Today I felt it first, and knew
> I could do anything.
>
> I laughed at adversity
> And, biting deep,

Shook the throat of life,
Drinking blood.[26]

But there are also first-rate student poems, as well as short stories, descriptions of off-campus projects, and extraordinary accounts by student or faculty travelers presented to a readership taught to revere travel as both adventure and international education. They make a magazine that is readable still.

Prewar English reading lists were daring for the time. While most prep school students (particularly girls) continued to read Milton, Wordsworth, Shelley, Scott, and *Idylls of the King*, Putney's seniors read all these *plus* Lawrence, Shaw, a series of British tracts on prison reform, Ibsen, Pirandello, Arthur Koestler, and contemporary American works by Upton Sinclair, or Eugene O'Neill, which few traditional schools would touch in the 1930s and 1940s. Every Putney student through 1950 must have read Steinbeck's *The Grapes of Wrath*. Most English teachers also required students to be reading books of their own choice throughout the year at the rate of 150 to 400 pages a week. In 1938–39, one tenth grader read sixty-three books (including the *Odyssey* and Parkman's *Oregon Trail*), another, seven (*Tom Sawyer, Tom Brown's School Days* . . .). This free reading imposed obligatory periods of isolation for which some students were deeply grateful.

Like the English curriculum, the course of study in history looks conventional at first glance: four years of standard ancient, European, and U.S. history. Ewald's example proved powerful, however. Though his three-year world history course was shortened to two when he left in 1943, many of Putney's succeeding history teachers also strove to embrace intellectual as well as political and social history within their courses. A senior's reading list for the 1945–46 American civilization course reflects the breadth of concerns. Berle and Means's *The Modern Corporation* keeps company with Davis's *Capitalism and Its Culture*, WPA oral histories, and the Lynds' *Middletown*. There is a book on black Harlem, another on the TVA, Henry Wallace's *Sixty-Million Jobs*, Mumford's *Culture of the Cities*, Chase's *Rich Land, Poor Land*, and novels by both Upton Sinclair and Santayana. It was clear to all that history and social science had Mrs. H.'s strongest support. Cruising around the grounds, she came upon Judy Gregory one day rapt in a Latin epic poem. "What are you studying all this stuff for?" asked Mrs. H. "Why aren't you studying social sciences?"[27]

English teachers required writing for or in every class. Most English and history teachers also assigned frequent essays and research topics that demanded unusual effort. Leta Cromwell (at Putney for four years in the 1940s) was particularly exacting and inspiring to writers. Ursula MacDougall set an example of requiring all students to correct and resubmit all their papers after she had commented on them or discussed them in her weekly conference, or (usually) both. Geoffrey Bret Harte, grandson of the renowned American writer, had a limited interest in formal pedagogy, having gotten his own education by reading in the Vatican library. He commented rather extensively on some history essays ("thorough and interesting, but . . . what about your *spelling* which seems to have taken ill? . . . Pleeze, deer Fillis, yuse a diksyournary!"), but appeared to have left others virtually unread. "Check here if you get this far, Mr. B-H," wrote students in the margins of their papers. The boxes remained blank. [28] Even as final exam giving diminished, however, Bret Harte's hour-long quizzes posed formidable questions for ninth-graders:

> If you were to compare the systems of government existing
> a. in Periclean Athens
> b. in the Roman Republic
> c. in present day America,
> which would you consider to be the most effective and which would you prefer to live under? Give your reasons.

Students minded neither his laxness nor his periodic firmness. "He was a great teacher anyway," they say. Ewald "puts a little of himself in front of his work, but he's a grand guy," wrote Polly Braun to her mother. And Janet Rogers (English history) "is the best teacher I have ever had." [29]

Every student was also required to devote twenty-eight hours of the month-long Christmas vacation to a project of her or his design, expecting no college credit; seniors could choose to spend up to half of their academic course time on a spring-term independent project, usually done under close adult supervision. Student projects came in great variety: a study of *Madame Bovary* written in French, laboratory work at the Brattleboro Hospital, the planning of "a practical policy of World Cooperation without World Government," serving as assistant teacher in the village public school, a two-week study of corals off the coast of Puerto Rico. In such a curriculum, experimental teaching could also flourish.

Perhaps it was only natural that the restless, idealistic teachers whom Putney so often attracted would go on to graduate schools or to other fields of work after a time. Several top-notch English and history teachers, including Leta Cromwell, eventually abandoned their efforts to communicate historical and contemporary issues to others and plunged into the world of events, often committing themselves to international service work or similar endeavors. Janet Rogers left in 1940 when her husband found (like two other men before him) that the assistant head position Mrs. H. had assigned him was untenable.

One voice for a rigorous pedagogy was muffled when Ursula MacDougall found herself supplanted as Mrs. H.'s chief academic advisor by Jane Arms. Nora Sayre, now a writer whose biting recollections carry many of her points, found a postwar English department largely filled with "capsized writers" and "would-be semanticists." Certainly there were some who gave up requiring students to "wrestle with the language." Similarly, Mrs. H.'s beloved historical correlations could become circular redundancies wherein, as Nora put it, "anything may be explained in terms of anything else: King Lear is like Christ who is like Socrates." It was not enough, says an alumnus, for a teacher's major comment on one's writing to be "It's lovely because it's you." Fewer English and history teachers are vividly recalled by Putney alumni graduating in the later 1940s.[30]

"Languages!" exclaimed Carmelita Hinton, "They are most important in building the 'One World' for which we work."[31] And a few strong teachers did, from time to time, break out of the rather constrictive pedagogy of pre-1950s language teaching, which depended heavily on grammar drills and English explanations. On the whole, modern languages fared the best; to Mrs. H., as to John Dewey, Latin's "One World" was out of date. Mara Moser, who was at the school from 1943 to 1948, was probably the outstanding language teacher of this period. Herself a Swiss, she was equally at home in French, German, Spanish, and English, and her interests ranged as wide. Her homemade grammar exercises were so amusing that students hardly noticed the repetition of phrases and forms. Off to a conference one day, she left instructions for her Spanish class, along with a recording of a "magnificent" Spanish poem. "Listen several times to each stanza," she wrote, "first without, then with the text. Finally, learn it all by heart." Her closing directions: "So long, chums. Take dictionary along—pens and ears and brains and a heart full of joy. Love, Mara." She was dynamite! says a '50 alumna.

Before Mara arrived, the language tables, so lively and successful in the school's opening years, had lapsed. The German living room, established by Hans Hollstein so that each student could "live the language he learns," had also closed down.[32] German House was tactfully renamed "Red Cottage" after war was declared and was emptied of German students. "Kelsie teaches French in English," wrote Polly Braun to her family. "I don't know whether to submit or go on to '*pensez en français*,'" as Madame back home had taught her.[33] This situation changed for the better during and after the war, when Putney became home to numerous scholarly European refugees and expatriates. Native speakers like Albert Raffanel, with his elegant lemon-yellow tie and cigarette-yellow fingers, his French songs and jokes, could seduce the most jaded youngster into a respect—even a love—for French. It is rather surprising that Putney did not pick up sooner on the oral-aural language teaching techniques that were developed so successfully by the U.S. Army during the War; but then, very few schools did so until the late fifties, when Putney would also board the bandwagon.

Latin, grandfather of the traditional school curriculum, remained Putney's stepchild. "Latin is so dull," wrote one student. "The class is too big and too impersonal." A limp Latin course added to Nora Sayre's "stupendous" boredom in her first year. She failed it. "We were supposed to work from inspiration, and I just hadn't felt inspired," a cop-out specific to Putney with its devotion to learning for its own sake. [34] A '47 alumna recalls how grateful she was to her Latin II teacher, who said he'd pass her only if she promised not to take Latin again. She did. Yet, as always at Putney, there were a few exceptions, Latin students and teachers who reveled in the subject. In a school where teachers' idiosyncrasies were so warmly welcomed, even dull teachers sometimes became interesting.

In *The Child-Centered School,* by Lawrence Cremin's account the key progressive work of the 1920s, Harold Rugg and Ann Shumaker celebrated "the historic battle of the artist against the superficiality and commercialism of industrial civilization." [35] All of Putney School fought the same battle, and the arts were in the front lines. Putney's sixteen-hour schoolday meant double time for the arts. Evening activities allowed both students and adults to discover or pursue interests often excluded from, but to Mrs. H. at least as important as, the college credit curriculum. [36] The line between evening and daytime programs was deliberately left fuzzy: students might rehearse with the madrigal chorus at night and by day spend two terms of Music II singing through and discussing virtually every piece in the *Harvard Anthology of Medieval and Renaissance Music,* or sculpt the same lump of clay in the studio for art class and art activity. During fall and spring project weeks, an equal amount of time was expected by the activity teacher and the classroom teacher sponsoring the two projects to which the student was committed. Soon this meant "double projects" in all the arts. "Today was Bach day," wrote one boy in his journal. "I did nothing all day but play and sing Bach." [37] In addition to the project week harvest, concerts, plays and dance exhibitions were seeded throughout the year; student poems were read during Sunday meetings; student and faculty art work was always on display.

Professional poets or musicians presented their work during all-school meetings as frequently as did other outsiders. Almost anything went. "Wednesday night," wrote Janet Thompson, a seventy-five-year-old Englishwoman "spoke to us on the Greeks' basic principle, HARMONY of the soul and body, and illustrated her talk with contortions."[38] At times, to be sure, the fragility of the creative process became an excuse for student sloth, the only real consequence being an audience disappointed or a blank space on the wall where a painting should have hung. Where everyone was assumed to be an artist until proven otherwise, garbage sometimes passed for self-expression. On the whole, however, the arts were as much respected and as disciplined as any other form of work at Putney. They permeated the culture of the school.

"The final basis of art is the vitality of one's own life," said Luke Gwilliam. For seven years, Luke's boundless energy enlivened the visual arts at Putney.[39] Luke worked in a style reminiscent of WPA murals, a 1930s realism approach that demanded close attention to detail. He designed his basic course on a series of exercises in color perception and line- or shape-making, moving systematically from one medium to another, then setting students free for their own painting or photography projects, as he turned to his, for he was often preparing for exhibitions of his own work. By comparison, Mrs. H. found Luke's successor, the English sculptor Oliver O'Connor Barrett, a little too lenient with students. They often idolized him for his kindness and his work (including a string quartet carved in high relief, which still hangs in the school assembly hall), but, says one alumnus, Barrett believed in free love as a legitimate philosophy for adults, and the principal did not. "Wouldn't you like him?" Mrs. H. wrote Cranbrook Academy of Art after a year.[40]

Meanwhile, Genevieve Hamlin, who ran the pottery workshop, made ceramics students her apprentices in a serious commercial enterprise. She worked like a fiend, her hair flying as she dug clay from the Connecticut River bank or plied her wheel, turning out hundreds of pieces a year.[41] Hamlin was one of two art teachers before 1950 who stayed five years or more. Although by far the best teachers were working artists, it was hard to find and keep them, given the demands of a Putney teacher's life.

Drama and music competed for students' attention as did no other two disciplines, partly because student talents overlapped, partly because their teachers' voices were so loud in the school. "People are theater," wrote Vivian Johannes in her call for a Putney Theater Workshop during Putney's third year. She and Mrs. H. proposed housing the workshop in the Lower Farm barn. Johannes had a curriculum planned that included training in breath control, eurhythmics, and pantomime to precede the actual rehearsal and writing of plays. It was this vivid, emotional little woman who engaged the steady engineer, Hugh MacDougall, to design and build Putney's theater with student help. "We all thought Vivian a marvelous kook," says Dan Morris. She left Putney's academic year program after a single year, however; it was Bunny White (teacher of English and Drama, 1943–51) who carried the workshop into reality after the war. Vivian returned to help Bunny in both the Putney Summer Theater and the school English department. While Bunny proved her faith in her students by "driving and driving us," and now and then "blasting everybody to hell," Vivian and the gentle Arthur Lithgow found their young actors and actresses so interesting that they became interesting to themselves. "Arthur is one of the few people here who really treats us as his equals, and yet makes us realize that there is an awful lot to be learned," one student wrote her family.[42]

Drama filled every crack in many student schedules. Mrs. H. had envisioned rehearsal of classic plays and music so thorough that Putney students could carry culture to town halls and granges all around southern Vermont. Local audiences may have found Chekhov and Synge and Palestrina puzzling, but they came, and came back. The students did more with some adult help: they arranged performances at the Brattle Theatre in Cambridge and in New York and carried themselves and all their scenery in trucks, often paying their way through ticket sales. Where there was a drama contest to be won, Putney generally won it.

Putney School aroused the interest of artistic parents, whose children set standards for others. Barbara Bel Geddes might put on airs and be disliked (at first) by most of the upper dorm, but all agreed she was a wonderful actress—so good that she won parts even when she failed to turn up for rehearsals. In the winter of 1941, much of the upper dorm traveled with the theater group to New York to see her in a professional production and to greet her backstage.[43] Other Putney School stars such as David Eames and Kit Lukas, who began their careers on the Lower Farm stage, became documentary film directors, television producers, or playwrights, joining the eighty alumni who eventually chose drama or filmmaking as a profession.

"Music should fill the air," said Mrs. H., and it did.[44] Hal Sproul had given it a strong start, and had in his person joined music with the larger life of the community. Boys admired Hal's skill on the baseball diamond. Janet Thompson loved having a creative writing teacher who was an equally good musician, and Hal, in turn, respected her writing as much as he did her musicianship. ("*Good*," he wrote at the bottom of one of her shorter compositions, "This, I suppose you know, is a poem.") Summer work campers, moved equally by Hal's conducting and his conversation, interviewed him about his educational philosophy for the *Putney Worker*, their magazine. "You can't teach without understanding," he told them, "and when you really understand anything—a horse, a person, a tree, a test-tube reaction or a curve of musical sound—you can't help loving it. It becomes a part of the self."[45]

Hal was also a man of dark moods, however. Though he would return to the Work Camp, he left Putney School abruptly in 1938 "after a terrific argument with Mrs. H."[46] There was an interim year in which the excellent piano teacher tried to fill in, but failed as music director: "he's a kind of nightclub guy who smokes *toujours*, . . . a salesman . . . too soupy in everything," wrote one talented ninth grader to her family. That was October 1938. In June she wrote, "Swimming is grand and everything is swell. We're getting a wonderful bird to teach singing next year. He came Friday. The guy is simply marvelous. It was the best singing of the year. His wife who accompanies him beautifully seems a dear."[47]

The "wonderful bird" was Norwood Hinkle, who, with his wife and copilot, Cornelia, would spend thirty-three years making music central to Putney School. Mrs. H. had found the Hinkles through Yeomans, a devoted amateur cellist, who had come to know of them through G. Wallace Woodworth and Thomas W. Surette's Concord Summer Music School. Surette was one of the few Americans who understood what young musicians could do with music, and he had made it his life's mission to teach others, with the help of such gifted teachers as professors Woodworth and Archibald Davison of Harvard and Putney's Hal Sproul, cellist for nine summers at Concord.

"Music is not mere sound," Surette had written in 1898; "It is the voice through which all the deep feelings and purposes of life speak."[48] Woodworth's conducting was energized by the same principle during the summer Norwood Hinkle spent at Concord. Convinced that good music itself would carry the message, Hinkle worked for years as an assistant editor in the Oliver Ditson music publishing house. Though Ditson had good music for sale, Norwood became increasingly disillusioned with the school music buyers, who continued to order "this JUNK!" (he says, still spouting).[49] He decided to try teaching instead. While training to do so under Davison and Woodworth at Harvard, he sometimes brought his young wife Cornelia to Davison's class. Cornelia had also received most of her formal music education at Radcliffe and Harvard and had participated for two summers in Surette's Concord School. Now she was discovering her own high standards by assisting Concord-trained teachers at Beaver Country Day School, which then had the finest student orchestra in the Boston area.[50]

For two years after taking his Harvard master's in teaching, Norwood directed music at Pinkerton Academy, the public high and junior high school for Derry, New Hampshire. Meanwhile Cornelia, New Hampshire–born, drove from one Derry elementary school to another, bringing singing, music reading, and folk dancing to over three hundred pupils. "The superintendent hired me because he knew I could drive in the snow," she says. When Carmelita Hinton came to Derry to approach the Hinkles about teaching music full time at Putney, Norwood was just beginning to realize how difficult it was not to become simply a band leader in a public school.

"Can you play first violin in a Mozart quartet?" asked Edward Yeomans of Norwood on the Hinkles' first visit to Putney. "I lied," says Norwood. And the Hinkles were hired. Soon no one doubted Norwood's first violin. He was undaunted by conventional teachers' fondness for "*preparing* students for Bach's and Mozart's music instead of *doing* it." Says Cornelia, "We just pitched in and taught, . . . and we were lucky to engage a series of unusual instrumental teachers to do the same," professionals like George Finckel, who could sit down with three struggling string players and, by his own cello playing, transform them into an inspired string quartet.[51]

So extraordinary a gift was the Hinkles' teaching to so many hundreds of Putney's people that one often finds graduates' musical reminiscences overwhelming all others. "How did Norwood do it?" generations of Putney alumni have asked.[52] He wasn't a polished conductor. He yelled at his sopranos when they sharped, and he told his woodwinds after a sloppy entrance that they sounded "like a cold fried egg." "An obsessed tyrant!" says one alumna.[53] But precisely because of Norwood's obsession with excellence, because of his passionate, colorful, and often humorous expression of it, his music sounded ever more clearly in the school, ever more complex and more beautiful.

The outside world heard it too. Young people who would not have left traditional schools for any other reason began to come to Putney for music. Once arrived, their reward was threefold: hard work (whether in daytime courses or in performance preparation), the warm appreciation the community accorded all artists, and usually the Hinkles' friendship as well. For all his public rages, Norwood's private kindnesses were as abundant as Cornelia's. Eventually over seventy of the twelve hundred graduated between 1935 and 1965 made the composing, performing, or teaching of music their career. Many times their number become devoted amateur musicians.

"At Putney, I discovered I was a musician," writes one. In the early days, one-third of the school was in the orchestra, including Mrs. H. ("Jesus! Can't you *count?*" Norwood demanded of his second clarinet[54]), about a quarter as the student body grew and orchestra became a regular evening activity. Many more took lessons. Teachers played too. "What are *you* doing down there?" Norwood shouted to Anne Holden when he saw she had joined the second violin section. "Playing every fourth note!" Anne shouted back. Cornelia transposed endless oboe parts for clarinet so that Schubert symphonies could still be played when oboists were scarce. Like it or not, every single student had to take a part in Friday night sing and (in 1948 and 1953) practice roulades from Bach's *Christmas Oratorio* in preparation for an hour-long performance of this difficult piece with one ringer (the first trumpet player) and 180 amateur musicians. A '54 alumnus, who came to Putney School in 1950 a shy and solitary boy, wrote in his journal of the 1953 performance from his station among those basses not part of the more select madrigal chorus:

> Friday evening was the Christmas Oratorio. It was we singing. It was Madrigals with the happiest faces I have ever seen singing wonderful things. It was the soulful voice of the Orchestra, trumpets and cellos and things. It was Norwood standing there giving them rhythm with every fiber in his body. . . . It was the wonderful togetherness, the rhythm of perfect, happy cooperation. It was Bach—but it was also Putney—the way they do things there—the diverse, united expression. It was great.

But there was a coerciveness about it all that even some eager musicians couldn't take. In rebellion, "Someone swizzled round the wires in my car so I couldn't start it," recalls Norwood. Several Friday sing resisters knew who it was, but they weren't telling. Eventually the music itself broke down almost everyone's resistance. "The *sound* of Friday night singing at the year's end! I couldn't believe it," said one recalcitrant who returned in June after a month's illness. Listening to homemade recordings of cantatas and concerti grossi, one still hears a rough, energetic brilliance that carries the music over its imperfect details, like a fast-running stream rolling pebbles along its bed.[55]

Norwood nearly always knew how far to push each individual. "You're coasting along on your excellent abilities," he wrote to John Moyer, '51, in his counselor's report. "You're just *pigheaded!*" he told him to his face. ("And I was," says John.) Norwood knew one casual trumpet player would wake up if he fired off a cap pistol at him in the middle of a rehearsal. Cornelia, a marvelous teacher, acted as comforter of those few who had suffered more heat than they really deserved. With her help, Norwood, as Nora Sayre writes, "infused the whole school with a devotion to music—and to his shouting, irascible self."[56] When Norwood Hinkle was awarded Harvard University's 1966 prize for excellence in secondary teaching, no one was surprised—except the man himself.

"Mrs. H. was wonderful," say the Hinkles, "way ahead of her time" in her insistence that the arts be essential to the work of Putney School. Their importance posed both hazards and opportunities for Putney's students, on whom the burden of synthesis fell: somehow they must combine college preparation with daring intellectual exploration and with artistic endeavors of many kinds. It was not always easy. One alumna who was simultaneously headwaiter, henkeeper, *Magazine* editor, and striving student writes that at Putney she "learned to do three things at once. This disabled me from reading forever."

Some students began building their syntheses early in their Putney careers. Jane Arms's first English report on Dick Campbell: "He is hampered by the inelasticity of his major premises." Dick's reaction? "By mid-winter my major premises began to . . . dissolve in the face of evidence that I had not begun to think for myself. Putney exacts thinking."[57] "A few very strong teachers in an atmosphere of close encounter" induced many to integrate self with academic work.

For others, the total impact of Putney's academic program—whether good or bad—became clear only when set in a series of educational experiences. A few found it lacking. "I coasted through my first two years on my elementary school preparation," several have said. Classes were "much more conventional than at Dalton, my previous school, the ideological climate narrower," writes a '46 alumna. Another "was made to feel pretty far down on the ladder of intelligence." Students' classroom experience depended even more than is usual on the teachers they were assigned because most teachers ran free of departmental constraints. Putney "probably rescued me from academic incorrigibility, but I am less than grateful because this was done with condescension," writes one who became a successful professor of veterinary medicine.

Other students were "too much preoccupied with living to be studying." "I was a terrible student, but Putney I loved," say two of these. Some of these alumni were among the 20 percent who received the general rather than the college preparatory diploma before 1950, or who didn't graduate at all. But well over half of those reporting found Putney's academic education the best they ever had, including, for some, years of graduate school (and for one, three years at Phillips Exeter Academy). "Perhaps we became a bit harsh and critical in our judgments," writes one alumnus, "but that may have been the other side of the self-reliance, the love of truth we learned in Putney's classrooms and Evening Activities."

For the slow growers, the system could be bent to apply pressure where needed. Mrs. H. might be adamant about withholding grades, but quite often the college advisor or a faculty counselor would leak low grades to a laggard in need of stimulation.[58] As each term progressed, as many as a third of all students were assigned to the daily make-up session. Seniors crammed for College Boards by flashlight for hours after curfew. Most alumni say they found Putney splendid preparation for college. Certainly Putney students entered demanding colleges in large numbers in the school's first fifteen years, 95 percent graduating with bachelor's degrees or more. The pattern of college attendance from 1938 to 1941 is typical of Putney's first thirty years, except that both the larger state universities and Harvard/Radcliffe gained in favor during the forties and fifties, with ninety graduates entering Harvard/Radcliffe between 1945 and 1955. One each attended twenty-five other colleges. About one-third of all alumni won college scholarships.

True, colleges were not so hard to get into when only 15 to 20 percent of the entire student population tried, especially from a school whose students' IQ scores averaged over 120. Besides, conventional colleges impressed by the records of students from the Eight Year Study schools were hospitable to Putney graduates and increasingly pleased with their overall college performance. "Putney Chemistry took me half way through the freshman Chem course, and my Putney French met the college graduation requirement," says a '40 graduate. A '52 alumna writes, "It took me three years to learn how to take exams, so I just missed *cum laude*—but that didn't really matter to me

College Attendance, 1938–1941[a]

Yale	5	Wellesley	3	Reed	2
Harvard	5	Brown	3	Dartmouth	2
Swarthmore	6	Radcliffe	3	Middlebury	2
Smith	7	St. John's	3	University at North	
Bennington	6	Vassar	2	Carolina	2
				Rhode Island School of	
				Design	2

because I *had* learned that such measuring rods were less important than learning itself." Honor grades rained down on her in graduate school, when she most needed them to launch her career. A comparison of Putney's 193 male graduates from 1940 to 1950 with a similar number of Hotchkiss School alumni shows that the Putney men as a group won higher college grades and over twice as many academic honors as the prep school men did. A higher proportion of Putney men went on to earn graduate or professional degrees (56 percent to Hotchkiss's 39 percent, also exceeding Andover's 50 percent). These disparities in graduate degrees are similar when Putney women are compared with 1940s graduates of Abbot Academy, New England's oldest girls' boarding school (Putney's 28 percent to Abbot's 19 percent). Alumnae of New York's academically elite Brearley School show a slightly higher proportion of master's degrees (25 percent to Putney women's 21 percent), but Ph.D. and professional degrees are equal at 7 percent.[59]

Some alumni now think Putney's preparation too good. "After graduating," writes a 1930s alumnus, "we may feel for a while that Putney was the only really complete experience we shall ever have." College could be a terrible letdown, a superficial world with "infantile courses." One alumna knows "no one who wasn't unhappy in the first year of college." "I suffered enormously at Harvard," says an alumnus-architect who left after three years to seek again the strengthening combination of theoretical and practical work he'd been nourished on at Putney. Another neared college filled with doubts about the relevance of four more academic years. "I'd rather find a job and get my degree through extension work," she wrote her mother.[60]

"You Putney people just don't belong here," a Harvard proctor told one graduate. The author of the Hotchkiss-Putney comparison and other observers reveal the strikingly different routes taken by Putney males and graduates of traditional prep schools through the social world of the Ivy League college. Putney alumni entered college with broader interests and more diffuse goals than Hotchkiss alumni, and they tended to pursue them in a far wider array of extracurricular and solitary activities. In the Putney sample, 21 percent transferred to other colleges, and four percent dropped out altogether, while none from Hotchkiss did either. Putney graduates refused the friendship and security that Hotchkiss and other prep school alumni almost universally sought in team sports, fraternities, or final clubs. "There are virtually 'two nations' at Harvard," wrote one social historian in 1959, "The private-school boys, with their accents, final clubs, and Boston debutante parties—stand aloof and apart from the ambitious, talented, less polished boys who come to Cambridge each year from public high-schools over the nation."[61] Yet the

Putney men, by their repudiation of "upper-class" social activities, did sometimes let themselves in for loneliness. If they joined anything, they joined the
public school nation. They also found friends in outing clubs, drama societies, ski teams, orchestras, or madrigal groups, sometimes starting their
own if there were none.

Eventually, most Putney alumni seem to have hit their stride at college.
The girl who had wished for a job found herself happy to have landed in the
Radcliffe yard after all. The many graduates who headed for large state
universities discovered how valuable were the intellectual independence and
the desire to see for themselves nurtured at Putney School. It was not always
easy to put off applying one's knowledge when Putney had in so many ways
insisted that thought and work are one. "The main thing, however, was
learning how to learn," says an alumnus, "keeping the whole in mind
always. That has been very beautiful."[62]

Chapter 5

Work II

Outside the classroom, students' work expanded toward the adult economy. Putney followed the example of most nineteenth-century utopias by setting itself within a local agricultural economy, largely heedless (at first) of the diversification and complexity that the machine was bringing.[1] "When worlds are tottering," Carmelita Hinton had written, "to have rural roots cannot but be a good thing."[2] New England farming itself changed greatly during Putney's first fifteen years; therefore the farm's role within the school changed, too. This was essential, for the farm's educational value was a function of its usefulness in maintaining the land, supporting the farmer-teachers, providing wholesome, low-cost food and, if possible, income that could be turned into scholarships or salaries.

Hutch was a skilled accountant, and her summer 1936 farm accounts had her worried. They suggested that she was not the farmer Putney School needed—a possibility she had felt in her tired bones. She had come intending primarily to teach agriculture, but she was working mostly as a farmhand, and an expensive one at that, with only two or three hours of student supervision a day. "Can you use me after chores in dramatics or English teaching?" she asked Mrs. H. in June. "We're not farming, we're just playing at it," she continued. She felt she was a good manager who was not being allowed to manage the farm as a whole. The "hasty appropriation of man and horse labor" by the garden or poultry staff, Mrs. H.'s penny-pinching resistance to hiring emergency help when tons of hay might depend on it, and her demands that Hutch "raise this crop or that crop" were all wearing her down. Besides, she couldn't seem to work as a friend with any of the farmhands except Clyde.[3] It had been a bold move for some of the men to sign on with Mrs. H.; to take orders from a second woman boss may have been too much. Dry-humored and rather shy, "Hutch kept people on edge," Ed Gray has said. "She'd only pay attention to the rest of us when she wanted something," and even then, she was often sounding alarms about problems that could have been forestalled by watchfulness.

One day in the middle of Putney's first summer, Isabel Stephens had sounded an alarm of her own. She'd been up in the cram-full haymow and noticed how hot was the hay that had been piled in the week before. Isabel told Hutch, who shrugged. Hutch and John Holden had taken the hay's temperature through most of the summer, and Hutch was convinced there was no danger. The second summer Hutch felt she had been equally cautious. But on the afternoon of September 4, 1936—whether from spontaneous combustion or some unknown cause—the big barn, the backbone of the school, went up in flames.[4]

Work Camp was over; fall term had not yet officially opened. Someone sprang to the one telephone to call the Putney and Brattleboro fire departments. Mrs. H. cranked up her car and careened down to the Lower Farm to pick up the sap buckets, though the water tank was perilously low. Others began leading the terrified animals to safety. At the last minute, Hugh MacDougall managed to rescue the bull from its stall. Wind carried gobbets of burning hay all about, and only by soaking the roofs of the sheds and the White Cottage could these buildings be saved. A milk tank truck appeared as if from nowhere; its driver had been alerted by the town telephone operator and had filled his empty truck from Sackett's Brook. A bucket line went straight to work, and the White Cottage was spared, but the barn and all the feed and equipment stored inside were ashes, a $10,000 loss.

After such a blow, any sensible school would have cut its losses and sold its livestock. The barn's insurance was nowhere near its replacement cost: strapped for cash in these tentative first years, Mrs. H. had taken a chance. ("No business sense," Perry Dunlap Smith had often grumbled to his family in Winnetka. "I told her so," he added, when he heard that the barn was gone.[5]) The morning after, however, Mrs. H. and Ed Gray were puzzling over how the Lower Farm barn could be made an adequate temporary shelter for fifteen milk cows and as many heifers, twelve horses, and numerous pigs, sheep, and goats. Already the fire was becoming, in Mrs. H.'s imagination, a part of the canon called "The Putney Spirit." She greeted returning students at the first all-school meeting with a description of the night-long fight against the fire, ending "It's a terrible misfortune that the barn is gone, but it was a MARVELOUS fire! If only you could have been here to see it!"[6] The animals were moved, fresh grain, harnesses, a new cultivator, and eighty tons of hay were ordered to replace some of the losses, and work began on plans for the largest modern barn in southern Vermont.

Then, somewhat to Hutch's relief, Mrs. H. released her from the farm manager's job, keeping her on until year's end as 4-H Club director, farm accountant, and assistant in the English department. Hutch would later return as part-time horticulturalist, but Ed Gray took over the dairy, adding it to his other responsibilities. Though Mrs. H. and he made several attempts to find a new farm manager, he kept the job till 1941, ably assisted by Roscoe Hodgdon, who first came to Putney School as its herdsman in 1937 and with his bride, Ruth, Putney's expert bookkeeper, stayed on for forty more years, two sea anchors of the school. Thus the integrated management Hutch had wanted was finally accomplished. [7]

Putney's friends sent barn-building contributions, and students raised money on their own through concerts and magic shows. The new barn went up fast—there wasn't time for much student labor on a building that had to be ready for next summer's hay crop—and the animals were settled into its spacious platforms and pens. Anne and John Holden, who had lived in the Lower Farm apartment attached to the Houghton barn, no longer woke to the lowing of cows or heard the bull tune up when John practiced his double bass. Students had a much shorter walk to their chores or their horses. Their heroic efforts to cope behind them, there was time for pranks. "One day," says Liebe Coolidge, "I and my little clique painted designs on all the white spots on the heifers with merchurochrome. It didn't come off easily. The herdsman practically cried." Letters home resumed their more ordinary farm news. "The mother pig I've been caring for will soon be butchered because of infanticide (she had lain on and crushed one piglet after another till only two were left), and I will raise another sow. That, my dear Aunt, is the Putney spirit."[8]

Ed Gray began gradually expanding the now "certified" herd with heifers born out of the breeding program Hutch had begun, until there were thirty milkers and as many nonmilking stock. Still the books said the farm only just broke even. "It must show a profit!" said Mrs. H. one faculty meeting. Replied Ed, "It *can't* make a profit when the school kitchen pays only 6¢ a quart for a type of milk that brings 8¢ everywhere else!" Hugh MacDougall settled the argument, contending that the farm was integral to the school's education program, and that for it to pay for itself was accomplishment enough. This attitude mirrored a view central to John Humphrey Noyes's Perfectionist community, which, while it made handsome profits on its steel traps and later its Oneida silver, cared less about efficient production than about work's role in tightening community bonds and allowing all Perfectionists to "live as God intended."[9]

Over the years, Putney's farm did more than pay for itself. Besides maintaining the land's fertility, it provided the machinery and the adult workforce for numberless projects. So much wood was needed for fenceposts, for maple syrup production, for school fireplaces and, later, for construction that Ed's brother Charles Gray signed on as woodsman. Charlie came in after the 1938 hurricane to help students and farmhands make useful the tens of thousands of board feet blown down that year. Though painfully shy, he proved a teacher as extraordinary in his own way as his brother. His reserve vanished when he explained the care of an axe or when his boys pestered him to show them how he could split a match in half. One of his tricks was to chain a mired truck to a hefty tree and then chop with a precision that slowly, simultaneously brought down the tree and pulled out the truck. One of several men who found Charlie their most important teacher at Putney School says, "I watched him over a year and a half. He was the first—and perhaps the last—person I'd known who could deal with the universe successfully."

Maple syrup was the farm's surest crop, in spite of yearly variations that turned on the early spring weather. This had much to do with students' eagerness to work with Clyde Hulett and his horses, to help with the sap gathering, to watch the boiling far into the night, and to be rewarded with syrup thickened on the snow and eaten inside a sugar house glowing with fire and steam—even to stay over on a low-paid spring vacation to see the job through. It had still more to do with the price of wood at the time ($4 a cord) and a total materials cost of 85¢ per gallon for a normal 1500-bucket run of 275–400 gallons of finished syrup. Though most was sold outside, the school bought 50 gallons, a small item in the enormous amount of provender that came out of the barn, the gardens, the root cellar, and later, the school's twenty-ton freezer.

Bill Hinton thought the farm was slated for some real profit when he came with his agricultural science degree to manage it during the middle years of the war. Bill was a conscientious objector. He returned to the school from a C.O. camp, still carrying about him suggestions of the hero's role in which his original Putney peers had cast him: a ski champion and an adventurer who had worked his way around the world as deckhand and farmhand in a year between Putney and college. He got on well with most of the students, knowing from his experience under Hutch when to prod and how. ("A poor worker, not unwilling . . . but born tired," he reported to one set of parents.[10]) Most agree that he made a good farm manager.

The farm books looked very good in 1943, but the surplus came largely from the sale of the Guernsey heifers Ed Gray had been raising, as Bill switched the farm over to the larger Holsteins. This innovation was the last straw for Ross Hodgdon, who felt more loyalty to the Guernseys than to the new manager, and moved forthwith to head all mechanical maintenance work. The farm slipped in and out of the red as the extra team was replaced by a tractor and a hog house was built—wartime construction materials costing more than the total sum required to buy the Rogers House dormitory. "Give up the farm," an agronomist parent urged Mrs. H. in 1943.[11] A year later, however, the dairy operation was strong, and the twenty-five hogs were earning their keep. The farm had a future in an agricultural economy that had begun to exclude smaller, unmechanized dairy operations altogether. Through the next three years it started to pay again. It also continued to provide forty percent of the school's and camp's food. It offered invaluable experience for the "little hordes of labor," as the nineteenth-century utopian Albert Brisbane had called them: hundreds of student workers joining (some, to be sure, a bit short on the childish enthusiasm Brisbane envisioned) in a complex, successful enterprise.

By 1944 Bill Hinton decided that some wars must be fought. After he had left to join the war effort, Mrs. H. began to wonder if there was such a thing as a good farm manager who would stay. Finally, in January of 1948, she found one: Larry Titus, farm foreman for the Mount Hermon School and master dairyman. He turned her down once, but she didn't give up. She drove down to see him a second time; this time he agreed to come.

At first it was hard for Larry to switch from Mount Hermon's graded farm classes to managing six different Putney farm crews and their student crew heads, but soon enough man and school shaped up as a near-perfect match. For years, the thirty-five Elm Lea milkers had ranked among the five highest-producing dairy herds in Windham County, and surplus cows sired by Putney Dauntless fetched twice the standard price at auction. Now the Putney School farm moved to the top and stayed there, the herd average having risen from 10,000 to 14,000 pounds of milk per cow annually. It took 350 tons of Elm Lea hay and ensilage to accomplish this, along with a good deal of bought grain, but by 1950, farm income had risen to $33,500, with the yearly profit at $4,000.

The new machinery changed things for students and work campers. A mechanical potato digger, a side-delivery rake that only a tractor could pull, a manure spreader, a hay loader, and eventually a hay baler put a small aristocracy of student drivers at the top and made some other jobs seem duller. The 4-H Club lapsed; there seemed to be neither time nor need to supervise students who might have wanted to "own" a single calf for a year, when the big, placid Holsteins appeared to thrive about as well in a group. Not again would Mrs. H. rouse a student out of sleep to care for a newborn calf.

Human error often rumpled Putney's pastoral scene. There were sluggards who felt they were doing something real only when they had gotten Larry in a rage. There was one work camper whom Larry found in a field of bush beans building little piles of bean blossoms all along the rows. The campers had picked two tons of beans—and she had decided enough was enough. As a farm crew head, Nora Sayre ran "a dangerous little band, which achieved some expensive damage," prematurely pulling apart electric fences on a refencing job and "releas[ing] cows into realms of disaster," among other sins. Finally Larry set them to cleaning the chicken house, where they could do no more harm than the breaking of a few eggs.[12]

Nevertheless, a myriad of jobs remained by which a student could learn the intricacies of farmwork. A new ninth grader fresh from the lawns and tennis courts of Scarsdale might be plucking chickens before even unpacking. And just as formerly, a farm emergency could bring out the school to meet it. One evening a thousand tomato plants arrived unexpectedly at suppertime. Assembly was cancelled, and everyone in the school worked an hour to set them out. The farm often provided the theater for dramatic individual acts of heroism: two truckloads of sawdust shoveled and delivered on a single Saturday afternoon, for example, or one occasion, on a stormy night in 1949, when two girls heard a horse crying in the wind, went down to the barn to investigate, and found half the north windows blown into the cows' mangers; they spent an hour sweeping mangers and removing glass from the cows' mouths. A boy ready to prove his manhood could volunteer to help Larry slaughter pigs. The monthly Farm Association meetings and the weekly farm planning council still provided some of the specialized agricultural education that lent meaning to dark winter mornings spent cleaning gutters on an empty stomach. For most students, farm and school remained inseparable.

There was plenty of other work to do. The popularity of Ross Hodgdon's maintenance crew supported two nineteenth-century utopian premises: shared work lowers barriers between sexes, and children love throwing trash, and outside skeptics often criticized Putney's insistence that girls join boys in the roughest, dirtiest tasks, but Carmelita Hinton considered such sharing an essential prerequisite to equality. The Perfectionist communities of Putney and Oneida had discovered its benefits amid fiercer criticism a century before. "Loving companionship in labor, . . . will be both economically and spiritually profitable," wrote Noyes. "When the partition between sexes is taken away, and man ceases to make woman a propagative drudge, when love takes the place of shame, . . . men and women will be able to mingle in all their employments; . . . and then labor will be attractive."[13]

Two major buildings, the classroom (library) building and the KDU (Kitchen-Dining room Unit) were built between 1939 and 1943, both of them planned and supervised by Hugh MacDougall in consultation with David Barnes. Tom Morse, a highly skilled carpenter who had first come down from northern Vermont to help build Mrs. H.'s house, was the steady center of the KDU project and of many others through the 1950s. "He was a gentle man—a beautiful workman," recalls one teacher; an alumnus who made sure to work under Tom on carpentry crew through each of his three years at Putney says, "He got his status from his skill."

Hutch had set out the berry plantation on the crest of West Hill, but now it was scraped away to make space for the foundations of the KDU. Tom Morse found the barn timber construction plan familiar. With scorn for inferior workmanship and slow, frank praise for jobs well done, he brought neophyte carpenters far beyond their own expectations. He built oak library tables for a school he must have expected to last a century or two.[14] The students who gave work afternoons, and many of their Saturdays as well, to such construction projects often found them milestones in their lives. It was "a child's dream" so to spend oneself, says one of these. "Small boys long to be real people." Student and camper crews finished both building jobs working under Addis Robinson, for ten years one of the most warmly respected of Putney's housepainter-teachers (and a decent double bass player too).

The new academic building made space for the fast-growing book collection necessary in a school comitted to independent student research. Marion Leonard set up a library that would soon become larger and more diverse than many college libraries, with over 10,000 volumes by 1953. And in his kitchen, the chef, Roy Bailey, at last had the space he needed. Little came readymade into the Putney School kitchen. Roy presided loudly and cheerfully over the breaking up of animal carcasses and the breaking in of student kitchen crews. When he left in the middle of the war to join the army, all the students conspired to give him a surprise party and a really good watch. (When he came back two months later, 4F, one boy wanted to know if he would give the watch back.[15]) Roy raised miniature Shetland ponies, which walked in and out of the smaller dormitories. Roy was one of the major reasons why Putney's kitchen-dining crews found their useful work rewarding to themselves.

In many respects, it was the continuing summer Work Camp that made both farm and farm kitchen possible. The eight-week camp flourished even through the war, regularly attracting a hundred or more campers, about half from public high schools, who wanted more than the traditional kiddie-camp fare. They worked through a four-hour morning on every job a farm requires, also undertaking major maintenance on the buildings that school and camp shared, then dispersed to tennis courts, stables, hills, and rivers much as the first labor campers had done. Someone kept a record of the campers' garden work in 1952:

Weeded 2 miles of vegetable rows.
Froze 1 ton of strawberries
          660 lbs. of blackberries
          816 lbs. of green beens
          1218 lbs. of wax beans

The Work Camp pulled more than its own financial weight, providing both summer staff salaries and care for the summer crops that would feed winter-bound cows and students. (The ingratitude of a few academic-year snobs bleeds through their remarks about campers: "They were the people who left the lipstick on the walls."[16]) There was time for a rich evening activities and trip program, a student-run newsletter, a self-government system, and a camper-run discussion series—in short, nearly all the activities that many academic-year students, along with Mrs. H., considered the most important aspects of their Putney educations, but without those pesky academic classes to interfere with learning by doing.

For most of the 1930s and 1940s, the camp was directed by someone close to the Putney School—Hester Crawford (Putney's first business manager), John Holden, or Warren Leonard—aided first by Putney faculty, then by an ever-increasing corps of college-age counselors, about one-third Putney School graduates. The staff-camper ratio was 1:2. The camp extended a Putney education to hundreds of young people for whom a school year's tuition, well above the average for boarding schools, was more than their parents could pay. Campers showed how they felt about their experience and the friends they had made by returning in droves each October to celebrate the harvest festival—much of it *their* harvest—with the school.

Putney School could thrive only by living lean. Arthur Green's chicken house became the dormitory for the summer theater and a winter hostel for alumni with very warm sleeping bags. Kelly and Allen house residents woke some winter mornings to find snow piled on their beds, their ink frozen in its bottles. By night, the Rogers House rats would steal students' apples from their bureau drawers and roll them across the floor. The most aggressive boys fought and killed them. This was a graphic form of sharing in the school's economic problems, as Mrs. H. had wanted students to do from the first.[17] For however Spartan students' physical circumstances, Putney's rich educational fare did not come cheap. Parents usually had a better idea of how much it cost to support simple living for their children at Putney School. As Liebe Coolidge recalls,

> My father was bemused at the idea of a school where kids paid to come and work like day laborers. One time Mrs. H. was bringing a group to Cambridge to a play or a concert or something. Mother asked my father if he'd mind if she put up eight or ten kids in sleeping bags in the attic. "No, I don't mind—how much is she going to charge us?"

In 1946, the school broadcast an appeal for funds to replace the madeover machine shed that was the "temporary" boys' dormitory; forty years later, the dormitory still stands. These were, perhaps, better accommodations than Mrs. H. had first envisioned. She had hoped about half the students would eventually build cabins of their own to live in, and she lent her own tools to the cabin builders to help their projects along. But only a handful were built, some too far away to be useful year round. Of the five most promising ones, one burned, one became a center for illicit smoking, and a third was appropriated by an outsider.

Though enrollment climbed steadily, no major dormitory was built until after the war. This was in large part the director's decision: Mrs. H. insisted for ten years that plant improvements be made only as funds came in. To borrow was to "become enslaved to your creditors."[18] Who could effectively contradict the woman who owned most of the land and all the Lower Farm buildings? But she never denied the school when it was really in need. On the contrary, she was an impulse buyer—of things essential to her vision. Hester Crawford writes of one such purchase.

> Perhaps the lowest point I ever reached (as business manager) was one day when I had just managed to plan "to get by" until camp tuitions were paid. Mrs. Hinton came in radiant with the news that she had just purchased a Blacksmith Shop complete with all nuts, bolts and the blacksmith himself (Carl Carlsen, wheelwright, sledge and tool maker for farmers thirty miles around). I am afraid I didn't show the proper enthusiasm. Mrs. Hinton's face fell as she said, "it was such a bargain, only $1500, and just think what it will mean in the life of the boys and girls"—and so it did and some way we paid for it.

And in every year of Hester Crawford's management, Dun and Bradstreet came to audit Putney School and left having rated the enterprise A-1.[19]

Mrs. Hinton's own generosity (three acres deeded here for a faculty house, some Wrigley stock sold there to pay a needy cellist's tuition) inspired wealthy parents to come through in emergencies, such as when the barn burned, or when the water system broke down so completely in the fall of 1936 that students dug temporary privies to replace the flush toilets. The school paid all the original Elm Lea mortgages in the first five years—except for the $15,000 lent without interest by Mrs. H. herself.

In many ways Mrs. Hinton seemed impractically kind. To keep her valuable experiment afloat, however, almost any penny-pinching seemed fair to her. Like a good capitalist, she pushed tuition as high and salaries as low as she dared, almost always paying the least she knew an individual would accept and still stay on. Jane Arms writes that Mrs. H. failed to notice salary inequities because she didn't care what she was paid herself.[20] Though the Putney School corporation owned two-thirds of its Elm Lea assets free and clear by 1942, cash was always in short supply. Mrs. Hinton found salary funds wherever she could. Years after one teacher left Putney School, she discovered that Mrs. H., who had paid most of her salary in free tuitions for her children, also solicited funds from the mother's friends for the same purpose, never telling the teacher that she was doing so. "Carmelita used _____ as bait," writes an alumnus who knew the family and is still resentful.[21]

Salaries in the 1930s and early 1940s were not, as Jane Arms says, unusually high for the period.[22] For all but a few they were unusually *low*, especially if one counts salaries for the nonacademic teachers who counted so much in the school. Mrs. H. guessed rightly that the Grays would not leave an enterprise in which they had invested so much of themselves, so she kept Ed Gray on at $75 a month plus housing for twelve years. It is true that some private school teachers worked gladly for room and board during the Depression in boarding schools that would otherwise have closed down altogether. Mrs. Hinton took no salary for herself in the first years. But Putney teachers knew privation even as their salaries were gradually rising. They found snow on their beds as often as the students did. Six early teachers shared one bathroom; another competed with eleven students for the sinks well into the 1950s. To one young faculty couple, home was a single room with a double-decker bed. These problems were rarely discussed in faculty meetings, which were devoted—with few exceptions—to the director's agenda. So heavily did they weigh on Hugh MacDougall that he was ready to quit when, to his relief, John H. Caldwell took over in 1941 as Putney's professional business manager. Now a few more building improvements were planned. Salaries rose by 7 percent in constant dollars from 1935 to 1948. Jack Caldwell brought more rhyme to the consolidated balance sheets, though there was little more reason in Mrs. H.'s salary column.[23]

For students, straitened circumstances were good education. They were consistent with the school's ideal of simple living, with the trials of a Vermont town and a nation in Depression, then with a world at war. Besides, many students vaguely understood that their school, though poor in things, was extraordinarily rich in people and educational offerings. All around them they saw adults doing "maximum work for minimum pay."[24] They sensed a direct line between their own work on farm and grounds and the benefits they enjoyed, such as the unusually large proportion of scholarship students. Compared with their peers at other private schools, few took their privileged education for granted.[25]

Chapter 6

A Way of Life: Religion, Sex, and Other Essentials

"Putney stands for a way of life," its Director and teachers agreed. Its students have used the same words. [1] But Putney School was more than a system of ethical culture. Its founders, and all those teachers and students who continually re-created it, were defining reality even while they talked of education: the nature of human nature; the qualities of truth; relationships between the individual, the community, and humankind; the interplay of artifice and the natural world.

Carmelita Hinton might revere the scientific method, but she dealt abundantly in *givens*. Not that she was preoccupied with God or church. Her surest, simplest faith was in herself and her school's mission. She seemed to embrace John Dewey's vision of the teacher as "the usherer-in of the Kingdom of God." [2] What better place to be such a teacher (and teaching principal) than in a boarding school on a hilltop, a community mutually chosen by its participants and herself? "Why do we talk about the Kingdom of Heaven on Earth if we don't try to make it so?" she asked Jane Arms soon after her school had opened. [3]

This was a faithful (if unintended) replication of John Humphrey Noyes's motives in launching the Putney township's first utopian community a century before. Though the Perfectionists were surer of God's favor than were Putney School's communitarians—and more often criticized as a "deadly influence" by outsiders—the similarities are striking. At the height of their success, the two communities were at once big enough to make their weight felt within the wider culture, yet small enough for consensus to appear decisive in everyday planning, whether of work, of dress, of eating habits (no coffee, tea, or alcohol allowed in either group), of study or play. In reality, much was preordained by both founders. Noyes's Sunday evening "home talks" served purposes similar to Mrs. H.'s speeches in Sunday night or all-school meetings. (One Putney boy writes in his journal, "Mrs. H.'s talk was down to earth, simple and . . . a little embarrassing, as are all her speeches—but we get used to that at Putney, and love her for it.") Both leaders prescribed sexual behavior. Noyes was probably more successful here than Carmelita Hinton, for she hoped in vain to curb her students' abounding libidinal energies, while Noyes laid channels for sexual expression within his system of "complex marriage," preaching coitus reservatus to his young men and initiating virgins into this form of "Christian love" himself. Both communities accorded females a fuller equality to males than did the larger society. Both were peopled by socially secure, relatively well-educated participants who pooled their talents to create a rich and self-sufficient cultural life.[4]

Intensive social interaction seemed workable to most of Putney School's communitarians partly because—like their nineteenth-century predecessors—they found ready escape and inspiration in surrounding nature. "Nature framed our lives," wrote Cynthia Deery Russell. "We were always surrounded by beauty." Few could walk from the main building to the assembly hall without taking in either Mt. Monadnock twenty-five miles to the east or the span that stretched between school and mountain. Nor could they experience Vermont's weathers unmoved. Alumni and faculty recollections, students' school writings and letters home are filled with references to morning mists and moods of sky and earth. "We're having a perfectly terrific wind up here. . . . How it does roar and drift the snow." Then, as "the earth awoke in March, we knew the restlessness and longing of Spring,"—or, more prosaically, "We are in the muddy season, and it is so gooey and squdgy."[5] When the mud lay deepest, Elm Lea was an island: delivery trucks and cars had to be met by tractor at the Darrows' farm. It is no wonder that even the most skeptical were piqued to interest by Edward Yoemans' Sunday meeting assertion that this earth "is the body of God."[6] At every stage of life, Putney folk might enter contemplation of all creation along the road through the woods between the White Cottage and the barn.

Intermediaries between known and unknown worlds were many. Music and other works of art seemed at once human and beyond-human in their beauty or *thing*ness. Farm animals were mysterious as well as useful. When a cow was about to calve, people gathered quietly in the barn to watch. Mrs.

H. and other faculty communicated their passion for nature both with and without words. Mrs. H.'s favorite recreation was to take long walks alone, lunch in her rucksack. Seeing her returning from one walk in the pouring rain, students asked why? "Oh, I wanted to see how long it would take to walk from Townshend," she said, her smile full of the day's accomplishment.[7] In the middle of one of her graduation speeches, she suddenly fell silent, and the whole multitude did the same, to listen to a bird sing.

A sense of apartness came along with Putney School's involvement in nature. The student who had survived the battering of a storm on the flanks of Mount Washington or had ears frostbitten while walking up to breakfast began to feel sorry for all those who had never been so tested. "We felt rugged and independent, superior to the city slickers back home," says Liebe Coolidge. Just standing in awe under a winter sky set one beyond others. "When the moon was out, casting a glow over the snow-whitened fields, we seemed to be at the very top of the world, in a space so vast and silent we could have been the only people on earth," remembers Cynthia Russell.

Far from disapproving this stance, the school appeared to strengthen it. At its most receptive to beauty and understanding (Yeomans told the students), "the mind of man is the mind of God," an *"upper mind* [which is] the only safeguard of any civilized society." Though evil was seldom mentioned aloud at Putney School, the specter of "debasement"—of alternatives to the Putney way of life—hovered always at the edges, heightening the upper mind's struggle toward perfection.[8] When Mrs. H. urged her students to seek "truth" or "spiritual awareness," this is one thing she seems to have meant. "Out there" lay the corrupt and corrupting world, with its cruelties, its urban squalor, its hucksterism. Only the courage of the enlightened individual was proof against it.[9]

These Emersonian themes had sounded repeatedly in the nineteenth-century American mind. They are likewise found everywhere in both Perfectionist and Owenite utopian writings, which inevitably add prescriptions for the kind of environment leaders must deliberately create to condition the enlightened individual.[10] But paradoxically, one of Mrs. H.'s givens was her faith in the innate power for goodness, spiritual awareness and creativity to be found in all young people.[11] She would have agreed with Francis Parker that "the spontaneous tendencies of the child are the records of inborn divinity,"[12] even while she believed that much adult manipulation of the adolescent was required for those tendencies to reach toward healthy self-fulfillment. Her faith, shaken but not destroyed by the horrors of World War II, extended to all humankind and to the future: just allow the people of every land to know one another and appreciate the unique potential of each individual, and all will eventually be well. Most Putney teachers shared this faith, and many students absorbed it. Students also absorbed the responsibilities it implied. One, now a teacher, has said, "I learned from Mrs. H. to look at a student, to forget the obvious, to reach deep into the essence of that person, to love that person's beauty, to guide (and) nurture that person, and when the person begins to bloom, to stand back and say, 'Wow!' "[13]

Experience and reason might undergird the Putney School ethos, then, but its ground was faith: faith in each person, in the power of love and responsibility within communities of equals, and in the encounters of a growing person full of health and strength with the natural world.

"The ideals of democracy and religion are the same," wrote Carmelita Hinton.[14] To be the "model home, complete community and embryonic democracy" that Francis Parker had envisioned in 1894 as the ideal school,[15] Mrs. H.'s school must be open, if possible, to youngsters of every land and every income group. In reality this was not possible, but Putney School certainly tried. While about half of its students came from Vermont, New York, and Massachusetts, the others' homes were scattered over the nation and the world. From ten to seventeen foreign students attended Putney in each of the war years.

More than half of all students received tuition reductions during the first year; as staff salaries inched up and applications increased, the proportion of income devoted to tuition reductions fell, stabilizing at about 15 percent in the late 1940s, while the fraction of students receiving the reductions reached one-third. These two figures remained constant through the 1960s; they exactly match the scholarship effort maintained by the Phillips academies, Exeter and Andover, each over two centuries old and heavily endowed. Lacking endowment, Putney's rich paid yearly for Putney's poor.

In theory, the roster of tuition-reduction holders was kept secret, even from the teachers: no scholarship student was meant to feel any different. In fact, Mrs. H. expected more from at least some of those brought in at a sacrifice to the school. "She never let me be unaware of my scholarship status," says one graduate speaking for several early students. These students' peers treasured the illusion of an income-blind microsociety, however, and strove to maintain it. It was easier before the fifties, when train travel declined and the Cadillacs began to arrive at vacation time to pick up the children of the nation's elite. Within a decade of the school's founding, black students on both full and reduced tuition began to join the handful of

Catholics, the Jews, the hundred or more WASPS, the urban and rural and foreign students that made up small Putney's diverse crowd. Their presence revealed the perils of an innocence that pretended no differences existed. Naiveté could hurt others, as one WASP alumna wrote: "Not knowing prejudice, we did not appreciate the pain of it."

"The development of democracy demands that . . . there be no barriers built between different groups and occupations," wrote Evelyn Dewey in *New Schools for Old*.[16] One aspect of Putney School's embryonic democracy seems to have been an unqualified success for the students: its commitment to a teaching force of social equals. The school's work program was fundamental to this commitment. The gap between the salaries received by academic and nonacademic staff was successfully concealed from students and generously ignored by most of the adults who taught outdoors or in the kitchen. Though distinctions of dress and dining rooms held in the evenings, it was easy to forget them entirely in the afternoon, out on work jobs. The Putney custom of calling nearly all adults by their first names obscured divisions of age and station. Cook, painter, and farmworker were welcome at faculty meetings (though most found them a waste of their time); nearly all the most important committees included nonacademic staff.

There were many adult friendships that crossed lines of social status or education. "There was always something jolly going on up there," says Alice Holway, who did everything at Putney School from cleaning offices to supervising the Work Camp gardening crews. She would visit kitchen friends, partly for the fun of "watching the kids throw dishes at each other," or go to the Hinkles to baby-sit and then stay for an hour talking with them after they got home from rehearsal. It did no harm that Ed Gray's speaking vocabulary was at least as complex as the average English teacher's written one, especially where younger outdoor teachers thought of him and Mabel as "leaders of the staff in all categories."[17] The community on West Hill was too small to obscure each individual's dependence on the other's effort. "Each person stood or fell on merit," recalls the nurse, Maria Phaneuf. How could one fail to admire the work of a cook like Minnie Wood, who had to be replaced by two people when she finally resigned to take a factory job for twice the pay? "Everybody was as good as everybody else, no matter what they did," says Minnie now. And students who spent their high school years in an environment that confirmed this assumption tended to continue behaving as though it were true once they reached adulthood.

The school's community government did more than play at democracy. Students had some say about all matters; in a few areas they had a great deal.

Though academic and disciplinary decisions rested ultimately with the classroom faculty and Mrs. H., students served on the academic policy and disciplinary committees from the beginning. The Community Council was chaired by a student elected by the entire community (after student-only elections had been tried for some years); the younger, newer students tended to classify him (it was always "him" until 1945) with the adults in authority and dignity. The dormitory head committee and its chairman (usually "her") also had considerable stature. In most years the council met twice in every week, the dorm committee once. More important, however, than the school constitutions written and rewritten, the succession of smoking and no-smoking ordinances, or the delicate proportions of students and faculty on the council and its committees was the constant interchange between teachers and students. Because the founder was a woman of principle and had retained a veto, discussion often became argument, and students often—eventually—lost. Yet for the young to know themselves worth arguing with was crucial.

Student leaders weighed in on deliberations over tuition raises and the establishment of new language offerings. "We made policies and felt powerful," says one. Elected leaders were impressed enough with their own status to maintain it with the faculty. More than one dorm committee chairman fumed in her righteous bed while dormmates cavorted in the May moonlight long after bed hours. As a newly elected council member wrote her family in 1939, "It's a damn nuisance to be good all the time." One student dorm head was so good that he wrote his adult dorm counselor a note scolding him for keeping a messy room. [18] Mrs. H., a charter member of both the council and the disciplinary (later standards) committee, took almost every student representative aside to impress him or her with responsibilities. These encounters are well remembered.

Everywhere, the director loomed large. "The fact that her judgments were often quite irrational was a source of confusion," writes one alumnus,

> but it also made me realize for the first time that those set in authority above me were human, too, and could be fallible. I think that no one will ever forget the occasions upon which she burst into tears in front of large sections of the student body because at some supposedly democratic election they had voted in a way she didn't want them to.

To make your principal cry: *this* was power. That the offending vote was mysteriously offset a year or two later by new administrative interpretations of the "basic ideals" written into the school constitution did not vitiate the sense of agency students gradually built within themselves. Among Putney's most valuable contributions to one alumnus "has been the perception of myself as a responsible member of successively wider communities, and of my capacity to influence their/our destiny."[19]

A community, like a religion, requires its rituals and festivals. Putney School had plenty of both. In addition to Sunday meeting ("a wonderful substitute for piety of the usual sort," writes one alumna), a series of celebrations punctuated the school year. The year opened on the top of Putney Mountain, up which young and old walked as on a pilgrimage, to gather in wonder at the center of a far circle of distant hills for the Director's welcome. Though sleeping outdoors would soon become "the natural way of doing things," more than one new student "trembled far into the night from a mixture of excitement and penetrating chill."[20] It was a rite of initiation.

The farm's seasonal requirements undergirded several rituals. Every day's chores reminded students that animals' needs require an ordered response. Thanksgiving followed harvest festival as a celebration both of nature's abundance and of Putney's larger family. Parents and siblings swelled the crowd at the tables set—first in the assembly hall, then in the theater, and finally in a KDU bedecked with evergreen boughs—for as many as five hundred. Alice Holway calls Putney's Thanksgiving "a Roman feast." Dinner was preceded by games and scavenger hunts and relieved by between-course music or dances. Typically one sat down at 1:30, Roy Bailey called "Turkey's up!" to the parade of father-waiters about 2:00, and everyone got up groaning after the March of Fruits and Nuts at 6:00 P.M. to return to the Lower Farm for the fall play—then went back to the square dance.

At Christmas time, perplexed sheep, calves, and oxen became actors in a Christmas pageant, serving as always as bridges between inanimate nature and the world of human beings. (In some students' lives, they were preferred to humans.) And for March's maple sugar pageant, whole forests of students—two roots per maple trees—might cavort upon the Putney community center stage, taking turns with child actors from the West Hill P.T.A. or a town square-dance set. Later a town or hill caller would summon townsfolk and hillfolk to dance together. Sugar on snow, pickles, donuts, and coffee followed the entertainments, which, in the years before television, drew between 250 and 300 people ready to break out of winter's torpor. For years, Putney School also took part in the Windham County 4-H tradition of observing Rural Life Sunday once each planting time. After the war, Hutch made sure that Rural Life Sunday coincided with the agricultural conference organized by the Farm Association.[21] She wrote a 4-H hymn that was sung in local churches as well as on West Hill.

Oh Thou who storeth nourishment
Within the quiet seed
To start it toward designed ascent
In garden, wood, and mead,
So store in us Thy wondrous food,
Thy grace and love and light,
That we may use Thy amplitude
To speed our growth aright.

Thou who excites the bud to flower
And lengthens branch and root
And grants the verdant plant the power
To triumph into fruit,
Oh bless us now with eagerness
Thy graces to perceive,
Thy love and light may we express,
And fruitful life achieve.

There were also surprise holidays. A display of northern lights might become the occasion for the director's joyful summons to Water Tower Hill, bed hour or no bed hour. Square dances were a monthly festival. New students were introduced early to this mix of art and athletics, which gathered the community in a shared rejection (until spring social dance night) of conventional teen entertainments. Mrs. H. was "a powerhouse" on the square-dance floor. So closely was Putney identified with square dancing that one graduate who decided he had gotten over Putney School told college classmates he would "never go to another square dance as long as he lived."[22]

The school year closed with another all-school journey up Putney Mountain and a graduation day rich with the spring's drama, dance, and music. The program might include a Mozart or Beethoven symphony, an entire Bach cantata and more, or the Magnificat, or the Kyrie and Gloria of the B Minor Mass. For many, commencement made it harder than ever to move beyond Putney School.

Each thread knitting together this community, each celebration, made one of Putney School's major goals more difficult to fulfill. This was a school set up to forge genuine connections between the young person and the larger world. Yet even before graduation, some students knew that all was not well in the relationship between school and town. Carmelita Hinton's ideal educational village should have worked in friendly cooperation with native neighbors. But once Putney School had become an educational village, it didn't much need its native neighbors—or was too busy to pay them much attention.

It seemed to some student consumers, for example, the height of re-belliousness to escape to the school's store one full mile away at the lower farm and spend a rainy afternoon next to the store fireplace with hot choco-late and "Helio" (Esther Morris, a favorite storekeeper). With the store just close enough for comfort, it would have been absurd to walk down to Putney village. Not that the school's enterprises made much money—the files reveal storekeepers (not Helio) who were constantly under threat of dismissal. (Or even legal action: as one manager responded to Jack Caldwell's threatening memo about a large discrepancy in store accounts, "I would like to drop the Store and go back to the chickens."[23]) But students got the message that Putney School was self-sufficient, if not superior. Its solidarity grated on Putney townsfolk much as Noyes's Perfectionist enclave had done a century before. Like the Perfectionists and the transcendentalist/intellectuals of Brook Farm, West Hill dwellers saw no need to look outside for play read-ings, music, or other entertainments.

If anything, the school became more ingrown with time. By 1939, nearly one-third of all Putney students were brother-sister pairs, younger siblings of former students, or faculty children. The proportion would stay much the same through the 1960s. "Our scrutiny of 'outsiders' could be ruthless," writes one alumna.[24] Some students present even resented students past, those few alumni ghosts who had gone to nearby colleges only in order to return every other weekend to haunt the school. The summer work campers, rubbing elbows with other hikers in a Mount Washington hut, observed that "the children of these camps are a totally different type than at Putney."[25] It is thus no surprise to read of one student's scorn for the local drama club production she was forced to watch in return for the privilege of presenting *her* one-act play to the natives, or of another bright remark made after a square dance in East Putney: "We ate impure foods and drugs off synthetic plates . . . and we had some ducky partners, old farmers and such, whose breath was as of the odor of fermented silage."[26]

The flurry of daily life readily turned the school community in on itself. Mrs. H. did not set a good example. "She was always *charging*," remembers one alumnus, and sometimes things got left behind, including a few impor-tant visitors. One summer camp day a "Mrs. Fisher" came over from Camp Arden to visit the new and intriguing Putney School. When she finally found someone who would stand still long enough to speak with her, she learned that the director was busy and would see neither Mrs. Fisher nor anyone else. No one offered to show her around, so Dorothy Canfield Fisher turned around and left, greatly disappointed. Soon Mrs. H. realized that the school could be hospitable without toadying to the famous, a common habit of private school principals in which she refused to indulge. This was one reason she persuaded her gracious Winnetka friend Hester Crawford to become Work Camp director and school business manager. Mrs. Crawford was soon hostess to a stream of visitors from the Progressive Education Association and to interested skeptics like Frank Boyden, headmaster of Deerfield, who left pronouncing Putney good.[27]

On a few well-remembered occasions, Mrs. H.'s preoccupation with her own goals involved means which some townspeople found flatly unacceptable. One day in 1950, she was packing her car for an important meeting in New York when she realized that her license plates had expired. Frantic, she took the fresh plates off the school station wagon, drove down to the service station in Putney village, and had them switched to her own car. Eight miles south of the village she was stopped by the Brattleboro police. Interestingly, she handled her regret over this aberration by making it public. "I have to be all of a piece," she once told Jane Arms. Her restoration in this case meant describing the incident to her Senior Discussion group: dishonesty doesn't pay. Unfortunately, while everyone in town soon knew of her arrest, few could know of her repentance.[28]

It should be said, however, that Putney School tried much harder than do most boarding schools to cross gaps between town and gown. It helped that gowns (even Austrian dirndls) were often less in evidence than were work-clothes donned to help paint the town hall or the community center or to clear the town roads after a storm. Mrs. H. and other West Hill women joined the women's club at the Federated Church. Faculty spoke at town literary clubs, and several school actors "offered their plays [wrote Mrs. H.] to the meek and astonished nearby villagers."[29] Nurses helped out in the public school, the orchestra played concerts in Brattleboro for the Children's Repair Fund, and seniors worked with patients at the Brattleboro Retreat. Though most faculty shunned the public elementary school, Mary Titus taught there, and there was always a Gray or a Hodgdon child enrolled. The Hodgdons joined both the Putney Grange and the masons and did a lot of square dancing.

On Putney Town Meeting day, classes were suspended so that all students and adults could walk down West Hill to attend. After 1948, students more often scattered to different towns, "for the Putney townspeople [one girl wrote to her grandparents] are rather sore when 160 school kids pour down into the town to take up all their seats. . . . I think on the whole they dislike us."[30] Certainly some townsfolk were overquick to condemn the outlandish school on the hill. There it was, perched up next to the Experiment in International Living, whose founder really did have Nazi contacts abroad (how else could German Experiment trips be arranged in the 1930s?). "To townspeople, we had to be Communists, or Fascists, or both," says Hugh MacDougall.[31] However, as the years and their shared festivals went by, and more town residents were hired to work at the school, friendly gossip began to make the rounds of the larger community. It also helped that Putney village gradually waxed more prosperous and perhaps less defensive. In the mid-thirties, state medical staff had found 70 percent of all Putney Central School children malnourished or suffering from serious, untreated health problems,[32] but by 1950, wartime prosperity had reached most of the town. Public schools now had twice the funds in real dollars to work with. A senior serving as a fourth-grade teaching apprentice in 1952 saw only a handful of too-thin boys nodding over their desks in the morning, already tired from hours of morning chores.

On Putney School's tenth anniversary, the Brattleboro *Reformer* summarized the antagonisms between West Hill and the larger community before congratulating the school on its achievements. The last paragraph tells how,

> with dignity, patience and excellent good nature, Putney School has created for itself its national reputation and its local friendship. And even though it may have gained part of its strength through rubbing against some of our cussedness, maybe we have learned a little bit about the weaknesses of a few of our habits of judgment when it comes to making friends with new ideas.[33]

So happily—so obsessively—did some students cling to their place on the hill that "We used to have trouble getting these kids *out* of here when vacation time came," says Ed Gray. One antidote was the Trip. Trips were adventure, and adventurousness lay high in the canon of Putney virtues. If a Putney student's imagination tended to leap over Putney village and to scorn the city slickers back home, it alighted gracefully in far places: up mountains and down rivers, northwest to Alaska and northeast to Cape Breton and Scandinavia. A Chinese peasant was apt to be more real than the man who ran the corner drugstore. "Songs of the People" were mimeographed for the campers and were sung by all Putneyites under Hal Sproul, songs (as the songbook's index said),

1) From the Negro
2) From the Cowboy
3) From the Sea
4) From the Railroad
5) From the Canal Boats

Of course wonderful songs came from all these sources, and wonderful men of the sea were Putney trippers' neighbors and friends in Cape Breton and beyond. Of the two dozen trips sponsored by the school during its first fifteen years, the longest took place during the summers to learn new languages and cultures, going to France (with the MacDougalls), bicycling through Scandinavia (with Mrs. H. and Henry Webb), paddling around Finland in kayaks (with Hans Hollstein). Others headed west to the Rockies or further. All were organized on shoestring budgets ($2.72 per person per day in Paris, for example, and 70¢ per day during a week of camping in Brittany). Home stays, Experiment style, were arranged wherever possible. It was as though Mrs. H. hoped to extend to all Putney students the adventures the Hinton family had enjoyed together ever since they "had come out of the West like a bombshell."[34]

At Putney School's farm on Cape Breton, Nova Scotia, possibly because the Putney group came most of all to experience the island and the sea around it, Mrs. H.'s dream of happy, cooperative relationships with a larger community seems to have materialized. She bought the primitive farm in 1948 for $1250 at a time when Cape Breton had few summer residents. The Scottish farming/fishing culture was still intact, the Gaelic-speaking inhabitants hospitable to a group of strangers who clearly admired their ways. Judy Gregory went on the first trip there:

> We're fabulous all over Cape Breton now [Judy wrote in her journal], and anywhere in Inverness they say, "Oh you're one of those out at Sight Point, are you?" and they become very chatty at once, for most of us go to the square dances which pleases them immensely. A week ago, farmers came over to help out with John Alex's hay, and in return we gave a feed and a square dance. Over 100 people came. They left 3–4 in the morning.

According to Nora Sayre, who went both to Cape Breton and to Europe, this was a far cry from the European trips, on which Putney travelers were encouraged to feel a "jubilant scorn for tourism": "you went abroad to help the poor, shiftless Europeans upgrade their farms. There were many shocks when the French or the English showed that they were being patronized—or that we were simply a nuisance."[35] Dozens of traveling Putney students felt no such shocks; these are still grateful for intercultural experiences that few Americans then enjoyed. Nevertheless, Cape Breton made a deeper impression on most than did any single place visited on the fast-moving European trips.

For those many who could not or did not travel abroad, there were other students' travel sagas to envy in assembly or *Putney Magazine* accounts of stays in Spain or China or Mongolia. There were heroes like Billy Hinton, whose remarkable dispatches from his round-the-world trip by freighter and thumb brought 1938 *Magazine* readers images of three continents lurching toward war. And finally there were both the optional weekend trips and the two (later three) major seasonal camping and ski trips, required of all but the infirm, including the faculty. Even a jaunt over the mountain to Scott Nearing's cooperative community could bring one into another world; and since this was one of Mrs. H.'s favorite places, one had the additional thrill of a drive with her. "She feels, I'm sure, that a car *cannot* go slowly even on the wildest roads," wrote one student in her journal. "One of the boys said, 'You can't see over that hill, Mrs. H.' 'Oh yes I can,' she said lightly. You surely couldn't tell her anything."[36] Alumni still marvel at her stamina on a bicycle ("I couldn't keep up with her, and *she* was 52 years old!"), her loquaciousness in a canoe, or the plain fun of a few days next to the kindness and enthusiasm that blossomed in her on a camping trip.

For Putney's adventurers, the more hazardous the weekend trip or the more thoroughly lost and chilled the trippers became, the more rousing the welcome they got returning late to school. "Daniel Boone types like Warren Winkelstein, also Rolie Marburg" (killed at thirty-two in a kayaking accident) were everyday heroes. So were two boys who challenged each other through the fall and early winter of 1950 to see which could go shirtless the longest on trips, on morning barn crew—everywhere outside of classes, meals, and assemblies. (Both made it until Christmas.) Though no one was ever gravely injured on a school trip, two young alumni, Steve Wasserman and Chris Reynolds, died in a fall the summer following their graduation, while trying a difficult route up the cliffs of Mt. Whitney. Soon they were legends.

The many overnight trips were a revelation to those new to camping. One fearful girl managed with various ills and pretexts to evade all but one, and that one changed her. "I awoke one morning after a terrifying night in those woods in a sleeping bag to see a porcupine swaying enchantedly at the extreme top of a birch tree." Though teachers longing for a rest sometimes encouraged clandestine luxury trips to someone's family vacation home, most Putney students learned what it meant to try to live up to the school catalogue's promise that they would "grow indifferent to wind, rain and cold." A New York camper on Putney Mountain once complained to Warren Leonard (then Camp Director), "Mr. Leonard, it's raining, isn't it?" "Raining?" said Warren, "Can't you see the sun's out today?" "Well, how come I'm getting wet?"[37] A '36 alumna remembers a Mt. Washington trip as "miserable, dangerous and gorgeous." Long before other schools were building Outward Bound exercises into their curricula, Putneyites knew the rigors, the social challenges, and the joys of being brought near the limit of their outdoor skills and endurance.

Robust health, "the foundation stone of any life," according to Mrs. H., was indispensable to the Putney way of life.[38] Not to be healthy, or to be struggling to *become* healthy, was a kind of sacrilege. The "Health Authorities" of the school were outside the democratic process by which all others instruments of nonacademic school governance were chosen. According to the 1944 school constitution,

> The Health Authorities of the School shall be selected by the Head of the School. It shall be their function with the Head of the School to make all decisions and regulations affecting the health of students living at the School. Such regulations shall include bed hours and requirements for outdoor exercise.

Any procedure involving health and safety could be dictated by Mrs. H.— and many were.

Carmelita Hinton had come by her obsession honestly, having been brought up at a time when American educators were thrilled to have discovered how strong and healthy women could be. It was a jubilant reaction against the pallid, corseted, Victorian woman, her flutters and her vapors, a reaction that had set in about 1890, had strengthened on the German and Scandinavian physical education movement, and had merged with the moralism of "muscular Christianity" as it was increasingly practiced on the playing fields of boys' boarding schools. Physical exercise, wrote Groton's Rev. Peabody in 1899, was the best guarantee of "pure and clean and righteous living in the school."[39] Mrs. Hinton would certainly have agreed.

Mrs. H.'s own blooming health stood as the students' chief example. But for generations of students she disingenuously drew lessons she knew to be lodged in myth. "We've always assumed that the barn burned because some students were smoking in the hayloft," she would say, though she knew that spontaneous combustion was the more likely explanation. Seniors went away from Senior Discussion convinced that the mysterious Mr. Hinton had been gravely weakened by smoking, if he hadn't died of it.[40] In those days, when medical evidence was meager, defiant student smokers experienced instead the full weight of Mrs. H.'s personal disappointment in them. "As a smoker," says one who was finally caught at it during senior year, "I was in Mrs. H.'s eyes a sham," not a student leader at all. "I thought she was going to expel me." Since that traumatic day, "I have guarded all that was good about my Putney experience with a feeling of guilt and heartache, as if it were not rightfully mine." Healthier, perhaps, was Mrs. H.'s swift reaction to a confession of secret smoking elicited from a whole set of dormitories. She suspended all forty-five penitents for a week, getting up early the next morning "to see them off, and [crying] because they had made her do it."[41]

Until the fifties, drinking seemed no great problem. If now and then "a student came in from a weekend high as a kite," most respected either the prohibition of alcohol or Warren Leonard's rigorous enforcement of it once he had become assistant director in 1946. The incorrigibles did their beer drinking in the woods.[42] Though the smoking issue made some school meetings as contentious (and seemingly as genuine) as the Athenian democracy, obsessive drinkers were shunned by other students. Mrs. H.'s lectures to seniors on the temptations they would soon face in college seemed unnecessary to many. As one alumna writes, "We took for granted the purity of our lives."[43]

Eating was another matter. Food was the only material thing the Putney community had in abundance. Many girls would have looked at home among the peasants in a Brueghel painting; boys grew thicklimbed from axe- or shovel-work and pancake-eating contests. It was natural for a farming school to make a festival of feeding, even when the steaks were cut from retired dairy cows. One girl, "a pathetic creature, weighed exactly 90 pounds in her first year." One of her friends recalls that for the monthly weighings "she stuffed her pockets with stones to escape the nurses' closer scrutiny. Within a year that device was no longer necessary, and by the time she graduated, she was strong as a buffalo, at a weight of 170."[44]

Though good health was the general rule, the strenuous life had its penalties. Letters home must have been hard on parents at times:

Today in the haymow we worked too close, and I'm lying in the infirmary now with a 2" deep hole in my calf.

For your general info, I got thrown off a very jumpy horse on Saturday, a runaway. It only scraped my back and sprained my wing . . . boy there was a horrible crash.

It's the most fantastic thing the number of people who are limping. The total wreckage of the year [1938–9] is

 2 boys ran away (one for good, one four days ago)
 1 boy died
 2 broken clavicles
 8 serious leg ailments.[45]

The medical staff—a resident nurse (later two) and a physician on call— were busy, called as they were to act as buffers for individual students against the school's demands. Every student lined up every day for inspection at the infirmary. A few nurses relieved their anxiety over the dangers of Putney's vigorous life by forcing daily vitamins and administering a tetanus booster for every scratch that broke skin; others were more subtle. The extraordinary Maria Phaneuf, Putney's nurse from 1936 through 1943, set a pattern of cautious, kindly response to student ills which brooked no hypochondria but served to forestall illness as well as cure it. She allowed one sickly girl passionate about ski meets to watch the home contests on warmer days, but kept her away from those at other schools. On her orders the same student was ensconced in a comfortable room in the inn for three days to study for exams. In the winter of 1940, one unfortunate came down with measles, and half the school got gamma-globulin shots and went into quarantine. Maria seemed to know when a student with a sniffle could ride it out and when he needed to "bask in the solitude of the infirmary." She was something of a psychiatrist, an essential confidante for many troubled youngsters who came for an aspirin but left comforted by a long talk.[46] Maria and a later nurse sensitively handled the two pregnancies that became known to Putney adults, advising the girls to go home and helping their parents to help them. There were surely others (alumnae speak of two others in thirty years), but nothing like the epidemic that coeducation's detractors had predicted.

Putney asked a lot. "Every hour misspent is lost forever," went a CCC Camp adage, and Putney's motto might have been the same had mottos been in. Many alumni recall being tired, mentally and physically, most of the time. Students saw that there was play in the system, however, and they used it when the pace became too fierce. They could choose birdwatching as a spring sport and make most of their observations from a prone position near Garland Pond. They could ask at the infirmary for afternoon "Rest." Cynthia Russell writes,

> It was not hard to get "Rest" if one knew how to space requests for it skillfully, varying one's symptoms appropriately while doing so. We all felt we were entitled to a certain amount of "Rest", and as some of us were consistently healthy, this system seemed a just one to us. After the authorities had been by to check on us, and found us all apparently sleeping soundly in our beds, we would jump up, dash out of the rear door, and across the fields to Mabel Gray's to buy a homemade cake. . . . You could smell her delicious cakes baking as you climbed up the last hill.

They could also join Cornelia Hinkle's cooking activity, where one could go to cook up a cup of cocoa and talk about whatever one wanted.

Week by week, the athletic program continued both to build health and to draw on its capital. As fields and courts were leveled, sports became more various: in time the boys started a soccer team with John Holden's help, and the girls got the hockey field to themselves—though some of them missed the rough, racing coed games. Jack Caldwell created a formidable baseball team. His two older sons, Johnny and Peter, enjoyed their father's rigorous training, as did several other boys, and wished for more.[47] With the help of carefully trained student ski teachers, John Holden and his successor, John Caldwell, Jr., built Putney's ski program into one of the two or three strongest in any Eastern school. Both men's contribution was underlined by their roles as officers in the ski associations. Ski meets brought some of the traditional trappings of competition: daily wind sprints, honed equipment, even beefsteak breakfasts before the big meets. Through thirty years, Putney would place in almost every New England and Eastern interscholastic contest.

As the trophies piled up, the school's efforts to underplay competition began to seem hollow. However, the ski program's strength was its depth, for almost everyone skied. The simplicity of early equipment dulled the panache. ("I wish you would bring up my skis and some old straps which I could rig up into a harness," wrote one student to her parents.[48]) Skiers who broke a leg were not made heroes, observed Jane Arms, "only regarded as victims of the good life." One boy—Vermont's downhill champion for the year—who had failed to get a long-finished paper into his teacher's hands by the due date was refused permission to go to the national trials. As the Caldwell, Gray, and Hinkle children matured and cross-country racing waxed ever more popular, Putney became the major Nordic racing center of New England, but the lovely trails funneled more amateurs than racers through the woods. As with so many Putney activities, the doing was all: the passionate interaction of body, mind, and surrounding nature. An article in an early *Putney Magazine* opened, "Skiing has become a religion."[49]

To Carmelita Hinton, a healthy attitude toward sex was central to the development of the whole individual. It is almost certain that, like so many of her generation, she feared what she called "those lower physical lusts" and their power to undermine what was "highest in man." As a young woman, she surely heard or read Jane Addams' anxious words on the failure of the urban young to master their appetites.[50] However, her stance toward sex was not merely a function of fear or personal prejudice. Far more than most adults, she had thought out the implications of sexual relationships within a small, complex community. If her wishes for her students were unrealistic, her determination to engage sexual issues was courageous. To many—even to those who ridiculed her words—that mattered.

Most messages got across without words. Those students who thought about it at all accepted the basic need to protect a coed school's reputation; some alumni even recall guessing at the time that Mrs. H. had designed her school's arts, outdoor, and recreational programs partly in order to open safe outlets for the brimming sexual energies of the young. Like these implicit messages, the director's explicit statements on sex were chiefly grounded in her concept of the well-balanced adolescent for whom no one avenue of growth should be closed by excessive concentration on any other. She was also repelled by the commercialization of romance. Students heard much of her antipathy to hucksterism of all kinds, sex "for sale" being only one of the corruptions of individual integrity that Putney School was founded to oppose.[51] Finally, her ideal of community led her utterly to reject conventional teen dating patterns. As Noyes had urged on the Perfectionists a generous and restrained form of free love, wishing to ensure that no one felt excluded, Mrs. H. hoped that repression of explicit physical sex would diffuse affection throughout the school. Given the forces of adolescent nature, it is remarkable how many graduates of both sexes speak of "being in love with a dozen wonderful people at once."

In public Mrs. H. preached the good clean fun of group activity. Usually she spoke as though confident that sex would never intrude on community, occasionally, after an "outbreak among a few sophisticated students," expressing her horror as she explained why one of these had been dismissed. "I can't understand why you all don't go around in a group the way everyone used to do when the school began," she earnestly told Senior Discussion classes, drawing on her most convenient memories.[52]

The second line of defense she drew in private conversations with each member of a new couple as soon as their relationship seemed to her to have reached the point of excluding other friendships and activities—sooner, if Mrs. H. thought a girl needed a "sex talk." To eschew such tender traps was to be strong-minded, remembers an alumna who had to be told this too often. On several occasions, expulsion was used as a last resort. To the dismay of her friends, Barbara Bel Geddes was dismissed after being discovered one too many times with a boy in a darkened classroom.

Mrs. H. admitted some befuddlement to colleagues or graduates ("We are not at all wise about sex," she wrote to one), but she plunged in anyway, making some inevitable misjudgments in the process. A '49 alumna who lived in Hinton House still feels defensive about a long "talk about the birds and the bees" she received one night after coming in late from an innocent conversation with a male friend. A teacher was "horrified at the grilling" one of her counselees got after being caught petting in an attic and even more shocked when the couple were then suspended.[53] Alumni also remember Mrs. H.'s remarkably sharp perceptions about other situations, especially more extreme ones which really did involve the exploitation of girl by boy or vice versa. "I don't know how, but she knew just what was going on," says one alumnus for several. "It was her watchfulness that freed us from the need for elaborate rules."[54]

The boys complained the loudest, a noise one begins to understand as her meaning becomes clear: she was telling them that no double standard was acceptable. A few boys defended it as hotly as she attacked it. Asked in Senior Discussion, "What are your sex standards?" one wrote, "This experience [intercourse] should be practised by the male. A decent girl should be a virgin up until she is married. Then the husband knows he is getting something brand new." Another declared it was "none of your business." "My own sex standards are to get as much as I can for as cheap as I can in the shortest possible time." But most boys answered that "sex should be sincere and mutual," or that "nothing should be forced on a girl." Thirty years later, an alumnus writes, "We knew she was old-fashioned; then after Putney we saw that she was right to be old-fashioned."[55]

No one person could hold back the tide alone. Mrs. H. asked every teacher to keep tabs on couples, though many were reluctant informants. "What were _____ and _____ doing in the back of the truck?" she'd want to know after a trip. "Uncle Phil" Chase, Carmelita's younger brother, was only the first adult whom Mrs. H. sent "sulking in the bushes with his flashlight" to discourage couples coupling. Though the elite boys boasting access to the fire truck and its heated garage could command warmth for winter trysts, neither truck cab nor root cellar was ever completely safe. One couple was discovered in an unlikely way. They had repaired to the haymow after the Harvest Festival square dance. So absorbed were they that they didn't notice the hay chute, and they slipped down, landing on the barn floor just as the teacher on flashlight duty came through to inspect the barn. "The next day they were gone from school just as though they had never been," says Alice Holway.

A Russian teacher made her mark on Friday evening record dances by sliding up to pairs who were dancing too close and warning, "*Seex eenches*, please, *seex eenches*." Even these efforts would probably not have sufficed if students hadn't been "kept exhaustingly busy," writes Nora Sayre. As a rule however, "virginity was (sometimes barely) maintained, really because we had too little time to lose it—a bell rang, horses had to be groomed, or a meeting on World Federalism began, an arts conference opened, there was a rehearsal of Auden or Pirandello. Reeling and gasping out of one another's arms," they rushed on to something else.[56]

Many faculty who spent little concern on students' virginity per se were experts at discouraging the distractions of sex. Norwood's disgust with "lovers" who mixed handholding with record listening was famous among the musicians. When a performance neared, he scrapped the usual deadline for ending evening rehearsal, and, at about 9:30, would turn around and yell to all those halves of couples impatiently waiting at the back of the KDU, "And I don't want any of this nonsense about walking people home!" The rehearsal would then go on to 9:50.[57]

Strange to say, the system often worked. Di Lasso madrigals really did hold and express beauties that many young students were just learning to feel. Arts could enrich the subtle, erotic messages that male and female conveyed to each other, often without knowing they were doing it. Both boys and girls could be in love with their horses, and no one even blinked. Over the years, Putney young who found Mrs. H.'s ideas on sex hilarious absorbed the values behind her repressive stance. Even Nora Sayre was as "grateful for coeducation as anyone else."[58] Some selection was at work, of course. Early fifties Work Camp recommendation forms asked, "Does the candidate have an extreme interest in the opposite sex?" If so, the candidate was not likely to be admitted. Still, one is impressed to read an editor of the Work Camp's *Putney Weeder* for 1947 deploring the rapid pairing off in the camp that summer. In ten days, he complains, "almost a dozen new twosomes have already been formed"; it seemed that going with a boy or girl had "become virtually a social necessity." It was clear to this writer—as it was to other student commentators on the same topic that summer—that the rich friendships they had come to expect at camp could not be built in so short a time. "Physical attraction will wear awfully thin," he finished.[59]

Putney was no monastery. Girls' letters home are full of chat about blouses or nylons worn proudly to dinner for the first time. One who had experienced "several broken hearts" was continually assuring her parents that she and her current boyfriend shared an interest in chamber music at least as important as romance. Male graduates recall the panic that preceded the spring social dance as couples formed and broke and almost everyone scrambled for a partner before all had been spoken for; they also write with delight of the fun of the dance itself, including faculty waiters' antics (the younger Caldwell once poured new-hatched tadpoles into his students' glasses with their water). Where boys and girls shared so much of daily life, deep, mature friendships formed in spite of anything Mrs. H. could say, and nearly fifty of the couples later married. These friendships were admired and intensively discussed by others. Two 1940s alumni remember the pleasure of seeing Holly Forbes and Gonzalo Leon toast each other with orange juice every morning at the early dish crew breakfast, at least three years before their wedding. Many other cross-sex friendships flourished, sex or no sex. "The platonic relationships were great," says one alumnus. Another remembers "being in love with about half a dozen wonderful girls [at once]—there seemed to be an incredible concentration of them at Putney."

After all, there was no way adequately to police the long house party which to the most sociable, the Putney community appeared to be. For every individual individually (and kindly) scolded after sleeping out in a coed group, then assigned to a faculty home for a week's closer supervision, there must have been dozens of couples who simply moved farther out into the woods or did their loving by day. Ultimately, trust in students' better judgment was the only practical resort. There is evidence that the trust was rewarded: recollections of alumni and alumnae who felt supported in decisions to refuse heavy sex and of others (or the same ones) who entered intimate relationships far more thoughtfully than rebels would have done. And Mrs. H., like her school, was too full of life for her students to take her repressions overseriously, unless, perhaps, they had been prepared so to be harmed by parental teachings along similar lines. After a while, one got accustomed to Mrs. H.'s apparently unquestioning belief in her ideas and forgave her periodic insensitivities to individuals. For many, such extraordinary self-confidence made her an exception, an authority figure too distinct from parents and all others for her more extreme positions to be threatening.

Putney's male graduates remark on Putney's broad sex education less often than do Putney women. Perhaps the female director's messages to boys seemed less personal, more abstract. Putney men are more apt to put them down to Mrs. H.'s Victorian attitude toward sex or to scoff at her don't-touch policy. It is also likely that girls needed the messages more, being more vulnerable to those distortions of social life and personal image that Carmelita Chase had herself experienced as a girl in Omaha or had watched her peers suffer as they reached the dating age. Feminist ideals of equality and self-fulfillment could not possibly be realized for Putney alumnae without direct attention to such harassments. Surely the school's attraction for many girls was its promise of release from some of the conventional pressures without the added artificialities an all-girl school imposes. However, some male applicants and their parents mention equivalent benefits for boys as factors in their choice of Putney School; several Putney men speak of the modern women's liberation movement and of their own enduring marriages as though they had learned to appreciate feminism's essential ideas while at Putney School.

A few Putney women have gone so far as to say that modern feminism could add nothing to their Putney experience. They are often the same girls who were thrilled to have a "motherly" Carmelita Hinton running the school "when most women were still in the kitchen." These alumnae may have been lucky enough not to notice the myths and put-downs so much a part of life at Putney School (as of all of American life) during its first fifteen years and more. Daily routine sustained the myths. In the forties, girls groomed the cows while boys shoveled manure. Girls were not supposed to try ski jumping for fear of damaging their internal organs. The boys drove all the big trucks until Warren Leonard trained the first female truck driver about 1953. The chef was a man, his helpers women, and a senior boy ran the dishwasher. After 1941, the business manager was male and all the secretaries were female. Girls never made up anything like half of the advanced physics classes, and several sections were all male. The opposite was true for dance classes. Girls tended toward diffidence in class discussion, and some teachers never bothered to notice.[60]

Yet Putney School was a good place for girls and women, as places went. Mrs. H. was such a powerhouse that she was probably wise to favor men in her hiring and promoting of teachers. Women teachers and teachers' wives found room for a growth and learning in the West Hill community that was far harder to come by in the world outside. Girls subverted some needless sexist distinctions by ski jumping and shoveling manure whenever no one who cared was looking on. Everywhere in their Putney lives they could find examples of daring individuals who happened to be female; nor were such models lost on the boys, who needed them just as much. Utopian assumptions had educational utility: behaving for three or four years as though sexual equality was real prepared people to bring it about in adult life.

As Mrs. H. grew older, the Christian God to whom her parents had prayed disappeared altogether from her life, and she refused comfort from any supreme being. Yet "that of God" was all about her in nature's beauties and in the heroic goodness of ordinary human beings. "You, Man, have to become divine!" she would say.[61] And one can be, she implied, by disciplining body and mind toward the goal of a better world for all. Thus did respect for persons—both as individuals and as sexual beings—take its place at Putney beside love of nature, the school's commitments to health and strength, democracy and community, and above all, to each student's growth toward his or her largest possibilities.

Chapter 7

Time Passing

To be viable a utopian community had to answer the needs of its times. Did Putney School do so? It must have been doing something right, because students kept on coming. By 1941, there was a heartening surplus of applicants. "Your friends' parents' eyebrows went up when they heard you went to Putney," says a graduate—but the next year the same parents might be writing for application forms.[1] Enrollment rose gradually through 1949, when it briefly leveled off at about 165.

No generalization is possible about the parade of parents who found promise in Putney School through its first fifteen years. Opinions abound: "They were artists." "They were New Deal Liberals." "Mine were conservative, convention-bound." "They were also Boston and Concord . . . there was a tremendous transcendental energy at Putney." "They were all closet radicals" who saw the progressive spirit fading as war approached, and wanted their children, at least, to catch and hold it. But "all" is always too many. Says one friend of Putney, "There were plenty of conservative parents who just thought it was a damn good school."[2] Certainly there were men and women living in the thick of public affairs who offered their children to Putney, among others James Conant, Ellsworth Bunker, Paul Hoffman, and later, Owen Lattimore, Helen Lehmann Buttenweiser, Allan and Eleanor Lansing Dulles, Alger Hiss, Abraham Ribicoff. Labels fail. Perhaps Putney families had nothing in common but a certain daring.

For some harried public servants, the school may have looked like a haven for their children, an island of innocence safe from the ominous events in the outside world. Yet Putney School inevitably reflected that world. The Putney community was too committed to world peace to escape awareness of approaching wars. In the very first issue of the *Putney Magazine* (and years before most American students gave a thought to foreign wars) is an article by

114

a boy trying on pacifism for size. "Would you join (if) Japan declared war on the United States?" he asks. Another 1935 writer describes the new Germany, whose rulers are destroying the rights of Jews and of labor unions.[3] Early in 1937, a few students joined three hundred citizens at a peace rally in Brattleboro and returned to organize discussions and speakers at the school. By this time at least one article on the conflict in China or Spain appears in every *Magazine* issue. Soon two school assemblies a week were being given to such current events. While a 1934 survey found almost nine in ten public school superintendents agreeing that high school history texts "should omit any facts likely to arouse . . . questions or doubt concerning the justice of our social order,"[4] early Putney students were learning U.S. history from one Marxist and many skeptics. They also read social protest novels in English classes.[5]

The 1936 election found most of Putney School parading to town and back. Wearing red, the socialist students and teachers walked, some ringing alarm clocks, others carrying the dummy of a malnourished woman and "many swell banners." The Democrats played "Happy Days Are Here Again" on their violins, and the Republicans filled a haywagon with brass players to blare their way down the hill in style.[6] Student actors put on a radio play in Assembly dramatizing the shortage of housing for the poor. Soon after Roosevelt's second term began, students turned to international issues with a new earnestness. In the 1938 *Magazines*, they read of Bill Hinton's travels through China and across the Siberian border in the midst of the Sino-Japanese War. His comment on the terrible cruelty he saw in the Japanese soldiers was, "Americans do the same to the people they hate. Look at the lynchings in the South." But by June, Bill saw no turning back. He wrote from Central Europe that "Warsaw seemed choked and dying." A German youth hostel that the Hinton Experimenters had enjoyed in 1934 was "no fun any more . . . it's a military camp." The warmth and élan of the German youth movement had given way to "ruthlessness. . . . They've been fed on nothing but Hitler for too long."[7]

Three months later, as though to match the gathering storm in Europe, the worst hurricane ever recorded slammed into New England. The wind began rising late in the afternoon of September 21. Before long trees were cracking, breaking, and falling all over Elm Lea Farm. The barn door blew out and across the road, and the huge barn itself began swaying in the wind; students led the cows to the safer wing of the barn. Ross Hodgdon drove up the hill from his Lower Farm chores as fast as his truck would go, trees falling behind him. The roof blew off the chicken house and all fifty chickens were blown away. "They'll come back," Mrs. H. told distressed students. But they never did.[8]

Years later, someone remembered Mrs. H. out in the storm, her hair streaming wet in the wind, shaking her fist at the sky and shouting "This *can't* happen! We can't afford it!"[9] But it did happen, and before long the hurricane became yet another educational challenge. The community gathered in a candle-lit assembly hall to sing the evening away and make plans for clearing up the chaos.[10] After the sixteen biggest trees fallen across the hilltop had been cut up and hauled away, the students threatened to go on strike unless they were allowed a second day off classes to help town volunteers reconstruct the roads washed out near the roaring Connecticut River. It was a week before electricity was regained. "We loved it," several alumni say of the dramatic destruction and the work of rebuilding that followed: the construction of a sawmill to turn windfall trees into useful lumber, the ditching and draining, the shoring up of the school against another such assault.

But the next assaults were manmade. Putney was readier than most schools, which had hardly noticed the darkening world around them.[11] The Second World War would change many faces, many moods, many routines, but would not touch Putney's core. Central to the school, after all, was a practiced commitment to world citizenship. As the nation's internationalists veered from crusading in vain for peace to making war, Putney crusaders moved with them, some suffering deeply over the perversion of the German culture that Putney travelers had learned to admire and that had nurtured several refugee teachers and students. Many mourned the wreckage of international friendships that had held such promise in the heady days of Experiment trips and World Youth Congresses.

The crisis abroad turned personal as Spanish and German families on the receiving end of fascist aggression escaped to America and sent their children to a school that seemed to embody the purposes for which they had struggled. The older of the two Leon boys, son of one Spanish Republican fighter and brother of three others, was the first to come to West Hill. Several Jewish refugees followed. Before long, a teacher was hired to tutor foreign students in English. When Werner Warmbrunn arrived to teach history and German in 1944, he felt he had " 'come home' to the generous idealism of the early German Youth Movement"—even to its lederhosen and hiking songs. Though the press continued occasionally to criticize Putney's German connections, its faculty managed to ignore this unwanted publicity.[12]

Compared with the alternatives, it was small humiliation for Werner, Ewald, and other Germans to have to register as "enemy aliens" with town officials and report in every time they planned to leave the township. Having survived threats to their lives, the newer refugees appeared to thrive on Putney's challenges. A German boy proved the most brilliant math student Putney had ever known. The gentle Werner did wish Mrs. H. would allow him more solitude to write the poetry that had been driven back into his soul by the stresses of Hitler's Germany, but Dwight Boehm, another refugee teacher, brought the proper Teutonic zeal to Putney's rigors. "Come on," he'd call to his Allen House boys, "Get up! It's only 30° below." Dr. Sandels (always "Dr.," even at Putney) had been head of a school in Germany. If his English was incomprehensible to some, he knew his Latin cold.

The school's internal political divisions faded for the duration, and with them some of the town's criticism. Mrs. H. had voted Socialist for most of her adult life, but FDR had become her president by 1936, and now she exhorted her school to back his war preparations in all ways possible. She herself bought as many War Bonds as she could. She heard of English families seeking safe homes for their children during the bombing of Britain in 1940, and her immediate response was to invite a group of the children to Putney School. With help from patriotic townsfolk, she rented a big old house in town, soon known as "English House," and engaged one of the children's mothers to be houseparent for eight British refugee children, eleven to fourteen years old. The children had a comfortable, familiar home life and became full-scholarship day students at Putney School.

Another Putney mother who took charge of English House for six weeks has left an amusing account of her stay. At first the children seemed un-naturally charming—flaxen-haired characters out of *Swallows and Amazons*. Gradually, however, they relaxed, and their temporary housemother found mischievousness with a British accent as exasperating as mischievousness anywhere. They also grew more and more at home at the school, loving square dances, farm animals, and festivals.[13] Their presence there was a reminder of Americans' good fortune. True, fuel shortages put a crimp in the longer trips, and building projects came to a halt. Summer trips went west instead of east, two successive groups working their way as haymakers and harvesters from upper New York state to Wyoming. The ski tow rested. The skiers climbed. While enrollment expanded to include impoverished European refugees, tuition income dropped. In 1943–44, 173 students attended Putney. A few science classes grew to nineteen students, "too many for lab work," complained one harried teacher.[14] But Putney already prided itself on living lean, and to live leaner still, with clear reasons for so doing, only strengthened the ethic of frugality that had made the school possible.

It was hardest to lose people. After Pearl Harbor, Warren Leonard, John Holden, Hugh MacDougall, and other men left for the war. Altogether about 130 Putney graduates joined the armed services or nursing corps— about half the total number of alumni. Eleven ski heroes volunteered for the mountain troops. They were among the few Americans accepted for this difficult training, and great was the disappointment of the last lot to join when the European war ended before they were needed, so that they were sent instead to swelter in the Pacific theater. Three alumni died in the war, heroes forever.

On West Hill, dislocations hurt here and there: a historian pressed into the teaching of chemistry, a storekeeper teaching ancient history, a relaxing of Mrs. H.'s determination to keep males preponderant in the teaching force. There were 26 men and 12 women in 1940; 20 men and 17 women in 1942. Yet some extraordinary people came, too, including such powerful characters as Mara Moser, and Jim and Flo Angell. Mrs. H. continued to welcome European refugees, pacifists, and other dissidents whenever their teaching skills were needed. Thus Putney weathered war far better than many schools, which often had to pull teachers from the very bottom of a small employment pool. (In 1943, Smith College's teacher-placement service could fill only 20 of 720 requests.) Putney's faculty turnover was swifter than ever as young men were drafted and wives followed husbands away, but some single-year teachers have always been among Putney's best from the students' point of view.

A Red Cross unit opened at the school, and later on a fervent refugee relief group headed by Mara Moser was able to raise as much as $4000 a year for its causes, with almost everyone, even "all the boys . . . madly knitting—some knitting socks and some eight-foot scarves, just to be dumb."[15] Camping trips left the school by foot, by bicycle, or on horseback instead of by truck, and found overnight accommodations in any hayloft instead of in select ones. ("My sleeping bag stank of sheep and chickens for years afterwards," writes one alumnus about an especially crowded barn). Mrs. H. and a crowd of students became apple pickers in Darrow's orchards, since so few men could be hired to bring in the harvest. Otherwise life went on much as always. In certain ways, the outer world's preoccupation with momentous events had the effect of increasing Putney's utopian apartness. Few outsiders had time to ponder or criticize what was going on up there on West Hill; the school could plot its course with a minimum of impingement on its freedom.

Yet the war was always present. Most dorms had a single radio for classical music and war news, and both were avidly followed. When Allied victories began at last to turn the war, few of Putney's adults could enjoy them, for they thought too deeply of the costs. Even some students rejected the newsreel war so many Americans cheered. Marie Wasserman wrote an extraordinary article about Japan in a 1942 *Putney Magazine*, describing the complex, orderly culture behind the "brutal, beast-like soldier" rampaging through China and searching for a synthesis of the two. War had brought out the worst in warmakers on every side; a school that assumed the best of humankind had few metaphors to make the worst comprehensible.[16]

News of President Roosevelt's death came in the middle of evening activities. One student remembers leaving off chamber music rehearsal in the middle of a piece and going to the assembly hall, where Mrs. H. wept and spoke of FDR, then wept again. Only then did most realize how deep her faith in him had grown. For the first time in her life, she feared for the future, and said so.[17]

The dropping of the first—and still worse, the second—atomic bomb stopped hearts that summer.[18] One person who knew all too much of the Bomb was the youngest Hinton daughter, Joan, who had graduated from the school in 1939. While still in graduate school, she had been asked to join a small group of the most promising physics students in the country, who would help to plan and construct the world's first nuclear weapon. She had agreed because she knew that the alternative might be Nazi control of the Bomb.[19] But almost as soon as 150,000 Japanese deaths had demonstrated its success, Joan Hinton, with many of her Los Alamos colleagues, began to work for peace with a vehemence comprehensible, perhaps, only to those others who thought themselves partly responsible for the massive slaughter. By 1948 the movement for international control had failed. Joan decided to continue her personal crusade by joining her brother Bill, now driving tractors for UNRRA in China. Peace work there quickly became war work again, however. The time came to choose sides. Joan saw no contest between a corrupt, dictatorial American ally and Mao Tse-Tung's peasant-soldiers, and with Bill's help, she moved north through a kind of underground to build farm machinery out of scrap metal and serve as an amateur agronomist in the primitive villages that kept the Red Army fed.

"I would continue always to love and miss physics," Joan has said of her thirty-eight years in the People's Republic, but she could not regret her decision to leave "the Science of Destruction behind" for her work of building better lives among peasants who had nothing.[20] By the early 1950s, when Joseph McCarthy rode high, red-baiters would assume that "Peking Joan, the spy who got away," had gone to China to give nuclear weapons secrets to the communists.[21] For several years, however, the American press left her alone with her broken windmills and her wild Chinese dairy cows (first tackle, then milk). Her mother read her letters to Putney students in Assembly or in Senior Discussion.

Joan Hinton's mission was only one intensive version of a widespread yearning to create an international order that would make war obsolete. In the months between V-J Day and the Soviets' rejection of the Baruch plan for international control of atomic energy, almost anything seemed possible. Schools and colleges all over the nation heard Bernard Baruch, Eleanor Roosevelt, and a host of lesser figures teaching the lessons of two world wars. The Indian independence movement strengthened idealists everywhere before Ghandi's assassination; the U.N. Charter seemed to doom colonialism abroad and racism at home. Cautiously, the fashionable prep schools opened their doors to a black student here, a Jew there, some so fearful of parent reaction that they surveyed parents ahead of time, then tried bravely to swallow their chagrin when a few parents did indeed withdraw their children.[22]

Putney School had been open to all races from the beginning, but not a single qualified black candidate had applied. Now, slowly, they began to arrive, and most felt wholly welcome even if never wholly understood. In 1946, a black veteran took over the complex post-office job; soon he was a central participant in Civic Action Committee (CAC) discussions and, with the CAC, a major organizer of Putney's first conference on racism. Activist students visited the managers of every large store in Brattleboro, asking each if he would be willing to hire negro workers. (Most said yes, if one ever applied.) "One world" at Putney School also meant a prophetic concern for natural resource management and population control; the CAC and Farm Association cosponsored a two-day conference on these topics in the fall of 1948 that hundreds attended.

A reader of the *Putney Magazine* in these times was certain to find at least two or three articles on the race issue in every number. Just after the war, fantasies of Armageddon by A-bomb or germ warfare alternate with calls for world government as the only possible strategy for survival. A few pieces, perhaps, substitute doggerel for thought: The final couplet of a sonnet, "The People" finishes

> Wealth in fine dress may last a little longer,
> But the rising spirit of the poor is stronger.

One article showed precisely how folk dancing could bring world peace.[23]

Many students were putting their convictions directly to work. The senior who chaired the new CAC insisted, "We, at Putney, can do a great deal to influence the leaders of this country." Twenty-five of the CAC members conducted a poll in the town to assess its inhabitants' willingness to prolong American rationing in order to relieve hunger in Europe; a third of the students and faculty ate a four-cent meal of gruel and potatoes one evening every week in order to raise money for European food programs. A group of summer campers initiated a "heifer for Belgium" project. With Hutch's help, they solicited gifts to buy an exemplary calf, which would be raised by students through the next school year and trucked to the Brethren Service Committee in Pennsylvania for shipment abroad.[24]

A year after V-J Day, interest in war relief was as keen as ever. It even extended to a special effort by Experimenters to send C.A.R.E. packages directly to hungry ex-Nazis who had been host families for Putney travelers before the war. The complications, however, were building. To many of Putney's students and faculty, world stability began to mean resistance to Soviet expansion. Others, equally thoughtful, insisted that "Americans, for all their manufactured fear and hatreds, want peace, not war." These called for "respect for the Soviets' local interests in Eastern Europe."[25] A heated argument began between the anticommunist moderates and the leftists, a discussion with no conclusion that would engage much of the Putney community in a years-long process of self-education.

Late in 1946, students Karl A. Schuman and Hugh MacDougall, Jr., started the *Putney News*, a mimeographed weekly ("Price, 0 cents"), including reports and editorials of their own and letters from all over the world. To Hugh and Karl, Putney's aim to make the world a better place involved more than daily education in the Putney mode. It meant a concentrated effort to inform oneself and others of the problems to be faced in that world.[26] Soon the *News* (later the *Press*) was an evening activity. The ever-larger editorial board followed the liberal movement at home and reported on the civil war in Greece, then in China, abroad. Bill Hinton wrote from his UNRRA post in China to warn that U.S. aid to Greece and Turkey was defending not democracy but Standard Oil's pipelines. The *News* outlined the U.S. germ warfare plans and at first approved several aspects of the "Soviet experiment"; but it also printed letters critical of its editorial views. The editors meticulously described both sides of the argument they had heard at a Williams College conference on the future of capitalism. Most impressive are the many news articles, striving always for objectivity even where detailed evidence inconvenienced a favorite editorial viewpoint.[27]

The *Putney Magazine* also reflects the growing confusion and students' valiant efforts to clear it. Articles from 1947 describe summer experiences: a student who went with Mrs. H. to the World Youth Festival in Prague; another who left the festival with "four Britishers—two Conservatives and two Communists" to join an international student construction crew. For a week they helped rebuild the Czech Jewish village of Lidice, totally destroyed by the Nazis along with its inhabitants.[28] Such themes or events are mentioned in other contexts, too. One senses from alumni and faculty recollections that they reverberated through the school.

In 1947, some of Putney's internationalists took a new stance. The 1947–48 *Magazine* editors reproduced a Sunday night talk by Bruce Menefee, a history teacher and *Putney Press* advisor just returned from helping to lead a Putney trip in Europe, a young man whose sensitivity and passion for human betterment brought him unusually close to students who shared his concerns. "Greed appears to be running America," Menefee told Putney School, "[Democracy has] apparently fail[ed]." In the fight Lenin began "for the liberation of mankind," he came "closer to Thomas Jefferson than any modern American leader has done."[29] Student editors of the *Putney Press* described a world too complex to fit such sweeping statements, but several of them responded to the challenge their faculty advisor had presented by founding a Putney chapter of the World Federalists, inviting speakers, filling bulletin boards with WF news, and canvassing in Brattleboro to get 286 shopper-citizens' views of world government and the U.N. By 1949 the Federalists constituted a small but noisy organization with a publication of its own, for which several future journalists and foreign service officers plied their pens. With the help of a Brattleboro lawyer, the group managed to get a resolution favoring world government on the Putney town warrant. Hours into town meeting, with only the stalwarts left, it passed.[30]

An overlapping group, including at least eight faculty members, threw itself into the Progressive Party's presidential campaign for Henry Wallace. As early as October 1947, Wallace spoke in Brattleboro and Putney, spent a night at the Hinton house, and took breakfast there with a crowd of eager

Putney folk. "The bulk of Europe looks on America as the center of World reaction[ism]," Wallace told his well-prepared audience. "There is ten times as much danger in the administration's suppression of civil liberties [as] in the Communists.'"[31] One weekend the following spring, Mrs. H. and Bruce Menefee drove together to the Wallace headquarters in Montpelier, where Bruce drafted the candidate's state platform and Mrs. H. helped to organize the campaign. West Hill Wallace supporters continued through November 1948 to campaign for him as though he were the last hope for a sane world order.

The school community polled itself the day before the official 1948 election, with the following results:[32]

Republican	73
Progressive	71
Democrat	36
Socialist	17
Vegetarian	7

Putney townsfolk once shocked by Nazi flags had now begun to think of the school on West Hill as a center of communist agitation, but it is much to Putney's credit that Republicans also flourished at this time, warmly supported by Jack Caldwell, an active citizen-politician. Caldwell spoke for the Taft-Hartley Act in Assembly; Republican students debated current events and contributed often to the *Putney Press*. A faculty family became permanent host parents to two Czech students who had fled the communist coup of 1948. A large minority of political infants may have nodded through Assembly as MacDougall and small David Dulles indulged their informational mission, yet even these back-benchers were impressed with the importance granted to public affairs at Putney School. By 1946, Russian had been added to the language offerings, and global politics vied for attention with ingrown adolescent conundrums in Mrs. H.'s Senior Discussion groups.

In the two years after V-J Day, most of the school's soldiers returned. John Holden, Warren Leonard, and their wives, Anne and Marion, brought with them the most welcome gift Mrs. H. could imagine: a sense that the emergencies were over. Unaware how much she had depended on these two men earlier, she now recognized them by giving John new responsibility for the afternoon program and making Warren assistant director of the school. Small resentments seeded themselves among some of the newer teachers who had brought the school through the war, but as yet, nothing was said out loud.[33] Where there was so much to be done, brooding seemed out of place. For Putney School, peace in the world meant also building on West Hill. As early as spring 1945 a pair of generous parents had contributed $10,000 toward a science building, and the blasting of the ledge behind the old one had begun, to the delight of the boys allowed to help with the foundations.

The school's most immediate need was for better student and faculty housing. Since 1936 only a few small spaces had been renovated for student rooms. For the most part, adults not in dormitories had built their own homes. Now that building was possible, the school corporation's directors determined to fill this need even if it had to *borrow from a bank* to do so. Mrs. H. swallowed hard before agreeing to this risky break with precedent. Virtually all of the school's "miraculous expansion" (as Jack Caldwell remarked when he arrived in 1941) had been accomplished with surplus funds: earnings from farm and camp, and Putney's pioneer tuition payers investing in Putney's future. The long construction timetables required for student labor allowed receipts to keep pace, with the help of small parent gifts at critical times. Now, however, the outlying farmhouses and the original boys' dorm seemed suddenly decrepit beyond usefulness. In the summer of 1945, the school hired an architect and launched its first campaign: *Putney School Needs $250,000 for New Housing.* Eight dormitory/faculty houses were to be built by contract as quickly as money could be raised from Putney's extended family.[34] Jane Arms, ill now and unable to teach, ran the campaign from a corner of the business office for the cost of printing and stamps. If parents sent no gift, she simply mailed them another booklet. That year the first of the "New Dorms" was begun.

It would be the last for many years. The $78,000 that eventually came in for this tenth-anniversary drive almost exactly matched the cost of a single dormitory with faculty house attached. Postwar inflation had more than doubled the estimated costs. That $78,000 was $74,000 more than Putney had ever raised for any purpose failed to dispel the regret that students had been kept from hammering a single nail into the building. The whole project left a bad taste in many mouths—a bad smell too, for it would be twenty years before the new dorm's sewage field was functioning as it should.

Nevertheless, other projects went ahead. The corporation's Executive Committee borrowed $20,000 to continue the dormitory and $7,000 more for an army-surplus prefabricated house and a huge deep freeze. The rusting water tower came down and concrete tank was planted in its place. The new science building was begun. In 1946, 130 of Putney's 320 graduates returned for harvest festival; they made clear to each other and to the school their desire to winterize Arthur Green's old chicken house, now the Summer

Theater dormitory, for alumni use during the school year. Barbara Barnes and Donald Watt, heads of the new alumni association, organized the renovations, and by 1948 the first alumni house was as ready as it would ever be. Despite all efforts, pipes froze, and body heat remained the major source of warmth for many winter reunions to come.

The new structures rising on West Hill seemed to symbolize Putney's safe passage through depression and war, while its confident borrowings and solicitations suggested its solidity as an established secondary school. Reminders of the hard years surfaced poignantly now and then: the absence of founding teachers like the MacDougalls, who had gone on to new work at the war's end, the presence of people still suffering its wounds. These included several students who had lost whole families to violence, as well as a violin teacher who had been hung by his thumbs under Nazi torture and was only now beginning to play again.[35]

While the progressive education movement as a whole became increasingly rigid and unresponsive during the late 1930s and 1940s, the war's end found Putney renewing its commitments to progressive ideas. The school had been praised in the 1940 *Vermonter* for serving as "a check in our decadent national life, . . . going back to first principles," and infusing its children with the "all-around dependability of sixty years ago."[36] Yet Putney seemed far from the static utopias of the nineteenth century. From the "children's" point of view, the school appeared largely to fulfill Dewey's requirement that education in a mobile, rapidly progressing society nurture both personal initiative and adaptability.[37] Soon after the war, an English teacher asked several students to define Putney. In response, they tried to convey the continual re-creation taking place within selves and school.

> *Putney is*
> a place for living without pause or peace
> a place where things begin at the bottom of reality and grow from there
> a place so separate that it is right in the middle of things
> a place where people are taught so that they can grow by themselves.[38]

Living inside bodies that changed almost daily and with minds to match, warmed by Putney adults' friendly respect, few if any students noticed that their teachers were struggling against static forms of faculty governance. The old habits had been adequate in the early days, but if Putney School were continually to foster health and growth in its adult members as it did in its young, one woman's utopia would have to become many people's institution, capable of broadly considered change.

Part III
A Hinge
1948–1949

"It was almost war, and no holds barred." It "shattered Putney's golden age."[1] Thus have one teacher and one student assessed the year of the teachers' strike, 1948–49, when most of Putney's faculty determined radically to change the distribution of power within the school community. Supported by several long-term teachers, the founder mounted a resistance so stubborn that, together, the antagonists nearly broke the Putney School. Certainly they changed lives, some of them drastically. Neither Putney's adults nor Putney's young were ever quite the same afterwards. Ultimately, however, the school emerged from this turning point stronger than before.[2] While the most ragged wounds took years to close, new forms of governance born on the battlefield proved equal to the challenges the future would pose: to survive Carmelita Hinton's retirement and build an enduring, self-renewing institution.

Chapter 8

Strike

There is a type of nineteenth-century farmhouse, quite common still in Vermont, which combines a wood frame and clapboard siding with a solid brick lining. The brick is laid between the studs of the frame and covered on the inside with lath and plaster. Older Vermonters say such a house is "honor built": the wood frame gives strength, and the siding protects the whole, while the hidden brick walls hold heat in winter and coolness in summer. From the beginning, Putney's three-layered system of school governance was much like this. This was no question who had framed the school, "no question who was the boss."[1] But as in an honor-built house, the clapboard siding and the brick core were also essential. If Mrs. H. ruled like "a benevolent despot," community decisionmaking was genuine.[2] Discussion in faculty-staff meetings was often freewheeling; where teaching was at issue, it could be decisive. As has been seen, students had both the illusion of responsibility and responsibility itself. Putney School attempted so much that responsibility had to be spread about if this complex organism was to survive at all.[3]

Perhaps the storm-window or shutter system of the honor-built house was Putney's legal facade. Beginning in 1937, all formal power lay in the small board of directors minimally requisite to any nonprofit corporation in Vermont. Mrs. H. chose its members—usually her closest friends—and held 90 of its 100 shares of stock. While the stock was financially worthless, the votes it conferred could be crucial. As John Holden points out, Mrs. H. "wanted things to be completely democratic"; at the same time, "she also wanted them to go the way she wanted them to."[4]

Since her school's beginnings she had felt she should share authority. A succession of assistant heads seemed always about to fulfill her original promise of a male codirector, but this one was too weak, the other too amiable to be an equal partner. The final assistant head, Warren Leonard, was too strong, though he and Mrs. H. would work in tandem for ten years. "He had courage to face the conflicts Mrs. H. tended to evade," says Ed Gray. "When he had to, he'd disagree with her, and in the end she could never forgive him for that."[5] The corporation board was enlarged in 1940 to include several teachers, but the rules of the game remained much the same. Mrs. H. held the high cards.

Near the end of the war, a small group of parents approached Mrs. H. with their concern that the school had become too dependent on her. What if she should suddenly die? Anyone inheriting her stock "could do anything he liked with the school." They pleaded with her to appoint a parents' council that could help raise money and a board of trustees or at least a board of directors' Executive Committee made up of four or five faculty stockholders.[6] At last she did appoint an Executive Committee to advise her on administrative decisions, finding it easy to choose the new stockholders once John Holden and Warren Leonard had returned from the war, fresh and confident from their years as naval officers.

From 1946 to 1948, then, Putney's legal Executive Committee consisted of Anne Holden, Norwood Hinkle, Warren Leonard, and John Holden, joining two of the original corporation, Mrs. H. and Jane Arms. The Executive Committee seemed to fulfill Mrs. H.'s ideal of a faculty-run school, an image inextricably connected in her mind with academic freedom. It was this ideal she invoked against those friendly parents and lawyers who urged her to consider an independent group of trustees much more broadly based than the corporation board.[7] The new directors took their advisory role seriously. While the original board rarely did more than join itself for tea once a year to ratify decisions already made, such as Jack Caldwell's recommendation on tuition and Mrs. H.'s salary decisions, the Executive Committee met weekly and, wrote Jane Arms, "tackled things with gusto, settling fates." Its members investigated other schools' pension plans and governance systems with an eye to the reorganization of Putney School. Throughout 1947–48, they considered at length how a board of trustees might work; a board to which Mrs. H. would turn over all corporate stock, keeping in return a veto over all trustee decisions.[8]

Ironically, this new exercise of teacher power only increased other teachers' feelings of being left out of the old-timers' deliberations.[9] And much was not discussed at all. Mrs. H. still owned more than half the corporation's stock and two-thirds of "the school's" land, including the entire Lower Farm; the corporation directors ruled only on the improvements made to all this private real estate in return for Mrs. H.'s grant of continued school use. Basic policies concerning hiring, housing, and salaries were set by the principal.

In theory, a united teaching staff could have assumed far more power than it did; after all, the faculty had traditionally had a loud voice in academic, admissions, and disciplinary decisions. However, Mrs. H. had found the individuality she always looked for in her teachers, and true consensus was rare. ("She had the extraordinary ability to pick wonderful people with whom she couldn't agree," says Dan Morris.) While the group could pull together warmly on single projects or in response to some loss such as a barn's burning down or a beloved colleague's being taken by cancer, divisions abounded. Mrs. H. tended to increase them. "She was astonishingly competent with students," but naive and rather "less adept with adults," say Dan Morris, Jane Arms, and John Holden as with one voice. "Good friend, constant adversary," adds Morris, who found that the excitement of the Putney experiment more than compensated for the "general unease [he saw] within the faculty" during the latter half of his nine-year stay.

No one expected the woman who hired and fired to be everybody's pal, but the distance Mrs. H. kept was uneven. She often gathered favorites around her and abruptly stopped consulting others whose knowledge and energy were crucial to the school.[10] Her personal and professional attachment to Jane Arms, who by 1944 had become her administrative assistant and successor to Edward Yoemans as official educational advisor, was so divisive that it set Jane herself to worrying about it.[11] Jane was still an exciting colleague to some, or "too far out to be taken seriously" by others, but a few found her influence on their founding principal downright ominous. Given that she went off to be briefly married in the late thirties, again left active teaching in the middle of the war, and was, when she returned in 1945, limited by ill health to being no more than a shadowy presence— given that she and Mrs. H. had a falling-out soon after ("Even gold rusts," Jane wrote a friend at about this time)—it is surprising to find Mrs. H. still bearing in 1948 the legacy of mistrust that Jane Arms's exclusive friendship had provoked years before.[12]

In 1948, additional and more rational grounds for resentment had accumulated among a committed group of teachers hired three to five years earlier to fill the places of ten key faculty who had left in the course of the war. Three of them, Geoffrey Bret Harte, James Angell, and Florence Angell, were older than most recruits and ready to settle in to complete their teaching careers at Putney. Jim Angell, the gentle, highly experienced educator who had assumed overall supervision of the academic program from Warren Leonard in 1942, had particular reason for pride in the part he had played bringing Putney through the difficult war years. Jim and Flo were also tied to the school by the students' deep affection for them. Mrs. H. herself found them "an unusually fine couple" and admired Jim's "rare sense of humor." To a colleague, Jim was one of "the steady pillars of the school."[13] Yet, when the soldiers returned, Warren climbed into the assistant head position as though he had never left, Jim remaining college advisor. The erudite Geoffrey Bret Harte, who lacked a college degree, was originally happy with his job teaching the youngest students (and with the salary, handsome for Putney, that went with it). But by war's end he felt his success as a ninth- and tenth-grade history teacher had earned him the right to teach senior students, and he was much frustrated by Mrs. H.'s resistance, against which there was no appeal. He began to wonder whether some kind of collective protest might help all faculty.[14] Other wartime teachers felt "displaced from important titles and committee posts by the returning veterans," according to Jane Arms. Arms later wrote that she and Warren, when they reappeared at Putney, seemed outsiders to such capable and well-entrenched teachers.[15]

"People in the community have changed since the War and I go right on the way I was," said Mrs. H. to Jane Arms as the 1948–49 school year opened.[16] It is true that Mrs. H. readily became everyone's alibi when delegated authority failed. But people probably changed less than they simply got fed up with their principal's going right on the way she was—her seeming unwillingness to work with them toward lasting solutions of such perpetual community problems as faculty housing, inequities in salaries, and hiring and staffing procedures that failed to include those most concerned. Nor did the board of directors appear to address these issues effectively. Of the 1948 executive committee, for example, only Warren Leonard lived in a dormitory, and his apartment in the new dorm was one of the few that was really adequate for a family. The others, including Mrs. H., had built or occupied houses of their own, while most of the newer teachers, married and single, continued to move from one cramped living space to the next. As for salaries and staffing, Mrs. H. had, like most principals of other struggling schools, simply made one special deal after another. How else could she fit special people to a special school? She could have consulted long-term teachers in the department concerned. As it was, she spoke only with department heads, whom she herself had chosen, and always retained the last word.

Special deals that had seemed fine at first sometimes looked like exploitation as time went on. In particular, women—divorced or widowed women with adolescent children to educate, retired teachers with no place to go— might beg Mrs. H. to let them come and, say, tend a small dorm and teach an evening activity in return for children's tuition, or "love and room and board" and $100 a year.[17] Then, if the fit was good and the special person generous and interested, her duties expanded with no change in the contractual arrangement. Or, for the apprentice teacher, duties had been geared to a sixteen-hour day to begin with, and $75 a month (or $150 or $175 for the more experienced) was no longer enough. Meantime, a handful of special deals went the other way to insure that the school kept highly skilled individuals who might otherwise move on.[18]

For those with power in the school as well as commitment, material rewards could be sacrificed. Living in "a permanent state of emergency," as Ed Gray calls it, suited other heroes, especially younger teachers who gave all they had to Putney for just two or three years, then left to grow old in other schools. It was the principle on which Carmelita Chase's college president, M. Carey Thomas, had largely built Bryn Mawr's high reputation for scholarship and teaching, though Bryn Mawr's emergencies were fewer, its average teacher tenure longer than Putney School's. And the principle worked wonderfully for Putney's students. There were, however, two problems with this pattern of rapid turnover as it applied to Putney's faculty. One was the inordinate power that it gave to the person who had done most to create it: Carmelita Hinton.[19] This power—to hire and hire again, to deal, to rearrange—was probably not one that Mrs. H. consciously sought, but it was there. Mrs. H. "liked to have fresh people," says Nancy West. She often felt too busy helping her new teachers to take time to consult her veterans; the short notes of encouragement and appreciation she wrote to these youngsters are moving testimony to her generosity toward them.[20]

There is another problem with a high-turnover school and its peculiar patterns of authority: What if newer teachers don't want to turn over? What if they come to a school that seems no longer a dashing experiment but an admirable institution with a long future in which they hope to share? This was the situation in 1948. It was to bring to a crisis the problems in school governance and personnel practices that had been brewing for a decade. For an honor-built farmhouse has one drawback. If it catches fire, as frame houses too often do, the brick lining wall becomes an oven, drawing and holding ferocious heat. The conflagration is over in minutes, often before the fire trucks have arrived.

No single person can be labeled incendiary. Mrs. H. and John Holden have alleged, however, that one man began as early as May 1948 to collect dry tinder. He was a history teacher named Edwin Smith, hired after giving a stirring Sunday night talk on the strength of his rich experience with the world;[21] a CIO labor organizer with a Harvard education, fresh from the oil fields. Earlier in his career, Smith had been Commissioner of Labor and Industries for Massachusetts, where he had played a crucial role in getting a minimum-wage law passed and child-labor laws enforced. In 1933 he was appointed—supposedly as a model of impartiality—by FDR to the National Labor Relations Board. Soon the Wagner Act gave broad powers to the nation's first National Labor Relations Board, and Smith became one of its three members. After the war, he had served as economic liaison between American unions and the Polish ministry of trade and as director of the National Council of American-Soviet Friendship. Surely such a man could become a teacher of history, thought Mrs. H. She felt concerned for Smith personally because he was being hounded by the FBI and by Communist hunters in the press. She was particularly encouraged by her daughter Jean's friendship with Smith, Jean having herself become president of a Federated Workers local union.[22]

After Ed Smith's first eight months as a secondary school teacher, Mrs. H. called him in for a conference and (gently, she said later) passed on her worries about his teaching. She had heard plenty from students. "He was an unbelievably poor teacher," recalls one alumnus. "We tried to keep our history classes going on our own—we taught each other," drawing on the wide range of readings Smith assigned. "He never did anything but lecture or read aloud, and that badly," says another.[23] Mrs. H. wished to follow her usual practice and give Smith one more year to improve his teaching. She assigned Una Buxenbaum, an experienced and highly effective history teacher, to help him. If he could not make substantial progress by midyear, he would have to leave the following June.[24]

Smith must have realized that he was not much of a high school teacher and never would be, that his number would be up by the end of 1948–49. But he also knew he was a good labor organizer. Organized teacher power might help him save his job. It could also help the school fulfill its founder's democratic ideals, ideals which (he has written) he deeply respected.[25]

Soon after his May 1948 conference with Mrs. H., Ed Smith and his wife Marion seem to have begun asking questions of teachers all through the school. Marion was personable, kind, and fond of Mrs. Hinton; she was also admissions secretary. Thus she was the one to give John Holden, then admissions director, "the treatment." John remembers her opening. Sure, she said to him, he "was a stockholder on the Executive Committee," but "didn't he know that the pay scale was unfair? Weren't he and Anne feeling the pinch?" (They were, of course, especially with postwar inflation.)

Wouldn't Putney be great if Mrs. H. gave over much of her power to the faculty? John refused the bait, never having caught on to why it was thrown in the first place, and "was labeled *Administration* from then on."[26]

Others bit. Marion's access to school files gave both Smiths the talking points they needed. And after all, many of their questions were good ones. They had impelled a few veteran teachers, including the "brilliant" Mara Moser, to foresee a crisis and leave Putney before it broke. The questions had been whispered for years within the circles of discontent quite outside the Smiths' orbit, and most recently, talked over at the convivial wine-and-conservation evenings held by the Bret Hartes at their house off-campus. The Smiths occupied the apartment in the Bret Harte house, and Geoffrey Bret Harte, gentlemanly, urbane, hospitable to all, soon became their closest ally.[27]

"As I remember, the trouble began with Sunday breakfast," says Ray Rice, Putney's principal art teacher in 1948. It had become a tradition for teachers to allow themselves one break from the institutional meal routine each week by picking up the makings of Sunday breakfast from the kitchen and taking the food back to their dorm rooms or apartments to eat any time they pleased. Early in the fall, Mrs. H. decided this was too complicated for the kitchen staff. The Smiths dropped by the kitchen one Sunday and were the first to be refused their box of food—though, unaccountably, other teachers received it as usual. "Unfair hiring practices!" said Ed Smith to Ray Rice, only half in jest. Ray was ready to wonder if Smith had not hit the mark. Ray had had his share of employer-employee wrangles during the summer, when Mrs. H. had asked him to teach an extra art course for 1948–49 with no change in salary. It had taken several exchanges of letters for him to convince her that he could not accept this. As faculty friends sat around and discussed the Smiths' Sunday breakfast, they counted up many similar small inequities as well as the larger ones that the Smiths had previously uncovered. The idea of a faculty association was born.[28]

The Smiths' role should not be exaggerated, however, for many of the dissidents had little connection with them at first. The most eager younger critic of the status quo was Gabriel Jackson, an extraordinary English-Spanish-flute teacher who had served in the war and then come straight from Harvard College to Putney School at the age of twenty-five. Students responded warmly to his intellectual passions. Under his hand (and immersed in the world of *Moby Dick*, *War and Peace*, or Mann's *The Magic Mountain*), some saw literature as philosophy for the first time. Jackson "valued reverie" and helped his students do the same.[29] Because he loved teaching at

Putney, he wanted to improve the school. In addition, he was engaged to be married to another Putney teacher and was making ready to settle down at Putney for a while. To Jackson, as to other young teachers, deepening his commitment to secondary school work meant understanding more clearly where he stood in relation to the school. This need was even greater at Putney School than for teachers elsewhere, devoted as Putney was to that taxing egalitarianism which so enriched teacher-student friendships—and which often complicated those with administrators or parents.[30] Bruce Menefee, already mentioned as *Putney Press* advisor, shared Jackson's hopes. So did Ray Rice, the drama teacher, Vivian Johannes, and many, young and old, who were ready to respond to the concerns that the Smiths and others had voiced. Excited and hopeful, twenty-six Putney adults secretly began work on their plans to create a new balance of power within the school.

Gabe Jackson remembers that "the political atmosphere of the time [also] played a big role." While Putney's teacher-citizens held views all over the political spectrum, a small, active subgroup had drawn particularly close to each other through 1947 and 1948 in their work for Henry Wallace's Progressive Party campaign. This was no surprise at the Putney School, where Mrs. H. herself was, says Jackson, "pro Wallace, pro Mao, and a left progressive on every domestic U.S. issue." So were most of the people who wanted change within the school.

> To us, with considerable doses of both truth and naiveté, it seemed a flagrant contradiction that [Mrs. H.] could hold such political positions and yet run her school as a completely arbitrary "boss," benevolent to be sure, but still completely unlimited in her authority over salaries, working hours, residence assignments, et al.[31]

Ed Smith had become chairman of the Vermont State Wallace for President campaign about the time of his spring talk with Mrs. H. Bruce Menefee and one other teacher, both socialists at this time, had worked closely with him, many activist faculty and students rallying to their side. The bitter disappointment the pro-Wallace teachers felt as the hopelessness of the campaign became clear may well have intensified the emotion with which they discussed school issues.[32]

On November 9, 1948, a week after Harry Truman's triumph and Henry Wallace's ignominious failure to win a single electoral vote, Mrs. H. received a delegation of six teachers in her office. They presented her with a mimeographed letter and waited while she read it.

> Dear Mrs. Hinton:
>   We know that you as an educator realize that there always exist among any group of teachers certain problems which can best be solved by an orderly presenta-

tion of them to the administration after the collective judgment of the group has been reached. The teachers believe that these problems include such matters as the exercise of their professional responsibility in serving the best interests of the school, salary scale, tenure, etc.

Therefore, the teachers and other members of the academic staff have formed a Putney Faculty Association. The Association will present to you, from time to time, proposals from the academic staff relating to the above-mentioned problems.

We are confident that by enabling teachers to deal with these matters which hitherto hampered their efforts in behalf of the best interests of the Putney School, this Association will contribute actively to the morale and the spirit of this community.

Respectfully submitted,
The Putney Faculty Association

Upon finishing it, Mrs. H. burst into tears. There was a brief, awkward conversation before the delegation quietly left.[33]

It soon became clear that three-quarters of Putney's classroom teachers and five of its staff had become charter members of the Faculty Association. The group's agenda was full of matters pertaining to "professional responsibility," which its members felt had been neglected in faculty meeting. They suggested a system of elected department heads who would serve fixed terms and, they hoped, would intelligently correlate courses within each department. They asked a voice for these chairmen in the hiring of teachers. They outlined a plan for orienting new teachers to the school.

With Association membership came a fateful requirement, almost certainly suggested by Ed Smith, but endorsed by many others who felt that the customary informality of in-school communications had failed to solve serious in-school problems. No one was to speak privately to any nonmember about any topic related to the Association's issues. All were to be represented instead by selected Association spokesmen: Chairman Gabe Jackson, Jim Angell, Vivian Johannes, Ray Rice, and, later, Bruce Menefee and Geoffrey Bret Harte. Thus were the usual knockabout exchanges by which the Putney community zigzagged toward its myriad goals—conversations over the KDU lunch table or faculty room coffee table—expressly forbidden.[34]

Throughout this opening week, Ed Smith remained in the background. The silence grated on everyone. A few phone calls to other school heads brought Mrs. H. no comfort: not a single Eastern private school had ever hatched a faculty association so determined as this one. She quickly grew anxious.

Just after the announcement of the Association's existence, John Holden had left for a week on an admissions office trip. When he returned, all of Putney's adults had chosen sides, and Mrs. H.'s initial surprise had become something like panic. She and Warren Leonard had brought to the November 11 faculty meeting their own formal statements to the Faculty Association, Warren first assuring them that "Mrs. Hinton does honestly feel faculty members should have a real voice in the affairs of the school," Mrs. H. putting her reaction to "the explosion of our troubles" personally.

> I am ashamed that I have been blind to some of your needs, and that in carrying the heavy and time-consuming load of daily details, I did not sense that my actions were lagging behind my real intentions, that I was not using your potentialities to the full, knowing that you must for your own best development carry heavier responsibilities for yourselves.[35]

Before November 9, Mrs. H. had felt quite confident that all the recent gropings toward better school government were bringing a "democratic and more or less flexible" system, even if not "utopia;" a system that could be gradually improved upon by all concerned.[36] Now both Mrs. H. and Warren feared that the Faculty Association could only be a devisive force in the effort to realize a mutual goal: the betterment of the school. The exclusion from the Association of all five teaching members of the Executive Committee was already fracturing useful alliances. Of course, Mrs. H. stated, there will be times when teachers can rightly meet independently, but not in an adversary relationship to administrators, "not on a union basis. In a hard world run for profit and power with very questionable politics dominating it, [unions are] necessary. There I'd be in the vanguard, but such organization is not necessary here . . . in our small community." She went on to propose that an ad hoc committee be elected by all teaching faculty to suggest changes in governance acceptable to all parties. "In our struggles upward, we stumble around, but in our stumbling we do the growing," she wrote. "I hope I can accept criticism bravely, whatever it is."[37]

In the next few days, the Association members met to consider Mrs. H.'s proposal. On November 16, the "Administration" met with their spokesmen, and the principal reiterated her idea of an ad hoc governance committee. She emphasized that, while no Executive Committee members could serve on it, they would be voters with all others. "The base of any committee was to be *the faculty*." Warren Leonard suggested that the election be held at the November 18 faculty meeting.

The election never took place. Thursday morning, Bruce Menefee reported to her that the overwhelming majority of the full faculty thought Mrs. H.'s ad hoc committee too weak and unrepresentative. Within the next four hours, Mrs. H. became convinced that she must take a much tougher line. When all had gathered at her house that afternoon expecting further progress, she opened the faculty meeting by reading the following ultimatum:

To the Faculty:

When teachers or other staff members originally came to the school, it was assumed by the Director that such adults would work harmoniously within a certain
framework.

If any teacher or other staff member feels that he cannot work effectively in such a
framework, this framework, at the moment, including my proposal as given in the
Sunday letter and clarified as I described Tuesday morning, and at the same time
perform his teaching and other duties conscientiously while maintaining his own
professional standards and personal integrity, his resignation will be accepted.

Those who wish to resign please leave a note on my desk in my school office by
6:30 tonight, resignations to take effect immediately or at Christmas vacation.
Anyone who has not left a note on my desk by 6:30 will be assumed not to wish to
resign. Negotiations are over. The meeting is adjourned.

As she made her way out, she spoke to two Association leaders, telling them
that she forbade the Association from meeting again.

What had happened to propel Mrs. H. toward such a rigid stance? Cool
carbons of memos back and forth surely conceal a tangle of fears and hurt
feelings. Ever since 1935, Mrs. H.'s nightmare had been that somehow,
sometime, her school would be taken away from her. Or perhaps her message was simply an extreme example of what one alumnus calls "her stub-
bornness or willfulness in the face of hard facts." The facts were the teachers'
grievances, which were many. That their strategies were abrupt did not
cancel the grievances. The intensity of Mrs. H.'s emotions on November 17
and 18 is perhaps made clearest by John Holden's penciled note at the
bottom of the ultimatum: "alternative was CH's resignation."

"I always get where I want to go, Geoffrey!" Mrs. H. had once exclaimed
as she blew in with the snow through the Bret Hartes' door, speaking in
response to the worries her host had expressed over her having walked
through a blizzard to reach the party. "I believe it, Carmelita! I believe it,"
Bret Harte had returned. But this time, she didn't. Furthermore, for some
teachers, her ultimatum focused diffuse fears that, in the end, Mrs. H. could
not be trusted. John Holden calls it "the one mistake."[38] It was certainly her
most serious one.

Now it was the Association members' turn to be in shock. Bruce Menefee
and one other teacher had submitted their resignations within the three
hours given. Fourteen others wrote letters of protest, simultaneously expressing their anger over this "violation of civil rights" and their devotion to the
school's ideals.[39] Over the weekend, Mrs. H. reread the letters. She held
tearful talks with her closest allies, most of whom backed the hard line she
had taken, struggled with herself, and made a valiant decision.

"Pardon for calling you together at 9:30 P.M.," she told the assembled faculty the next Tuesday evening, November 23. "I could not bear to enter Thanksgiving with the faculty in such a tragic situation." Whereupon, she formally rescinded her ultimatum, rejected the two resignations, and promised to "bring no pressure to bear on anyone" before an election by secret ballot of the ad hoc committee could take place. "This is the way I see the situation," she explained.

> You, who were trying to form an organization, were harsh in your methods. Then, at the last faculty meeting, I was harsh. That kind of action towards each other will never get us anywhere. My action was meant to be a thunder clap to clear the air and show my insistence on keeping the faculty together as a whole—undivided. It was not until I read *this* in one letter to me—"I am not offering you my resignation because I can scarcely afford it"—that I saw my blind spot. I had put you into an economic trap. I don't know whether you will believe it or not, but that idea had not entered my mind. I am therefore withdrawing my statement on resignations.[40]

But it was too late. While the faculty meeting went through the motions of endorsing the idea of a separate Faculty Association by a vote of 26 to 15 after Thanksgiving was past, the community gradually drew further apart. Every gesture of reconciliation seemed to fail. The Holdens went to one Association meeting but felt that their loyalty to Mrs. H. made them unwelcome. Cornelia Hinkle was invited to another meeting at the home of her old friends, the Bret Hartes, but little was said. (Someone later remarked, says Cornelia, that there had been "a spy in our midst.") The Association's "vow of silence" now became the custom, if not the law, for *all* informal conversation between members and nonmembers. Bruce Menefee's piano lessons with Cornelia, which he had loved, came to an end. Other faculty fell silent if the Hinkles sat down with them in the KDU. As late as April, when Cornelia's father died, only Flo Angell of all her Association friends would break the silence to express her sympathy.

It was something of a miracle that the school made it through a project week that seemed to students as rich a climax to fall term as any other. The senior who played Petruchio in *The Taming of the Shrew* remembers very clearly Gabe Jackson's devotion to his responsibilities at the time. "Gabe decided that the Petruchio role had gone to my head. He took me aside and gave me unshirted hell for about 20 minutes for the argumentative tone of voice I'd adopted in speaking with Mrs. H. I had no business speaking to her that way, he told me."

Nevertheless, over Christmas vacation, Gabe resigned, along with his fiancée and one other teacher. "I simply couldn't continue the emotional discord," he now recalls. Gabe's respect for Mrs. H. had been his major

reason for accepting leadership of the Faculty Association. While he valued
the concept of a truly representative faculty committee such as the one she
had first proposed, December's futile negotiations convinced him that "Mrs.
H. would not accept *any* representative committee that would . . . limit her
options by their advice."[41] In his mind, and in those of most other Association members, the group was "founded with the most genuine and bona fide
intentions to help the school." So he stated in the letter he wrote to Putney's
seniors through the student chairman of the Community Council, convinced by mid-January that he should "spike the rumors" students were now
hearing. "No personal question of salary, duties or authority was involved,"
he assured the seniors.

> You must think that I broke with Putney easily. It is an agonizing thing to learn that
> a person whose ideals and whose accomplished work you intensely admire is also a
> person who rationalizes the most arbitrary power, at some times recognizing that
> power to herself, at others, masking it as a better than democratic ideal. . . .
>
> The way in which we were consistently misinterpreted by Mrs. H. and our acts
> misrepresented to her by persons around her forced me to a most deep disillusion-
> ment.[42]

Jackson's final reason for leaving was that he had indeed married over vac-
tion, as he and his fiancée had planned. "I could not afford a real honey-
moon," he says now, "but decided at least not to spend the first months of
my marriage in a bitter labor conflict."[43]

And bitter it was. Over the holidays, Mrs. H. had continued a series of
individual contract conferences with Association teachers, which she had
begun in early December. She had hoped to mend fences; instead she laid
herself open to the charge that she was trying to split her opposition. She
suggested to Ed Smith that he begin seeking another job for the following
year; he in turn accused her—seriously this time—of unfair labor practices,
assuming her main complaint to be his role "in the development of the
Faculty Association."[44]

Mrs. H. had also written a letter to all parents, having consulted no one
but her closest allies. It was probably necessary to assure parents that the
three teachers who had resigned had been replaced by experienced people
who knew Putney well. It didn't hurt (though it obscured issues of power) to
remind them how democratically the Community Council went about its
constitutional business, how appropriate a forum the full faculty meeting
could be for addressing faculty issues. However, Mrs. H.'s explanation of the
midyear resignations was, naturally enough, a justification of her stand. She

denigrated the Association by which "some members" of the faculty had chosen to press their interests, "one of the strongest underlying principles of Putney being, wherever possible, to avoid formal divisions." Maximizing the impact of her fourteen allies, Mrs. H. added that "quite a number of the faculty, particularly those who had been in the school longest, saw the question in this light also, some even more strongly than I."[45]

A few Association teachers were furious to learn of the principal's initiative with the parents when they returned to school. Their anger only increased when one of their number was—they were convinced—forced out unfairly by Mrs. H. after a ninth-grade boy stated that the teacher had made homosexual advances.[46] Cooler heads put together a set of "suggestions, . . . the carrying out of which might demonstrate to the members of the Association that Mrs. Hinton is acting in good faith."[47] The first two were mild enough. One asked equal school Assembly time for spokesmen from both sides, who would tell the students "that the Administration and the Association are working together in the interest of the school"; the other proposed a similar approach to the new teachers, who would have to decide whether or not to join the Association. The third "suggestion," however, asked what the administration had steadily refused for two months: "that Mrs. Hinton recognize the right of the Putney Faculty Association to determine eligibility to its membership."

The final "suggestion" reflected teacher fears of another administration move as precipitous as the November ultimatum:

> We ask that any proposed dismissal of a present member of the Putney Faculty Association be subject to a review and final determination by a majority vote of a group composed of the Director of the School and four duly elected members of the Putney Faculty Association, and that this committee be in operation for the rest of this school year. Written letters of rehiring should be tendered to members of the Association before leaving for Spring Vacation.

To Putney's founder, the proposals looked more like labor union demands than Faculty Association "suggestions." The last one "put fear in her," says her daughter Jean. It required a show of good faith on a request that could not be granted without completely changing the character of the school. "How can teachers hire and fire each other?" asked Mrs. H.[48]

Nonetheless, on February 4, Mrs. H. wrote a memo conceding much. Beginning with the caveat that "this reply to your suggestions cannot be a means of proving my good faith," stating instead her feeling that "your belief in my integrity can only come as a result of the work we do together" on common school tasks, she formally granted recognition to the Association.

She invited its delegates to discuss how students should be kept informed. She added that she would concede "the right of the Association to determine eligibility to its membership," pointing out only that nonteaching staff (Marion Smith and two others) could not logically be a part of "a *Faculty* Association."

The Association's "suggestion" on the rehiring of teachers she flatly refused. She could only promise that "before spring vacation, *all* faculty members will be notified about returning next year."[49]

No Association delegates ever came to talk over the announcements to students, though Jim Angell tried nightly to arrange such a meeting. Instead, routine encounters between Association members and nonmembers became infected with suspicion. Apparently the dissident teachers' fears for their jobs had begun to obscure all other considerations.[50] Their next memo was brief: they set a six-day deadline for an agreement on the problem of tenure. They asked Mrs. H. to meet with the group's job security committee that very afternoon to begin talks.

Lacking agreement about how students should be informed, Mrs. H. simply decided she must discuss Gabe Jackson's resignation with a group of anxious seniors in Senior Discussion. When Jim Angell objected privately but vehemently, she invited him to the other two Senior Discussion groups and repeated her remarks. He later told her (John Holden has written) that her presentation was "unprejudiced and fair."[51] Phyllis Watt, West Hill–born and loyal to Mrs. H., remembers this midwinter revelation as a portent of a new adult perception: There was such a thing as evil in her world.[52]

After this all issues were on the table, and events moved fast. When the six-day deadline had arrived on February 11 with no job security agreement to show for several delegates' meetings held, Mrs. H. sat down and penned her final communication to the Association. In it she asserted once more her responsibility for "deciding who shall and who shall not teach at the school," but she held even this generally approved school practice up for revision by any new, mutually acceptable school governing body that might emerge from the discussions the board of directors had begun the year before. She proposed that these discussions be broadened to include "the best thinking of all of us"; she looked forward to the reorganization's being completed by the fall. She put in writing her verbal promise "that membership in the Association will not be considered by me as cause for the dismissal of any person or for non-renewal of contract." Finally, she warned everyone of "our first obligation: . . . to the students in this school." Learning could only take place in an atmosphere of mutual trust. It was clear to her that faculty disagreements must be kept out of classrooms, work crews, and any student-faculty discussion anywhere. [53]

The Association reaction showed how narrow and how sharp the basic dispute had become.

February 14, 1949

Dear Mrs. Hinton:

The Putney Faculty Association has voted unanimously that your letter of February 11 is almost entirely unsatisfactory in that it gives no real assurance of job security to members of the Putney Faculty Association for the coming year because it fails to approve the principle of review of any alleged unjust dismissal.

I suggest that you contact Geoffrey Bret Harte if you wish to see the [job security] committee.

Sincerely yours,
Bruce Menefee, Secretary
Putney Faculty Association

Mrs. H.'s concessions and promises on all the broader issues of faculty governance had been swept aside, [54] much as she had reduced the conflict to a procedural issue in her November ultimatum.

The same day the Association members took their turn at a letter to all parents, explaining their position. The letter concluded that only concessions by Mrs. H. on the vital job security review process could prevent "any future development that may interfere with the continuity of life at the school during the balance of the year." This was coming close to threatening a teachers' strike.

Two days later, words fit realities more precisely. On February 16, the Association voted to become the Putney Teachers Union, CIO Public Workers Local #808. Announcing their decision, Geoffrey Bret Harte, classics scholar, aesthete, bond-coupon clipper, and now union president, expressed the Association teachers' hope that Mrs. Hinton, "who had persistently refused to deal on any meaningful level with an organization of individuals in the school, might be finally disposed, because of her liberal declarations, to deal in good faith with a CIO union."[55] While the CIO connection was originally Ed Smith's idea, the other teachers adopted it willingly. It is almost certain that their decision was influenced by Smith's contacts with CIO colleagues, who must have kept him in touch with developments outside Putney School: the continuing shortage of teachers, which put school union organizers in a strong position, and the success of CIO organizational efforts in public schools. The CIO had garnered 180 new charters since 1946—over half of all new teachers' unions in the nation. [56]

"Now it was U.S. Steel vs. Putney School," writes John Holden. This was the moment, say Mrs. H. and Warren, when they concluded that Bret Harte was "the false front"; that Edwin Smith, the "incredibly smooth" CIO organizer, must have been prime mover for the whole dissident group.[57] Mrs. H. embraced the explanation with a fervor that suggests her desperate desire to find simple causes for the school's complex problems.[58] She began to suspect Smith of determining that "Putney School would be the first Communist boarding school in the United States." Although colleagues say it is absolutely untrue, Mrs. H. felt sure that another key union member was also a communist sympathizer. This assumption had never worried her before: After all, she herself certainly sympathized with the Chinese communist revolution, and this valuable teacher had assiduously avoided partisanship in all teaching. But now it began to needle her. While she was ruminating, one anti-union teacher declared that "fighting Communism" was part of his cause. At least one union member told two of his friends that he had had to accept Ed Smith's communist associations as the price of solidarity. Mrs. H. confronted Smith with the question of his Party membership, and (she later insisted) "He never denied it."[59]

To some union members, even the cursory expression of such suspicions seemed shameful in a school that had stoutly resisted the red-baiting already pervading the nation. "How could you *take* it?" Ray Rice asked Smith. "I've had my civil rights fights before—it's nothing new to me," replied Smith, in the calm, fair-play manner Ray had always found admirable.[60] The communism issue, combined with the announcement of the union's formation under a CIO leftist, swung the entire remaining staff behind the non-union group. On February 18, thirty-three nonacademic staff signed a letter rejecting any union, and giving Mrs. H. welcome support from many of the community's longest-tenured members.

To her credit, Mrs. H. made no attempt to pursue her concerns about Smith's politics or to use them against him. True, to draw attention to them might have inflamed outsiders' habitual suspicions of "that school in Vermont." However, say her friends, uppermost in her refusal to capitalize on the "Communists at Putney" issue was her long custom of ignoring a teacher's politics, whether right or left, in favor of her own judgments of the person's merit as a teacher. As a result, the communism bogey soon died down except in the minds of a few panicked parents and many distant critics.[61]

The older students were discussing the issue among themselves and beginning to defend their school against these few parents' questions about communist infiltration. They did it, say two of them, in a political vacuum, because the union teachers, themselves a group with diverse political opinions, had been so careful not to become classroom advocates on the larger political issues of the day. Though several were deeply interested in socialist experiments and in the Chinese revolution, neither these nor "splendid Russia" were in the academic curriculum. Putney School's internal divisions were beginning to close in, however. Even before the agreement to protect students from the conflict had broken down among some union members, even though classes went on and ski trips took off as usual, it was impossible not to notice the silence that had fallen between groups of Putney adults, impossible to ignore the separate tables in the KDU or the union teachers going around in pairs and refusing to greet Mrs. H. on the paths.[62] Mabel Gray took care of both the Hinkles' baby and the Rices' baby while the two couples were at faculty meetings. Her cooking class soon learned how awkward this was for her.[63] A few students started worrying over their faculty friends. "Something about Ed Smith made me rather sad," says Nora Sayre, "I think he knew he was boring in class." Those close to Vivian Johannes knew how distressed she was by her inability to win a definite renewal of her contract from Mrs. H. Next year, Mrs. H. would call her typical of those whom Ed Smith had "made to feel they weren't the success they should have been." Vivian's efforts to keep her thirty-five student actors humming through those terrible months had exhausted her, she now told her favorite students. Those students who had long admired Bruce Menefee's passion for teaching or shared his socialist faith found his distress and disillusionment wrenching.[64]

It was natural for these few aware youngsters to side with the union at first, since nearly all of their teachers were union members.[65] Thus, it was perplexing indeed for the new young partisans to learn that a major union figure, Jenaro Artilles, had resigned from Local #808 in mid-February. Artilles, with his classics Ph.D. and his long experience in university teaching, had headed a Spanish teachers' union before being expelled by Franco. "This union does not act as an honest union should," he explained to John Holden and Mrs. H. as he stepped across the boundary between the two factions. "Most unions are willing to make reasonable compromises; this union does not ring true."[66] "Once we knew of the conflict," recalls an alumnus, "those of us who were in Ed Smith's classes simply couldn't understand how he could have gotten himself into this embarrassing teaching position for which he was so ill-fitted, or how others could be trying to help him perpetuate it."[67]

Some evidence suggests that Geoffrey Bret Harte, too, might have pulled away from the union at this point had he not been so deeply involved in its creation. "We had no idea what we were getting into," said Kit Bret Harte to Helen Chase, Mrs. H.'s sister-in-law. "We *never* meant it to go this far." When a CIO field advisor arrived on campus, Kit saw their crusade passing out of the hands of committed Putney teachers to outsiders. "We've been taken," she told Anne and John Holden, breaking the gag rule.[68] Mrs. H. didn't learn of these doubts till later, but Artilles' principled stance seemed to shed a single beam of sanity and hope over her life during this stressful February.

"The disintegration of personality was frightening" even to a worldly-wise parent, Felix Pereira, who came with his wife for the Washington's Birthday weekend to visit their two Putney children. Pereira heard people from one side swearing at people from the other. He found himself moving through the gap that had opened between Putney adults and trying in vain to close it. With Helen Lehmann Buttenweiser, another parent and an experienced labor arbitrator, he offered to help the contending parties make one last try at agreement on the job security issue.[69] The two sat down for a seven-hour meeting to reason with both parties, a New York labor lawyer on the administration side of the table and a professional CIO organizer sitting with Bret Harte, Bruce Menefee, a woman teacher, and Ed Smith on the other side. "The CIO man knew *nothing* about education", protests Pereira.[70] He had a lot of negotiating experience, however, and he would do his best to win an agreement acceptable to both sides.

Finally, a contract review committee was born. In cases of conflict over the nonrenewal of a union teacher's contract, two *parents* would be chosen by each side and one by both sides together to submit a finding of the facts to both union and administration. A sizable group of parents who had come to ski or visit over the holiday had made clear their readiness to do almost anything to help steady the pitching wagon that was Putney School. The five-parent review committee seemed to them a big step forward; Mrs. H. and Geoffrey Bret Harte together described it as such in a brief, reassuring letter to all parents. So at first did a planned statement to students, to be signed by Bret Harte and Mrs. H. and intended to close student debate on the issues.

But the union members had new plans. First they insisted on "reserv[ing] the right of freedom of speech" with students; this prevented the posting of the long-promised joint statement for students. They studied the faculty contract at the ultraprogressive Little Red Schoolhouse in New York, where teachers had been given a powerful voice in all hiring and firing.[71] Then, on March 11, they presented their proposals for a union-administration contract. The union contract provided for

Union recognition

A Union shop (all employees must join the Putney Teachers Union, except the Assistant Director, the Admissions Director, the kitchen, business office and outdoor staff); binding arbitration of all grievances.

Tenure for all Union members after two years; dismissed employee may appeal to the Union.

A clear definition of teaching loads. (Leading trips shall be voluntary.)

A salary schedule exactly geared to years of service, including extra pay for dormitory duty, weekend duty, and extra evening activities.

A definition of housing and dining benefits.

A pension plan.

With the contract came a proposal for a faculty advisory council, which was formally submitted to faculty meeting for its approval. The procedures for electing the faculty council were remarkably similar to those suggested by Mrs. H. in November.

Almost immediately the five Executive Committee faculty sat down with Mrs. Hinton in her living room to discuss the proposed contract, joined by Mrs. H.'s brother, Philip Chase, her daughter, Jean, Jack Caldwell, alumnus Donald Watt, Jr., and Mark Lauter, the administration lawyer. Everyone in the room now knew what would happen if agreement was not reached before spring vacation began March 26: the union would strike.

Anne Holden's notes on this meeting reflect a collective distress and anger so acute it is hard to decipher her prose. Hadn't the union just been given what its members most wanted? Jack Caldwell and two others insisted that *no* union contract could ever be acceptable at Putney School. Philip Chase argued that all 24 union members should be fired and the school reopened after vacation with a fresh group of teachers. Norwood said he was "prepared to meet a strike tomorrow" and to "go along until spring vacation" with the nine non-union teachers taking all teaching duties if he knew the twenty-four would not be rehired for the following year. "I don't understand," said Mrs. H. of the union members to Jean afterwards, "It's like a whole pack of wolves chasing a scared rabbit."[72]

A full day of formal but fruitless negotiation followed. Mrs. H.'s hopes rose briefly when the union's next step turned out to be a strangely benign "explanatory" meeting with the administration group the next day, the explanations to be completed the following afternoon. But the union cancelled the second meeting, instead deputizing Geoffrey Bret Harte to demand that Mrs. H. agree that very evening on three general principles: union recognition, the union shop, and tenure. They also asked for a timetable for negotiations at the end of which all unresolved questions would be submitted to arbitration. An interim agreement on these points was essential to any future negotiations, Bret Harte stated.[73]

The administration refused such precipitous action. They denied the moral right of the union to act for all teachers when no formal all-faculty vote had been taken since December. Federal labor law offered little guidance, and mutual trust was gone. Beginning on Monday, March 14, each side hurled challenges at the other for a week, accusing each other of deliberate delay, Mrs. H. pointing out to Bret Harte how inadequately the contract comprehended the complex responsibilities of Putney's classroom and outdoor teachers. Black humor larded union members' conversations. "Putney is a place," went one joke, "where the farm dogs are treated like children and the children are treated like adults, while the adults are treated like dogs." The union president, Bret Harte, made a weekend trip to New York to meet with the CIO representative. Mrs. H. "curtly and severely reprimanded him" for missing his Saturday class without the customary prior notice to her. Non-union secretaries refused to type for union teachers. Meanwhile, Marion Smith typed and mailed a long letter to every parent in which Mr. Bret Harte explained the union position—with no copy this time to Mrs. H. Jack Caldwell did some counting and concluded that the new salary scale would add $65,000 to next year's budget, a 20 percent rise over 1948–49. "Take it out of the frills!" the CIO advisor responded. Caldwell insisted that there were no frills, and the CIO man gave up. Perhaps no one anticipated that there would be a 19 percent surplus in Putney School's accounts by the close of the 1948–49 fiscal year.[74]

Ironically, while the lightning bolts flew, the two sides' professional representatives were at work, finding an unexpected stretch of common ground. This was no surprise to the administration. As John Holden writes, "We knew from the beginning that most of the Union demands were reasonable, and we were ready to agree with them."[75] Mrs. H., who had so long "regarded obstacles as mere scenery," who had believed that any problem could be solved with "courage and work,"[76] had begun to accept due process as a principle essential to cooperation with teaching colleagues. This point won, it appeared that the salary scale, the pension plan, the job definitions, and more democratic forms of faculty governance could eventually follow.[77]

With a week to go before spring vacation began, Mrs. H. made what she considered a positive reaffirmation of her promise to meet with every individual teacher on his or her contract for the following year, asking only that the union teachers notify her by March 25 as to whether or not they wished to return. By Monday, March 21 (she said later), she had managed contract interviews with all but seven union teachers and had made plans for the remaining appointments. She had told one of the union teachers brought in after Christmas ("a known troublemaker," says Pereira) that his contract could not be considered until June; she had reminded Vivian Johannes, whose correspondence with Mrs. H. had suggested to Vivian a longer-term commitment, that her job as theater teacher would end when Bunny White returned from her leave of absence. Ed Smith (Mrs. H. has repeatedly said) had been told some time before that his contract would not be renewed. All the remaining union members would be rehired.[78]

The union would soon disagree with Mrs. H.'s account on nearly every point, insisting that she had resisted all attempts to arrange interviews with the last seven, including Ed Smith. "She was already taking steps that would make it impossible to return," Bret Harte wrote Putney's parents, "and in fact had begun to reduce our numbers by dismissing us."[79]

The following day at 11:15 A.M. twenty-four Putney teachers went out on strike. Most students got the news from the union members teaching their classes. One recalls her astonishment as her French teacher pulled out a piece of paper and read the announcement from it. Tears came to his eyes; he put the paper down and walked out of the room.[80] Geoffrey Bret Harte presented Mrs. H. with the union's reasons for taking this extreme step: first, the administration's "uncompromising hostility" since mid-November; second, its recent attempt to drive union teachers into an "untenable position" by holding individual contract conferences in the middle of union contract negotiations—and simultaneously insisting that they notify her of their intentions to return. He gave Mrs. H. the strikers' four demands, the last three to be satisfied "either before or after Spring vacation":

> (1) that the notification deadline of March 25 be abandoned; (2) that the unjust dismissal of Vivian Johannes be retracted; (3) that because of the recent unethical rehiring procedure on your part, we repudiate all antecedent agreements as to rehiring and demand that letters of rehiring be tendered to all Union members by March 25; and (4) that you agree with us on a time table for future contract negotiations.[81]

Who was to blame? Helen Buttenweiser remembers her sad surprise as the strike opened. She had attended a meeting at the Bret Hartes' house to hear the union's grievances, "But no one talked 'grievances'; they just talked 'strike.' Yet there didn't seem to be any real *reason* for a strike." She found Smith "very far left, very rigid" in all his dealings, "not a labor organizer but a labor *dis*organizer." On the other hand, "Mrs. H. didn't want to talk with anyone who wasn't with her 100%. . . . It was almost as though she didn't *hear* the Union teachers," and this surely contributed to the deadlock.[82] The two sides' seasoned representatives, returning together from New York on the first train they could catch, both expressed astonishment that a strike they thought they had averted should happen at all.[83]

At Putney School each side now openly blamed the other. Since the nine non-union classroom teachers, helped by secretaries and others who pulled their high school French or history out of the trunk, were doing their best to handle all scheduled classes, they had a forum that the union lacked. Though they agreed to make their answers to students' questions short and simple, great was the satisfaction of a few still seething over the long discussions of the conflict that a handful of union members had allowed. At least one of these would later be accused of "devoting whole classes to his (or her) support of the Administration."[84] One of the seniors in Ed Smith's course took over Smith's history class.

The most dramatic incident occurred on Tuesday evening. During dinner, striking teachers entered the KDU lobby for just long enough to put a mimeographed explanation of their position into every student mailbox. In the middle of the meal, a non-union teacher discovered this and quickly mobilized colleagues to pull the memorandam *out* of all boxes. John Holden strode into the dining room and called for silence. The union memo had been broadcast (he announced with heat) in defiance of the principle that students "taking sides will not contribute" to a resolution. As he sat down, the usual buzz of community conversation became a roar of exclamation and dispute. "The students became adults and the adults kids," says one alumnus. "What fun," thought Nora Sayre, who—"as a timid rebel"—had felt "a certain initial glee" when the strike was announced. "I loved the idea of grown-ups rising against grown-ups." At lunch on Wednesday, Bruce Menefee tried again for the union in the KDU, with an announcement of the union's purposes—to the loud hisses of one non-union teacher.[85]

That evening the Bret Hartes held an open house at their home. They invited no one, but word spread among the students.[86] There was wine there, and intense conversation, as well as distribution of the memo that had been suppressed. The memo, a long calendar of events, decried administration refusals to cooperate with the association and adhere to "democratic,"

"ethical" practices "in personal and group relationships." In the middle of
Ed Smith's explanations of how the NLRB might be brought in to supervise a
fair union election, an alumnus named Charlie Humpstone remembers that
"the telephone rang, and union president Bret Harte, in his tweeds and his
grey flannels and his goatee, got up and went to the phone. 'Yes?' . . . he
asked, 'I'm busy right now. . . . What? You say it's gone up? SELL!!'"

It was the last of the light moments, for Charlie, who held school office,
cared strongly about all those most deeply implicated and now, with a few
other seniors, began moving from one adult to another, trying desperately to
mediate between the two sides. Charlie was one of Vivian's favorites, and he
had been trying for weeks to cheer her. Others concentrated on comforting
the Bret Hartes' son John, who was "terribly upset" by the strike. Still others'
thoughts were with Bruce Menefee, who (unlike most strikers) had moved
out of his dorm room and was already missed by his counselees. They told
each other how Bruce had come into dinner following the decisive union
meeting before the strike, "looking absolutely shattered. His voice broke half
a dozen times as he tried to explain to us what was going to happen."[87]

John Holden says simply that "students were in the middle being crushed."[88]
The youngsters' excitement over "the revolution" and all the union songs
and position papers that went with it faded to anxiety as the implications of
"solidarity forever" sank in.[89] The more aware students shared their teachers'
pain. Since "the school had blown wide open" anyway, Mrs. H. felt free to
talk with some special student friends, including Nora Sayre. Nora could see
that the teachers felt treated like children; she would still be on the strikers'
side as she packed to go home for spring vacation. But through the spring she
would do "a lot of listening throughout the faculty, and would gradually
come to feel that the Hinton group was right" in opposing the union—that it
was the Hinton group who cared most about the students and the school.[90]

Two youngsters, as much concerned for their continued education as for
who was right or wrong, got eighty-three signatures on a student petition the
second day of the strike and presented it to Mrs. H.:

> We think it would be impossible for you to hire new teachers during Spring
> vacation who would be able to uphold the fine standards set by the present teaching
> staff.
> This being the case, we hope you will consider the terms of [the Union's] letter
> of March 22 for acceptance, and will come to an agreement that will be to the best
> advantage of everyone concerned.[91]

Several of the petitioners, most of them ardently pro-union, pledged not to
leave school for vacation until agreement was reached.

A large group of younger students was simply stunned by the whole affair. Most of the ninth graders, unable to imagine their new school closing down for good, took the strike as just one more marvel in the series of novel experiences Putney School had dealt them through the year.[92] Judy Gregory recalls her amusement at the gruff summary offered by Hutch, now the school horticulturalist. "It's just because Wallace lost the election," Hutch grumbled. "They have to let off steam somehow."

After one more informational meeting arranged for by Mrs. H. to "balance" union presentations,[93] Putney School closed for spring vacation. The only students who stayed on (beside those helping with the maple sugaring) were five petitioners who set up a student information center. There was no agreement in sight—in some cases, no information about whether students were passing or failing, either, for several union teachers refused to turn in their student evaluations. Parents all over the United States had already been alarmed by national news reports of the strike, for the press had decided that a private school union organized by the hard-slugging CIO was news indeed.[94] They had received long letters about it from both Mrs. H. and Mr. Bret Harte, Bret Harte's describing the essential conflict as one between authoritarian leadership and the democratic process.[95] Their children's accounts agitated them further. How could Putney open after vacation with most of its teachers missing? What would colleges do about unrecorded grades for not-yet-admitted seniors? Parents in three cities responded eagerly to news that Mrs. H., John Holden, or Warren Leonard was ready to meet with them.

Several union teachers arrived without invitation at the Buttenweisers' New York home hoping for a sympathetic ear, though not always finding it. "We weren't taking sides," says Helen Buttenweiser, "There was no side to take." Students dropped in too, especially children of divorced parents, who seemed "destroyed by the strike. They came around day after day as though they'd lost their home."[96]

The administration felt tremendous pressure from parents to settle quickly, a pressure only aggravated by the letters sympathetic to the strikers that Marion Smith had solicited from ex-Putney teachers everywhere whom she knew to have left Putney discontented. In spite of an equal number of supportive messages from parents and former teachers, Mrs. H. feared that large numbers of parents would withdraw their children, and that the school would have to close.

The various vacation meetings suggested that even the parents were becoming polarized. Felix Pereira recalls the meeting at his house as hysterical. "'Mrs. Hinton,' one parent finally said, 'All this talk is a lot of nonsense. You're the *one* and the union people are ciphers. You should sack the lot of them!'" A New York father expressed his grief over this "snake in Eden." Meanwhile, John Holden's meeting with sixteen Chicago parents proved to be one of the toughest encounters of his life. As he tried to explain the paradox of a "strong believer in unions being faced with a union that wanted to take the school away from her," he heard only angry demands that the school be given over to Local #808 to keep it going through June. They considered Geoffrey Bret Harte the epitome of respectability, which was exactly why (John argued) Edwin Smith had made sure he was union president. "They couldn't believe we'd already offered almost all the concessions the union was asking for."[97]

Afterwards, exhausted, John went to the home of Charles Gregory, a law professor, who had not been able to attend the meeting. Hearing John describe Ed Smith, Gregory went to his bookshelf and pulled out the printed transcript of a 1940 congressional investigation into the partisan behavior of Edwin Smith and one of the other original NLRB members. Smith had gone so far as to help organize a CIO local of the United Public Workers within the NLRB staff itself. President Roosevelt knew that the investigation had been mounted by Southern conservatives and AFL advocates hoping to discredit him, but a few raw facts seemed to confirm that Smith had indeed acted intemperately in his pursuit of justice for workers. FDR and Frances Perkins agreed that Smith could not be reappointed to the NLRB.[98]

This clinched the case against Smith for John Holden, and shortly, for Mrs. H. and Warren Leonard as well. When attorney Lauter next conferred with Mrs. H., he asked her, in one supreme effort to get the whole dispute unstuck, "What, at this moment, do you want most in all the world?" "For Ed Smith to leave Putney School," she answered. "That will be hardest," said Lauter. "When do you want him fired?" "Right now." And he was. It was not just the sacrifice of a scapegoat, for clearly Smith did not belong in high school teaching. From most of his students and colleagues, and from contemplating his stormy Washington career, one has the sense of Edwin Smith as a man so hardened by conflict that he had no warmth left for Putney School, no more energy for compromise. He moved on to become the uncompromising and effective director of the National Teachers' Division of the CIO's United Public Workers Union. His abrupt dismissal cost the school Smith's salary through June and $6,000 in lawyers' fees, but, said Mrs. H., it "had to happen."[99]

This done, Mrs. H. found the heart to respond to parents' pleas that she try negotiation once more, even though she was still smarting from union assertions that it was she, not they, who had broken off all talks. On March 27, she invited Millicent C. McIntosh, long-time principal of New York's Brearley School and now dean of Barnard College and a Putney parent, to be the new mediator and to meet with her in her New York hotel room the following morning.

Mrs. McIntosh is a Quaker and deeply committed to reconciliation. She had intended to use this meeting to begin the process of learning each side's position. But when she arrived at the hotel room at 11 A.M., Mrs. Hinton was just getting up, so distraught after a night's brooding that she shed far more tears than light during the conference. However, within a few days, Mrs. McIntosh had arranged a mediation meeting of union and administration leaders at the Barnard deanery. There Mrs. H. stated that if Ed Smith would stay away, she was ready to recognize the union as the sole collective bargaining agent for faculty and academic staff, except those serving as directors. All parties also agreed, as a start, to a permanent grievance and job security committee set up along the lines of the parents' committee already established. Almost immediately after this meeting, negotiations resumed on all points still at issue. The union teachers, now as concerned about their students as about their fast-diminishing strike fund, promised no further strike actions. They also agreed that the opening of school would be delayed a week to allow progress to ripen.[100]

It was not all smooth going. Millicent McIntosh would be accused by each side of taking too soft *or* too hard a line against the other.[101] She found the bitterness of union leaders alarming. In a final conference with Geoffrey Bret Harte, she became convinced (as she wrote him on April 17) that his "relations with Mrs. Hinton [had] reached an absolutely impossible status." To have watched him lose his temper and attack Mrs. Hinton during negotiations was one thing to Mrs. McIntosh; but it disturbed her still more that Bret Harte should have become so obsessed with Mrs. H.'s "dictatorial" pursuit of "bogies" (first Smith fired—Bret Harte must be next!) that he could talk privately to the mediator of nothing else.

"On the other hand [the letter went on], it seems clear to me that Mrs. Hinton finds it impossible to accept the principle of working with the Union. . . . She cannot forgive its actions," nor the bitterness and schism it had spread under Bret Harte's leadership. Mrs. McIntosh suggested a compromise: on the administration side, "making acceptable places for the two union members who feel they have been improperly treated" (including

Vivian Johannes), and guaranteeing Bret Harte his job for the following year. In return, Bret Harte had to be ready to resign in June 1950 and had to resign his presidency of the union immediately, making way for a leader "of moderation and patience" who was willing to assume the best of Mrs. H. rather than the worst and to move forward on the basis of common interests.[102] These were harsh terms for a man who thought he had settled down at Putney for a lifetime, a man of whom Hugh MacDougall has said wonderingly, "It was so foreign to his nature to be the antagonist."

Putney School did reopen as scheduled, to everyone's relief. Whatever the mediator's current status among adults, to such students as Charlie Humpstone, she was the "Dream Girl." Ultimately, John Holden, one of her critics, would call her a godsend.[103] In any case, reconciliation seemed to be underway at last: the alternatives were all too clear.

And for Putney's students, life resumed much as usual. The long-planned conference on racism was a success. The swimming pond warmed; the young cavorted there by night and day. Judy Gregory went back to work on Esmeralda, the 1919 Buick convertible she had bought from two older boys the year before. The union members resumed their teaching. Mrs. H. blamed union teachers' encouragement for students' futile efforts to swing the Community Council toward lax interpretations of the rules, but students say they were always trying to do that anyway.[104]

In spite of Mrs. H.'s fears, only one student had dropped out over spring vacation. Another boy learned that his parents planned to send him to a conventional prep school in September, a fate his friends scorned. "The indignity of being plucked out by your parents because of the Strike! It suggested that you couldn't handle life's problems!" an alumna remembers thinking. While some alumni recall the strike itself as a terrible time, more of them—especially the older ones—think otherwise. "It was the fireworks at the end of the fair," says one. Several drew strength from the experience. Charles Humpstone now remembers feeling the greatest excitement about the school that year, a sharper sense of its purposes and its value to him than he had ever had before. "What I discovered was that two groups of people could be [equally] idealistic," equally committed to the labor movement, and still "come out on opposite sides of the issues. I realiz[ed] that . . . there is no reconciling of some conflicts, and that the struggles which go with growth can't be avoided."

Most of Putney's adults were also busy, clearing the debris and beginning to rebuild. As she withdrew from her judiciary role, Millicent McIntosh had added her weight to Felix Pereira's suggestion that Putney School be reorganized under "a strong Board of Trustees with a democratically chosen membership."[105] Preliminary discussion of such a board took its place among the other changes being gradually worked out. "What do you want to strengthen the school?" Mrs. H. asked the faculty.[106] While the union held together under its new president, Mary Bartlett, both union negotiators and individuals cooperated to develop a salary scale that rationalized Mrs. H.'s informal procedures and—to universal acclaim—brought the maximum classroom teacher's salary above $2500 for the first time. This was close to the average for the smaller boarding schools. A faculty questionnaire having shown how common was the sixty-five-to-ninety-hour work week, faculty duties were specifically outlined. Tenure would be granted after three years of service. Most important would be the invention of the Administrative Council, a governing body more powerful than the faculty council Mrs. H. had resisted so firmly when the union first proposed it.[107] The new council would eventually replace the old Executive Committee; it consisted of four members appointed by the principal, three elected by the academic teachers and office staff, one by the outdoor teachers and household staff. The council would elect two of its members to represent Putney's adult community on an independent board of trustees, which in turn would delegate week-to-week responsibility for school operation back to the council and the faculty. Mrs. H. was careful to consult all teachers as she began casting around for the trustees who would launch the new board once the details of the charter change had been decided. She would signal a new direction when she appointed a *banker*, Felix Pereira, whose arguments for such a board she had many times opposed.[108]

Through all this time, negotiations on the union contract continued in tandem with the broader discussions. On May 18, the directors met, including three new parent directors, "to read and discuss the contract between the Putney School, Inc. and the Putney Teachers Union of Public Workers, CIO, Local #808. Upon a motion duly made and seconded, a majority of those present voted to accept the contract." The union had gotten virtually everything its members had hoped for.

Now, strangely enough, the union teachers began one by one to make plans to leave Putney School. Geoffrey Bret Harte made the first move, perhaps because he felt sure he would want to leave in a year's time anyway. As early as April he had received a letter from Mara Moser, on leave from Putney at the new Verde Valley School in Arizona and sympathetic both to Mrs. H. and to the union teachers' stated purposes (if not their methods). Why not join me here? Mara asked. Mrs. H. sat down on May 6 to write the first of twenty letters of warm recommendation for the twenty union teachers who, by October, would decide to forfeit their hard-won contracts and leave.[109]

And so, the union teachers—not by design, but just as surely as if they had planned it—did finally deal a terrible blow to Putney School, one perhaps more damaging than the strike itself. Non-union faculty and staff who had longed for reconciliation with old friends found the opportunity evaporating as the friends disappeared.

Why? "They were ashamed," said Mrs. H. "They were embarrassed," said Warren Leonard. Certainly, adds Warren, some were convinced that Mrs. H. would never regain confidence in them.[110] But Ray Rice, who must have known Mrs. H.'s opinion that he was "the best art teacher we'd ever had,"[111] says that it "just wasn't worth working at Putney any more." The ambience, the élan—everything that made cold winters and low salaries bearable—was gone out of the adult community. Ray, like Gabe Jackson, would continue for thirty-five years to realize that "I have never enjoyed teaching so much anywhere else." As Gabe writes, "One does not know with a *first* job that in some spiritual ways it will be the best job one ever holds. Wellesley, Knox, UC, University of Madrid, wherever—I have never had better teaching experiences than at Putney."[112] Nonetheless, Ray would follow Gabe away. Teachers from each side sum it up. "There was so much hurt left," says a union teacher. Say the Holdens, left behind, "There was just too much bitterness."

Most people did hold out until mid-May when Jane Arms circulated a scurrilous news clipping headlined "GOOD BYE, MR. SMITH," about the strike and the "Communists" who were behind it. The clipping carried "nasty anti-Semitic innuendo," Ray Rice and Ed Gray remember. For those who had hoped to stay, it was the last straw. Albert Raffanel took up the college job he had refused the year before. Vivian Johannes found new work as head of the Catlin-Gabell School's drama program. Bruce Menefee accepted an invitation from Werner Warmbrunn to teach seventh and eighth grades at California's Peninsula School. He shared a house with the Angells, who each took a year out for graduate work, Jim at Stanford, Flo at San José. In 1950 they joined Vivian as principal and librarian at Catlin-Gabell, "a terrible loss to Putney," Mrs. H. said. Vivian would no longer infuse Putney students like Judy Gregory with "the new notion that I might be able to *write* [an idea that] stayed with me for twenty years until I *did* begin to write." Nor would the dapper Raffanel be for those like her "one of the very few men" who really enjoyed her for herself. One pair of union members stuck it out at

Putney through September of 1949, hoping the school could recover its original sense of tolerance and shared purpose. Instead, they found only "suspicion and red-baiting" when they returned, and decided at last to leave. [113] Just two union teachers stayed through the following year. One was Mary Bartlett, a brilliant graduate of Putney School. The other (say colleagues) couldn't find another job. [114]

Eventually, most of the departed teachers did get back in touch with Putney friends. Only two remained utterly apart, too much haunted by their memories of the strike year to wish for any further contact with the school. And as years passed, Mrs. H. wrote to several teachers who had once belonged to Public Workers Local #808, asking if they would like to return to Putney School. Each declined, with regret. Ray Rice was persuaded to teach at the Work Camp one summer—but he didn't come back for a second. "Mrs. H. was at Cape Breton," he explains, "and the guts had gone out of the place."

Thirty years after the strike was over, tears still sprang to Carmelita Hinton's eyes when she talked of it. One can never be sure exactly how her work as educator was affected by the strike and the suffering before and after. Some friends say her "innocence" was lost forever, and with it her overweening confidence; others point to new enterprises launched with the old ebullience soon after the emergencies had ended. To students who arrived after 1949, the strike was only a rumor of times gone by. The school was theirs, and their principal was extraordinary. [115]

Mrs. H. tried to draw the curtain on the past. By May 1950, she was announcing to alumni the health of the school and of its new forms of governance. She would assure her constituency that "the student body is as large as ever"; she would report that the annual union election held in February proved the union no longer "represent[ative] of a majority of the faculty, and therefore the contract was not renewed." [116] Yet simultaneously, and often unseen, she was struggling to recoup the school's losses and to adjust to the relinquishment of her final authority to the trustees. There was heroism in these efforts, but there was an undermining bitterness too, which softened in time to a simple inability to understand how the catastrophe could have overtaken her. [117] Though her confusion makes sense, given that some of her antagonists behaved so irrationally, her feeling of betrayal [118] probably weakened the lessons the catastrophe offered; so did her desire to blame a single agitator and "you union people" for the final breakdown of a whole system. She wrote Mary Bartlett in the summer of 1949 that the new salary scale was more of a hindrance than a help—she'd like to have paid Mary *more* than the scale allowed. And she finished with a

> Note: We are still eight boys too few for the school year next year. I don't think any of you union people realize what a blow you dealt Putney and how hard it is to keep our clientele standing behind us. You ask for more money, more furniture, and then the pupils that give us just the little extra surplus are lacking.

Mrs. H.'s tendency to exploit people did not disappear overnight any more than did the school's need for unusually generous-hearted (therefore easily "exploitable") adults.[119]

However, the improvements brought by the costly conflict were greater than the lingering problems. "Things were better after the strike," says Ed Gray, the longest-tenured teacher of all. Perhaps one can only conclude that *both* Putney School *and* the upheaval that ultimately, painfully made its future possible were the function of one woman's single-minded vision. No leader less stubborn could have launched such an experiment; no leader so rooted in her convictions could escape a reckoning. The tragedy was in the inflammatory character of the reckoning, its heedlessness, once ignited, of real human beings: teachers, students—and Carmelita Hinton herself.

Carmelita Hinton, Harvest Festival, 1948
(photo by Rudolph Furrer).

Garden Work Jobs (Putney School Archives).

Allen House: A Boys' Dormitory
(photo by Allen C. Hawkridge).

Ed Gray Repairing the School Bell, 1960s
(photo by Ed Shore).

Spreading Manure, 1930s
(Putney School Archives).

Chores, 1940s (Putney School Archives).

Picketing in Brattleboro
(photo by Ed Shore).

The Carpentry Shop: Tom Morse and Student
(photo by Ed Shore).

Sugaring with Clyde Hulett
(Putney School Archives).

Ski Racing: Hester Goodenough (Caldwell),
Class of 1946 (By permission of
the *Brattleboro Reformer*,
Judson B. Hall, photographer).

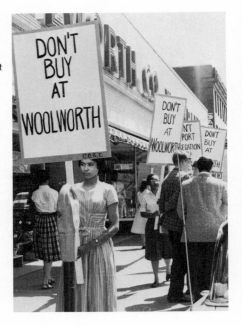

Folk Dance Group, Harvest Festival
(photo by Ed Shore).

Performance of Synge's *The Playboy of the Western World*, 1960s
(Putney School Archives).

Painting the White Cottage
(Putney School Archives).

Chemistry Laboratory
(photo by Ed Shore).

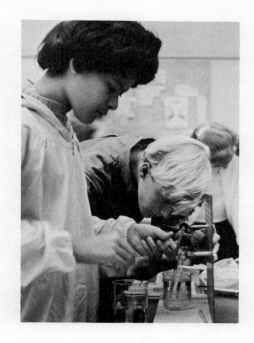

H. Benson Rockwell
(photo by Ed Shore).

Norwood Hinkle Conducting Madrigals Chorus,
Commencement at Lower Farm, 1960s
(photo by Ed Shore).

Part IV
Learning Endurance
1949–1965

Carmelita Hinton's original Putney School had been unique. The institution that emerged after 1949 was also one of a kind. Its new governmental framework, as unconventional as it was hard won, proved capable of sustaining the extraordinary variety of persons and opportunities that had been the school's chief strength from the beginning. Fresh teachers came—and stayed. With the veterans, and with much help from the friends Mrs. H.'s utopian experiment had made, they recreated Putney School. The community's "density of purpose" did not significantly diminish when Benson Rockwell took Mrs. Hinton's place in 1955, though Rockwell's profound acceptance of individuality allowed for individual rebellions against many of Putney's purposes.[1] For all its innovations, its continuing trials and errors, the school maintained its original definitions of progressive education. Its movement through the next sixteen years of history would run a steadier course than that which history itself was taking.

Chapter 9
The Pioneers Dig In

While Mrs. H. sought eighteen new teachers through the summer of 1949, John Holden began the spadework needed to build an independent board of trustees. The corporation directors had already renewed the search for some model of institutional governance that would suit Putney School. Over two dozen inquiries were yielding a stack of college and school charters, constitutions, and faculty manuals. John secured the help of an able Brattleboro lawyer, soon to be joined by Mark Lauter, the labor specialist who had helped the school through the strike. The union contract outlined classroom teachers' responsibilities and rewards, but much more was needed.

The colleges, which took for granted their faculties' interest in policymaking, proved better models of governance than the schools. Antioch College offered the most promising scheme, no great surprise considering the depth of Antioch's commitment to democratic forms. Antioch's trustees numbered twenty-seven—"scientists, labor leaders, businessmen and other professional people chosen for their ideas and ideals," not for the size of their bank accounts or their loyalty quotient in the alumni office. While the Antioch board retained ultimate responsibility for the college, it delegated virtually all policymaking to an administrative council, which assisted the college president (also the council's chairman) in carrying out these policies. [1]

The Antioch system built hedges around executive power far higher than Carmelita Hinton had ever dreamed of. However, such an organization comported well with Putney's tentative plans for a faculty council. It could only strengthen the student-adult Community Council, and it promised so clearly to guarantee faculty involvement with administrative decisions that no separate faculty association or union would ever again be necessary. "Good!" wrote Mrs. H. next to the Antioch plan for all-faculty election of administrative council members. [2]

Under the prospective Putney charter, short-term decisions fell to an

Administrative Council; so did the obligation to reach agreement with the school's new Board of Trustees on most of the crucial long-term ones, such as the choice of each new head of the school. By mid-October, Mrs. H., her veteran teachers, and the corporation directors had decided to adapt the plan to Putney School. The full faculty and staff gave its approval just before Thanksgiving.

There were fears. The Putney plan gave the director the right to choose half of the eight Administrative Council members and allowed Mrs. H. a veto over council decisions as long as she was head. Before the first set of revisions, Felix Pereira wrote Mrs. H. of his grave doubts whether the State of Vermont would sanction "a Board of Trustees whose executive authority is limited to the power to dismiss the head of the school." At the parents' meeting held the morning after Thanksgiving, several parents added their loud objections to those of the few teachers who remembered all too well what tares and snares Mrs. H.'s uses of power had sown the year before. "I know," wrote Pereira, "that you gave the impression to many parents at the meeting that you were quite unwilling to modify any of your powers."[3] He implored her to distribute authority, so that Putney's director could keep parental and faculty support, for without such support, her remaining powers would be useless.

A small group of experienced educator-parents sat at the same meeting, struggling (say two of them) to envision how this charter unique to the secondary school world would work out in practice. At last, Millicent McIntosh said what was in their minds and told Mrs. H. that Putney School should "go ahead and pioneer in this thing."[4]

And Putney School did. With the doubters' warnings in her heart, Mrs. H. determined that whatever the state's ruling, an experimental Administrative Council should go to work as soon as possible in order to *show* faculty, staff, and parents that the school could be cooperatively run. She promised herself that she would use her veto rarely, if ever—and she kept that promise. She moved quickly to hold faculty and staff elections for the council and to insure that her own appointees were people well known and trusted by all of Putney's adults. She chose Warren Leonard, John Holden, Norwood Hinkle, and Mary Bartlett (who was still president of the Putney Teachers Union) to join the elected members, Anne Holden, Jack Caldwell, Ross Hodgdon, and a capable new science teacher named Larry Boothby. Thus half of the council that began work in early February consisted of the four most active faculty stockholders from the old corporation, a roster that insured continuity with the best work done under Putney's original corporate organization.

The state education officials proved unexpectedly benign. Their promise of eventual approval hastened the search for a group of trustees who would be glad to serve as balance wheel for the Administrative Council and final authority for the school. Mrs. H. made a crucial decision in choosing the trustee who would become the first board chairman, Richard Brett. Brett's two daughters had attended Putney and had known the school at its best. He liked and admired Mrs. H., but he was not overawed. His experience as a big-city banker and as business manager (first of the Macmillan publishing company and now of the New York Public Library) made a rich complement to hers. His assumption that "man is basically crooked" nicely balanced her faith in the ultimate goodness of all. He could laugh at her as readily as she could laugh with him. "She didn't approve of businessmen running schools," says he. "Neither did I." Finally, Brett loved Vermont's land and shared its maverick leanings, having made a summer home and an experimental forestry plantation in the hills fifty miles to the north of Putney.

Brett's style was not to dictate but to converse. As the moment in May approached when Carmelita Hinton would give over her corporate stock to the board of trustees she had so long resisted, her talks with Dick Brett assured her that the school might after all flourish under the guidance of such a man and under the board gathering about them both.[5]

Fifteen of the twenty pioneer trustees arrived at Hinton House on a sunny, windy day in June 1950. Though strangers to each other, several were Mrs. H.'s old friends: Margaret Coolidge and Ursula MacDougall from Putney's earliest days; two lawyers, one banker, one professor of religion and philosophy, the assistant chief of the U.S. Forest Service; an old Bryn Mawr classmate now a specialist in labor economics at Smith College; and Edward Yeomans, Jr., the new director at Shady Hill School, who had been one of her first nursery school pupils back in Winnetka. Ten of these six-year trustees were parents of present or former Putney students. Jean Hinton Rosner represented the three Hinton children, as the new charter required. She continued to serve into the 1980s. Administrative Council members Anne Holden and Jack Caldwell were there, elected trustees for 1950–51 by the faculty and staff. William Uptegrove and Barbara Barnes represented the alumni, having been elected for two-year terms. Dick Brett looked around the living room and said to himself, "It's just as she planned: there's not a common thought in the whole mob."[6]

There was plenty to discuss, however. The board was legally responsible for Putney School's earning, spending, and borrowing as well as for its educational function. It was final custodian of the Elm Lea property and lessor of all the land and buildings still owned by Carmelita Hinton. While the Administrative Council was already discussing most of these things and weekly determining policy for the school, the camp, the inn, the store, the farm, and the pottery, the council was obliged to advise with the trustees twice each year and with the trustees' Executive Committee at least twice more. And money was tight now. During the year that followed the strike, Putney had run up a $12,000 deficit, its largest ever. "A good school never has enough money," Brett says. "The plant is always about to fall apart. There are not enough closets for the extra students to live in. The staff is overworked. Putney's raw material was a group of very bright teen-agers"— and teen-agers are volatile stuff.[7]

Nevertheless, the polyglot board began its delicate task of helping at a safe remove to shape that raw material without unduly disturbing those actually working with it. The board and the Administrative Council had five years before Mrs. Hinton planned to retire in which to shore up the school and choose her successor.

The five years appear to have been well spent. The major powers having been redistributed, the council and the board took up one by one those issues of adult responsibility and compensation that had so radically upset the Putney School community during the year of the strike. The new group of teachers did not want to continue the union but did vote enthusiastically to continue the union contract. Though this was a logical and legal impossibility, the message to Mrs. H. and the Administrative Council was clear. Five months before the first Trustees' meeting, Mrs. H. made a formal promise to the faculty that the school would "adhere to the substance and spirit" of the contract.[8] Within the next two years, the council and the board had made virtually every one of the contract's provisions, and more besides, permanent school policy, all set out in a twenty-page faculty manual written by Mrs. H. with others' advice and reviewed by the entire teaching staff. The salary scale was made more flexible than the union scale by allowing a range of salaries within each group in the seniority spectrum, leaving exact salary awards to be decided by the director, often with Dick Brett's advice. Mrs. H.'s salary was raised from $5400 to $6000. Generous maternity leaves were incorporated into the compensation system for both tenured and nontenured teachers. With the faculty's consent, the three-year trial period before tenure was extended to five years. Finally, the manual spelled out the exact procedures by which school food could be obtained outside regular dining room meals: there was to be no more confusion over Sunday breakfasts.

The sabbatical leave and pension provisions took longer to realize, for after a decade of small annual surpluses, Jack Caldwell's cupboard was bare at the end of each year. Postwar inflation had taken its toll, as had a general raise in all academic salaries following the strike and the hiring of a few extra teachers to reduce each individual's work load slightly.[9] But by 1959 these last two benefits were firmly in place, the pension plan having been painstakingly worked out by Felix Pereira and a subcommittee of the Administrative Council. It helped that the Social Security Act had already been extended in 1950 to cover teachers and that many other independent schools had also developed pension plans since the war. Putney School was not pioneering here.

The Administrative Council recommended that the grievance procedure set out in the union contract be dropped altogether, since no union now existed to appoint half the committee members. So successfully did the council function as a conduit for faculty-staff concerns that formal appeals to either council or board were almost unknown. Members of both groups informally received grievances both personal and professional. Jane Arms wrote one of the latter, mincing no words, to Margaret Coolidge in 1951. Jane's anxiety over the antiquated fire safety system and the dilapidated school vehicles had reached the limit.[10] The trustees took the heat, as trustees are meant to do; at their request, the Administrative Council handled the details of repair with Jack Caldwell. Chairman Brett was particularly skilled at fielding the more personal appeals.

Putney's new governance procedures might look cumbersome to outsiders, the weekly council meetings impossibly long and dull to a few insiders (Norwood Hinkle resigned from the first year's council, protesting the time subtracted from his music teaching). Trustees complained from time to time that they were "no more than rubber stamps," and indeed, their most common function was to advise rather than to control.[11] Yet taken all in all, the system worked remarkably well.

None of these supports was firmly in place when twenty new teachers arrived at Putney School in the fall of 1949. They came for the fresh approaches to schooling and to life that Putney seemed to offer; they came on the strength of the school's reputation in spite of the general knowledge of the school's upheaval. By its refusal to join the many progressive schools that scrambled back to safe ground after the war, Putney had made itself the more attractive to adventurous teachers.

A few accepted appointment as impulsively as Mrs. H. appeared to have hired them. Tom Wendel's father had expected his son to follow him into the world of business. The senior Wendel was amazed that Tom should be heading for Putney School in mid-October to take the place of the latest union teacher to resign. "But what will they pay you?" he asked. "$1500," was Tom's reply. "$1500 every what?" "$1500 every year." (Stunned) "Tom, have you no . . . pride?"[12] Allen Thomas came to Putney an "intellectual peasant" (he says) virtually free of teaching credentials. But he had plenty of experience as a weather forecaster, a logger, a poet, and a lover of literature, and Mrs. H. signed him on as an English teacher at the close of a twenty-minute interview. Partly because the supports for teaching grew ever stronger, nearly all the new crowd stayed for at least three years, long enough to lend the school a desperately needed sense of stability. Five would join the Hinkles and the Grays in remaining at the school for twenty more years, and by the time Mrs. Hinton retired in 1955, seven more teachers had arrived who would stay as long.

Not all teachers who join a school on two months' notice can do the job: there were a few sad cases whom students remember all too well. But over five years, Putney managed to gather a rich and uncannily familiar mixture of dedicated academics and colorful characters. Just as several wartime refugee teachers had done, Felix and Marisa Lederer came almost straight from the boat to West Hill, carrying the best of European culture with them. Much as Ewald Schnitzer found Putney School granting him "a second youth," Marisa says she experienced "a kind of rebirth" at Putney School. "Do you like children?" Mrs. H. asked Marisa. No was one of the few English words Marisa knew; it was also the truest reply she could manage to this "incredible woman—bright, energetic, with big holes in her cotton stockings." Mrs. H. may have hired her for her frankness as much as for her doctorate in history and her experience as an archivist-librarian. But Marisa proved herself wrong about children after a few months in the new boys' dorm surrounded by boy-jokes and boy-problems and by the three-part boy singing that sounded through the shared bathroom wall. "Discovering these boys—their whole inner life—learning later from my girl counselees, woke up the maternal part of me," says Marisa now.[13] Felix soon knew English as fluently as he knew Italian, French, Latin, and his native German; his "delight with excellence," his demands on himself and his students set standards, however kindly expressed, that younger faculty repeatedly mention as a major influence on their own teaching. Both Lederers were "dearly loved" by all who knew them well.[14]

So were Fernando and Stepha Gerassi. Fernando was Putney's last Spanish civil war refugee: he had been a general in the doomed republican army. Yet his paintings and his teaching of art were so ebullient, so bright with color and courage that students soon flocked to the art studio. His wife, Stepha, originally Ukrainian, had, like her husband, an international education in philosophy and history, with degrees from four different European universities and the language skills to match. Both Gerassis were short and squat, toughened by the privations of their adventurous lives; but their minds moved in two directions. "I'm glad Eve ate the apple," Stepha told her Russian students. "I like this knowing the difference between good and evil. But Fernando? Fernando would rather to be back in the Garden of Eden eating the banana!" Say several alumni, "They were like parents away from home. You could talk about anything—*nothing* was forbidden."[15] These two, along with the Lederers, Jeanne Case, and other new language teachers picked up the internationalist intellectual thread so vital to the school in its first fourteen years and carried it into Putney's future.

Nor was Putney long without its traditional socialist leaven: a pacifist Unitarian minister, a man of two races and many nations named Jeffrey Campbell, who knew his native country to be "the fellowship of the human race."[16] Jeff joined the English department in 1951 with Ray Goodlatte, who would be one of the last of the longer-tenured teachers to come from college-level teaching or doctoral work (in Ray's case, as an instructor at Harvard) to Putney School, as so many past Putney teachers had done. There were other academic teachers of equal importance to the new Putney School, of course, and over the years, many one- or two-year teachers who would by their origins or their educations similarly help to link Putney with its past. At this transitional time, however, these six, so familiar and yet so individual, seemed to give special reassurance that the school could sustain some of its liveliest human traditions.

The other adults whose continued presence was crucial to Putney School were the many outdoor teachers and staff members who had never even considered leaving during the difficult years. Ruth Hodgdon would no longer be called by Mrs. H. at 10 P.M. to take dictation. as Ruth had often and happily done during Putney's exciting opening year, but she was as essential as ever in her new job as the school bookkeeper and as the new clerk of the trustees and contributor to all their meetings. For many years either Ruth or

Ross Hodgdon sat as elected staff representative on the Administrative Council. Nancy West, who had arrived in 1936 to be Ruth's successor as Mrs. H.'s secretary, quietly and powerfully supported the founding principal through all Putney's transitions. In her many roles, Nancy would be for thirty-two years a still center of Putney's turning world, depended upon by students, alumni, and teachers alike.[17]

Clyde Hulett's last team of horses was sold in 1953, but Clyde stayed on as a night watchman—who knew exactly when to look the other way. Students loved him for what he ignored. Tragically, Charlie Gray shot himself in April 1956 after a season of ill health and despondency. There was no replacing him, so Putney School didn't try. His brother's family grew in numbers, however, one Gray son eventually joining the teaching staff for a while, another becoming U.S. District Attorney in Vermont.

As staff salaries and benefits began at last to reflect staff contributions to the school,[18] as the five Gray children grew to be Putney School students, Ed and Mabel Gray gathered a measure of material reward for their long years' work in the school's establishment. It wasn't all roses. When Ed Gray lost parts of two fingers in a carpentry accident, he couldn't afford to rest. He took his $400 workmen's compensation check, bought three pieces of machinery for his small farm, and went right back to the paint shop. But they stayed. Students continued to be astonished by Mabel Gray's ability to talk for twenty minutes straight while weeding her garden with one hand and picking flowers with the other, getting up to kill a chicken or comfort a child, then sitting down again to weed. Her candor was legendary. "Each time Mabel had a baby, every girl in school learned the details in short order," writes one alumna.

A major reason for adults' willingness to stay on through the years was that Putney School was proving a good place for growing. "One thing about this place," says Ed Gray, "you may get angry but you'll never be bored." Almost every teacher who came after 1949 speaks of the delight of learning new skills, of trying out new courses or evening activities, and especially of fitting one's life to the beauties of nature, its catches and its changes. Like most Putney adults, Tom Wendel learned to ski from his students—at night. Tom recalls, that "Everyone said it was easier to learn at night because one didn't see the little bumps and ridges that might scare him off during the day." Already a gifted pianist, he took up the cello and entered a new world of chamber music performances. He was Westmoreland in Bunny White's *Henry IV, Part 1*. "'So shaken as we are, so wan with care. . . .' I can still remember the lines," he says. For several Chekov plays, "The only time we had to rehearse was after hours, when everyone was supposed to be in bed." One scene in Ibsen's *Peer Gynt* found Ray Goodlatte and Jeff Campbell among a group of "international bankers," wrote Jeff, "huddled in the African desert, planning to trim the hero of his shirt and make a getaway on a disappearing liner."

"Mrs. H. never allowed you to be just a cellist," says George Finckel. "You had to be a *person*." A math teacher learned folk dancing and joined a Vermont troupe that eventually toured Europe. Teacher-poets shared their work with students; Robin Spry Campbell jealously guarded the time Putney granted her for her own sculpture—but set up her small studio in a room off the larger teaching room, so that students could watch each new piece evolve. Ten years before other schools mounted Outward Bound programs, Robin was learning, then teaching, white-water kayaking on the rivers of northern New England. "The danger brought a group together," she says. As it happened, Robin herself was the first and only Putney person to meet serious danger in thirty years of river-running. She almost drowned when her kayak overturned and her life jacket got caught in tree roots underwater. A student saved her. She took just one more white-water trip to put her fear behind her.

The new sabbatical and summer-study grants, minimal though they were, offered weary teachers a season of self-renewal. Charles Brickley forwarded his own education at no cost by traveling to Cornell and Deep Springs for three summers' work as director of the Telluride program for gifted high school seniors. Women looking up to Carmelita Hinton found courage to try work they had never before imagined doing—starting as a cook and becoming head of the dining room or moving between secretarial or library work and classroom teaching. [19]

Money was needed to support teaching and learning, more money now than ever. Salary outlays, never more than half of each year's budget at any time before 1960, did not rise as fast as one might expect, for many of the new teachers began at beginners' rates. But these soon climbed the scale, their raises outpacing inflation. It took the full five years that followed the strike for tuition income to stabilize. While "a flood of girls" continued to apply, scholarships had to be offered to almost twice as many boys as girls if they were to come to a coeducational school at all. [20] The school added to its own difficulties by refusing to compromise on the policy of filling each graduating class by the beginning of tenth grade. At least three years at the school (it was assumed) were needed for every student to absorb Putney ways and learn to take Putney responsibilities.

In time, however, Putney's good name seemed to clear. A stepping-up of recruiting trips may have helped. In January 1954, Mrs. H. took the longest of these herself, driving to Omaha by stages and taking the train to the West Coast, staying with friendly alumni and parents, and giving dozens of talks about her school. She was particularly anxious to increase the number of foreign and black students, and she had some small successes here. Since most schools' applications dropped off as the Depression babies entered high school, it is possible that Putney would have had difficulty finding uniformly strong students even if the strike had never occurred.[21]

In any case, self-selection worked well throughout these lean years. There are indications that Putney more "closely approached the ideal type of the progressive school" in the public eye than did any other Eastern school.[22] In the mid-fifties, well before the baby boom was offering high school age children, and in spite of the widely read "Conant report" whose author, a Putney parent, urged all parents to send their children to comprehensive public high schools, applications began suddenly to increase. By 1960, there were four serious applicants for every place in a school of 185 students, a ratio even more favorable then that enjoyed by the two Phillips academies, Exeter and Andover.[23]

Pressed by Felix Pereira, who thought it disgraceful that ill-paid teachers should be "subsidizing prosperous families,"[24] the board and the Administrative Council raised both tuition and scholarships again and again. By 1956, when Pereira took over as Chairman of the Board, Putney's full fee stood higher than that of any Northeastern boarding school except for the most elegant all-girl schools. As Pereira had predicted, however, the raises made no difference either in applications or in the average economic circumstances of Putney's full-paying clientele. Increasingly, mothers appear to have taken jobs to earn Putney children's tuition.[25] Less wealthy families learned that Putney's scholarship program was one of the five most generous among New England boarding schools relative to its size. Putney School continued to give tuition reductions to one-third of its student body and did without 15 percent of potential tuition income. Only Northfield and Mt. Hermon offered more.

Even with its high tuition, money ran short at Putney School—$16,000 short in 1953. This was 4.3 percent of the total budget. Clearly tuition alone could not cover the ambitious educational and scholarship program or the resulting deficit of $5,000–$25,000 every other year or so. Neither could Putney's auxiliary enterprises make the difference Mrs. H. had envisioned. Despite careful oversight by the new authorities, only the farm and the camp showed a surplus. First the commercial pottery, then the inn were given up, new technologies and new tourists' tastes having begun to demand more capital investment than a small school could justify. The trustees went to work to raise the needed funds, the weight of their determination overwhelming Carmelita Hinton's initial fear that a school selling itself to its public had to become a school for sale.

Endowment funds kept tuitions down at the older boys' preparatory schools, even though their real costs per student were up to 65 percent higher than Putney School's.[26] However, a larger endowment did not seem possible for a young school, four-fifths of whose alumni had joined the education, health, or social-service professions, become musicians, artists, or craftsmen, or begun small businesses (including about two dozen farms and ranches by 1970).[27] The trustees followed Mrs. H.'s lead in resisting any help that might compromise the school's freedom, as some forms of endowment inevitably do. They chose the only alternatives: periodic fund drives to raise building and operating funds and an annual giving effort run entirely by the school.

Counting the 1946 fund drive, there were three campaigns in the first thirty years. In 1950, Putney still needed $250,000; under Pereira's leadership, the trustees decided to try again. And again this goal proved overambitious, though not by much. Half of the $190,000 the drive brought in was given by Libby Holman Reynolds as a memorial to her mountaineer son Christopher and went to the science building. The Wasserman family helped to double the size of the library in Stephen's honor. Parents fell to as never before, approaching foundations and sending endorsements. Millicent McIntosh praised the "cooperative management" of the school to all who would hear. "O Putney parent, now's your chance," wrote Edward Dodd, father of three Putney students (and later grandfather of three more) in a solicitation-by-rhyme.

> The plant is in a sorry state,
> Worn by a seventeen-year old spate
> Of students so hefty and hilarious
> That even with patches multifarious
> The buildings now are really precarious
> . . . .
> Think now of the things your kids have had
> And been spared the things that drove you mad.
> . . . .

Remember all the drivel and drool
We used to suffer at our kind of school?
Those rah-rah sports we had to grapple?
Those stiff collars we wore in chapel?
Then think of God in a Vermont apple.

"Why it's worth a super-colossal grant / just to be rid of all that cant," the parent-fundraiser went on. The money he helped to raise was spent even before it had all come in: on building and sewer repairs, on scholarships and salary increments, on finishing construction begun in 1946. In 1953–54, the school's cash position was so poor that it had to borrow $40,000 to meet its payroll and had to suspend its $2,000 voluntary tax payment to the town. In 1957, the trustees declared a five-year moratorium on general mortgage payments to gain the cash needed to run the school.[28]

The three-parent foundation committee had labored long, presenting one large foundation with a scholarship proposal, another with a request for $131,000 to provide equipment for Putney's exemplary out-of-class curriculum, everything from a grand piano to a new manure spreader. Only small foundations seemed interested, however. Putney father Rudolf Serkin played his third benefit concert in the KDU to raise funds for the piano; farm and evening activity programs tightened belts and made do. The trustees looked modestly for another $200,000 in a twenty-fifth anniversary drive, and got it all and more. This time, one-third of the funds came from a single family.

Fortunately, annual giving was proving successful. Tom Wendel organized it, his one visible concession to his upbringing before he returned to business during the drive's first year. Nancy West, now alumni secretary, continued it with much help from parents, other staff, several trustees, and the alumni committee. The first goal was $15,000. Mrs. H. did everything wrong, allowing the Administrative Council to run the drive on a shoestring budget, apologizing for asking for alumni's money in the 1954 issue of the *Alumni News*, and often making herself too busy to meet with possible parent donors. But it worked anyway. The 1954 goal met, sights were gradually raised to $35,000—the equivalent of usable interest on a million-dollar endowment—ten years later, and would be raised again to cover virtually all of the school's scholarship (or tuition-reduction) budget. Though alumni contributions stayed relatively low (never more than 40 percent of the total dollar amount), the number of alumni donors had reached a high of 41 percent of all graduates by 1965. Parents, friends, and small foundations gave the rest.

Given hope and love and constant vigilance, then, Putney School was a viable economic proposition. Week by week the Administrative Council played watchdog on all expenses, tightening department budgeting procedures, refusing special requests.[29] Trustee-faculty financial and planning committees gradually made hand-to-mouth operations a thing of the Putney past. The *willingness* needed to make a tight budget work was a function of Putney's adults knowing themselves represented in the policymaking bodies of the school. In the toughest years, Dick Brett and Mrs. H. would assemble the entire faculty and staff, Dick "putting himself on the griddle" for hours to talk over financial problems with them and gather their solutions.[30] The school floated, nose above the waves.

Chapter 10

Looking Outward

The years from 1949 to 1955 found Putney School reaching in new ways toward the outer world. Despite the buffets it received in a political climate grown hostile to many of its assumptions, the school was making its mark on the larger society. Each year more alumni grew into work of their own. As if to put the strike far behind her, Carmelita Hinton seemed to be hurtling through her final Putney years, spending her energy as much to enlarge the scope of the school as to strengthen it for the future. Failures sprouted here and there among her successes, like weeds in a fertile garden. But the garden grew.

Alumni were much more than open wallets for Putney School. "I'd never seen anything like Putney alumni's love for their school," recalls one teacher. Mrs. H. wanted Putney to be a "tenacious part of them," wanted them all to think of West Hill as home.[1] Almost two hundred alumni joined a huge harvest festival crowd six months after the strike. Their show of confidence clinched a decision Mrs. H. had put off during the troubles. Soon afterward she donated land and lumber for an alumni house, hoping that the alumni themselves would be able to raise funds to complete it. When they couldn't, in spite of many contributions of money and construction work, she dug deeper into her own pockets and persuaded her colleagues to allocate funds to finish the job. Only occasionally did she allow herself to wonder why every graduate was not helping out, why about a fifth of the alumni group considered themselves to have learned Putney's lessons in independence so thoroughly that they need not keep in touch with the school at all. It was enough for her to hear of the majority spreading the word that Putney School, whatever its shortcomings, was a place where one could grow as a whole person, where happiness was possible. Great was her joy when alumni children began to attend Putney School in 1958. By 1965, thirty had enrolled, with many more on the way. For all her adventurousness, the Putney family was her home too, and she wanted it to endure.

While it is impossible to separate a school's influence on its students from that of their families, patterns were emerging among alumni of the first twenty years, light brushstrokes that gave a clearer image of the school itself. Putney graduates make a striking contrast to those coming out of some boys' prep schools. Nearly 60 percent of Hotchkiss graduates from the 1940s were in business or finance, for example, half of these on their way to the top of large firms, while the 21 percent of Putney men who had entered these fields tended to be running their own small businesses, including farms. The Hotchkiss junior executives lived up to their income in "manicured suburbs," writes their collective biographer; most Putney alumni had settled in cities or small towns. Three times as many Putney men had become teachers. Of the 18 percent (to Hotchkiss's 16 percent) who were physicians, many more were teaching in medical schools.[2]

A twenty-year comparison of Putney alumni with Exeter and Brearley graduates combined may be a better indicator of Putney's influence, because together the three schools served both boys and girls. Furthermore, there is almost certainly some overlap of parent constituencies among the three. Available figures suggest that the proportions of Putney graduates in business are only one-third those of the Exeter-Brearley average, while percentages of Putney men and women in health fields (12 percent) and the arts (17 percent) are two and three times larger. The disparity is smaller for teachers: 13 percent for Putney, 12 percent for Brearley, and 7 percent for Exeter. Carmelita Hinton would have been glad to know that the proportion of research scientists, though small in all three schools, is five times larger for the Putney group than for either of the other two.[3]

"The independent school's mission is [to] 'forge ahead with more and more valuable experiments,'" Carmelita Hinton told her faculty in March of 1954.[4] That very year she was fostering an experiment particularly close to her heart: a "Little School" for the children of West Hill as exciting (she hoped) as the nursery and elementary schools she herself had been involved with early in her career. Though she wanted Putney School to connect with the town and its public school—and there were several trustees who insisted that the public school could improve only if Putney teachers would get behind it—she wanted even more a stable faculty who would gladly raise their families on West Hill.[5] A good elementary school seemed essential to this plan, and several key teacher-parents were ready to help carry it out.

For eight years, Philip and Helen Chase ran such a school six miles from Putney School. Putney School paid one-third of each faculty child's tuition to Hickory Ridge. But Hickory Ridge included boarders among its twenty to thirty pupils, a few of whom were troubled children. One set two fires, and the second entirely destroyed the school's main building in 1951. The Chases' school closed down.

It was Mrs. H.'s style to build even more energetically on ashes than she did on bare ground. She remembered a pair of acquaintances, Eleanor and A. E. Hamilton, who had founded, then abandoned, a successful elementary school in New York City. The Hamilton School attracted children in love with life and fostered their curiosity instead of quashing it. It was so much sought after that after fifteen years the Hamiltons began to feel like the prisoners of their wealthy and enthusiastic parent clientele. They bought a farm in Sheffield, Massachusetts, and started a boarding school and summer camp (as well as a large family of their own). The move freed them to experiment with a host of educational ideas based on Wilhelm Reich's theories: the full energy, intelligence, and adventurousness of childhood could only be released, they felt sure, in young persons wholly at home in their own sexuality. Free children unafraid of nakedness or of adult mysteries could make the best of the wonderful devices "Ranger" and "Tajar" (they went by the children's names for them) had developed for teaching reading, writing, arithmetic, and science.[6]

Meanwhile, West Hill was proving itself "an ideal place to bring up small children," says Cornelia Hinkle, mother of three of the forty youngsters who now enlivened Putney School. With Hickory Ridge gone, a little one-room school for ten of them became a stopgap. Their parents lobbied vigorously for a larger school to inhabit the renovated chicken house now that Putney's alumni were soon to get their own quarters. Just a month after the Hickory Ridge fire, Mrs. H. wrote Ranger and Tajar Hamilton.

It took only two letters back and forth for her and Ranger to become fast friends, recognizing each other (wrote Ranger) as "woman-doers . . . steam engine kind of people."[7] Carmelita Hinton probably needed such a person in her life at just this point, her ardent friendship with Jane Arms having cooled. It had been a difficult season for her. She had broken her back falling off a sofa while decorating her house for the school Christmas party in 1950. She refused to believe it until she finally went to the Cape Breton hospital in June and was put to bed for the summer in the cast she should have assumed six months before. And there were moments when she still allowed her memories of the strike year to bleed her. Thus the warm-hearted Ranger's confirmation of her worth was particularly welcome. Couldn't the Hamiltons move their four children, their horses, dogs, and cow to West Hill, Ranger to run the Little School, Tajar to be the nearby psychotherapist the Putney School almost surely needed now?

First hope, then skepticism spread through the faculty-parent group as the Hamiltons warmed to the prospect. Did Putney need more pioneers, looking for "the roots of education that could change society" in *their* children? And what about the whispering that suggested Reichian "obsessions," the Hamilton camp and school children running naked about the swimming pool, or being invited to watch Ranger give birth to a new Hamilton child?[8]

Carmelita Hinton had learned some lessons in consultation since 1948. She wrote Putney parents who knew the Hamiltons' work, including psychoanalyst Erik Erikson; she made inquiries of such Hamilton Farm School trustees as Governor and Mrs. Thomas E. Dewey. The replies were reassuring as well as cautionary. "Handle the money yourself," "make no long term commitment to Tajar Hamilton as a psychiatrist," and these two might be exactly the people needed for the new school to succeed.[9]

Troubled by the delay, Ranger Hamilton mourned to Mrs. H. the fact that "no one but yourself has the guts to risk bread and butter in favor of the search for more truth," but Tajar stated himself willing to put the "cowardly smears" behind him.[10] By spring 1953, the faculty-parents had agreed to invite the Hamiltons, and they had agreed to come.

So the new Little School was begun, in a turmoil and excitement not unlike that which had attended the opening of its sponsor school. The energy required by the initial leaps of faith seemed to power the school throughout its five-year career, even though Ranger Hamilton lost her health after a single year and the Hamiltons themselves had to leave.[11] The school and its twenty-one pupils were taken over by Elizabeth Burns, an extraordinary Scottish teacher, Joan Shore coming fresh from a teaching post in the Tongan Islands to assist her. The Little School continued growing under Joan until a new public school building and an expanded public school curriculum made a private elementary school seem redundant to most faculty families.

The most ambitious of Mrs. H.'s post-strike initiatives was to lead Putney School in the founding of a graduate school of teacher education. She plunged into this project even before the last of the union teachers had left the school. Perhaps she wanted to have the graduate school in place before a board of trustees could say no. Whether or not this is so, several developments coincided in the fall of 1949 to send her into action.

The first was the continuing national shortage of good teachers, and the paralysis that, to many commentators, appeared to have seized the teacher training schools. Even Mrs. H. acknowledged a few excellent apprentice programs, the best of these at the elementary school level. Most, however, were living off the intricate state certification requirements designed to keep incompetents out of teaching; they had tried to codify Dewey and jam him into their methods courses, and it couldn't be done; they were further constricted by the conformity expected of the education profession in times of national emergency, an expectation which most of the dwindling P.E.A. membership seemed ready to satisfy, no matter how earnest the efforts of the group's remaining internationalists.

Now a new emergency appeared: soon after being won from the Nazis, Eastern Europe had been lost to the Communists; China was also in the grip of the world conspiracy. South Korea and who knew what other free nation would soon follow? In 1949, the House Un-American Activities Committee published its pamphlet "100 Things You Should Know About Communism and Education":

> #1 *What is Communism?* A conspiracy to conquer and rule the world by any means, legal and illegal.
> #2 *Is It Aimed At Me?* Right between your eyes. . . .
> #95 *Are Communists Very Active in Teachers' Unions?* Yes. . . .

Joseph McCarthy was preparing to show how dangerous free speech and free association could be. It was safest to keep quiet and to have as few ideas as possible. The pall reached West Hill when two FBI agents attended the school's conference on Soviet-American relations in the fall of 1949, an intrusion that influenced the faculty's decision to cancel the annual conference for several years following.[12] Carmelita Hinton took the fearstruck national mood as a challenge: now more than ever, the world needed Putney School and the ideas it represented. For Putney to teach teachers would be to spread progressive concepts of schooling far and wide.

Another factor was the availability of a man of many ideas named Morris Mitchell. Edward Yeomans, Jr., head of both Shady Hill and its teacher-training program, had known Mitchell as a teacher of teachers and a visionary organizer of school-based rural cooperatives in Alabama and Georgia. He had been greatly impressed by this tenacious Southern Quaker, who had learned war as a shell-shocked First World War soldier and had lived his resistance to it ever since.[13] Mitchell had also organized study tours of underdeveloped nations, run a conventional private school in Buffalo for two unhappy years, and taught at New College, Columbia University. Now he was dairy farming in one of his Georgia cooperatives, but his family was growing. When Mrs. H. came to see Shady Hill's teacher-training program in action, the younger Yeomans suggested she contact Morris Mitchell.

She found the slow-moving, bold-thinking Morris as irresistible as some others would find him incomprehensible. She wholly agreed with him that preparing to teach "in a world of contradiction and crisis" meant more than learning pedagogical technique, however important that was. It also involved knowledge of self, of the world and its peoples, a "deep sense of the fundamental unity of mankind" no matter how fiercely divided the postwar world, and the capacity for great love.[14] Education was as much an engine for social betterment in Morris Mitchell's eyes as it had been to early political Progressives. What if such a man could bring young teachers-in-training to the Putney School and turn their enthusiasm and their accumulating skills to Putney's good? A number of Putney School faculty and trustees-to-be found promise in the idea and pledged to back the graduate school project.

A place was needed—not too near the Putney School, for it began to look as though the new Putney Graduate School of Education should ultimately be an independent entity. But not too far, either. Almost miraculously, the ideal place was offered. The two Andrews sisters, who had, with their Elm Lea tenants, welcomed Carmelita Hinton and Putney School to Elm Lea Farm in 1935, knew how long Mrs. H. had contemplated some kind of apprentice teaching program. They proposed to sell her Glen Maples, their beautiful old family home in the hills just southwest of the school. Consulting few people outside Jack Caldwell and the remaining stockholders, Mrs. H. decided to buy it. The surplus funds from 1948–49 provided a down payment. After a healthy majority of the faculty endorsed the idea of a graduate school, teachers began preparing to supervise the promised apprentices. Successful application was made to the state for the right to grant the master's degree. The first year's students, nine in all, arrived in June to begin making Glen Maples usable, and the Putney Graduate School was underway.

"What good is an independent school unless it's pioneering?" Dick Brett wanted to know.[15] By definition, pioneering is risky. The graduate school lasted fourteen years before it was absorbed by Antioch College's teacher education division. It brought problems as well as help and excitement to Putney School: at the simplest level, a continued need for loans—$2000 one year, $4000 the next, a total of $46,000 counting the Glen Maples mortgage—to tide the place over its six first years of under-enrollment. "Things look very hopeful for next year," Morris kept saying, always waiting for, but only twice getting, the sixteen students he considered ideal.[16] The study tours to the Tennessee Valley and Mexico proved expensive; so did visiting philosophers, beekeeping projects, and, most of all, marvelous candidates who could not pay tuition. While Jack Caldwell fumed, Putney's small coffers leaked money to Glen Maples, and the Administrative Council endlessly discussed the graduate school's problems and possibilities, trying to improve the return the Putney students and teachers got from Morris Mitchell's presence and the apprentice teachers' help. Putney's original loan was of course secured by Glen Maples' valuable real estate, but to give up and sell Glen Maples would be a larger failure. Such are the dilemmas of which innovative education is made.[17]

Early groups of apprentices mingled young people of daring and energy with adult-sized children who had nothing else to do. Morris Mitchell's faith and kindness supported the stronger graduate students and rescued several of the weaklings, whose number diminished as the years went on. For a majority of the graduate students, Mitchell's emphasis on experiential and international education opened unimagined territory, exploration of which proved useful through years of later teaching.[18] It was another problem to link the ten to twelve apprentices with Putney School's already complex program. Mrs. H. engaged an experienced and efficient graduate student advisor— who threw up her hands after struggling for two years to square the details of the teaching craft with Mitchell's world-sized dreams. Then Mrs. H. asked Isabel Stephens to do the job. Isabel had supervised Shady Hill and Wellesley College teaching apprentices for years, and had helped through 1935 to launch Putney School. But she was ready to quit after a single year. To her way of thinking, a neophyte teacher was hardly the best person to begin "changing the social order." Morris Mitchell "is subverting education to his own specific ends," complained Warren Leonard, usually the first to hear from those Putney teachers who could not work with a particular Glen Maples apprentice. Others agreed. At least one veteran refused to work with *any* apprentice. "Mrs. H. hasn't learned a thing from 1948–49!" exclaimed one teacher, who felt much more time was needed to build a stable group of expert teachers able to work well with novices.[19]

Yet fully half the apprentices made themselves indispensable to their master teachers. Given Mrs. H.'s enthusiasm for the graduate school, the dissenters never could find votes enough on the Administrative Council to close it. Those who had known Carmelita Hinton the longest appreciated the sincerity with which she had put her dictatorial impulses aside to work cooperatively with the council and the faculty. Such people were willing to bend to this one powerful wish of hers to retain the Putney Graduate School.

The difficulties eased as Horace Reed, the longest-tenured graduate student advisor, arrived to assist Mitchell. Reed was also a first-rate science teacher and Work Camp director for Putney School. Though still struggling for money, the graduate school trustees, already legally independent, resolved to cut financial ties with Putney School in 1956. Alternate apprenticeships were found for student teachers whom Putney could not absorb. Through the years, eight graduate students who had grown strong on Glen Maples' rich fare were hired as full-time Putney teachers after finishing their masters' theses in June. Over two-thirds of the graduate school's debt to Putney School was gradually repaid. Morris's wife, Barbara, gave volunteer help to Putney School's trip program while working as admissions secretary. Morris Mitchell himself led evening activities and sat in on Administrative Council and trustees' meetings. Putney students and campers who visited or worked at Glen Maples marveled at the ingenuity the Mitchells and the graduate students brought to their communal life: together they refurbished the old house, reconstructed the top-floor dormitory after a fire had burned it out, built and sold the strong leather-and-metal "Putney" chairs to reduce the debt, and grew much of their food in a large, carefully irrigated vegetable garden. Morris spoke his philosophy to Putney School at many Sunday meetings. Some students dozed, but a few were deeply stirred by his "gentle politics."[20]

In 1963, a group of northeastern Quakers invited Mitchell to be chief organizer and first president of the Friends World College, based in Long Island. Antioch College was eager to take Glen Maples under its graduate program, provided that its remaining $15,000 debt to Putney could be cancelled. The Antioch-Putney Graduate School promised a program very like the one almost 150 young teachers had known under Morris Mitchell: the students would spend half their year at Glen Maples studying civil rights issues and economic development in the United States, half in international travel and in apprentice teaching at Putney School and elsewhere.

Putney's trustees thought long on this proposition, then accepted it. Richard Brett's warm support of the merger was probably decisive, since he had been a central figure on the graduate school board from 1950 on. They voted away the $15,000 second mortgage, asking only that Antioch keep the graduate school going for at least five years, and reserving the right of first refusal on the property.[21] By the summer of 1964, Morris Mitchell's successor had arrived fresh from his post as Peace Corps field director in Cameroon. Morris could not have been more pleased—or several Putney School trustees more relieved.

Perhaps the graduate school's most important gift to its parent institution was its peaceful but unrelenting radicalism. Neither Morris Mitchell nor his students needed always to be right (or wrong) to help provoke discussion of issues that most Americans refused to consider during the 1950s. Before the Supreme Court had ruled on school segregation in 1954, for example, an integrated study trip including several Putney School teachers and students was already traveling through Alabama, insisting that service stations with "whites only" restrooms serve all alike or none at all. Mitchell loved Putney students' music, but he told them that "we cannot sing with true inner joy knowing 75 percent of the earth's people to be chronically hungry." To be constantly reminded of the inviolability of individual conscience and of the unity of the world's human family was, for Putney School, to be challenged with its own first principles. [22]

Such reminders were more than ever needed during the early 1950s. It was an age when Putney pollsters, organized by J. Anthony Lukas, found 87 percent of their Brattleboro interviewees hoping that Chiang Kai-Shek's troops would join the Korean war effort. Almost two-thirds wanted an invasion of mainland China. [23] Joseph McCarthy and friends had provoked fears that America's schools were molding young communists for Russia's and China's benefit. Every state without a teachers' loyalty oath left over from the 1930s hastened to require one. Vermont's State Department of Education hoped to avoid the panicky legislative battles that New Hampshire and other states were undergoing by quietly telling all school principals that their teachers must "solemnly swear" to support the Constitution and laws of the United States and Vermont, "so help me God," or face the possibility that their schools would close. A defiant school would certainly lose state accreditation and all tuition reimbursement for Vermont children attending.

By April 1954, Putney School could no longer avoid the issue. Three Quaker teachers refused to swear to anything. They and several others feared that the right to bear arms could easily become an obligation in the present national mood. No teacher who took Thoreau at his word could resist resistance to the oath. [24]

A flurry of constitution-reading finally convinced the holdouts that they could go along if they were allowed to "affirm" rather than swear allegiance. The state gladly adjusted the oath to Putney's demand and that of a handful of other schools, and the issue subsided. It had sounded like a mere word-storm, but as it blew over West Hill, it taught both teachers and students to stand against the wind when they had to.

And the wind soon rose. Putney School felt the repressions of the McCarthy era most sharply through Joan and Bill Hinton's experience as targets of virulent press criticism. Bill Hinton had compounded their shared sin of remaining in Communist China by taking notes for a book on the revolutionary transformation of Fan-shen, a north Chinese village. *Time* called him "an idealist gone wrong"; the Brattleboro *Reformer* pictured him wrapped round by the "tentacles of Communism."[25] When he returned to the United States in 1954, his notes were impounded by Senator James Eastland of the Senate Subcommittee on Internal Security, and he was grilled before the subcommittee concerning everything he knew about suspected "fellow travelers" in China, including his wife and his sister; about his own "party membership"; about J. Robert Oppenheimer, who had lent his ranch to the Hintons for a family vacation while Joan was a research assistant at Los Alamos; even about Alger Hiss and the "Pumpkin Papers."

Bill refused to answer seventy-nine questions on First and Fifth Amendments grounds, hoping to protect associates and family members from enduring what he was enduring. He answered no questions about himself—he wrote soon after—so as to defy the subcommittee's "star chamber proceedings" and to spring free of Senate investigations so that he might continue speaking all over the country about the real China, one-fourth of the world's people. But this course would also convince headline readers throughout the nation that Hinton had something sinister to hide. Wasn't he really a puppet sent back to the United States to propagandize for Red China? Didn't this show that the "fashionable and successful" Putney School that Hinton's mother had founded was suspect too? And the stakes were high: hadn't the "cruel" Chinese communist regime just proven once again its aggressiveness by attacking American planes patrolling near the southeast coast of China?[26]

Dick Brett's first response to the spate of news stories was to protect the school in his trust. In all talks with reporters, he dissociated it from Bill's and Joan's politics, and he prepared a statement defending Putney School in case of direct attack. While several trustees and teachers were spending their anger on reporters' characterization of Putney as "fashionable" or "exclusive," Brett pondered the larger accusation. He invited Bill to come see him, hoping to persuade him to lie quiet for a while. Let the world forget about both him and Putney School, he suggested during their long talk together.[27]

Bill refused. This was exactly what Senator William Jenner and his associates were trying to accomplish, he wrote Dick Brett from a lecture stop in Nevada.

What Putney has stood for is intellectual freedom and active participation in the life of the community and the nation. . . . The School has been involved in

controversial issues because it is a live, vigorous place where ideas and personalities
meet and clash. Such a place is a menace to McCarthy and all he stands for. . . .

No, I think the School must stand up boldly . . . on the whole of its 20 year
record and defend it without apologies and without equivocation. . . . It should
never retreat one inch.[28]

And Bill continued his speaking tour. His mother said nothing. Three
alumni traveled to Putney to talk with Mrs. H., intending to persuade her
publicly to establish some distance between herself and Bill. "We stayed up
most of the night," writes one of the three, "and she routed us completely.
She said that even if she disagreed with some of the things Bill said, he was
her son and she would stick by him." She had no interest in the sympathy
extended her by *Time* and the Brattleboro *Reformer*. Teachers took similar
stances. A *Life* reporter, ready for bear, arrived while Mrs. H. was away. Jack
Caldwell and Ray Goodlatte listened to his allegations concerning Bill, Joan,
and the school. "How *red* is this school anyway?" he wanted to know. "I'm a
very conservative man," Jack answered; "I wouldn't send my children to a
school such as the one you're describing." The reporters were easy for
Caldwell to handle; he had had plenty of experience fielding more challenging questions from the FBI. As a good Republican he had felt it his duty to
do so, and as a committed Putney staff member, he was equally ready to
defend the school.[29]

Such defenses were successful because they were truthful. The loudest
critics counted on Putney's principal and teachers backing down, on Putney's
parents abandoning the school. When they would not, the critics had nowhere to go. They couldn't even force a dairy farmer out of his job: Bill
Hinton worked for no one but his cows.

Though none knew it at the time, it was lucky for Putney School to have
been most fiercely attacked at the peak of Joseph McCarthy's successes, just
before his disgrace in the Senate at the hands of Army lawyers, a television
debacle that several Putney students were furious not to be allowed to
watch.[30] However well the school was protected by its isolation, it is impossible to say how it would have fared had the hysteria continued at the same
pitch. As it was, nothing that the red-baiters could deal to American schools
through the rest of the 1950s seemed to dampen Putney's self-confidence.[31]
Mrs. H. excitedly presented Norwood with a copy of *Git On Board*, a
folksong book with a hefty share of songs from the Chinese revolution, and
tried to persuade him to use it in Friday night singing. The FBI needn't have
worried, however, for Norwood saw that it combined propaganda with plain
bad music and turned it down. The list of outside speakers suggests the

breadth of community interests as well as the faculty's fearlessness: it runs from John Carter Vincent and Owen Lattimore, two of McCarthy's earliest targets, through free spirits such as I. A. Richards, Erik Erikson, Eleanor Roosevelt, and Ralph Nader (then a law student interested in federal American Indian law), to moderates like Max Lerner and Howard Mumford Jones. Instead of narrowing discussion of international issues, as the pressures of McCarthyism had subtly but inexorably done in most other American schools and colleges, the assaults on Joan and Bill Hinton provoked more consciousness of students' and teachers' need freely to speak and learn, whatever their political positions. While there is no doubt that the outcry also smudged Putney's public image for a while, the faculty's refusal to be cowed probably strengthened the school over the long haul. And four years after his Senate hearing, Bill Hinton successfully sued Senator Eastland to get his notes back and sat down to write his book.

Thus, in an age when progressive education as a movement had fractured and all but died, Putney School's persistent faith in free human discourse, courageous individual actions, and international cooperation continued to link it with the optimistic temper of early twentieth-century political progressives. As these reformers had surrounded and supported progressive pedagogy in those early days, so Putney's broad curriculum drew strength from their political assumptions. After all the years between, with their eighty million dead by war and genocide, by execution and manmade famine, perhaps only a school community could sustain such hope. Only a school is renewed each year by the hopeful young.

Similarly, only the illusion that the world can ultimately be reasonable could nurture people willing to try to make it so. Evidence suggests that most Putney students managed to grasp their own significance as evolving adults capable of acting on what they learned, just as John Dewey had thought they could and should do in a truly progressive school. A '55 graduate's summary of her Putney years conveys the conclusions of many others.

> Putney taught me the excellence of variety as well as the pleasure of achievement. Although I often felt a sense of failure while there (when papers received less than enthusiastic comment, when I didn't get my favorite part in a play, when the lights were out before I had finished something), what I feel in retrospect is the elation of learning and of victory! Over what I do not know. It is difficult to give it a name. As the years pass it will seem to have been the victory over bigotry, racism, egotism, isolationism, and ignorance.

No affirmation of Putney School's success could be more welcome than the number of educators who carried its principles forward in other settings.

Many of the more than two hundred alumni who chose careers in education did this daily, in ways both small and large. Other schools also took courage from Putney's strengths, embarking on new programs or revising old ones; this in spite of the caution that seized progressive schoolmen after the war and the general rejection of experimental curricula even by schools that had participated in the Eight Year Study.[32] In the period between 1945 and 1965, eight new coeducational boarding schools were established in New England. While each had its own special impetus and character, there could be no doubt of their indirect debt to Putney School.

The most dramatic extension of the Putney idea was the advent of four new schools founded by Putney teachers or alumni during the school's second fifteen years. The first was Colorado Rocky Mountain School, John and Anne Holden's "Putney of the West." They spent the last two of their fifteen Putney years planning it, finding a place in country rugged enough to demand allegiance to familiar ideals of physical toughness, cooperation, and individual and community self-sufficiency, then hiring teachers who would sustain a strong academic, arts, and outdoor program. By September 1953, sixteen students had arrived at the mountain ranch that was the Rocky Mountain School. There would be 125 students—a full house—when the Holdens handed it on to a successor head in 1967 and moved to new work in Woodstock School and inner-city Boston.

The next teachers to found their own school were Doris and MacNiven Conard, Putney teachers from 1954 to 1959. Though West Hill ways had been entirely outside their teaching experience, it took just a year at Putney to set Mac Conard planning. "There should be more schools like this, and I'm going to start one," he remembers thinking. The Conards' school need not match Putney's size—indeed, says Doris, "By the time we left, we felt Putney was too big for the kind of education it offered."[33] They built the Mountain School virtually from scratch on a Vermont hill farm, engaging young people of a softer era in learning and outdoor work as demanding as that which early Putney students had accomplished. They found between twenty-five and thirty-five students at a time to fill classrooms, farm, and woodlot, and to continue building the school through its twenty-year lifespan.

Putney ways also pervaded two successful elementary schools. The Putney Grammar School was founded by Dick Richardson ('40) and former Putney teacher Jerry Pfohl, with George Shumlin, to take over and take off from the Little School in 1960. Carmelita Hinton had applied the most powerful ideas she had found in elementary education to a high school. It was thus particularly heartening for her to see many of the same ideas put back to work in elementary schools. She was thrilled by the Manhattan Country School founded in 1966 by Augustus Trowbridge and his wife, Martha Dwight Trowbridge, both Putney graduates. The Trowbridges determined that a racially and economically integrated school was possible in New York City despite the dozens of failed public and private efforts to achieve such schools. Energetic help from parents and foundations has sustained a bustling school of two hundred children, over 60 percent on scholarship. About half are black or Puerto Rican children whose families, like all families, pay 10 percent of their gross income, whether that is $100 or the maximum tuition of $6500. Each year, each child travels north and lives for up to three weeks at the school's farm in the Catskills. "My school was Putney in the city," said a Manhattan graduate who had won admission to Putney School, just as virtually all his classmates had earned entrance into competitive public and private high schools. [34]

As any institution becomes known in the world outside, it is in danger of losing concentration on its own tasks. Stretched though they were, Putney faculty tried consciously to improve daily life and learning. There was a communal tightening up of project weeks, evening activities, and study schedules (successful) and, in June 1951, a three-day faculty review of curriculum (less successful, for the new teachers were fully as independent-minded as those who had left).

Carmelita Hinton was anything but quiescent as she crossed into her sixties. She initiated another festival to ornament the spring, staying up all one night to pick flowers with the secret help of several students and arranging them in May baskets for every single person or family in the school. On May day itself, students found their flowers, and walking toward breakfast, rubbed their sleepy eyes to see the flagpole become a Maypole streaming with ribbons. A few teachers were beginning to waltz, pulling the youngsters— always more conservative—into the fun. While Mrs. H. gave up her once inevitable conferences with new student couples, she was as watchful as ever. "I have a beaming light through my troubles," wrote one new tenth grader to his parents. "I have found a true friend at long, long last. Her name is _____ and she is thirteen." But

> Mrs. Hinton was very blunt the other night when we were all just about to embark on our trip to Putney Mt. "Any known Sex Relation [during the night], physical or otherwise, will be punishable by immediate expulsion of both offenders from the school." I nearly went through the floor.

Mrs. H. wrote her own letter to the boy's mother five weeks later.

The Putney School
Elm Lea Farm
Putney, Vermont

Oct. 23, 1953

Dear Mrs. _____:

Your boy is going through a period of depression because he has broken up with _____ who did not want to go with him steadily. He came to me Sunday night a week ago and was very depressed. He said he could laugh at himself but felt too sad to do it. I have had his counselor, his dorm head and [a student] all trying to help him over this spot and think he looks much better now than he did at the beginning of the week. I told him that he would have these crises more than once in his life and that he would have to pull through without his parents. Sunday night he wanted to get hold of one of you immediately.

I am hoping to get him interested in working for the Hallowe'en Party which comes October 31st. They need artists. . . .

Sincerely yours,
Carmelita Hinton[35]

Another boy was equally impressed by his quite different encounter with the director:

For our Senior Discussion course with her, Mrs. Hinton asked me to talk and reflect on my childhood experiences as a Jew in occupied Holland during the Holocaust. I wonder if she ever realized what she gave me by asking me to do this? It was for me a profoundly important opportunity to be listened to, a chance to report and express everything I had witnessed and felt, including, for the first time with any adult seriousness and honesty, my hurt and fear, disillusionment, anger and bitterness. I remember how confirming it felt to be allowed to say it all and be heard and acknowledged. But when I finished I was astonished by the impact I had had. The group was silent and Mrs. Hinton was crying silently. . . . I suddenly wondered if perhaps I had been too rough, too "realistic" for [her]. I felt guilty for hurting her or spoiling her vision.

But at dinner time that evening she came up to me once more. She looked very much o.k. again, serious and yet smiling at the same time. "Thank you for what you shared with us today," she said simply.

Again, I felt acknowledged and confirmed as a person. And I don't think I ever got around to saying: Thank *you*.

Students, after all, are a school's main business, no matter how large and pressing the world's concerns. For above all, Carmelita Hinton wanted her school to be strong for her successor. The closer she got to the moment of transition, the stronger the school appeared, and the more clearly the trustees and faculty realized they wanted a new director who would carry on Putney very much as it was. There was irony here, for Putney School had been founded by a breaker of precedents.

The search began late in 1953 with over a hundred letters sent out to educators and Putney friends all over the country. Ninety people were proposed. Thirty willing candidates were good enough to be seriously considered, most of these traveling to the school to be interviewed. They included a college professor (the former mayor of a Vermont town), a specialist in Cherokee Indian politics who had taught at both Black Mountain College and North Shore Country Day School, two former Putney teachers now doing anthropological fieldwork in India, a mine-manager-turned-elementary school teacher, an aspiring U.S. Congressman, a former college president, and several heads of progressive coeducational schools. An old progressive pioneer, principal of Cherry Lawn, could suggest no one because she thought Carmelita Hinton "nearly irreplaceable." One correspondent's solution was for Bill Hinton to replace his mother. Meanwhile, another wrote privately to Dick Brett to muse on the plethora of strong applicants, explaining it by noting what an attractive school Putney would be once freed of Mrs. Hinton and her children's leftist political associations. [36] And indeed, applications poured in from able but somewhat conventional educators, most of them heads or assistant heads of boys' schools. Several couples applied, hearing that Mrs. H. had hoped for a husband and wife as the ideal co-heads for a coeducational school. [37]

Why no women not already attached to a likely man? Dick Brett felt that a director "oriented to boys" would "strengthen Putney's appeal to boys." Many agreed, though they dared not say so. True, very few experienced women educators were available at this time: the hardy and committed generation of unmarried women who had come to maturity in the heyday of the early feminist movement was nearing retirement; almost all younger married college graduates were at home during the fifties, minding their kitchens and their volunteer work, as the feminine mystique directed. [38] Finally, there are indications that the founder knew herself (as two alumni have called her) to be "an original." She realized her job would have been easier had she been a man, and she wanted her successor to have every advantage. "I was enough to put up with," as she told the trustees in her last report to them. [39] The decision to give up early on the search for a woman director was almost certainly a practical one: the surge in student applications that followed it looked like a reward for foresight. But it was also a retreat to a school less in tension with the assumptions of its times; a more ordinary school.

It was Mrs. H. who made the final moves. After the long, outward-reaching search, both the Board of Trustees and the Administrative Council concluded that the real choice lay between two Putney teachers: assistant director Warren Leonard and H. Benson Rockwell, a history teacher since 1952, Putney's admissions director, and head of the boys' dorms. Warren was the logical successor. He had been Mrs. H.'s most essential partner since 1939, the navy lieutenant commander with the habit of cheerful command, the man best known to parents and most relied upon by new teachers learning the ropes in dormitory or classroom. He was an accomplished flutist who could show students the rewards of discipline. He had all of Mrs. H.'s energy, and the focused will to carry through, twenty-four hours a day if necessary, on the wonderful ideas she sowed for others to cultivate.[40] But a few (Al Thomas was one) had already spotted Ben Rockwell as "the shy, retiring heir-apparent" when he arrived in 1952, the "weaver of dreams" Mrs. H. had told students she wanted for the new head.[41]

Both men were spontaneously endorsed by many outsiders. Both had warmhearted and highly intelligent wives, busy with young children for now, but promising future coleadership. Letters to Mrs. H. and Dick Brett underlined the differences between the two finalists. "The best Putney teachers are devoted to Warren" and "the pupils respect [him]. . . . They go to him knowing he will get things done, and most of them like him." He was extraordinarily kind in handling their problems "without being vulgarly familiar." Each virtue had its difficulties. "As can be expected, the slovenly, half-baked faculty and staff don't like Warren, for he tries to keep them in line."

"Students love Ben," another letter said. (Mrs. H. already knew that.) "He is a kind of philosopher. . . ." He was a wonderful young teacher during his fourteen years at Pomfret, though he lost by a hair his bid to be head of that school. "Not a dynamic person," but the faculty would welcome a head who did not abruptly press new ideas on them. "Ben would take forever to get others to understand what he wanted and hoped for"; thus forward movement would be strong, even though it would seem slow.[42]

Mrs. H. rejected the seasoned administrator-mathematician and chose the "weaver of dreams," Ben Rockwell. She and Warren had worked too closely. So often had he taken up where she left off on the details of running the school that she could not see him as the visionary she wanted.[43] And like the students, she loved Ben. In spite of dissenters among both trustees and Administrative Council members, her views prevailed. When the decision for Ben Rockwell was announced in an early October Assembly in 1954, there was a shout of joy that made the windows rattle, followed by minute upon minute of happy applause. The new era could begin.

Through that last year of overlap and preparation, nostalgia mingled with a special thoughtfulness of Putney's central values. There was the usual handful of students alienated from Mrs. H. and an equal number very close to her, but the large middle group now made special efforts to know their extraordinary founding principal. At a student-only Assembly, they voted a present for her: not to smoke for the whole year. If a few addicts could not carry through, they made sure she didn't know of it. December's Christmas party at Hinton House seemed a more jubilant occasion than ever, except for one crisis at the living room doorway. Several Hinton house girls thought it would be jolly to wear lipstick. Mrs. H. walked up to greet them, stopped, and burst into tears. They fled like terrified animals to their rooms to wipe it off.[44]

Instead of wandering the hills on their April birthday holiday, every student in school turned out to help arrange a surprise birthday party for Mrs. H. They set the luncheon tables in an H formation on the KDU terrace and greeted her with flowers and song as, astonished, she bicycled up to lunch.[45] To the beauties of Vermont's late spring were added a multitude of faculty-staff parties and other acts of appreciation and love.

"I hate to leave," Carmelita Hinton told a *Time* reporter, "but I have so many things before me that I'm boiling over."[46] How much better to retire at a mere sixty-five, full of strength and health for new adventures, than to hang on too long! For a year she stayed in her house, overseeing the agreement carefully worked out with the trustees on the transfer of some of her real estate (including the Lower Farm) and the rental of the rest. She enjoyed her American grandchildren (though most were in China), bringing one along on the school's yearly ski trip to Stowe. Some felt she was watching Ben. "Can't you get her out of her *house*?" a wrought-up teacher asked of one trustee. She soon got herself out and away on a study tour to Africa and India in a Volkswagen bus, arranged by Morris and Barbara Mitchell.[47]

Twenty-two years of active work remained to Mrs. H. before declining health would begin to limit the sweep of her affairs. Her travels in 1957 convinced her that world peace was the prerequisite to solving all other world problems. Therefore, she went to Philadelphia and walked into the national offices of the Women's International League for Peace and Freedom to ask if she might help. The league needed a chairman for its educational contacts committee; soon it also needed a top organizer for the centennial celebration of its founder, Jane Addams. Mrs. H. settled into both jobs with a will, happy to be helping to tell the world about her old friend and mentor who had accomplished so much for the poor and the powerless, whose very face held "all the sorrows of others' experiences" while her mind sought the causes and cures for these sorrows.[48]

Mrs. H.'s next move was to buy a farm not far from Philadelphia, a home base from which she struck out to learn and to teach for the next two decades. Her forays included a host of peace education meetings and rallies. At one of the latter she broke her hip while walking backward counting marchers, but the injury slowed her hardly at all. She longed to go to China to see her daughter Joan, but she could not get State Department permission, so in 1961 she simply went, getting to know her grandchildren and their adopted country. When U.S.-Chinese contacts began again in 1971, she got her confiscated passport back and accepted an invitation from Chou En-Lai to bring fifteen young people, including her American grandchildren, to the People's Republic. For the best part of a year they toured China, worked in its farms and factories, and, not least, came to know one extraordinary octogenarian. [49]

Though Carmelita Hinton kept in touch with many one-time Putney students and teachers and attended almost every Putney School trustees' meeting for twenty-five years after her retirement, neither the Pennsylvania farmhouse she shared with her son Bill nor her Cape Breton and Massachusetts homes, shared with Jean, held a single relic of her Putney School years. [50] Probably she needed none: her school had been her life, and it was impossible that she should ever be entirely apart from it. Nor did Putney School now need her to survive. Pushed by both friends and antagonists, she had made an institution that could run free of its founder.

Chapter 11

Turning Points

The Board of Trustees and the Administrative Council chose Benson Rockwell because they wanted Putney School to carry on as it was. There was no one more committed to Carmelita Hinton's Putney than Ben and Barbara Rockwell. Though their birthright had been an easy, affluent life, and though Ben's whole professional experience before Putney was fourteen years of teaching at his own prep school, they were ready to put all more conventional life chances behind them.[1] For many years, Ben had been working out his own concept of the ideal education. To come to Putney, many of whose goals coincided with his, was to bring his ideals to life. The Rockwells took on the job with the energy of the truly convinced.

It was a quiet sort of energy, for both were quiet people. Ben had read and reread William James and John Dewey. While he also read the Bible and saw Putney's basic ideas as primarily religious ones, he believed with James and Mrs. H. that "truth . . . is made true by events."[2] An adult's responsibility to children is to arrange the daily events of their lives so as to maximize their wholesome experiences. For all his firmness with students, Ben could rarely bring himself to dictate to them or to anyone. Both Rockwells felt certain that one teaches less by telling than by living, just as one learns through one's whole self so that each small thing learned changes all things. Mrs. H. agreed with the principle, but could not have assumed the style if she had wanted to. Deeply admiring Ben's integrity, she nevertheless felt he was modest to a fault.[3] Thus, in certain ways, Putney School would have to change. Gone was the clamor that the founder carried about her, gone. the vivid attachments and antagonisms she engendered. Putney School would never again paint itself in primary colors.

In other ways, however, the Rockwells' leadership freed the school to be more itself than ever. To care as deeply as Ben did about the sanctity of personality was to allow individuality, whether in teachers or students, to flourish, which was exactly what Mrs. H. had been aiming for. Often she got it, but not because she tolerated fundamental questioning of her values. Now Putney School was strong enough to be governed with a lighter hand, and one of Ben Rockwell's favorite words was tolerance. Under the continuing, rigorous daily and yearly schedule, under Rockwell's unbending stance on Putney's utopian expectations concerning health and work and community, was a passionate appreciation of alternate ways of being. Thus the classic utopian dilemma—the conflict between community needs or ambitions and those of individuals—would be more perplexing than ever in Benson Rockwell's Putney School.

Ben would spend hours in searching talk with a contrary student or teacher, whether or not he could finally approve.[4] Ben trusted, at least through the mid-1960s, that such rebels would eventually fashion lives he *could* approve, given the tools offered at Putney School. Whether awkwardly or eloquently, he spoke again and again of "the miraculous potential and importance of every single person in the world." He noticed things about almost every student and expressed his pleasure or his concern to each, often teasing (and delighting) those who knew themselves tough enough to take it. "Infinite time spent with faculty and students—that's what held the whole together," says Ben's wife, Barbara. Several other Putney adults use almost exactly the same words.[5]

There was also in Ben an apparently infinite fund of humor. To show both his disapproval and his appreciation of students, he sometimes teased the whole school. A '59 alumna recalls one notable piece of deadpan.

> Until one Harvest Festival, Ben's reserve and quiet watchfulness had always made me a bit uneasy. That fall . . . he had promulgated a "law" that there was to be no more do-it-yourself ear piercing. Mary Scherbatskoy appeared the following morning with a lovely gold ring through one nostril. Perhaps a week later, Ben answered her defiance by marching in the Harvest Festival parade in a black cape and stovepipe hat, with an enormous gadget attached to *his* nostril.[6]

Time and again, Ben's weekly Assembly talks gave way to faculty skits on every topic from packing for the long spring camping trips (dress shoes, electric razors, unabridged dictionaries) to announcing the fire code (Ben read it from a roll of toilet paper—only that was long enough). Ben knew that there are days when teachers must either laugh or give up.

Ben's ways had evolved over years of experience quite different from that of his predecessor, even while the Rockwells' every move seemed to nudge them closer to Putney School. They first came to the school in 1952, Ben as history teacher and admissions director, Barbara as mother of four small children and a ready architect who would help the school with many problems of material design. These were not their first jobs on West Hill, however. Barbara had been born in Vermont. Her family warmly supported her choice of a new and unconventional Vermont college: Bennington. There she met Jean Hinton. She had been quickly drawn to the Hinton family idea of education, different though it was from the schooling she had known before Bennington. Restless at Pomfret School and wanting to look at alternative modes of learning, the Rockwells decided to spend a summer at the Putney Work Camp. Ben worked in the woods under Charlie Gray. Barbara reported to Mabel Gray. "O.K.," said Mabel that first day, "your student crew is going to make twenty dozen toll house cookies by lunch time." It was an ideal way for a Princeton man and his wife to get to know the Putney way of life. They did their best to bring it back to Pomfret, where Ben initiated a work program and became assistant headmaster. Pomfret was the richer for their efforts, according to several who knew them there.[7]

Nevertheless, by 1951, Ben's quest for change seemed blocked. That year he lost his bid for the Pomfret headmastership. To come back to Putney after a year's graduate study at Harvard, with the possibility of becoming Putney's director, was more than consolation.

Ben felt ready to "make Carmelita Hinton's ideas work," as he had promised the search committee he would try to do.[8] The week his new job began, he started picking up some threads that had loosened a bit while Mrs. H. concentrated on other affairs both daily and visionary. Through his open office door walked students, teachers, and parents who had worries or inspirations they had not shared with Mrs. H. He listened to students bucking required Friday night singing, and he told them he would try out their complaints. He sang every Friday himself for a year before emphatically deciding that the requirement should remain, and he kept on singing (gladly if never very well) in years to follow to show his support for both Norwood Hinkle and his music. He heard a physician-father's assessment of gaps in the monitoring of student health and began his routine of visiting the infirmary every day to see who had come in, how they were doing, who should be watched and pampered a bit, whether in the infirmary or not.[9] A flu epidemic that flattened 120 students soon put his improvements to the test. They passed.

Ben and Barbara together made good on many of Mrs. H.'s aspirations for strong town-school connections. As one student put it, "Some of the antipathy is their fault, but most of it is ours."[10] With the Mitchells, Grays, and others, they supported the local public school with both their youngest child's presence and their own work. Barbara helped plan the move to the new school building and won a seat on the school committee in 1958, the year the school opened. The Rockwell's example inspired others to similar actions, including students who went in increasing numbers to tutor needy children or to teach skiing or crafts. Though changes in Vermont village culture (and television in Vermont homes) had eliminated some of the festivals and dances that town and school had once shared, the Community Council opened school square dances to the town's young people, adding these to the concerts, conferences, and plays to which they had always been invited. Some even came.

At the same time, those far-flung Putney vacation trips that had been given over to the Experiment came back under Putney School sponsorship. Though they would never involve so many students as they had before World War II, trips such as those to Italy, Alaska, Puerto Rico, the Soviet Union, and Japan brought far places closer in the persons of the teachers who led them and the few students who went along. As in the past, each trip was usually preceded by weeks or months of introduction to the language and culture, in a special evening activity if not in a language class. Cape Breton trips also continued until 1963. In the last summer of these, George Carow, a gifted math teacher, and his wife, Elizabeth, found private funds to bring eleven inner-city children and five Putney student counselors to Cape Breton's wilds.[11]

Ben had a poet-philosopher's love of the outdoors, Barbara a special way with animals large and small. "Ben is the sort of man," said Ray Goodlatte, "who secretly feels honored when a deer enters his garden."[12] One of the Rockwells' first decisions was to send every person in the school out on foot, horseback, or bicycle for a fall camping weekend in the countryside around West Hill. One group walked to the Connecticut River and climbed into the school's canoes; another bicycled eighty hilly miles in two days. More than any Putney School adventure, Ben loved the long spring weekend. One of these dawned in sheets of rain. An angry student confronted Ben at the bell while others climbed into the trucks, their ponchos streaming. "This is insane," he shouted to Ben. "We're going," answered Ben. "*I'm* not going," said the boy. "You're right," said Ben, "you're not going. You're suspended for four days till we get back."[13] The boy, amazed, went home. The sun came out that afternoon.

The Rockwells' prep school sports became something new and wonderful

at Putney School. Barbara revived a riding program that had been languish-
ing ever since 1953, making it easy and cheap for those not owners of horses
to join in. Ben introduced ice hockey—or rather, rink maintenance for the
ever-hopeful, with a bit of hockey on the side. For some, ice hockey served
as a dignified escape from skiing. So did winter camping. Ben knew that
student ski teachers had become more demanding than ever since Johnny
Caldwell's return to Putney in 1953.

   Johnny brought life and rigor to the entire sports program, and the whole
Rockwell family joined in. Johnny was an Olympic Nordic skier. Within
twenty-five years, four of his students (including Martha Rockwell) would be
Olympic skiers also; seven more achieved national team ranking. The cham-
pions helped to build the thirty-five miles of trails on which they trained.
Putney School became one of a handful of cross-country racing centers in
the East—all on a total yearly sports budget of less than $24 per student,
counting field maintenance and coaching salaries. This was less than half
what conventional boys' prep schools spent on equipment, referees, transportation, and office costs alone.[14] Though Putney was reaping some criticism
for having become a "man's place," it was Ben who coached the girls' hockey
team when he first arrived, Ben who found a superb successor coach and
quiet woman leader in Elizabeth Mills, Ben who made certain that the girls'
ski team was revived (it won the Prep School, State, and Eastern meets in
1957). Ben even allowed the girls to use the school's 25-meter ski jump,
though they could find no other jumping girls to compete against. He was
Johnny Caldwell's strongest supporter, as well as the man to make sure
Putney did not become the captive of its athletic successes.

   Ben kept Mrs. H.'s yearly drop holiday, but he dropped it in unexpected
places through the year. One April 18, he pulled some clothes out of a
family costume chest just after breakfast, mounted the Rockwells' chestnut
mare, and galloped up the school driveway past the old boys' dorm and the
White Cottage shouting "The British are coming! The British are coming!"
Students streamed out from their rooms and moved toward the main building. Ben and horse rounded the old girls' dorm and clip-clopped into the
assembly hall. Then, pushing aside the academic pressures of the season, he
forbade study. "Go out and *get lost!!*" he told 180 jubilant listeners.[15]

   Both Rockwells worried that the farm was becoming distant from the
school. They renewed Mrs. H.'s custom by holding Farm Association meetings at their house, and before long over a third of the students were members. Ben arranged for Larry Titus to take two consecutive morning assem-

blies in the cow barn. When the increasing press of academic work discouraged students from signing up for morning barn chores, Ben began assigning six weeks on the barn crew to every student who could walk.

Ben also did his best to maintain the founder's scrutiny of sexual activity, though he was less successful here. He could lecture in Assembly about how "exclusive relationships" undermine inclusive community; he could convey his belief that sex outside marriage was as wrong as married sex was good— but, say his former students, this was one thing he was too shy to talk of easily to the real, live individuals he often summoned to his office. His own clear views could not dispel the fogs that surrounded the issue in daily life. By comparison, smoking and drinking problems were a relief. Unlike Mrs. H., Ben often submitted health issues to community decisionmaking processes, and great were the wrangles that eloquent adolescents could weave. The air cleared in 1964 when the surgeon general's report came out. Ben got up in Assembly and announced the smoking policy for the following year. Seniors would be free to smoke given their physician's O.K., their parents' agreement, and Ben's permission—but Ben would give no permissions whatsoever.

The groans were brief because the discussion through the years previous had been so long. Perhaps Ben's chief strength was in his building (from the bottom up) a community of deciders. It's true that some decided on rebellion, and perhaps it was lucky for them that Ben's immovability on a few basic Putney ways gave them the causes that rebels require. Rebels found Ben exasperating. It was in his nature to care as much about how as about what. Mrs. H. knew her goals and fought for them. But the more Ben felt others pressing for change, the more he slowed down and talked of procedures, looking always for moral means toward worthy ends. When he couldn't find such means, the worthy ends joined his many "questions that have no answer."[16] This was a commitment to democracy far more profound and complex than that of most progressive educators. It expressed itself in respect for student leaders, whom Ben, like Mrs. H., saw as partners with the faculty and staff in the running of the school. He also took seriously the student-citizens who loudly contested his views in the school's town meetings. He urged more and more student participation in the committees that oversaw everything from curricular offerings to the school store. Students soon sat in on Administrative Council and trustees' meetings. A 1960s visitor recorded that the only phrase more frequently heard around school than "Ben said" was "I said to Ben."[17] Unlike Mrs. H., Ben welcomed the repeated rewritings of the school constitution. "It's another chance for people to find out who they are," he said.[18]

To some extent, Ben's democratic commitments were at war with his conviction that the young are vulnerable and need direction. The contradiction could be confusing even to those who most admired him. Insofar as synthesis could be found, it lay in his gentleness and his willingness to talk, gently, about almost anything.[19]

And so, many people loved Ben. Students remember him on a Sunday morning standing outside the old boys' dorm looking mournfully at a scattering of soda cans and crumpled papers that had accumulated through a Saturday evening's relaxation. He wouldn't say anything or pick up anything, but soon after he'd walked on, the litter was gone, just as surely as if Mrs. H. had swept several passing students into her orbit to help her clear the ground. "He was like a father," say several alumni (and three teachers who were also young in the 1950s). "We knew how much he cared about us, so we'd do what he wanted us to do just because he wanted it."[20] His kindness, his presence everywhere on West Hill, walking about with his lighted pipe in his pocket (after he had forbidden student smoking he set it in his mouth only when he was talking to an adult), the sure knowledge that one could find him any time of the day or night if the need for him was real—these were reassurances that gradually bound most students (though never all) both to Ben Rockwell and to Putney ways. Only late in Ben's fourteen-year tenure did any number of Putney's young grow too contrary for such a man to reach.

The "infinite time" and patience that Ben gave Putney's people had other consequences. Decisions often appeared to take infinite time, too; essential administrative acts lay undone while Ben talked with a troubled child or a colleague.[21] Issues close at hand were much more real to him than the money that needed raising to insure the future of the school or even the teacher who must be found to fill a coming vacancy. There are a dozen stories of aspiring teachers who wrote or visited Ben and heard nothing back until, say a year later: Ben Rockwell on the phone, asking "Are you still interested in teaching math at Putney School?" A husband and wife who had applied to teach cello and dance thought their interview had gone well, but they waited in vain for the letter that would tell them how well. In late August they called to ask, "Shall we come?" "Well yes, I guess you'd better," said the person holding down the summer switchboard. They had to hitchhike from New York City on Labor Day weekend, expecting who knew what. Ben was delighted to see them and show them to the dormitory quarters all prepared for their arrival. They were delighted to stay and surprised at their good fortune, unlike Ben, who seemed to have known all along that they would eventually show up. [22]

More serious, perhaps, was Ben's reluctance to evaluate teachers already long at Putney School. It was not just that Ben found good in everyone. It was a simple habit of putting off the hardest decisions a school head must make. Under Putney's faculty tenure system, if the evaluative moment was delayed long enough, tenure was automatic. Ben was often a skillful counselor of younger teachers. But as ever more teachers stayed the requisite five years, his reluctance to say a final goodbye to the few limp ones meant soft spots in the academic curriculum and probably weakened the program as a whole. [23] Similarly, the school's expensive abandonment of the summer Work Camp in 1962 was as much a result of Ben's refusal to tangle with its current director as it was of the camp's enrollment problems. The natural sciences camp that he and the Administrative Council designed to take its place was a gem, but too tiny a gem to repay summer running costs for the school. [24]

Part of the problem was the size of Ben's job. Warren Leonard stayed a year to help Ben get started but then moved on to be headmaster of the Storm King boys school. After that there was no Warren Leonard to do a large fraction of the things a principal must do. Ben found Lovat Cooper-Ellis, a gifted Pomfret colleague, at work as a Harvard admissions officer; he brought him in to assume Warren's college counseling role and put Charles Brickley in charge of the academic program. But the many hidden tasks that Warren had accomplished for Mrs. H. now fell to Ben. While he was a wonderful support to colleagues in their jobs, his powerful sense of responsibility prevented his delegating any of his own jobs to others. Once he had assumed the authority of the director, friends noticed in Ben a lonely seriousness never quite dispelled by the humor and love for others that still bubbled to the surface from deep-moving springs within. "Come on in and have a beer," called Joe Schaaf out the window of his dormitory apartment as Ben walked by one Saturday soon after he had become Director. "Oh Joe, I'd love to but I can't," said Ben, walking up to Joe's window. "Lots of work today?" asked Joe. "Not so much—it's just that I can't do those things any more." Continued close friendships might be seen as favoritism, Ben thought, or still more important, might narrow his perceptions of the school as a whole. No one could really share his authority, not even Barbara, though she and Ben did talk over many school problems together. Quite suddenly, and largely because of his own definitions of a head's obligations, he had taken on more than any single person could do. The air of sadness that seemed to gather about Ben is recalled the more poignantly by all those who loved him because he died at age fifty-nine of congestive heart failure, only five years after leaving Putney in 1969. To some, it seems that he was spending himself on Putney School—on them—and that the toll unwittingly exacted had simply been too high for one good man to bear.[25]

Fortunately, teachers often sought out Putney rather than waiting for Ben to seek them, and stayed and grew in strength. Fortunately, money came in too, including $100,000 that arrived unasked for soon after Ben assumed the directorship in 1955. It was a vote of confidence in Putney School, given all but anonymously by Benjamin and Helen Buttenweiser in memory of Carol, the oldest of their three Putney children. Fortunately, Ben would eventually do most of what needed doing, and do it well. "Once he'd finally made them, his decisions were usually right," says Ruth Hodgdon for many.[26]

The faculty and staff welcomed first and most the decisions Ben made concerning the conditions of their lives. Through his first months as director, he spoke to every adult on West Hill, asking where Putney should go and what they needed to help get it there. He was distressed by the disparities in salaries and housing conditions that had persisted despite the many improvements made since 1949. The Rockwell family might still be cooking in the bathroom of the old farmhouse they had bought, but this was their choice, and a temporary condition. Older teachers spoke of their straitened circumstances with resignation: it was the Putney way of life. Ben, usually slow to anger, was outraged.

Backed by the trustees and encouraged by the Administrative Council, he went to work on inequities.[27] The lower salaries were brought into line with those of most other independent schools. Walls came down between tiny dorm counselors' rooms and the spaces next door; bathrooms were put in. Mrs. H. had shooed faculty and their families away every summer, insisting that a change of place would refresh tired teachers (and free their houses or apartments for the summer's Work Camp counselors). Ben announced that school living quarters were homes and that no one would ever be cleared out of them for the camp's sake. He used much of the Buttenweiser gift to make such changes possible. "So this is what a principal does!" thought one old-timer who had never taught under any principal but Carmelita Hinton.[28]

The small renovation projects showed that student labor, carefully supervised, could still be made useful. Over the next ten years, students and adults working under Barbara Rockwell's leadership prepared building specifications for three comfortable faculty apartments with dormitories attached, two designs being executed by Putney friends (alumnus John Rogers and parent Eliot Noyes) as gifts to the school, the other by Barbara herself. Student crews accomplished over half the work on two of the new dorms—beginning, for Rogers Dorm, with felling and sawing the lumber—and on the additions to the art studio and library also built by 1965.

Ben Rockwell did much more than improve on the material gains made since 1949. Almost universally, Putney's adults were glad to work with him and admired his embrace of simplicity (knowing he was anything but simple himself) in his own life as he responded to their complex needs. "Ben was a revelation to me," wrote Maurice Leconte, a French teacher to whom "Putney's educational culture was as far remote from the education [he had] received as Chinese tradition is from American modernism. . . . Ben's sense of fairness, his concern for the welfare of all" were vital ingredients in the radical changes Putney brought to both Lecontes' lives.[29] All faculty were deeply grateful for Ben's courage in holding the line against restive students. Because Ben wore a tie all the time, they could leave theirs in their closets if they wished. Putney adults understood better than most how complicated were some of the decisions Ben pondered at such length. They loved him because he allowed them to be their best selves.[30]

And nothing is so important in a school as that. If Ben faltered in hiring new teachers and in firing the few weaker ones, the energy he gave to supporting the present adult community was crucial to Putney School's overall success. The decisionmaking structures that had come out of the year of the strike already conferred far more authority on teachers than teachers usually have. Ben's sensitive implementation of Mrs. H.'s belief in academic freedom maintained Putney's traditional teacher autonomy and the self-respect that can go with it.[31]

Autonomy certainly flowered in faculty meeting. Often it seemed that Putney School was the only thing these teachers had in common. Only 15 percent had gone to private schools themselves, for example. They came in eight nationalities and all ages. Argument was friendly now, but hot. Sometimes Norwood found he could take no more, and would get up and walk out; a neophyte history teacher remembers his astonishment as Norwood climbed right up on and over the refreshment table that was in his path to head for the door. (No one else blinked.) So many votes divided down the middle that Ben took to deciding many issues himself after thorough soundings of faculty opinion. In this situation, Ben's good humor was a crucial bond. The best faculty skits were saved for the jolly faculty-staff gatherings that now closed each school year. Ben was a major actor in all except those designed to make sport of *him*.

During Ben's first year, he and his teaching colleagues decided on a thorough review of curriculum, aiming "to raise standards without eliminating experiment and risk-taking."[32] Remembering past failures, they took care to organize it this time by departments. Some leavening was sorely needed here, for teachers knew the stakes. Ben was responding in part to parents' anxieties. The critics felt it was past time for Putney to have recovered from the curricular disruptions inevitable in the years after the strike. In addition, new, respected school accreditation associations had been asked to evaluate Putney School, as they are invited to evaluate any institution aspiring to endure. After each department had labored for a while, a young English teacher named Alfred Heller (Putney, '46) provided the humor in the form of "Departmental Reports to the faculty." Heller's English teachers agreed that only through English study "can one develop one's awareness, one's thoroughness . . . and one's oneness," that a major function of class discussion is "slyly [to] undermine the science department . . . that grammar is something none of us know and all of us teach." The next report described art as a "life urge. It starts at the toes and works out to the hands. Thus finger painting. . . ." The Putney math department promised to "teach algebra, but not too carefully"; the drama teachers ranted over their second-class status and pledged to fill every hour of the day for "everyone who is not in music." Music was "out for rehearsal": too busy to report to anyone.

But seriously, an overhaul seemed overdue. Putney's academic isolation had been breached by new pressures from outside the school. Mrs. H. had just finished reassuring the trustees in 1955 that "college requirements have softened remarkably and do not hamper us at all now," when colleges began rejecting students who should have been sure bets. This was happening all over the country as newly affluent families began swelling the percentage of college matriculants: their number would double between 1954 and 1964.[33] Further pressure came from the national humiliation engendered by the Soviet launching of *Sputnik I* in 1957 as well as from campaigners for academic rigor such as James Conant and Arthur Bestor.[34] In these pressures, Putney teachers, particularly those in languages and mathematics and science, saw opportunity to engage the attention of those students to whom Putney academic work had long been secondary.

Throughout his fourteen-year tenure, Ben Rockwell continued to press both for a stronger traditional curriculum and for academic innovation. For imaginative faculty ready to grow, Putney's habitual academic freedom, especially as it combined with the revived concern for academic discipline, was an invaluable gift. "Pat and I became teachers" at Putney School, Leconte writes. Invention flourished in many studios and classrooms, a creativity that was only enriched by the responses of an able and attentive group of students, for applications had more than recovered their pre-strike level. Teachers speak of the first eight Rockwell years as of a kind of golden age, not unlike the heady pioneering years of the 1930s school.

While the largest changes took place in math and the sciences, it is a measure of Putney's continued orneriness that the expansion of the arts program was equally notable. Two history scholars made it happen: Ben Rockwell and director of studies Charlie Brickley. Ben and Charlie knew that most Americans considered the arts a mere luxury. As the general public clamored for the three Rs, they arranged new daytime courses in the international languages of music, dance, and the visual arts,[35] and found strong teachers to staff them. Soon music had more competition than ever during project week, especially as theatre and sculpture teachers joined forces in designing the extraordinary sets that characterized some 1960s productions. Alumni remember with delight the day that Norwood stormed out of a specially scheduled rehearsal to pluck one of his best tenors from the boy's regular conference in the sculpture studio. Norwood was amazed when Robin Campbell refused to let the tenor go. It was exciting for students to know themselves so much wanted, exciting for everyone, including the Hinkles, to watch all the arts growing strong at Putney while most conventional schools pushed the more conventional disciplines and stood bewildered by the artistic enthusiasms of the sixties.[36]

The major contributors to the more intensive math and science curricula were a group of committed teachers brought in by both Mrs. H. and Ben from 1952 on. First-rate individual teachers had not before this dispelled the general mediocrity of the program, which had never fully recovered from wartime departures. There were exactly three science teachers in 1952–53, only two of them full time, compared with three full-time equivalents for a school 25 percent smaller in 1941.[37] If a student drew the wrong teacher, "science was inexcusable" as late as the mid-fifties: so says one who was talented in arts but anxious for a broad education. Several other alumni agree with her. "Ben hired our biology teacher the day before school opened," she goes on. "We had no microscopes. Phyla were unheard of. We dissected one worm. It was so easy that I started planning to be a doctor."[38]

Putney graduates Mary Bartlett and Anne Volkmann had been bright spots in a dim life-sciences picture during and after the strike year. Arriving in 1958, Robert Mills began to change Putney biology for good. He tied its systematic study to a broad land-use curriculum that many students pursued in work job, evening activity, and project time as well as in class. As other able teachers joined him, some of the gaps between farm and classroom closed. The seventy-acre Garland Pond Wildlife Preserve, an arboretum, and a hundred acres of tree plantations became laboratories for student projects, much as school lands had been under Olwen Williams. This was no coincidence, for Olwen had been Bob Mills's teacher at the University of Colorado graduate school, as she was to two other skillful life-science teachers who shortly joined Bob at Putney. A greenhouse and animal house for nondairy farm animals would be added to buck the "increasing encroachments" of commercial recreation and urban values on southern Vermont, now evident on every hand. (The Holiday Barn Boutique was moving into one of the finest farmsteads in north Brattleboro, while light industry claimed its hay meadows.) As under Bartlett and Volkmann, at least half of every biology course was again lab time, closely supervised; Mills made sure that Putney was one of the first few schools to test the teaching techniques that came out of the Biological Science Curriculum Study Committee and to receive lab equipment for the tests from the National Science Foundation.[39]

All of the new introductory physical science course was lab time. Edward Shore had come from college physics teaching to Putney in 1953, wondering what country living and bright high school students were like. He found both exciting. His interest continued because he was constantly rebuilding science courses, backed by the federally supported Physical Science Study Committee (PSSC), of which he was an original and continuing member. Ed had been brought into this small group by Malcolm Smith, who had taught physics at Putney from 1952 to 1956 before becoming a major figure among the university and secondary teachers gathered at MIT to recast the teaching of physical sciences. Before long, Ed was chief organizer for the experimental courses themselves. Thus Putney students were among the first guinea pigs for the three PSSC physics-chemistry courses, at least one of which would be taken by more than half of all American high school science students by the close of the sixties.

Ed's summer work often included the teaching of teachers. Encouraged by Ben Rockwell, he (like George Carow and several others) would introduce courses such as Advanced Placement calculus, then help mathematics colleagues take it over. Though there were few AP courses as such, several

Putney students took the exams each year. Thus Putney added its bit to national AP enrollments in the colleges, which rose sharply between 1949 and 1961. The collegiality among teachers brought coherence to the math-science curriculum as well as many opportunities for adult self-education. About half the Rockwell-era alumni who have described their Putney experiences volunteer their appreciation of what these adults offered. With his photography lab and homemade physics equipment, Ed Shore joined other math-science teachers in reversing the "snobbery about technical pursuits" that had disheartened a number of engineering buffs in the 1940s and made others into delightful eccentrics floating on the margins of the usual student hierarchies.[40] Along with several shorter-tenured women, the newer math-science teachers successfully taught advanced physics-chemistry and math to a significant proportion of Putney girls for the first time since the 1930s. Indeed, the basic principles involved in the "new" science, as in much of the "new math," were those on which early teachers like Daniel Morris and Eric Rogers had built their inventive teaching twenty years before.

All this did not mean a perfect math-science program. Occasional lemon teachers continued to come and go. One ebullient and admirable young man "made eleventh-grade math the end of my math career," recalls an alumnus. "He'd glance at a problem in the book and say, 'Let's make this a little more interesting.' He'd continue making it more and more interesting until he couldn't solve it. Then John R. and Dave G. would come out of the *New York Times* crossword puzzle long enough to solve it for him." Nevertheless, the general improvement in math and sciences was striking.[41]

As with the physical sciences, the boost to modern languages came both from individual teachers and from a new national focus on language teaching. Ben Rockwell added his own quiet concern with international affairs. The assembly of a small language laboratory signaled the final commitment to the oral-aural teaching that had always been used by Putney's best language teachers.[42] Thus, in spite of teachers' continued freedom, the quality of language teaching became more uniform, along with its materials. Language tables and language clubs thrived once more. Graduates found that Putney's language training easily satisfied college language requirements.

There was nothing uniform about the English department, ever, nor is there any agreement about its effectiveness. Its longest tenured members had no wish to cramp each others' style: if one's own language is one's most personal possession, then its mastery may indeed be—as several felt it was—a function of personal growth. "I feel, therefore I am!" scoffed one faculty wag. Yet there were other English teachers like Lovat Cooper-Ellis who felt free to disagree with this approach, and they are as warmly remembered as are the "role models for eccentricity" in which the department seemed to specialize.[43] Close, challenging reading went on in almost every classroom. Ray Goodlatte and Jeff Campbell picked their favorite texts early in their Putney careers and changed them little, giving each year's innovative energies to each year's unique young minds. Many students loved Ray and Jeff for the intellectual respect these men granted them and the hours and hours they took with individuals to show it. Students, especially if they already knew their grammar, reveled in the reading of complex literature that Ray encouraged or in Jeff's large ideas, his booming voice, and the kindly encouragement he gave them to construe themselves with equal boldness. "The teaching was much better than anything I'd known," writes a Swiss student. "We were taught to understand rather than to memorize." But a large minority felt disappointed in their English teachers. While reading and journal writing were often delightful, they say, the craft of writing was barely taught at all. They were building on sand. "If you can't write a sentence, try a paragraph! If you can't write a paragraph, try a whole essay! Or a term paper!"[44]

It was possible for the same students to move through one or more history courses in the same vacuum of usable skills; individual alumni are still bitter about all they think they missed, perhaps because they had such high expectations of the colorful Putney adults who were supposed to teach them spelling and paragraphing and note-taking. As in English, however, the demanding wordsmith some most needed might well teach next door to the seeker of overarching intuitions, or the two might be found in a single adult. In history, moreover, one could more often choose one's courses, and therefore one's teacher. Though neophyte teachers sometimes went unsupervised, there was a close, conscious effort to coordinate the teaching of writing and research skills and to engage the changing issues of the times. Mrs. H.'s powerful interest in China had first nudged non-Western history into the curriculum, and under Ben Rockwell these offerings were gradually expanded. Putney had company here: independent schools such as Exeter and Westtown also introduced Chinese and Japanese history, even though students could not take College Board exams in such subjects. Economics became regular fare in Charlie Brickley's European civilization sequence. Charlie also gave to the communist movements a close, dispassionate attention that was rare in private schools during the fifties and would have been unacceptable in virtually all public schools. One boy's journal opens a window on Brickley's senior history classes, and shows how Putney pushed (or failed to push) the bright, reluctant student.

> Today Charlie Brickley spoke to me in reference to the work I have been doing (?) all year. And also about the talk I gave (?) last week.
> We each were given a [choice of two] topics and ten minutes to prepare it. . . . (There was a little bad luck involved, I did know a little *something*.) I decided to take a chance, and so I talked on my second subject. This didn't bother me too much; I hoped that Charlie wouldn't notice it or that he would not say anything right away if he did. I stammered along and did the worst in the class. I had nearly no idea of what I was talking about and filled it with "covering" phrases.
> Charlie later told me that this was typical of myself and that my attempted effort at the beginning of the term had petered out. He said that this was the way of all my intentions and that that was the way it had been all along. . . . Charlie said that I could and should be at the top but that I am at the bottom.
> He is entirely correct.
> He said that someone should have screwed me to the wall last year in the hope that it would have done me some good. But they didn't. They just said, "You'll do better next year."
> Charlie hit me in the face with the realization that I am behind. . . . I really have to go. To get somewhere instead of drifting along on a smile.[45]

Hester Caldwell, like her husband drawing on her own student experience of such teachers as Norwood Hinkle and Anne Holden, also brought the gift of high expectations to her history students. In Hester, Johnny, and over a dozen shorter-term teachers, Mrs. H.'s original hope that many Putney teachers would be Putney graduates was partially fulfilled. History teachers were a restless lot; thus the department often had openings for one- or two-year teachers who came with a passion for, say, Yugoslavian culture or nuclear disarmament and organized exciting evening activities (or even Brattleboro peace marches) around their interests.

The History and English departments had no corner on political radicals. Roger Franklin, a Glen Maples–trained math teacher, "was just great," says Alice Holway (who was herself Roger's favorite back-kitchen friend). "I've never known anyone have so many tomatoes thrown at him and come up smiling." Roger gave Alice one of Edgar Snow's China journals to read. "I thought it would burn my hand," she says. But she took it and read it all. The receding of the McCarthy years made it easier to sustain the range of political ideas represented in all of Putney's departments. Spring conferences were revived in 1956, and the FBI stayed in Washington. With Ed Shore, leader of Putney's Russian trip, and Stepha Gerassi, history teachers played host to one of the first post-Stalin delegations of Soviet educators. The visitors stood up in Assembly in their square black suits discussing with their interpreter the safest responses to challenging questions; they were thrown off balance when they received a series of questions asked in Russian, realizing that their private discussions had been understood.

The Russians were also upset to visit the library and find Trotsky's book among those on the Russian revolution. "The only things you have on Russia are written by our enemies," they told Karen Goodlatte, Marisa Lederer's assistant. "We'd be glad if you'd send us some materials of your own," Karen told them. They did. The glossy Soviet magazines joined the *Nation*, the *National Review*, and other periodicals and books all over the political spectrum in this collection, now grown to 15,000 volumes under Marisa. By 1963 the new library wing had doubled the space in which to house it. As Marisa moved into language teaching and Karen Goodlatte took over, the collection continued to grow (25,000 volumes by 1980), an unusual resource for a secondary school of any size, but an absolutely necessary one where term papers and other independent projects were central to all students' education, along with (in most cases) the careful individual coaching that Putney's high teacher-student ratio allowed.

Putney students continued to get into good colleges in spite of the new competition. Encouraged by their college advisor, they applied to a greater variety of colleges. The favorites were still Harvard and Radcliffe (an average of seven admitted each year), but now three or four seniors who might before have headed for Cambridge went (gladly, they found) to Berkeley or the University of Wisconsin instead.[46] They were accepted partly because colleges had found that Putney graduates generally did well in spite of the shock of leaving West Hill. Both the Hotchkiss-Putney study and an informal inquiry made by Harvard in the 1950s proved Putney alumni's freshman grades poor predictors of four-year success. Once they had learned to take examinations and to care at least a little about grades, they moved, on the average, beyond conventional prep school graduates, the two curves crossing about the middle of the junior year. It was a replay of the colleges' experience during the Eight Year Study, and it gave their admissions officers confidence in some of the oddest, most windblown characters to come off West Hill.[47] Very soon, as the sixties rebels multiplied, most colleges would be happy to welcome Putney students who had been experienced in community government and well schooled in the complexities of choice.

There were some "failures" among the Rockwell-era alumni, who were half of all Putney alumni by 1969. The 4 percent who did not finish college might be considered failures for a college preparatory school, as might the girl who felt "incredible" pressure at Putney to go to "top colleges or none at all," was rejected everywhere she applied, and "turned in panic to the wrong school," only to drop out two years later. More serious for Putney's commitment to the "whole child," the competition for college entrance piled excessive academic pressures onto some youngsters who were already overburdened.

To the extent that such pressures undermined joy in learning, Putney School's ability to uphold ideals of progressive education was also reduced. Just before she died in 1961, Jane Arms, still doing battle with all things conventional, wrote her last peroration against "the modern Putney senior's" obsession with college entrance. For the third or fourth time, a senior boy had become so anxious about the grades he did not know that he had broken into the college advisor's files and copied a pageful of class rankings and friends' grades. Exams, long papers, College Board hysteria: it could be "any prep school," she wrote, disgusted.[48]

But these were surfacings of the familiar tensions between utopian ideal and hard reality that had pulled at the school for twenty-five years. Without such tensions Putney School might have moldered in complacency. Putney was, after all, not just any prep school. The informality of classes continued to seed self-confidence in most students even while it allowed some others to drift.[49] College hysteria seized few seniors for long; some teachers wished it would goad them more and sooner. Perhaps it was fortunate that Putney's progressive energies had never been systematically concentrated in the classroom, for the school was less vulnerable to the more reactionary academic pressures than were many once-progressive schools. Putney teachers had never wanted, nor could a small school afford, an array of glossy electives. The required course of study was much the same in 1965 as it had been in 1935. While some classes lapsed into conventional methods or slipshod nonmethod, these seem to have mattered less to students than the energy for learning conveyed by the community as a whole. The new pressures, fielded as they were by a collegial faculty under Ben Rockwell, helped the school recapture—and in some areas amplify—the academic strengths with which Jane Arms, the MacDougalls, and others had equipped the original Putney experiment. Though details were altered as the experiment became an institution, the basic design remained intact.

Chapter 12

Students: Notes from the Underground

How did students fare in these sixteen years when Putney School was learning endurance as an institution? This is, finally, the test of a school. Ideally one should know what graduates made of their lives afterward too, but Putney is still too young for such knowledge. The lives of the students who make a school while they attend it already defy institutional definition. One can only sketch out a few of their comedies and tragedies and color in some scenes.

The gaps in the script are not there for want of adults' efforts to fill them. It is a teacher's business to try to know what goes through students' minds, often to judge as well, and to communicate judgments. To some extent, Putney students saw or tried to see themselves as adults described them. Letters and journals recount many attempts to absorb adults' definitions. Students (especially girls) can be found puzzling over teachers' descriptions of a person of wonderful potential. "A scientist! I hadn't thought so," wrote one who later became a biochemist. "Putney taught me that I could do and be more than I had ever thought possible," concludes another, echoing two decades of similar reflections. [1]

Just as often (especially for boys), that most deeply learned was learned in tension with adult expectations. At least through the early sixties, Putney's students continued to live cheek by jowl with their teachers, and few words were minced between them. "Johnny Caldwell could be ruthlessly sarcastic on the playing field if a kid wasn't trying," says an alumnus, "but he really helped me into my body." Jeff Campbell was not the only teacher who felt it his right to describe a child in platitudes to parents and with entire candor in a separate report to the boy or girl in question: "You may have written some poetry this term but you're an infantile, egotistical brat," he wrote one boy. A beloved teacher's opinion mattered. The boy went to work to make himself the poet Jeff knew he could be. (He is now coordinator of California Poets in the Schools, working with about as many poets as there were students in Putney School.) Less happily, and less typically, a girl felt "blamed for not understanding the New Math." "We are all gifted," Ben Rockwell said at one commencement, but this girl thought she'd learned otherwise.[2]

Another boy, sixteen years old, hoped to turn around his writing (and his life) by beginning an English class journal. He showed it to Mrs. H. as though wanting her to see that he now recognized the faults that were holding him back. The note she wrote him may have made him wonder why he'd shared it:

March, 1954

John,

I've just finished reading your report and was very much disappointed in it.
It portrays the life of a soft sort of person, still very young and immature.
The best colleges won't want you I'm afraid.

Mrs. H.

He kept the note, however, and he wrote later that he held onto the criticism like a talisman as he made his way out of his worst difficulties the following year.[3]

Of course many academic sins—too many, say alumni—went unregarded. Many rules were successfully broken in secret, where conflicts with adults could not be joined.[4] But those that did surface got lots of attention. For good or ill, Putney tended to infuse errant students with a sense that they were betraying a community that belonged to them. A '54 alumnus describes crawling through his dorm window after a Saturday night binge in Brattleboro with some day-student friends and finding himself face to face with a senior. The senior "saw my condition and knew just what was going on. 'I think you'd better turn yourself in,' he said." The boy did so, knowing full well that the senior would bring him before the student-faculty standards committee if he didn't appear himself. Though it took time for the boy to accept his dormmate's role, he soon understood that this respected senior was "part of my solution." When the boy was suspended for a week, he was being banished by "his" people. "It was our school. We had built it," he says now. "That week gave me the most important moral lesson I had at Putney School."[5]

One form or other of banishment was the most common consequence of ill-doing. Some were so mild that they did no more (and no less) than make time for reflection. One boy's penalty for smoking was to live alone in the youth hostel for a week and have to walk to school each day from the Lower Farm. Another got something more like a reward for reading under the blankets after lights out. He spent two nights with Clyde Hulett above the milk house. "No curfew there, and we talked and listened to Clyde's radio late into the night." Or, put all by yourself into a Lower Farm outbuilding for smoking, a student could smoke all night once the nearby adults had turned in.

There was worse to come for a boy who got fed up with his roommate's alarm clock and took a hatchet to it. Mrs. H. told him that "if he was going to act like an animal, he should go live with animals." He spent a week sleeping in the chicken house atop the crust of manure, broken eggshells, and feathers that chickens lay down. The most unusual (but perhaps most logical) place of banishment was reserved for a boy who had been caught again and again wandering about after hours. None of the ordinary penalties made any impression. "Up in Hinton House Mrs. H. slept in one of two twin beds," writes one of his friends. "A small group of us boys found that out when _____ had to spend the night in the second bed. He swore us all to secrecy the next morning." One of the group notes, "Some things about Putney School seemed a bit much to a farm boy."[6]

It was the daily taking of consequences, however, that most consistently shaped students' lives. John Dewey had written long before that "the discipline of the school should proceed from the life of the school as a whole." At Putney School, in the 1950s, it still did so. "Do you realize that you hurt when you teased me?" a teacher asked her ninth-grade counselee. "That question has always been with me," the ninth grader says now. "In such a small community, everything you did came back to you," an alumnus continues.[7] Though he was quick to act in emergencies, Ben Rockwell's responses to everyday sins were slow in coming. Yet a teacher who left Putney partly because he thought Ben a terrible administrator found his many student friends absorbing Ben's expectations of them. "Given time, his own nobility . . . carried enormous weight and truth in the school, and for a while it worked." One of the students writes, "We were close to Ben as a man, and as he really was, since that was the way he presented himself. So as I have grown up since Putney I have not outgrown what Ben meant to me when I was there."[8]

Adults and students write counterpoint in a boarding school, and some years cacophonies pervade the music no matter what teachers do. The one constant theme that almost all students seemed to hear was the ideal of a humane community. Word quickly spread, for example, of how vehemently Mrs. H. or Ben Rockwell or Stepha Gerassi argued in faculty meeting for keeping and working with a troubled youngster in trouble with everyone else. Or the ideal might be expressed in subtler ways. Many boys knew, for example, that one of the most respected and generous-hearted men on the staff was a homosexual. He was a safe and reassuring presence to boys not sure which way their bodies were tending, and they kept his secret, much as he kept his homosexual friendships entirely outside the school. Both parties knew that known homosexual adults got fired from boarding schools in the 1950s and early 1960s. To their surprise, a few boys learned (through some tangled grapevine) that Warren Leonard also knew the secret and kept it. So did Mrs. H., the woman with the power to fire. The Massachusetts State Police had picked up the man for loitering late one night, and Mrs. H. had asked Warren to travel to the police station and try to learn if the charges might in any way affect the man's role at Putney school. Back on West Hill, the two administrators saw their colleague doing much good and no harm. He stayed. No Assembly talk or catalogue pronouncement could say more.[9]

Even while adults sought to shape them, students made their own lives. Central to their experience was the variety of young people around them. Though more and more applicants with Putney connections gained admission,[10] the student body remained remarkably diverse through the mid-sixties. It is true that fewer foreign students enrolled as international emergencies subsided, and the school's administration of Secondary School Aptitude Tests after 1956 virtually eliminated the wild cards—those "certificate of attendance" students who had colored the landscape for twenty years. But admissions officers consistently sought a richer ethnic mix, and to some extent they got it. More Jewish students came, more blacks, and a silent pair of Navajo Indian brothers. Most exotic were three Tongan Island students who came on full scholarship through Edward Dodd's generosity and Edward Shore's good offices. Purposely brought into the eleventh grade, the two boys and one girl had already crossed into adulthood by their culture. They had learned the separate languages of Tongan aristocrat and commoner that they would need to know when they returned to take up positions in Tongan government or education. With much support from the Dodd and Shore families, they were able to meet cultural shocks few Tongans had ever faced. Other Putney students gained much more from their presence than the fun of playing soccer until the snow flew next to a burly barefoot Polynesian or the salvation of the kindly tutoring in physics that Langi Kavaliku gave at least two struggling classmates.[11] The three brought another world into a community that on the whole welcomed international differences instead of trying to erase them; so did over a dozen Asian and African students who came to Putney School on their own.

There were stresses. American blacks were more vulnerable, their precious, ravaged culture more readily prey to their peers' well-intentioned attempts to find common ground. "Everyone was just treated the same at Putney," a black teacher happily recalls[12]—and for black adolescents this was precisely the problem. "There was no way of registering blackness," says Dick Evans, a black alumnus, "though the school helped a little. They made me caretaker of a new black student—we roomed together. And after that there was a lot of discussion, black and white together." One of Dick's black friends just felt bereft. From a well-educated Philadelphia family, she came to Putney expecting great things of herself, until a few of her teachers made clear to her (she says) that they expected virtually nothing. She had to straighten her hair with the dormitory iron, as no personal appliances were allowed. After Dick graduated, it often seemed she had "no one to date, no one to talk to." She did have some white friends, the Hinkles among them, for "singing was the only thing that made me feel special." (Norwood still calls her "my PRIZE soprano." For her part, she gave him an ebony baton to show him what he meant to her.) Several of the girl's friends were also outcasts, however: the frail, serious girl with diabetes, the wild girl who had grown up in the Far East. To her, trying to make it black at Putney meant going home and finding she didn't have a place there either. Now she is a successful professional woman, but "If I hadn't had Jeff Campbell, I wouldn't have made it through Putney," she says.

Most black students were happier, especially as their numbers increased and the dawning civil rights movement opened blue eyes.[13] A student-teacher-Glen Maples group out picketing Woolworth's in 1958 lent reality to race issues for Putney students all the time it was bewildering the citizens of Brattleboro. Even if real, life-enhancing racial differences were sloughed over, at least the school's egalitarian principles stood squarely behind black students' dignity. Though it failed them daily, Putney remained a better place than most of the other schools then opening up to an integrated world.[14]

There were other fissures and hierarchies peculiar to the social world of Putney School. A few of these appear to have reflected teachers' attitudes. While most arts teachers, for example, tried to welcome every aspiring painter, actor, dancer, or musician (indeed, Nora Sayre complains that West Hill was awash with pretentious "artists"), some could not resist concentrating on the most talented. The proliferation of the talented both enriched the school and brought it problems. One of the less talented gratefully remembers people "playing the KDU piano like gods before dinner." "Wally Shawn was my guru," says another. Many recall the young printmaker (dying, they learned later, of a chronic disease that haunted and quickened his efforts to have his say), whose only folio, "The Psalm Book of Charles Knowles," is now in the collections of Harvard's Houghton Library, Israel's national museum, the National Gallery in Washington, and New York's Museum of Modern Art.[15] Several alumni say that the Putney admissions office was also dazzled by the "stars." As it welcomed more and more promising young artists, heroes multiplied as fast in the studios and practice rooms as they did on the ski slopes. While many students were inspired by them—daytime arts classes multiplied, and between seventy and eighty took instrumental lessons each year—a minority hung back, discouraged. "I expected people to be valued for what they were," recalls one alumna. "Instead there seemed to be a special, favored group." "It was a fast track school," says another; "some of us got left behind." "You can't draw, you can't sing, you shouldn't be here," an alumnus remembers telling himself miserably.[16]

Some of this, some years, was probably teachers' fault, but students put pressures on each other too. While almost everyone was grateful that "strange people were considered interesting rather than bad," there were swift conformist crosscurrents. For every person who learned compassion at Putney, or who was "astonished by the friendliness of the place," or by "the freedom to explore, to be yourself," there are others who also remember keeping constant watch on themselves to make certain they did not stray from the ways their peers would approve.

Putney students' pressures to conform took on their own peculiar ethnic and ethical twists. Alumni disagree on their meaning. One woman still smarts from "the scorn of Putney's well-to-do-intelligensia." A boy from the South and a girl from Jewish Long Island lost their accents in less than a year, because "people laughed at me every time I opened my mouth." "Well so what," a Brooklyn man says, "I used to say 'Mudda' and people would walk around saying 'Mudda' to me all the time and it didn't bother *me*." "It was tough to have Jewish curly hair in a straight hair environment," the girl (now woman) rejoins. Another Jewish student who left Putney early agrees; a third says "That's nonsense!" A chorus protests, "I didn't even *know* you were Jewish." "I wished I *was* Jewish," one man exclaims, finishing the exchange. Again, adult intervention—and the simple presence of respected, unique adults like the Lederers (Felix was half-Jewish) and the Gerassis, or Ed Gray and other honored outdoor teachers—was often the best proof against cliques and loneliness. However, many alumni now recognize a "tyranny of style" in the school they shared: a constant undercurrent of self-congratulation for nonconformist airs, clothes, words. While this very pressure could liberate, one also had to learn to ignore it.

And what if you were simply depressed, as adolescents often are? "Why am I so miserable when I'm so happy?" one girl asked of the air around her. There was a special burden to being "unhappy in paradise" as one alumna puts it. Carmelita Hinton's prescription of constant if not frenetic activity could not work for everyone. Immobilized, some watched students and adults rushing around them, doing significant things. Several people maintain that "Putney did well with those who 'acted out' ": in a school where faculty "huffed and puffed about coca-cola and radios," the rebels had "plenty of things to push against." Most youngsters from the ever-increasing number of broken homes actively sought and found dear friends among the adults. Yet teachers seemed too busy to notice the sad, quiet ones, or the few who had not wanted to be loners, but were. A '64 alumna, still angry, says, "I could never understand how a school so deeply committed to self-expression and the arts could so entirely dismiss individual suffering." Even Jeff Campbell, who, like Ray Goodlatte, helped so many troubled students, could only say to one deadened boy that he was "insensitive." "Jeff didn't recognize depression when he saw it."[17]

The Putney faculty was not alone in thinking that as long as students met a rich curriculum and extracurricular program halfway, all *must* be well. This was an old tradition in American schools, especially in independent boarding schools. It was the rare school that offered easy access to psychological counseling or psychiatric help before 1960, and there were years-long faculty quarrels between those who saw such services as essential and those who disdained them as somehow demeaning to their own competence as educators.[18] At Putney, a few teachers had begun asking for a psychiatric consultant in the early 1950s. Both Mrs. H. and Ben Rockwell understood that the school physician was neither trained nor effective in this area, and tried intermittently to find help. A gifted psychiatrist, brought onto the Board of Trustees in 1956, came up twice to talk with the faculty. But it took him ten years to get Ben Rockwell to concentrate on the problem of engaging a permanent consulting psychiatrist. To both directors, Putney's daily life seemed so health-giving that it may have been harder for them than for

others to think clearly about the really ill. Both feared that a resident counselor would undercut the school's nonprofessional counseling system. "It's
risky" to tamper with people, Ben would say.[19]

It can be terrifying for an adult to watch a young person move beyond the
reach of loving concern. Ben's profound sense of responsibility, his reluctance to share his burden, made him the more vulnerable. An alumna who
had sent her daughter to Putney in the turbulent sixties traveled up to talk
with Ben when her child was experiencing psychological difficulty. "Ben was
more upset than I. He seemed frightened of the situation. He somehow took
the attitude [that] this can never happen here—and did not seem able to
cope. I was left feeling baffled and without support. Other incidents reported
to me [amplified the] feeling. . . . It was a difficult time."[20]

The difficulty here is that Putney's exciting intellectual and community
life was indeed healing for many, just as Mrs. H. and Ben assumed it to be.
And if town meeting or Bach or Tolstoy failed, one might have a long talk
with the school blacksmith, or with the Grays or Larry Titus, who always
seemed to have "time and kindness for students." Joseph Fineman's 250-
page journal makes a moving record of one boy's passage from fearful,
awkward childhood to young manhood at Putney School with little or no
help from psychiatry. Joe came as a ninth grader in 1950, sent by his parents,
he assumes, as "some kind of therapy."[21] Brilliant at science, he was both
terrified of and drawn to words. It was a science fiction character, a mutant-
supergenius hero who typed a page a day, that had inspired him to begin the
journal.

Joe wondered if he was insane: the journal was for him a lifeline linking
his most chaotic thoughts with the possibility of order. Joe's father, a writer,
had encouraged him to keep it going

> Oh, what a yummididy! Hwidllescrumpy YUMPydiddle of a MOMMYboxy
> YUMP GLUMP se a MOMMYboy waa. YUMP seeaMOMMYboy cwimple.
> GWUMp 2 da. YYYYYYYUMP! Hwiggk hwiggle. AAA quiet daddy you make me
> mad. phooey—illustrates changing moods—click click oh shut UP. Nuts to you
> nertz QUiet! nice littlere kitty cute yumpy old fuzzy bear. KIT THE DÜT. Jonny
> is the devil HE must be killed KILL THE JON Jonny MUST be kh hated hm that
> düt Jonny Must mbe killed Chop off his head. Bite off his nose KILL HIM. Listen
> to the düt KILL KILL Jonny. . . .

Early pages are not quite gibberish. There are times when one's brother
(Jonny here) doesn't deserve to live, and times when one's mother (Yum-
pyMommyboy) is life itself. "Dearest Momiboi" (Joe wrote his mother),

"Sometimes I wunder how I am so difrent frum evribudi. Iz it posible dhat I am rite and evribudy els rong?"

Many a thirteen-year-old is interested in other people's crotches. But few make up a new language to tell what they've seen, nor do they describe the thrill of discovering sexual climax alone between their bedsheets ("quietly, quietly now—don't bring your roommates into this"). Nor do they over time show their raw accountings to friends in order to teach themselves to communicate more and hide less, as Joe quite often did.

What is this "normal" world that adults have made? Joe wanted to know.

> . . . To THEM even a killing is nothing. Why? "Because it happens all the time; because I am used to it, BECAUSE I AM A NORMAL HUMAN BEING!"
>
> And why must everything . . . ever-happening be unimportant? . . . What am I writing about?
>
> A feeling.
>
> I am searching, searching, searching for another who has it. . . .
>
> in this lonely world
>
> Is the world made of THEM?

And next to this an English paper crumpled, restored, and pasted in:

> Here I am, O man like myself; come to me
> Are you honest? Completely honest?
> Do you disagree with many:
> Do you change your hates and loves every hour, every minute?
> Come to me. . . . Here I am.

Gradually, language heard in classes or sung on Friday nights makes its way into the journal. IDEO GLORIA IN EXCELSIS DEO. General MacArthur as THEM, prolonging the killing in Korea. After a year or so, the writing warms.

> GOD LISTEN TO THE SINGING O GOD
>
> I love. This is what is good. This is
>
> what is good. . . . But be careful)))). I
>
> love people people people men good stock all kinds making the language and not restraining it . . . this is what is good good YOWP! I am no longer a . . . . . .
>
> good kinds   all kinds some bad but not too many   THIS IS
> THE WORLD
> MEET THE WORLD

Joe didn't always want to meet the world. He skipped the first year's social dance and the next year's. He sat typing in his room: "I am not 'human' and never will be. I will always be alone . . . in the sense that no one else has my particular brand of insanity." And a while later, "I do not deserve any good girl and I don't want a bad one. Neither my body, nor probably my mind, is capable of giving any girl an interesting time." Still later, a friend (female) penciled a note next to the last sentence: "Proved wrong."

For Putney friends gathered around Joe, one by one. Teachers helped. Watch your "intolerance of others' ideas," said a biology teacher. "Forsake theory, face facts," Tom Wendel wrote on Joe's tenth-grade English report: "I am very concerned about your lack of literary insight. . . . As long as you see emotion as 'unsane' you will not understand literature." By June Tom was elated with Joe's growth: "You'd even like Richard II now!"

In Joe's third and fourth years the journal overflows with ever more complex perceptions, with poetry, with reflections on physics (he was mastering it and searching out its connections with his daily life), on music (he had come to love it), on politics, on sex and homosexuality. There are motions of reconciliation with his brother Johnny, and a pondering of his parents' suffering and gradual separation. "I felt the family rotten," he wrote. But this time he knew that it was not his fault: thus he could begin really to help them.

> With three things I am strongly sick:
>   hate,
>   guilt,
>   worship.
> For Jonny is not the enemy, but hate is.
> For my sins are not shameful, but shame is a sin.
> For the gap between me and my fellows is not infinite, but my hope is.

"I love Daddy and I will try to comfort him and keep him sane," writes Joe.

Joe goes to his first social dance and has a wonderful time. He grasps and holds "the unity and friendliness of Putney." Jonny is now a ninth grader; Joe's counselor, Jeff Campbell, sees Joe being "quietly helpful to his brother," and Jon "being very proud of Joe." Joe's article on the American-French partnership in Vietnam appears next to Jeff's in the mimeographed newsletter of the Brattleboro Fellowship of Reconciliation. He is secretary of the Community Council. He asks Mrs. H. if he might speak to the school in Sunday meeting about his concept of philosophical truth. She, very happy with him, agrees—no questions asked, no limits set—and he makes his speech.

As senior year ends, Joe looks back and registers some experiences that fit at last, such as his four spring camping weekends. "I remember even the earliest as if I were there, for they have been beautiful times." He recalls Fernando Gerassi ("How can one comprehend so rare and real a person?") bringing cheer and beer to Joe and the others, Joe feeling "all in myself . . . nothing," but *taking in* the possibility of sociability and happiness in the rain-soaked woods. And finally he describes graduation day: watching himself both loving Putney and hating the show of love for Putney. By the time he leaves in June 1954, he has made himself ready to do so.

Joe had weathered a tragedy during that last year. On October 28, his roommate Ives Hendrick shot himself in the bathroom adjoining their room in the old boys' dorm. It was the only student suicide Putney School had known, the awful fulfillment of every teacher's and every parent's nightmare. Through Ives's death, the nightmare entered every present Putney student as well.

Joe and most of his friends knew that Ives had a .45 caliber pistol. They had shielded him a week earlier when two ninth graders had reported another gun-carrying student to Ben Rockwell, who was serving as acting director in the absence of both Mrs. H. and Warren Leonard. When the standards committee confiscated the other boy's gun, Ives's friends told him he must give his pistol in confidence to Stepha Gerassi to keep for him until he could take it home. But Joe never checked up; he just assumed Ives had done so. ("One can so easily go so completely wrong," wrote Joe later in his journal.)

"Ives was no ordinary boy," writes another student to whom Ives was "one of my best companions."[22] Jane Arms had known this since becoming Ives's writing teacher and friend the year before. "Bliss," Ives wrote,

Bliss
Is the time
When you awake
Into the beautiful morning
And lie half awake,
With no time on your mind.
Bliss is the time
When you have no bonds
And the sky is blue and cool
With a very few clouds;
And the blanket above you
Is almost warm enough,
But all is clean
And clear.

This was the best of life for Ives. What was death? he wondered. He talked about that with dormmates. "Life is walking through sheets of rain, . . . death is the hot shower and the kiss," wrote Ives.[23]

Ives put his pistol to his head about 11:30 one October morning and discovered death. It did not take him instantly. An ambulance rushed him to the Brattleboro hospital, where he lay several hours in a deep coma. Ben gathered all the students in the assembly hall and gave them the flat medical reports. A teacher mopped up the blood in the bathroom. Three more times, Joe and Ives's other roommate washed the place where the blood had been, and still they smelled it in their room. Hardly anyone in school could eat supper while Ives lay dying. One girl fainted; many girls wept, and many boys struggled not to. Ives's "best companion" went to the library to look for a Bible or a prayer book. They were all gone.

"Ives is the first person I have known who died," Joe wrote his mother late that evening. "It is rather hard to imagine it—that we will no longer hear his banjo playing, and his singing of Handel and Bach and Mendelssohn at the top of his voice, and that this means not that he has gone on a weekend or a trip somewhere, but that there is no more of him at all."

Ives's parents arrived the next day and took their boy's intricate journal from the stricken girl to whom he had willed it. But they also told his friends that he would be buried in a Putney village cemetery. Their last few years with their only son had not been easy; they understood that Putney School had been the best of life for Ives.

The students' distress with Ives's parents, who had taken away all his things, equaled the parents' distress with Ives's friends, whose shock had closed them to the parents' terrible grief.[24] Joe Fineman, the boy who lived with the bullethole above the door, remembers no adult talking with him about the suicide after the first week, when Mrs. H. and he had talked long. Though other students' healing seems to have begun with the Friday night singing they dedicated to Ives, Joe moved woodenly through the days, wondering why he could not mourn. He described the death in the essay that helped him win admission to Harvard College. All that was left to Putney of Ives Hendrick was a grave, flowers lovingly planted on its surface, a sheaf of poems, and the fifty thousand bees that he and Morris Mitchell had kept together.

The "impulse toward self-destruction" by which Mrs. H. explained Ives's suicide to her students and herself[25] could not vanish from a community of human beings. But as the years went on, the school's vitality stood out in high relief. The many small acts of courage by which Putney had maintained its integrity during the McCarthy years had laid the ground for a period of consonance between the school and the broader culture—or so it would seem once a new president had been elected in 1960, once the stilted foreign policy debate of the Dulles-Eisenhower years had given way to a larger, more generous international concern, once many signs had converged to suggest that Americans might be able to live up to their ideals of racial equality. The sixties brought a brief renaissance of progressive education, expressed as much in pressures for change within old schools as in the founding of new ones. Community, artistic freedom, care for the environment, sexual equality, craftsmanship, freedom of speech and dissent—all these watchwords of the sixties had been Putney School's concerns since its beginnings.

And Putney School flourished in very many ways. Its success showed in ever-rising numbers of applications, in students' artistic and academic accomplishments through the school years, in a high level of political discussion and action, in college admissions statistics. Yet the sixties also brought tensions specific to a school of which great things are expected. It became increasingly difficult for Putney to maintain its traditional sense of community in an age when individuality, so highly valued for twenty-five years, gathered meanings for the young that few adults could accept: the right to have sex at any age, for example, or the right to wear or smoke whatever you pleased. While most Putney adults' standards remained as high as ever, students grew less likely to live by their teachers' convictions.

The Putney of the 1960s "was not a good place for children needing a lot of structure" says an alumna, now a parent. Large numbers of alumni and teachers describe a newly defiant brand of individualism—and a fiercer tyranny of style—filling the vacuum of adult arrangements. Both threatened genuine community as the Rockwell years went on, even though the school was full to bursting with wonderful enterprises. While the causes surely are multiple, and just as surely lie in part outside the school in the increasingly pervasive youth culture, one change occurred within Putney School that many connect with the increasing separation of peer pressures from adult expectations. Ben Rockwell allowed veteran teachers with growing families to move out of the dormitories, one by one. Most moved off campus as well, since there were so few school houses available. Whole families gained an identity apart from the school, the more so as rising real estate prices in the Putney township began sending them farther afield. This was good for families; for many teachers, worn by the twenty-four-hour demands of the boarding school, it was an essential move if they were to stay on. The change brought stability and individuation to adult lives, but it also weakened bonds between students and some of their teachers. The new policy was a trade-off, and no one was sure whether the losses outweighed the benefits—except for a few such as Mrs. H., who continually counted for her fellow trustees its costs in the quality of supervision and community.[26]

Some extraordinary young teachers came into the dormitory apartments and usually moved on after a year or two or three, often to college teaching, to law school, public service, or environmental protection groups, even to the U.S. Congress. The veterans drove in from their homes in the dark of winter dawns and stayed most evenings until 10 P.M. One can protest that adolescents always want more attention than they get. One can also ask why Putney did not do more of what schools have done for centuries: substitute rules for personal transactions, issue demerits and suspensions and dismissals, and let students like it or leave. Hundreds of other independent schools were being rocked by the new adolescent discontents. Some clamped down harder than ever. Some opened new ways for students to join in decision-making. Some lay like ships helpless in the roiling waters, all stays broken, all sails flapping and useless.[27]

Almost every school experienced wrenching political polarization as the sixties ripened. When Ben Rockwell saw Putney's leftward tilt crowding the moderates, he worked more anxiously than ever for tolerance. But the problems were more than political. The Putney faculty's bewilderment reflects the peculiar vulnerabilities of a school that has already granted its students all the responsibility that responsible adults should give. Putney had relied since 1935 on the friendship and example of its adults to guide its young toward acceptance of shared purposes. As the young began to insist on purposes of their own that adults could not share—and proudly used all of Putney's democratic processes to try to advance them, friendship often became exhausting, and example seemed irrelevant. The school bore the added burden of its identification as a pioneering progressive experiment, and didn't progressive education mean "permissiveness"? The Summerhills and educational communes multiplying in the forests and on the beaches had reinvented the "free child" of progressivism's Bohemian wing. The handful of loud and wearing youngsters who had come to Putney to escape all bonds saw only hypocrisy in Ben Rockwell's (and Carmelita Hinton's and John Dewey's) idea of freedom as a function of self-discipline, competence, and sensitivity to community needs.[28]

For these captives of the new urban-suburban affluence, the experiences unique to Putney School now became targets for resistance. To be made to sing Bach when you badly missed the stereo and TV set you'd just left behind meant that you might never wholeheartedly try it. Even to many classical music lovers, Putney's official rejection of a whole new world of popular music seemed ludicrous. Increasing numbers of youngsters from artistic-intellectual families came to West Hill feeling they had seen everything. Far from seeking an adult-arranged moratorium within which to find themselves, they were already immersed in the subculture their own generation had made. They chafed at Putney's utopian isolation. For some, the farm felt like a dude ranch, its self-sufficiency a needless anachronism, and the students who really cared about it phonies doing jobs machines should do. And there *was* hypocrisy in a school that celebrated equality but did nothing to discourage wealthier students from sporting $500 skis on the slopes. There was smugness in large plans for a better world, plans which later would seem so simplistic to a few ardent student reformers that they withdrew from adult political arenas altogether. Some forms of resistance made sense. Others, however, were powered by a soul-diminishing privatism that undermined the very community students had come to Putney to enjoy.[29]

A few older boys and girls found the school's constraints on sexual relationships incomprehensible. Their incredulity was contagious, because young people discovering their own sexuality are discovering powerful truths about self and about intimacy with others. An alumna writes of "being in love and getting a lot of disapproval, as if it wasn't natural or good for me at 17." Partly because of "the guilt we felt . . . we lost each other" after graduation. Few Putney adults could grasp the heartbreak that followed the collapse of an intense adolescent love affair.[30] It is true, as it had been true for years, that adults' denials did little to prevent much happy experimentation. For many, first love continued to be a central Putney experience—"metallic, searching kisses" between two sets of braces down in the boiler room or, more rarely, love in a sleeping bag, love under the apple blossoms on the way down from Putney Mountain. Nevertheless, several 1960s alumni feel sure that students' desire for ever more sexual freedom frightened Ben even while he resisted it.[31] It was impossible to recover the confidence (or the illusions) that had stiffened Mrs. H.'s backbone against sexual expression for so long.

The tensions brought benefits also. There was more excitement than ever within town meetings and faculty-student committees. Some teachers found they could teach through argument as well as they could through agreement. Many youngsters thrived on this kind of learning or happily settled into the quieter friendships with teachers that Putney students had known since 1935. For all those who continued to love nature and its wise uses, the new national concern for environmental protection lent special significance to Putney's land-use program, including its farm. It was also a time of asking,

"Is it right for me to buy a bass recorder when so many of the world's people are hungry?"[32] Putney's internationalists found a host of allies in the growing antiwar movement, inspiration in the large numbers of alumni, former teachers, and graduate students who had taken up international service work, whether for the Peace Corps (as both trainers and corpsmen), the United Nations, the American Friends Service Committee, or even the State Department.

Some older teachers who—like teachers all over the country—"had never even *heard* of marijuana" found ways to learn its meaning for a new generation, and, occasionally, ways to help students resist foolish experiment.[33] And finally, the incorrigible offenders were dismissed, at the usual cost to all those who had struggled with them and loved them. No school works well for everyone in it. In an age when schools all over the country seemed more and more distant from their students' needs, Putney's original vision of a learning community deeply respectful of each of its members remained its chief excellence. "You would leave Putney knowing . . . that no one could ever be ignored," Wally Shawn told a recent Putney senior class, "and then you'd go out into the world and you'd be horrified that the compassion you'd learned at Putney wasn't practiced there, and so the struggle between you and the world would begin." "Putney gave me a vision of excellence which I've striven to build over and over in increasingly complex situations," says another 1960s graduate. The school "kept you looking," says a third, "even if the searcher stumbled." That teachers' work was hard going did not diminish its value, nor obscure new delights to be found in youngsters who could enthuse about Ringo Starr and Brahms and Malcom X and Gandhi, all in the same breath.

The dilemmas that had surfaced by the mid-sixties would decide Ben Rockwell to give way to younger leadership in 1969, when he was fifty-four years old. The Putney School itself would go on, tough enough now to survive difficulties that would soon send many schools under. If the progressive education movement had long ago broken into its component parts, several of its most vital and most contradictory ideas could continue to flourish in a small, self-sufficient school. The contradictions tended toward resolution in the students themselves. The students were not ideas. They were living people, for whom support of community and scope for individuality were equally vital. As the sixties gave way to the seventies, many of the traditional preparatory schools would take on or strengthen the ways of teaching which had proved themselves at Putney School: student work programs; outdoor education; the arts as a major component of a secondary education; active student involvement in school governance; and perhaps most important, coeducation. Few in control of such changes will admit any debt to Putney, but one can find many private and public school teachers who have rediscovered progressive pedagogies and who are grateful for the role played by Putney and other progressive schools in keeping them vital.[34]

Where many of these pedagogies have become common coin, could a school so expensive, so intense in its preferences, continue to justify itself? It would depend. In a world more than ever in need of reverence for life and nature, a world whose most comfortable habits of thought may have endangered its very existence, it would depend, perhaps, on Putney School's continuing to live out its "passion for adventure."

Notes

Part I. Beginnings: 1890–1936

1. Story told by Barbara Barnes at a memorial service for Carmelita Hinton, Apr. 24, 1983. Title of chapter 1 (to follow) from Edgar J. Driscoll, obituary of Carmelita Hinton (*Boston Globe*, Jan. 8, 1983).

Chapter 1. A Passion for Adventure

1. Dr. James Blair, Jr., interview with Carmelita Hinton, July 2, 1981. All other quotations in this paragraph are from Carmelita Hinton (hereafter referred to as CH), "A New Secondary School."
2. Jane Arms, *Putney School Aborning* (Putney: Putney School, 1959), p. 8.
3. Liebe Coolidge Winship in Sunday night talk at the Putney School, Feb. 13, 1977.
4. CH to A. Katie Geer (hereafter AKG) in interviews, 1978–79.
5. CH, speech given to the Secondary Education Board.
6. Quotations in this paragraph are from CH, four interviews with Susan McIntosh Lloyd (SML), 1981–82.
7. Joseph W. Taylor, in will endowing Bryn Mawr College (1880). William James, *Talks to Teachers on Psychology: And to Students on Some of Life's Ideals* (New York, 1899).
8. Quoted in Lawrence A. Cremin, *The Transformation of the School* (New York: Knopf, 1961), p. 109.
9. CH's paraphrase of James, quoted in the *Boston Globe Magazine*, "Carmelita Hinton at 82: From Putney to Peking" (Nov. 26, 1972), p. 22. She was almost certainly summing up several of the ideas in the chapter "Emotion" in *Psychology*, James's own abridgment of his *Principles of Psychology*, designed for college students, and assigned for close reading by Dr. James Leuba in the education course Carmelita took at Bryn Mawr. "Refuse to express a passion and it dies," wrote James in *Psychology* (New York: Henry Holt, 1892), p. 382. See also "Will," pp. 448 and 451–52. Information on Dr. James Leuba's course is courtesy of Lucy West, Bryn Mawr College Archives.
10. CH, in interview with AKG.
11. Quoted in Cremin, *Transformation*, p. 88. Jean Hinton Rosner suggests that CH's optimism was reinforced by her mother, Lula Bell Chase, as well as her father. "I can certainly remember her (Mrs. Chase's) ingrained feeling that all was right with the world and the future was to be a glorious continuation of a glorious past—until the aftermath of World War I ushered in a different reality, which she did not accept" (letter to SML, Feb. 6, 1986).
12. This quotation and the following are from one of SML's interviews with CH.
13. Jane Addams, *Twenty Years at Hull House* (New York: Signet, 1961; [first ed., New York: 1910]), pp. 97, 98; J. Addams, "Women and Public Housekeeping," undated pamphlet, p. 36.

231

14. This quotation and the previous one are CH's in interview with AKG.
15. Addams, *Twenty Years* (1911 reprinting), pp. 440–42.
16. See ibid.; also Addams, "Public Housekeeping," pp. 36–37.
17. Cremin, *Transformation*, p. 220.
18. Jane Addams, "The Subjective Value of Social Settlements," *Forum* (November 1892).
19. G. S. Hall, *Adolescence: Its Psychology, Anthropology, Sociology, Sex, Crime, Religion and Education*, 2 vols. (New York: D. Appleton, 1904; reprint ed., 1916), pp. 533, 561–62, 610.
20. See Edward Yeomans, *Shackled Youth* (Boston: Little, Brown, 1916; reprint ed., 1925), p. 1; John and Evelyn Dewey, *Schools of To-Morrow* (New York: E. P. Dutton, 1915), pp. 170–204, 251–68. See also Mrs. Edward Yeomans' MS biography of her husband; Edward Yeomans, Jr., *A Teacher's Odyssey* (Cambridge, Mass.: Windflower, 1981), p. 9. CH gave additional descriptions of the Hull House inhabitants and guests to SML in interviews.
21. CH: "My Education for Teaching," *Bryn Mawr Alumnae Bulletin* (Spring 1951).
22. CH in interviews with AKG and SML; Joseph Lee, *Play in Education* (New York, 1915), quoted in Joseph F. Kett, *Rites of Passage: Adolescence in America, 1790 to the Present* (New York: Basic, 1977), p. 225. See also G. S. Hall, *Adolescence*; Jane Addams, *A New Conscience and an Ancient Evil* (New York: Macmillan, 1912), p. 105.
23. Arms, *Putney School Aborning*. p. 8.
24. CH, "My Education."
25. See Cremin, *Transformation*, p. 124. On early progressive educators' zeal for democracy, see Dren Geer, address to Putney School conference, "The Maturing of Progressive Education," June 12–14, 1986.
26. Neva Boyd, *Play and Game Theories in Group Work: A Collection of Papers*. Quoted in AKG, "The Progressive Origins of the Putney School," senior project, 1979.
27. Mrs. Dorothea Smith Ingersoll, in interview with AKG, December 1978.
28. Death certificate for Apr. 29, 1923, on file at the town clerk's office, Stockbridge, Massachusetts. None of the three Hinton children knew until 1983 that their father had committed suicide. The explanation given to all but the older generation of Chases and Hintons was that he had died of complications attendant on a case of adult chicken pox, intensified by pneumonia.
29. L. C. Winship, 1977; Jean Hinton Rosner (JHR) and William Hinton to SML, July, 1985.
30. CH, in interview with AKG.
31. Liebe Coolidge Winship, whose mother, Margaret Coolidge, taught third grade at Shady Hill. Also Sally Mattison Mitchell, at memorial service for CH.
32. Isabel Stephens, in interview with AKG, 1978; Sally Mattison Mitchell, ibid.
33. Quoted in AKG, preparatory paper for senior project, Dec. 5, 1978.
34. Accounts of the sheep's progress through Cambridge differ. The account given is JHR's.
35. CH, in interview with AKG.
36. John Coolidge, in interview with AKG, 1978. JHR assumes that her grandmother arrived soon after her grandfather Chase's death.
37. Ibid. Letter to AKG from Arthur Green, Oct. 19, 1978. Four alumni from the years before Mrs. Hinton's retirement recall hearing a similar message in Senior Discussion and in informal talks with CH.
38. John Coolidge, in interview with AKG and in conversation with SML. See also folder in JHR's archives labeled "Sex Customs," a collection of student writings (probably classes of '53 and '54) in answer to questions posed by CH during Senior Discussion.
39. JHR, letter to SML; CH, in interview with SML.
40. CH, in interview with SML; JHR to SML, letter, Feb. 6, 1986; Wallace "Carmelita Hinton at 82," p. 28; Otti Hirt, in Putney School faculty/staff questionnaire, April 1983.
41. There is a photograph of this scene which has kept the recollection alive (to their chagrin) for several of the participants. Arthur Green, letter to AKG; McGregor Gray, conversation.

42. Anne Holden, letter to AKG; Isabel Stephens and Betty Frothingham Moore, tape, Nov. 5, 1980.

43. Carmelita Hinton, "History of the Putney School," in *Putney School Needs $250,000 for New Housing* (1946).

44. CH to AKG, personal communication. Porter Sargent, *Handbook of Private Schools for 1935–36*, p. 986, lists 43 college preparatory coeducational boarding schools. Some of the boarding schools established by the Society of Friends had had "male and female" departments since the eighteenth century, and ran fully coeducational academic and extracurricular programs by the early 1930s. Even forward-looking Westtown, however, kept a handful of segregated classes (home economics for girls, shop and agriculture for boys) through the mid-thirties, a campus divided into "girls' bounds" and "boys' bounds" in order to separate dormitories, and the Orthodox Meeting for Worship (males on one side, females on the other). Information courtesy of Alice B. Long, Curator of Archives and Museum at Westtown; see also Thomas Woody, *A History of Women's Education in the United States*, 2 vols. (Science Press, 1929; reprint ed., New York: Octagon, 1966), chap. 1; and Reginald Snell, *Coeducation in Its Historical Setting* (London: Hogarth Press, 1939), pp. 145, 146. The Cambridge School in Weston had had a small but fully coeducational boarding department since 1931, and in 1933–34 this included 17 boys and 23 girls out of a total of 112 students (information courtesy of Karen Dorn, Cambridge School).

45. CH, "My Education."

46. Taped conversation between Isabel Stephens and Betty Frothingham Moore; CH, in conversation with Stepha Gerassi.

47. John Coolidge to AKG, personal communication.

48. John Holden, in conversation with SML.

Chapter 2. One to Get Ready

1. Arms, *Putney School Aborning*, p. 11. Arms dates this mailing "on a winter night in 1934," but she must have meant spring, because the mimeographed prospectus includes the first news that Elm Lea Farm will be the site of the school, a fact established in late spring 1934.

2. Wallace, "Carmelita Hinton at 82."

3. CH, in interview with AKG.

4. Mrs. Ingersoll, in interview with AKG.

5. In J. Arms's notes for a Putney School history, typed MS. See also George Finckel, in interview with Margot S. Shaw, May 1954, and numerous other faculty, staff, and student comments.

6. Penciled comments on copy of CH's proposal, "A New Secondary School."

7. Ibid.

8. Superintendent of the Harrisburg, Illinois Schools, quoted in David Tyack, Robert Lowe, and Elisabeth Hansot, *Public Schools in Hard Times: The Depression Years and the Last Decade* (Cambridge: Harvard University Press, 1984), pp. 45–47.

9. Ibid., p. 47. From 1930–34, public school funds fell 23 percent, to an annual average of $76.70 per pupil, with a 49 percent reduction in the poorest state (Arkansas), to $33.56 per pupil. Meanwhile, the number of high school graduates grew by 67 percent. See also Cremin, *Transformation*, pp. 259–63.

10. "The New Plan for Public School Social Studies" (1934), quoted in Tyack, Lowe, and Hansot, *Hard Times*, p. 57.

11. Ibid., p. 58.

12. Schlesinger, *The Coming of the New Deal* (Boston, Houghton Mifflin, 1958), p. 558.

13. Harold Rugg in "Creative America: Can She Begin Again?" (1939), quoted in Tyack, Lowe, and Hansot, *Hard Times*, p. 119.

14. Putney School catalogues, 1936–54.

15. Hugh MacDougall, letter to CH, Jan. 21, 1935; Ursula MacDougall, letter to CH, Jan. 22, 1935; Hugh MacDougall, in interview with SML. Arms, *Putney School Aborning*, also dates the MacDougalls' acceptance of their Putney teaching positions in November 1934.
16. Ewald Schnitzer, faculty questionnaire, 1982.
17. Janet Thompson Keep, (hereafter JTK), in interview with AKG; Wallace, "Carmelita Hinton at 82."
18. Arthur Green, letter to AKG.
19. Schnitzer, questionnaire.
20. Green, letter to Sue Mulcahy, Mar. 3, 1983.
21. Edwin and Mabel Gray, in interviews with AKG and SML; John Coolidge confirms the story.
22. Letter from CH, to Margaret Thompson, Mar. 18, 1935.
23. Quoted in Wallace, "Carmelita Hinton at 82," p. 28.
24. Among others, the North Shore Country Day School of Winnetka, Dalton, Walden, and City and Country schools in New York, and the Spring Hill School, a progressive boarding elementary school in Connecticut.
25. Quoted in Wallace, "Carmelita Hinton at 82," p. 19.
26. CH, "The New Schooling at Putney," *The Vermonter*, Jan.–Feb. 1936, p. 4; tapes of New York and Boston alumni history sessions; and JTK, in interview with AKG.
27. John Dewey, *School and Society*, 1899, quoted in Cremin, *Transformation*, p. 118; Joseph K. Hart, *A Social Interpretation of Education* (New York, 1929), p. 362, quoted in Kett, *Rites of Passage*, p. 237. See also Dren Geer, address.
28. Correspondence between C. Hutchins Maynard and CH, 1935.
29. John Holden, in interview with SML, Apr. 23, 1983.
30. John Holden, faculty/staff questionnaire.
31. Nancy West, conversation with SML.
32. JHR, letter to SML, May 1984; Vermont Public Radio series on traditional arts and song in Vermont, Aug. 1983.
33. John Holden in "Carmelita Hinton's Contribution," MS.
34. Arms, *Putney School Aborning*, p. 22. CH, taped conversation with James Blair.
35. In *A Room of One's Own*. See especially pp. 109–10. (New York: Harcourt Brace, 1929; reissued, 1957).

Chapter 3. Shaping Time: The First Year

1. Communications from Carmelita Hinton to AKG and SML; Roger Wilson; Liebe Coolidge Winship (LCW).
2. Quoted in Kate P. Wiggin and Nora A. Smith, *The Republic of Childhood* (Boston, Houghton Mifflin, 1896), vol. 2, *Froebel's Occupations*, p. 1.
3. Mimeographed "Rules etc.," written in September 1935, probably by CH.
4. Abbot Academy Archives in Andover, Mass., and interviews.
5. Peter Ringland, in the 4-H essay required of every animal-raiser, which had to be submitted along with the record book, Nov. 1935; JTK, in letters to her mother, Sept. 20 and Oct. 29, 1935.
6. Sally Bangs, in 4-H essay (1935 or 1936).
7. Quoted in Arms MS.
8. 1937–38 catalogue; CH, in interview with SML.
9. Mabel Gray to SML. See also letters written home, including Peggy Squibb to her mother, Dec. 8, 1935; Minnie Wood, in interview with AKG.
10. Ewald Schnitzer, in interview with Elizabeth Simmons, Aug. 4, 1983.
11. H. MacDougall, in interview with SML.
12. Alumni questionnaire (class not given, but assumed to be '37–'39).
13. Questionnaires from three alumni, 1930s classes; CH, in interview with SML.

14. Three-quarters of all questionnaires from faculty, staff, *and* from students through the class of 1941 mention the high quality of students, or "intellectual excitement not encountered again 'till graduate school."

15. McGregor Gray, questionnaire.

16. See Evelyn Dewey, *New Schools for Old* (New York: E. P. Dutton, 1919), p. 255. In the spring 1936 *Putney Magazine* CH wrote an article, "Is Putney too Visionary?" in answer to a parent's question.

17. Francis Parker, quoted in Merle Curti, *The Social Ideas of American Educators* (New York: Charles Scribner's Sons, 1935), p. 374. See also Dren Geer, address.

18. Ibid., "The Calf" by Walter Pettit, and Walter's 4-H reports (including chart of expenses) submitted to Hutch, May, 1936.

19. C. H. Maynard, "Farm Report" (to CH), July 5, 1936.

20. John Dewey, quoted in Cremin, *Transformation*, p. 225.

21. Letter, Mar. 18, 1983.

22. CH and E. Gray, interviews with SML.

23. First Boston alumni history session.

24. Clippings file, 1935–36.

25. From JTK's diary, Nov. 17, 1935.

26. JTK, letter, Jan. 29, 1936.

27. LCW, 1977. There is evidence (in "Rules, etc.," Sept. 1935) that the winter schedule was contemplated from the beginning, and that Liebe's encounter with Mrs. H. only triggered an earlier plan.

28. JTK, letters to her mother, Oct. 1935, and many alumni recollections.

29. Arms MS.

30. CH, in interview with Dr. Blair; CH to SML, personal communication.

31. LCW, questionnaire.

32. JTK, letter to her mother, Nov. 1, 1935; Peggy Squibb Stevens, letter to her mother, Nov. 3, 1935.

33. News clippings from "The Putney Column" in the Brattleboro *Reformer* (spring 1936).

34. CH, in interview with SML.

35. LCW, 1977.

36. See Addams, *The Spirit of Youth and the City Streets* (New York, 1912), p. 13.

37. Alice Holway to SML, personal communication, 1984; also CH and Hugh MacDougall, in interview with SML; Robert Darrow alumni questionnaire.

38. "The Putney Column," clippings, 1935–36.

Part II. "Utopia Was at Hand": 1936–1949 and Beyond

1. CH, "My Education for Teaching," p. 31.

2. See essay by Nora Sayre, "Boarding in Heaven," written in April 1968, a harrowing season for Americans, with Martin Luther King's assassination, the mayhem that followed it, and the Vietnam war as background; in Sayre's *Sixties Going on Seventies* (New York: Arbor House, 1973). Though I owe Putney's image as a twentieth-century utopia to neither Nora Sayre nor Carmelita Hinton, their contrasting definitions and evaluations are stimulating.

3. Arthur M. Schlesinger, Jr., Harvard College lectures on American intellectual history, Nov. 29 and Dec. 1, 1954; idem, letter to SML, Oct. 28, 1985. See also John Humphrey Noyes, *History of American Socialisms* (New York: Hillary House, 1961; reprint of the 1870 ed.), pp. 650–57. Schlesinger writes that his four criteria are adapted in part from Noyes's.

4. The best account of the Perfectionists' hurried escape from Putney is in Constance Noyes Robertson, *Oneida Community: An Autobiography, 1851–1876* (Syracuse, N.Y.: Syracuse University Press, 1970), introduction, pp. 11–13.

5. John Wirth, letter to SML, Feb. 2, 1986.

6. See James McLachlan, *American Boarding Schools: A Historical Study* (New York: Charles Scribner's Sons, 1970), p. 79, and chapter 2, "The Search for New Educational Forms."

7. See Mary Lyon, "To the Friends of Female Education," 1834; Kathryn Kish Sklar, *Catherine Beecher: A Study in American Domesticity*, (New Haven and London: Yale University Press, 1973), pp. 96, 321; Susan M. Lloyd, *A Singular School: Abbot Academy, 1828–1973* (Hanover, N.H.: University Press of New England, 1979), pp. 40–43, 144–45; Kett, *Rites of Passage*, pp. 102, 111, 137, 143, 152; McLachlan, *Boarding Schools*, chap. 6, "Innocence and Isolation: St. Paul's and the Victorian Educational Ideal."

8. Erik H. Erikson, "The Problem of Ego Identity," in *Identity and the Life Cycle, Selected Papers of E. Erikson* (New York, Psychological Issues monograph vol. 1, no. 1, 1959) pp. 116–18. Erik and Joan Erikson sent their children to Putney School.

Chapter 4. Work I

1. Richard Brett, in interview with SML, Aug. 7, 1981.

2. The Eight Year Study was managed by a commission on which several of Mrs. Hinton's old friends, colleagues, and/or mentors sat: Ralph Tyler (director of the study's evaluation staff), Perry Dunlap Smith, Flora Cook, Harold Gray (president of Bennington and father of two Putney sons), and Katharine Taylor (from archival material on the Eight Year Study in Cubberly Library, Stanford University School of Education, and Cremin, *Transformation*. Cremin discards the more exaggerated claims for the Eight Year Study in his analysis).

3. Letter from CH to John Holden, May 10, 1969; CH, in interview with SML. See also Cremin, *Transformation*, pp. 88–89, 181–83, 258–68.

4. Ralph Tyler, in interview with AKG, Dec. 28, 1977. See also Edward Yeomans, Jr., *The Shady Hill School: The First Fifty Years* (Cambridge: Windflower, 1979), p. 38. Yeomans describes Johnson's visit to Shady Hill in 1930 and her opinion that the school "was somewhat too structured."

5. John Dewey, "Discipline and Freedom," from *How We Think: A Restatement of the Relation of Reflective Thinking to the Educative Process* (reprinted in Reginald D. Archambault, ed., *John Dewey on Education: Selective Writings* [New York, Random House, 1964]), p. 256.

6. When Gerry Biddle retired in 1976, an expert math teacher tried to write a computer program that would schedule students' and teachers' appointments as skillfully as she had done with her system of pins and beads and personal consultations—and found it couldn't be done (Ray and Karen Goodlatte, in interview with Sue Mulcahy).

7. *Putney School Needs $250,000.*

8. Hugh MacDougall, in interview with SML; and Werner Heider, faculty/staff questionnaire; director's files.

9. See Sidney Hook, "The Case for Progressive Education," *Saturday Evening Post*, June 30, 1945. CH saved this article in her files.

10. Only one year's scores were available, and this list is incomplete, 17 of 120 upper school (ninth through twelfth grade) students having either been given individual tests (scores unrecorded) or missed the test altogether.

11. Testing file, curriculum reports, and correspondence between Ceci Brinton Roberts and CH.

12. From a six-page introduction Rogers wrote to his "General Science Course Outline," Sept. 1938.

13. Ed Gray, in interview with AKG.

14. Charles Hapgood, in interview with Peggy Squibb Stevens; Smith's reading lists and curriculum outline, Sept. 1947; alumni recollections of Hapgood and Smith.

15. Second New York area alumni history session; JHR's archives contain seniors' answers to CH's questions: What is the best method for teaching each subject? Have your teachers lived up to this ideal? (1953).

16. See Putney School prospectus, *A New School*, 1935, p. 2; CH, typed MS with handwritten revisions, undated (about 1936–37).
17. CH, in interview with AKG. See also Al Pfanstiehl, Physics I curriculum report.
18. D. Morris and Al Pfanstiehl's curriculum reports from June 1943 and June 1947.
19. Arms, course outline for 1938–39; 1940s alumni recollections; "Good Teaching" file.
20. Heider, curriculum report, "Chemistry X" June 1946; Williams, "Chemistry Curriculum Report," 1945–46. Other curriculum reports address the continuity issue.
21. 1930s and 1940s alumni questionnaires; Rogers' curriculum reports, 1939–49; Allan Hawkridge, personal communication to SML.
22. Polly Braun (Middleton), JTK, letters home in 1940–41 and 1936–38; conversations between alumnae and SML. Alumni questionnaires and other evidence (Peter Gill, interview with Margot S. Shaw, and George Carow, interview with Anne Jafferis, spring 1985) suggest that the problem of spotty upper-level math teaching worsened in the mid-forties and continued through the early fifties. More on this appears in the "Good Teaching" file.
23. Arms, MS, p. 24.
24. Jean Campbell, English curriculum report, June 1939; alumni recollections, two '51 alumni; Al Pfanstiehl, general science curriculum report, June 1948.
25. From CH's memo to students and faculty about the *Putney Magazine*, 1935.
26. Monica Owen, "Strength," the *Putney Magazine*, June 1936.
27. Judy Gregory, alumni questionnaire.
28. Phillis Watt Ingersoll, ancient history notebook, and many alumni recollections.
29. Polly Braun, letter to her mother, Mar. 13, 1941.
30. Sayre, "Boarding in Heaven," p. 194; alumni recollections, especially of the late forties and fifties; J. Arms, recording Charlotte Jossman's observations of the postwar English department, in MS, "1950–51"; comments of '48 alumni in their 15th Anniversary Report, the *Putney Post* (December 1963); "Good Teaching" file.
31. CH, typed MS with handwritten revisions. Original speaks of "the 'One World' for which we yearn."
32. Course outline for German II and III, 1938–39. See also Arms MS, p. 20.
33. Polly Braun, letter to her mother, Sept. 20, 1938. Several comments suggest that the early "language program was, in general, very poor" (questionnaires from 1936–38 alumni).
34. Polly Braun, letters to her mother, Sept. 24 and Oct. 1, 1939; Sayre, "Boarding in Heaven." Several other alumni offer similar opinions.
35. Cremin, *Transformation*, p. 183.
36. Arms MS, p. 26; CH, script for talk (c. 1947); and CH, in interview with SML.
37. Student journal, Dec. 8, 1943.
38. JTK, letter to her mother, Jan. 29, 1938.
39. Brattleboro *Reformer* (n.d.); Allan Hawkridge, personal communication to SML; Ottilie Hirt Rollins, faculty/staff questionnaire.
40. Director's files; William Wasserman, class of 1945, conversation.
41. Alumni questionnaires and Arms MS, "1945–46."
42. Interview with Phyllis Watt Ingersoll; Judy Gregory, alumni questionnaire; other alumni recollections; Polly Braun, letter to her mother, Mar. 13, 1941.
43. Polly Braun, letters to her mother, Sept. 24, 1938, Apr. 18, 1939, and Feb. 17, 1941. Mabel Gray also describes Barbara's eventual success in making close friends among other girls, and their regret at her departure.
44. CH, talk to Secondary Education Board, undated.
45. *Putney Worker*, July 24, 1945.
46. From Sproul's daughter Margot, Putney class of 1950.
47. Polly Braun, letter home, June 11, 1939.
48. In the September 1898 *Etude*, quoted in Kathleen Ulher Adams (with Dorothea Bowditch

Jones), *Thomas Whitney Surette, A Crusader for Good Music*, (Cambridge: Windflower, 1983), p. 121.

49. This and the Hinkles' account that follows are from their interview with SML, July 1982.
50. Adams, *Surette*, p. 93; C. Hinkle, in interview with SML.
51. C. Hinkle to SML, personal communication; Peggy James, in interview with Ted Dodd, May 1985, on Putney's bracing concept of the amateur; and G. Finckel, in interview with Margot Sproul Shaw, May 1985. Finckel played in the Stradivarius and Esteval quartets in addition to teaching at Bennington.
52. Alumni recollections in all history sessions; nearly all alumni questionnaires; interviews.
53. 1953 Alumni questionnaire; versions of this statement appear in nearly every class's questionnaires from 1936 on; "Good Teaching" file.
54. Joseph Schaaf, a violin/viola player, in conversation with SML. Marie Pereira, in conversation with SML, Nov. 1984, and many alumni have commented on Norwood's colorful language.
55. See also letter to Brattleboro *Reformer*, Dec. 15, 1951, on an "incredible performance" of music in the Putney Town Hall by Putney School musicians; the writer went by chance, knowing nothing of the school.
56. Sayre, "Boarding in Heaven," p. 195.
57. In *Putney School Needs $250,000*, p. 24.
58. Holden, "Carmelita Hinton's Contribution"; alumni recollections and questionnaires; Arms, MS, p. 20.
59. Christopher Fairbairn Armstrong, "Privilege and Productivity: The Cases of Two Private Schools and Their Graduates," Ph.D. diss., University of Pennsylvania, 1974, pp. 149–52. Abbot Academy, Phillips Academy, and Brearley School figures are courtesy of Jennifer M. Cooke and Mary Hamilton; statistics are based on questionnaires (incomplete returns for Abbot and Phillips academies).
60. Three questionnaires from 1930s and '40s alumni, second Boston area alumni history session, May 31, 1983; 1940s alumnus, who cited one classmate who did the same, in interview with SML; JTK; undated letter to her mother (context indicates March 1938). See also "The Putney Syndrome," *Harvard Alumni Magazine*, Oct. 10, 1964.
61. Questionnaires from 1930s–50s alumni; fifteenth anniversary reports of the Putney class of '42, compiled by John Quisenberry in 1957; Armstrong, "Privilege and Productivity," pp. 124–54 (includes references to E. Digby Baltzell, *Philadelphia Gentlemen: The Making of a National Upper Class* [1959], and idem, *The Protestant Establishment: Aristocracy and Caste in America* [1964]).
62. Stephen Sachs, '56, tape.

Chapter 5. Work II

1. Schlesinger, Harvard College, lecture Dec. 1, 1954. As Noyes wrote of the rural utopias, "We incline to think that this fondness for the land, which has been the habit of socialists, had much to do with their failures" (*American Socialisms*, p. 19).
2. CH, "Castles in the Air," original proposal for a new secondary school, 1934.
3. C. Maynard, "Suggestions for Next year," June 1936, and idem to CH, July 5, 1936. See also John Holden and JHR, in interview with SML, April 1983; CH, in interview with SML.
4. Isabel Stephens to SML, personal communication, October 1984; quotation from Ottilie Hirt Rollins, faculty/staff questionnaire. Ed Gray and others have remarked on Hutch's "built-in resistance to any suggestion." John Holden, on the other hand, thinks Hutch was very careful not to store wet hay (from interview with SML).
5. Dorothea Smith Ingersoll to SML, December 12, 1983. The old barn was insured for $5700; the new one would cost $7500 to build, and $1500 more would be spent to replace feed and equipment.

6. Two questionnaires from 1930s and '40s alumni; Nancy West to SML, personal communication.
7. Questionnaires from 1940s and '50s alumni.
8. LCW, 1977; Janet Thompson to her aunt Bertha, Oct. 29, 1936; Peggy Squibb's account of her sow, 4-H report, Oct. 13, 1936.
9. William M. Kephart, *Extraordinary Groups*, 2d ed. (New York: St. Martin's, 1982), 119.
10. Quoted in *Harper's Bazaar*, October 1943.
11. J. Arms, MS, "1946–47."
12. Sayre, "Boarding in Heaven," p. 192; alumni questionnaires.
13. Noyes, *American Socialisms*, p. 636.
14. Ed Gray in the *Putney Post*, May 1968; JHR and alumni recollections.
15. Nancy West to SML, personal communication. Roy had diabetes, which may have been the reason for the 4F classification. Several of Roy's assistants would stay almost as long as he, including Linnie Campbell, who retired soon after making her 2,500th birthday cake.
16. Questionnaire from 1955 alumnus; Cynthia Deery Russell (CDR), "A Way of Life and a Time of Life," MS on the Putney School, p. 68.
17. English journal, Peter Caldwell. Putney School catalogue, 1940–41.
18. CH, quoted by Jane Arms, MS vol. 2, pp. 17–18.
19. Hester Crawford, "Reminiscences of Putney School"; Arms, MS vol. 2, p. 21.
20. Arms, "Some Characteristics of Mrs. Hinton" (1954); confirmed by Warren Leonard in a letter to SML, Aug. 24, 1984.
21. Letters to 1940s alumnus, Dec. 18, 1980, and to Joseph Post, n.d., alumni files.
22. *Putney School Aborning*, p. 18.
23. From the business manager's consolidated balance sheets, beginning in 1941.
24. Crawford, "Reminiscences."
25. Evidence on this point is necessarily impressionistic, but it is interesting that it appears spontaneously in many informal conversations, as well as in alumni questionnaires, alumni history sessions, alumni notes in the *Putney Post* and students' letters home.

Chapter 6. A Way of Life: Religion, Sex, and Other Essentials

1. The words from the first sentence of the faculty manual, written 1950–52, and part of the title of CDR MS, "A Way of Life and a Time of Life." See also Paul A. Buttenweiser, "Ideal Community," *Harvard Crimson*, June 16, 1958.
2. John Dewey, quoted by Cremin in *Transformation*, p. 100. Dren Geer, principal of the Francis Parker School in Chicago from 1976 to 1986, says that Dewey, Parker, and other early progressives thought of their work as part of a broad-based evangelical Christian movement. Ralph Tyler sees CH in the same tradition.
3. Arms, "Some Characteristics of Mrs. Hinton." R. Tyler, in interview with AKG; Werner Heider, in interview with Jane Roberts Gill, Aug. 8, 1983.
4. W. Kephart, *Extraordinary Groups*, pp. 95–96, 110–14, 125–26 (including quotations from the Oneida *Handbook*). See also the Rev. Hubbard Eastman, *Noyesism Unveiled* (Brattleboro, 1849) and John Humphrey Noyes, *The Putney Community* (Oneida, N.Y., 1931). After being brought before his townsmen for violating Vermont's adultery statute, he reaffirmed to his followers, "The Kingdom of God is commenced." The Perfectionists needed no conventional moral law because, they insisted, "immediate and total cessation from sin" was possible given a beneficent environment. Noyes, *The Putney Community*, p. 340; Charles Nordhoff, *The Communistic Societies of the United States* (New York: Harper and Bros., 1875), p. 269.
5. Polly Braun, undated letter home; CDR, MS, p. 40; JTK to her aunt Laura, Mar. 20, 1938; also alumnus project week journal, Dec. 9 and 10, 1943.
6. Yeomans, "The Religious Idea in Education," *Putney Magazine*, Dec. 1935 (the first issue);

JTK wrote to her aunt Bertha about this speech, Oct. 1935. Jane Arms called Yeomans "Carmelita's good friend, preacher and adviser" (MS).

7. CH to SML, personal communication. Alice Holway remembers the same incident. (CH stopped to rest at her house in Dummerston. The whole trip was about seventeen miles.) Alice Holway, in interview with AKG; Arms, "Some Characteristics of Mrs. Hinton."

8. Yeomans, "The Religious Idea," pp. 2–3. See also Clara Brokaw (parent) in *Putney School Needs $250,000*.

9. See especially CH, "Castles in the Air," and Putney School catalogues, 1936–55.

10. Robert Owen, *A New View of Society: Essays on the Principle of the Formation of Human Character* (London, 1913; reprint, Everyman, 1927 pp. 14–90. Schlesinger, Harvard College lectures; Oneida *Handbook*; George P. Lockwood, *The New Harmony Movement* (New York: D. Appleton, 1905). Lockwood discusses the Owenites' commitment to an education as intensive as it was unconventional.

11. This theme is especially prominent in CH's notes for an undated speech (probably 1937–38).

12. Parker, quoted in Cremin, *Transformation*, pp. 134–35.

13. Muriel Seelye Heinemann, at memorial service for CH, Apr. 24, 1983; also CH, MS for talk given at Bryn Mawr College about 1946; JTK, in interview with AKG; alumni recollections of "Mrs. H.'s belief in us."

14. CH, "A New Secondary School."

15. Parker, quoted in Cremin, *Transformation*, p. 134.

16. E. Dewey, *New Schools*, p. 336.

17. Donald Dickinson, faculty/staff questionnaire; see also Arthur Green, letters and questionnaire. The Grays are mentioned more often in faculty/staff questionnaires from 1936–65 than any other colleagues, the Hinkles receiving the next most frequent comments. This is partly a function of both couples' long tenure at the school.

18. Questionnaires and recollections from 1940s and early '50s alumni; Polly Braun, letter, Oct. 1, 1939. Albert Raffanel, written complaint to CH concerning student note, Feb. 1949.

19. Dirk Spruyt, alumni questionnaire.

20. CDR, MS, p. 35.

21. For the 1946 conference, "The Future of American Agriculture," Edward Yeomans, Jr., returned in his role as secretary of the Eastern Division of the National Farmers' Union. Other speakers were Ralph Borsodi, economist and author of *This Ugly Civilization* and *Flight from the City*; Arthur Packard, president of the Vermont State Farm Bureau; and Frederick B. Coles, Commissioner of Agriculture for Massachusetts.

22. Conversation with Dorothy Lloyd Tyack.

23. CH, report to directors, June 16, 1942; store manager's reply.

24. CDR MS, p. 67.

25. *Putney Worker*, Aug. 12, 1938.

26. JTK, quoting a friend in a letter home, Feb. 1937.

27. Ed and Mabel Gray, in interview with SML; Arms, MS.

28. Alumni recollections (several from '50); faculty recollections.

29. CH, draft of "My Education for Teaching"; the published article in *Bryn Mawr Bulletin* says "the much astonished nearby villagers."

30. J. Gregory, Mar. 1948, and an article in vol. 4 of the *Putney Press* (unsigned), "Putney Snobbery towards Its Own Village."

31. Alice Holway and Hugh MacDougall, interviews.

32. Monica Owen, senior project report, "A Study of the Town of Putney, Vt." (1936), p. 45.

33. "J. S. H." in Brattleboro *Reformer* editorial, July 23, 1945.

34. LCW, Sunday night meeting talk.

35. Sayre, "Boarding in Heaven."

36. J. Gregory's journal and many alumni recollections.

37. *Putney Weeder*, July 11, 1947.

38. In *Putney Magazine*, Apr. 1936.
39. Quoted in James McLachlan, *American Boarding Schools*, p. 284. Other sources on the athletic ethos in boys' schools include the inspirational novels and book-length sermons written by headmasters. Two examples are Claude Fuess, *The Andover Way* (Boston: Lothrop, Lee & Shepard, 1926) and Alfred Stearns, *The Challenge of Youth* (Boston: W. A. Wilde, 1923).
40. Three alumni recollections, 1949–52.
41. Jeff Campbell; Bill Wasserman, at Memorial Service for CH.
42. J. Gregory, letter home, Mar. 11, 1948; alumni recollections.
43. CDR MS, p. 66.
44. Ibid., p. 54.
45. S. McIntosh, letter home, Nov. 1950; P. Braun, letters home, Oct. 19, 1938, and Jan. 29, 1939.
46. Letters home by J. Thompson and P. Braun; alumni recollections; parent's article on Putney School, "A Modern Plumfield," (n.d.), in Putney School archives.
47. P. Caldwell, English journal. Several other alumni also describe the elder Caldwell's prowess.
48. Peggy Squibb, Dec. 1935. Similar requests appear in two other students' letters.
49. By David Bradley, Dec. 1935.
50. CH, MS, "Evening Activities," c. 1947; J. Addams, *A New Conscience*, p. 106.
51. CH, "Evening Activities," also CH, "Castles in the Air," and CH, in interviews with SML.
52. Questionnaire from 1940s alumnus; many alumni recollections; Peter Caldwell, in letter to SML, Feb. 1985.
53. CH, in letter to Lucy Pary, Jan. 25, 1949; questionnaire from 1949 alumna; Marisa Lederer, in interview with M. Sproul Shaw, May 1985.
54. Alumni recollections; also Karen Goodlatte and John Caldwell, Jr., interviews on CH's constant watchfulness.
55. Boys' comments from "Sex Customs" folder; alumni questionnaire; JHR's reflections.
56. Alumni questionnaires and recollections; Alice Holway's recollections; conversations with Putney parents; Sayre, "Boarding in Heaven."
57. John Moyer to SML, personal communication.
58. Sayre, "Boarding in Heaven," and virtually every alumnus and alumna who addresses the issue in questionnaires.
59. *Putney Weeder*, 1947, issue #1.
60. Alumnae recollections. See also Sayre, "Boarding in Heaven": "Most girls muffled their minds in class."
61. CH, in conversation with SML. See also Wallace, "Carmelita Hinton at 82."

Chapter 7. Time Passing

1. Mrs. H. reported to parents in 1941 that the seventh and eighth grades had been dropped, but that in spite of this, applications were pouring in. "We could be a school of 400 tomorrow," she finished. 1948 figures appear in Arms, 1954 MS; Nancy West, personal communication. Arms writes that in 1948 three applied for each accepted. This application-to-admission ratio represents no primary documents, and Arms may be referring to the ratio of inquiries to enrollees, inevitably a more hopeful figure. Nancy West's estimate in the June 1948 *Putney Alumni News* is more conservative (about 2:1) and probably more accurate.
2. Alumni questionnaires; Boston area, first alumni history gathering; Mark Lauter, in interview with SML, July 1, 1985; *Time Magazine*, Aug. 4, 1954 ("The school has attracted the children of some of America's most alert and influential people").
3. Articles by Alfred Eipper and Dick Campbell, *Putney Magazine*, Dec. 1935.
4. 1934 Survey conducted by Frederick Bair; cited in Tyack, Lowe, and Hansot, *Hard Times*, p. 68.
5. Charles Hapgood, in interview with Peggy Squibb Stevens; English curriculum reports.

6. JTK, letter home, Nov. 3, 1936.
7. W. Hinton's letters to the *Putney Magazine* (June 1938), pp. 13, 22.
8. Ruth Hodgdon, in interview with Laura Heller, Mar. 25, 1985; SML, conversation with 1939 alumnus; David M. Clarkson to SML, personal communication, Jan. 26, 1985; recollections of Betsy Doolin Uptegrove; Arthur Green to SML, personal communication, 1985; questionnaire from 1940 alumnus.
9. In *Putney Post*, 1961.
10. Nancy West to SML, written recollections.
11. Survey reading of public and private secondary school magazines and newspapers, 1938–41, covering a sample of schools in Boston, New York City, eastern Kansas, and northern California.
12. Warmbrunn, faculty/staff questionnaire. See also Ewald Schnitzer, faculty/staff questionnaire. While Ewald's and Werner's recollections on this score are almost entirely positive, it took some time for Putney School to shake the negative aspects of its "pro-German" image. The most extreme manifestation of it was registered in the *New York Herald Tribune* in the Sept. 30, 1940 "Letters to the Editor" section, which was headed "DISLOYAL SCHOOLS: Nazi Influence Said to Pervade Some of Them." The anonymous letter was written by the aunt of two Putney School students. It accuses Putney (without naming it) of being a "fifth column stronghold," a "Nazi School," and finishes with a call to parents everywhere "who suspect their children's schools" to band together and simultaneously to withdraw their children.

     The Tribune letter brought an indignant reply from the two students' grandmother defending Putney School. Privately, at least one parent wrote CH to ask her for a reassuring word that would prove the hysterical chatter baseless. A similar (though not so colorful) exchange of letters appeared in the *New York Times* at about the same time (undated clippings).
13. M. Thompson, letters written from English House, fall 1941.
14. Antoinette Pels, curriculum report, June 1943.
15. J. Gregory letter to her family, Nov. 16, 1946.
16. Alumni recollections; *Putney Magazine*, Jan. 1942.
17. New York area alumni history sessions.
18. Arms, MS, "1945–46," and alumni recollections.
19. Joan Hinton in *Putney Magazine*, Dec. 1945.
20. *Washington Post*, Mar. 2, 1978, and *Sunday Globe*, Mar. 12, 1978, interviews given by Joan Hinton on her first trip back to the United States.
21. 1950s magazine articles, quoted by Joan Hinton to *Sunday Globe*, ibid.
22. Marguerite C. Hearsey, principal's reports (Dec. 7, 1944, and Apr. 8, 1949) to the trustees of Abbot Academy, describing other boarding schools' experience with black students and Abbot's obligation to admit them. A handful of Putney's friends advised CH to conduct a survey of parents, but she flatly rejected the idea.
23. *Putney Magazine*, June 1946.
24. *Putney Magazine*, Dec. 1945, articles by Waldo Frank and Alfred Heller.
25. *Putney Magazine*, Dec. 1946.
26. *Putney News* editorial, 1st issue, Dec. 15, 1946.
27. *Putney News*, Dec. 15, 1946; Jan. 29, Feb. 5, May 7, May 21, and June 6, 1947; survey of all issues through 1950. Bruce Menefee, faculty advisor to the *News*, found promise in socialism; it is thus impressive to note the range of opinion within the *News*.
28. David Lattimore, *Putney Magazine*, Nov. 1947.
29. Menefee quoted in *Putney Magazine*, 1947.
30. In March 1949; see Hugh MacDougall, Jr., letter to SML.
31. *Putney Press*, Oct. 8, 1947; Bruce Menefee, in interview with SML, Aug. 26, 1985.
32. *The Sphere*, Dec. 1948.

33. Arms, 1954 MS of Putney history, 1945–47. The following account of postwar difficulties is based on Arms and on conversations with and questionnaires from faculty, staff, and alumni.
34. J. Caldwell, in *Putney School Needs $250,000*, pp. 6–12.
35. Holly Forbes Leon, in interview with SML. H. MacDougall became engineer for various international projects.
36. Charles R. Cummings in the *Vermonter* (1940), pp. 261, 263.
37. Dewey, *Democracy and Education* (1916); quoted in Cremin, *Transformation*, p. 122.
38. Unidentified typed MS in English curriculum report folder, filed with 1946–47 reports. Student authorship is assumed because of the character of several "definitions."

Part III. A Hinge: 1948–1949

1. Arms, MS (1951): alumna at first Boston area history session.
2. Felix Pereira, in interview with SML, Nov. 1984; many faculty and staff observations.

Chapter 8. Strike

1. Alumni questionnaire, 1941.
2. Richard Brett, in interview with SML, and many other sources including Alice Holway, Felix Pereira, Daniel Morris, Tony Kray, Elizabeth Frothingham Moore, and alumni of almost all classes to 1956.
3. Dan Morris, in interview with SML; John S. Holden, "An Experience with Bureaucracy: The Putney School Strike of 1949," 1968 paper for a graduate sociology course at Harvard.
4. Faculty/staff questionnaires, and Holden, "Experience," p. 5.
5. E. Gray, in interview with SML.
6. Arms, MS, "1946–47." CH is referred to as principal instead of director in this chapter to distinguish her role from that of the directors on the corporation board, though she only occasionally used the title.
7. CH, in interview with SML, 1981. See also CH's explanation of the Executive Committee's purpose in minutes of faculty meeting, Nov. 11, 1948.
8. Arms, MS, "1947–48"; John Holden, "Random Notes of the Guy Who Was Away When the Storm Broke," 1948–49. Beginning in the summer of 1947, CH's secretary, Charlotte Mac-Donald, had been writing to other private schools and colleges to inquire about their charters, boards, and corporate governance systems.
9. Faculty questionnaires and Holden, "Experience," p. 2; Arms, MS, "1946–47"; Holden, "Random Notes."
10. See Holden, "Experience," p. 2; Hugh MacDougall, Ed Gray, and Dan Morris, in interviews with SML; Alice Holway in interview with AKG.
11. See Arms, MS, vol. 2, p. 10, and carbon copy of handwritten letter (or of original not sent), to Isabel Stephens, c. 1948; Alice Holway, interview; Nancy West's and Warren Leonard's letters to SML, summer 1984.
12. See student journal, '49 graduate; copy of undated letter (or original not sent), Arms to Isabel Stephens; and Arms, undated letter to C. Hinkle. Mrs. H.'s assessment of her old friend in 1981: "A peculiar person—an absolute individual" (from interview with SML). It should be added that at least one relatively new teacher (as well as most of Jane's students) disagreed with others' perceptions. To Ray Rice, "Jane was hale and hearty and open with everyone" (in interview with SML, June 1985). Arms resigned from the Executive Committee in the summer of 1948.
13. Alumni recollections, especially of the men who lived as students in Angell House; CH, in

interview with SML and in June 1949 letter of recommendation to the California State Department of Education; Werner Warmbrunn, faculty/staff questionnaire. See also Arms, MS, "1950–51."

14. CH, in interviews with SML; correspondence between CH and GBH, director's files; Joseph Schaaf, in interview with Margot Sproul Shaw, May 1985.

15. See Arms, MS, "1946–47"; Holden, "Experience." Holden put it this way: "When Warren and I came back, Geoffrey Bret Harte and Jim Angell had a lot of power. Our taking over old responsibilities made them feel left out." See also Arms, MS, "1945–46."

16. Arms, MS, vol. 2. See also CH, letter to Cameron Winslow, March 1949 (JHR archives).

17. Richard Brett, in interview with SML.

18. Random survey of Putney School office files with contract letters and other correspondence with CH; letter from 1948–49 teacher to SML, Aug. 21, 1985. During this era of teacher shortages, Mrs. H. paid one young science teacher $400 a month plus room and board for himself and his family. Werner Heider has spoken on the subject of serious teacher overload (interview with Jane Roberts Gill, Aug. 8, 1983) as have other former faculty; a letter to JHR from Gabriel Jackson, Jan. 25, 1949, explains why he had to refuse the special deal offered to him and his bride.

19. See Edith Finch, *Carey Thomas of Bryn Mawr*, (London: Harper & Bros., 1947). Also article by Barbara Barnes and Donald Watt, "The Strike at Putney," in *Putney Alumni News*, #3, written in May, 1949, p. 1: "The overall impression remains that good teachers leave Putney in large numbers"; Joseph Schaaf, in interview with M. S. Shaw.

20. The office files are filled with such letters. Often they are messages incorporated in yearly contract letters. Poignant examples are those written to Gabriel Jackson (June 28, 1948), Harris Buxenbaum (June 23, 1947), and others later involved in the Faculty Association and union.

21. CH, in interview with SML.

22. Documenting Smith's difficulties with the FBI and congressional committees are Mark Lauter, interview with SML, July 7, 1985; H. Rept. 1902, 76th Cong. 3d sess., and accompanying H.R. 1902; hearings of House Committee for Un-American Activities (Mar. 1, 1956); references to other congressional investigations of Smith ten years earlier in 1946. On Smith's organizing of oil workers, see letter to SML from S. E. Weinbrecht, Freedom of Information Officer, NLRB.

23. T. Ingersoll, in interview with SML; C. Humpstone, letter to SML, Jan. 1, 1986; several alumni remarks in first Boston and New York area history sessions; Peter Caldwell, letter to SML, Feb. 22, 1985.

24. Holden, "Experience," pp. 5, 6, and CH's added pencil comments; Tudor Ingersoll to SML, personal communication; and several alumni remarks in Boston and New York area history sessions. Smith's 1947–48 curriculum outline for History 12 (European and American history "from the Congress of Vienna to the United Nations") lists as principal texts Carl Becker's *Modern Europe* and Allan Nevins and Henry S. Commager's *Pocket History of the United States*. There are also documentary readings such as the *Communist Manifesto* and frequent assignments in Hazen, *Europe since 1915*, and P. T. Moon, *Imperialism and World Politics*. It appears to be a fertile approach to complex developments, and suggests that Smith might well have made a superior college teacher, had he had the chance. His major eleventh-grade text, says one alumnus, was Leo Huberman's *Man's Worldly Goods*.

25. See letter from Smith to CH, Nov. 11, 1948. Smith finishes, "I am very sympathetic with your personal distress" (JHR archives).

26. Holden, "Experience." Holden uses the first-person pronoun. Italics are added. To Holden, as to several others, including at least one union member, Smith was the villain. Gabriel Jackson and Ray and Miriam Rice minimize Smith's role, however, and feel he has been unfairly blamed for the 1948–49 upheaval (conversations with SML). One teacher wrote Mrs. H. that

she had accepted Marion's overtures not from any distrust or disloyalty but because she believed in unions. Rae Greenfield, letter to CH, Nov. 12, 1948.

27. Bruce Menefee says that the Smiths approached him together to propose a Faculty Association. "A bombshell," he says of the proposal. See Hugh MacDougall on the weekly evenings at the Bret Hartes'; Barbara Warren (Mrs. Hamilton Warren, cofounder of Verde Valley) on Mara Moser (conversation with SML, June 21, 1986).
28. Ray Rice, conversation with SML, June 22, 1985; director's files.
29. Questionnaires from 1949 alumni; J. Ingersoll, in interview with SML; Judy Gregory, alumni questionnaire; first Boston area history session.
30. Gabriel Jackson, letter to SML, Apr. 6, 1984.
31. Ibid.
32. Several informants have mentioned the disappointment over Wallace's showing in the '48 election and feel it intensified the divisions at Putney School.
33. Bruce Menefee, in interview with SML, July 26, 1985.
34. See Barnes and Watt, "Strike," for the effects of the "vow of silence," including the way in which "attributed reasons became more and more slanderous . . . as the tension grew" during November and December. Also Anne and John Holden in interview with SML; G. Jackson, letter to SML, May 5, 1985; and minutes of faculty meeting, Nov. 11, 1948. One former Association member (Ray Rice) describes the original limitation of discussion as nothing like a gag rule: "I would never have agreed to that," he says.
35. Memos to the faculty, "to be specifically considered by the Association," Nov. 11 and 14, 1948.
36. See especially CH, memo "TO WHOM IT MAY CONCERN," written Apr. 22, 1948.
37. W. Leonard, Nov. 11, 1948, and CH, who turned her statement into a formal letter to all faculty members on Nov. 14, 1948; minutes of faculty meeting, Nov. 11, 1948.
38. Penciled comment by J. Holden on his copy of the ultimatum. The ultimatum's significance is confirmed by memos and letters to CH from both sides, Nov. 18, 1948–Feb. 10, 1949 (JHR archives), and by Association letters to parents, Feb. 14, 1949. CH herself, in trying to explain later to three Association members why she refused to be rushed into a February decision, called the ultimatum an "unforgivable" result of being rushed in November. (Notes on two-hour administration-association meeting following CH's Jan. 15, 1949, letter to parents.)
39. Faculty/staff letters to CH, Nov. 18–22 1948 (JHR archives). The quotation is from Marion Smith's letter.
40. Carbon copy of CH's announcement rescinding the ultimatum. See also Barnes and Watt, "Strike," on the hard-liners.
41. G. Jackson, letter to SML, Aug. 5, 1985.
42. G. Jackson, letter to Peter Sloss, Jan. 24, 1949.
43. G. Jackson, letter to SML.
44. CH, in interview with SML; E. Smith, letter to CH, Dec. 16, 1948; Corliss Lamont, letter to CH, Dec. 31, 1948 (JHR archives).
45. CH, letter to parents, Jan. 15, 1949; JHR, her mother's almost constant consultant in the 1948–49 crisis, confirms CH's relative moderation.
46. From conversations with former union teachers. One insists, however, that there was no evidence that the teacher's dismissal had any connection with Association membership. Leonard confirms this interpretation.
47. Association "suggestions," Jan. 21, 1949.
48. JHR to SML, in conversation and by letter, May 1986. See also Barnes and Watt, "Strike."
49. CH, letter to the Putney Faculty Association, Feb. 4, 1949.
50. Faculty recollections; two memos to CH from A. Raffanel; two memos from J. Angell (JHR archives).

51. J. Holden, penciled note on CH's memo to the Association, Feb. 11, 1949.
52. Phyllis Watt Ingersoll, in interview with SML.
53. CH, memo, Feb. 11, 1949. A memo to CH from John Holden, Feb. 9, 1949, also testifies to her views.
54. See Barnes and Watt, "Strike," on the job security issue's predominance.
55. Also Ray Rice to SML, personal communication. The union members were:

> Florence Angell
> *James K. Angell
> *Fritz Bargebuhr
> *Mary Bartlett
> Harris Buxenbaum
> *Una Buxenbaum
> *Jean-Marie Chalufour
> *Calvin Goodman
> Florence Goodman
> Rae Greenfield
> *Jack Guthrie
> Frances Fistick
> Stanley Fistick
> *Geoffrey Bret Harte
> Vivian Johannes
> Sylvia Mendenhall
> *Bruce Menefee
> Esther Morris
> *Albert Raffanel
> Miriam Rice
> *Raymond Rice
> *Edwin S. Smith
> Marion Smith
> Virginia Vitzthum

Asterisks indicate full-time academic teachers.

Six other faculty, five of them classroom teachers, were members of the Association but not of the union. All of these except Artilles had left Putney School by the time the union was formed.

Joseph Schaaf recalls a coffee conversation among members of the new union at about this time, sitting in the faculty room before or after one of Joe's rehearsals with Norwood. "People began to come in and say, 'Now, the next move is a strike.' 'A *strike?!*' exclaims one of the new Union members. 'Yes, that's the way to move things along.'"

56. Bruce Menefee, in interview with SML. See also William Eaton, *The American Federation of Teachers, 1916–1961* (Carbondale: Southern Illinois University Press, 1975), pp. 126–47. The 180 charters included a private-school CIO union, which was that very February completing negotiations on a contract with The Little Red Schoolhouse–Elizabeth Irwin School in New York City, a cooperatively-run school from the beginning.
57. For opinions on Bret Harte as stooge, F. Pereira, Helen Buttenweiser, and alumni recollections; first Boston area history session; Mark Lauter, in interview with SML, Jan. 1, 1985.
58. G. Jackson, letter to SML, Aug. 5, 1985, discussing the reasons for CH's "paranoia"; Calvin J. Goodman, letter to SML, Aug. 1985; conversations with former faculty and students.
59. CH, in interview with SML; also Jane Roberts Gill, at first Boston area history session; Ray Rice on the anti-union teacher; Ed and Mabel Gray, in interview with SML, (on Jim Angell's concerns about Ed Smith at this time). There is, however, no proof that Smith was ever a Party

member, despite repeated charges by antagonistic congressmen and others. (At the Mar. 1, 1956, HUAC hearings, Smith had to plead the Fifth Amendment forty-six times.) JHR says "The 'Communist' issue was never one that [Mrs. Hinton] fell for, or was influenced by in this case" (letter to SML, May 2, 1986).

60. Ray Rice, in interview with SML.

61. Mark Lauter, in interview with SML; SML's conversations with former faculty and parents; personal observations; parent letter to CH, Feb. 1949, warning her that the CIO had proven it had the means to "provide outside protection" if there were communists on the faculty; letter from Adelaide Hering to CH, Mar. 18, 1949, on communists in labor unions.

62. J. Gregory and N. Sayre, taped conversation about political "vacuum," confirmed by other alumni recollections; T. Ingersoll, P. W. Ingersoll, F. Pereira, CH, John Moyer, all in interviews with SML; J. Schaaf, in interview with M. S. Shaw; first Boston area history session.

63. Mabel Gray to SML, personal communications; alumnae conversations with SML.

64. N. Sayre, tape; alumni conversations with SML; T. Ingersoll, P. W. Ingersoll, in interview with SML.

65. Alumni recollections in history sessions; T. Ingersoll and P. W. Ingersoll, in interview with SML; J. Gregory and N. Sayre, taped conversation.

66. Artilles' words as John Holden and CH recall them. Calvin Goodman believes that the union-administration conflict put Jenaro Artilles in an impossible plight, since he felt he owed Mrs. H. so much for "befriending him in his search for political asylum" (letter to SML, Aug. 21, 1985).

67. From first Boston area history session.

68. John and Anne Holden, in interview and phone conversation with SML; first Boston area history session; three references to Bret Harte's resignation from the Association just before the union was formed, from CH's personal correspondence in JHR archives; Warren Leonard, letter to SML, July 1985.

69. F. Pereira, in interview with SML. Alumni have spoken of the open use of obscenities among some faculty (history session tapes); also J. Moyer, in interview with SML; Feb. 1949 correspondence between CH and F. Pereira and H. Buttenweiser (JHR archives).

70. F. Pereira, in interview with SML. Ray Rice says that Mark Lauter, the administration attorney, recognized Smith with surprise, having been a young staff attorney for the NLRB in the 1930s. Lauter confirms this.

71. Memo to Mrs. H. from Bruce Menefee, union secretary, Mar. 9, 1949; JHR, in conversation with SML.

72. Anne Holden's notes for this directors' Executive Committee meeting; JHR, in conversation with SML.

73. Typed manuscript of contract negotiations, Mar. 12 and 13, 1949. Negotiators were stymied in part by "the absence of law specifically applying here [which] means we have no comparable situation to go by" (Lauter, quoting E. Smith, p. 17).

74. Letters: Bret Harte to CH, Mar. 14 and 22, 1949; CH to G. Bret Harte, Mar. 18 and 23, 1949; C. Goodman to SML; unsent letter to parents enclosing key documents, beginning with July 1948 Executive Committee reorganization proposals; CH, in interview with SML; Judy Gregory, tape; F. Pereira, Mark Lauter, in interviews with SML. Also Caldwell's Mar. 12, 1949, estimate of a 20 percent increase (JHR archives); final 1948–49 financial records.

75. In "Experience," p. 3.

76. Arms, MS, vol. 2, p. 12.

77. CH and JHR, in interviews and conversation with SML. That some specific points had been successfully negotiated by the two parties' outside counsel, the CIO's Alfred Katz and Mark Lauter, seems borne out by notes taken at the explanatory meeting arranged for students after the strike by Carroll Shepard. Shepard records Lauter's statement that "the two had agreed to return and discuss counter-proposals on April 2nd" so that things would be settled on the

students' return. Katz "had not yet told the Union of this agreement" when, to his astonishment (Katz: "I was literally sick at what had happened"), the strike was called. Mark Lauter confirms this now (July 1, 1985).

78. CH's and JHR's vivid memories of the appointments made; director's files; CH's letter, dated June 28, 1948; undated response from V. Johannes. The two letters support Vivian's interpretation. There may have been unwritten exchanges, however.

79. Bret Harte, letter, Mar. 24, 1949; also notes of Bret Harte's contract conference with CH, Mar. 22, 1949, made by two witnesses, one from each side (JHR archives).

80. M. S. Shaw, tape, May 1985.

81. Letter to CH, Mar. 22, 1949. See also the Brattleboro *Daily Reformer*, Mar. 23, 1949.

82. H. L. Buttenweiser, in telephone interview with SML, July 4, 1984. Mrs. Buttenweiser says that CH was "suspicious of Ben [her husband] and me" because of their background in labor law and the fact that both Buttenweisers believed that, in some circumstances, strikes are necessary.

83. Carroll Shepard, notes on Mark Lauter's description of his reaction. Lauter confirms (see n. 77, supra).

84. Shepard, notes.

85. Principle articulated by CH in brief, carefully impartial announcement in Assembly the night before; recollections of 1949, 1951, and 1952 alumni. John Moyer, in conversation with SML; J. Gregory, tape. See also B. Menefee's Mar. 23, 1949, letter to CH describing a mailroom confrontation with Caldwell and accusing Caldwell of threatening intimidation of "Reds" in the union (JHR archives).

86. Barnes and Watt, "Strike"; other alumni recollections.

87. T. Ingersoll, in interview with SML; Charles Humpstone, personal communication; John Moyer, in conversation with SML; first Boston area history session.

88. "Experience," p. 8. Similarly, a former Putney parent wrote the Brattleboro *Reformer* contending that "no matter what settlement has been made, the damage to the children cannot be erased" (March 1949).

89. Questionnaires from 1951 and 1949 alumni.

90. N. Sayre, from J. Gregory and N. Sayre, taped conversation.

91. Brattleboro *Daily Reformer*, Mar. 24, 1949. Michael Vidor and Maria Josephy initiated and presented the petition.

92. Questionnaires and recollections from 1951 and 1952 alumni, corroborated by Barnes and Watt, "Strike," and the account of one senior.

93. CH, four-page letter to parents, with enclosures, Mar. 23, 1949.

94. Putney School archives' late March 1949 clippings from the *New York Times* and Chicago and two West Coast papers (UPI and AP dispatches). The previous two years had seen far more strikes by public school teachers than the U.S. had ever known (12,000 teachers out on strike in 48 different job actions, as opposed to 1700 from 1940–45) but a private school, CIO-sponsored strike was unheard of (*Boston Globe*, Mar. 30, 1949).

95. CH, letter to parents, Mar. 23, 1949; Bret Harte, letter to parents, Mar. 24, 1949.

96. H. Buttenweiser, T. Ingersoll, in interviews with SML.

97. Holden, "Experience," p. 3, and in interview with SML; Warren Leonard, letter to SML. The "snake in Eden" quotation is from the New York meeting and a letter to CH, Apr. 6, 1949, from Thomas D. Eliot.

98. The local name of this vertical union was the NLRB Union, United Public Workers. See H. Rept. 1902, pp. 7–19, 24–25, 48–51, 57–60, 82–83. See also James A. Gross, *The Making of the National Labor Relations Board: A Study in Education, Politics and the Law, 1933–1937* (State University of New York Press, 1974; hereafter referred to as *Making*) by the same author, *The Reshaping of the National Labor Relations Board: Politics in Transition, 1937–1947* (State University of New York Press, 1981; hereafter referred to as *Reshaping*). Gross describes Smith's

service as "a bright and useful member of the pre-Wagner Act National Labor Board" (*Making*, pp. 109–10) and his deepening disgust with employers' attempts to evade Wagner Act requirements during his third term on the board. He offers ample evidence, including data from extensive personal interviews with Smith, that Smith did indeed take the CIO's side as both the AFL and the CIO "used the Board in their efforts to defeat one another" (*Making*, pp. 156, 203, 251–52; *Reshaping*, pp. 2, 167–69, 239). While the AFL cheered his "elimination," calling it "the crowning achievement in [its] long campaign to rid the NLRB of brazen favoritism toward the CIO," some employers also celebrated the removal of "Communist" influence and the NLRB's "retreat to a conservative labor policy" (*Reshaping*, pp. 167, 239, 251, 256). Gross finds no evidence that Smith was being manipulated by the CIO, the Communist Party, or anyone else. Two other labor historians characterize the climax of the seventeen-month investigation as "an ugly series of hearings" that offered no proof whatsoever of the charges of communist subversion—"Nor were they susceptible of proof." Frank W. McCulluch and Tim Bernstein, *The National Labor Relations Board* (New York: Praeger, 1974), pp. 29–31.

99. CH, in interview with SML; further information on Smith is from material obtained from the FBI under the Freedom of Information Act.

100. C. J. Goodman, letter to SML; conversations with former union members.

101. F. Pereira, in interview with SML, John Holden, letter to M. C. McIntosh, Apr. 22, 1949.

102. M. C. McIntosh, letter to Bret Harte, Apr. 17, 1949. H. MacDougall, in interview with SML. As early as March 22, however, Bret Harte told the Brattleboro *Reformer* (Mar. 23, 1949) that he did not plan to return to Putney School. Yet by mid-April he was ready to do so (letters to CH, Apr. 1949). Other pertinent letters are: to CH from parent Christopher Granger, Apr. 29, 1949, calling on Bret Harte to reinstate his resignation; to CH from Smith College's president, Herbert Davis, Mar. 28 and Apr. 27, 1949 (JHR and Holden archives).

103. N. Sayre, tape; alumni recollections, first Boston area history session; J. Holden, in interview with SML; Hugh MacDougall, Jr., letter to SML, Jan. 24, 1984; Edward Yeomans, Jr., letter to SML, Sept. 30, 1985.

104. See also John Holden, letter to M. C. McIntosh, Apr. 22, 1949, on union's suggestions to students "that they defy the authority of the school."

105. M. C. McIntosh, letter to John Holden, Apr. 29, 1949.

106. CH, in interview with SML.

107. CH, letter to parents, Mar. 23, 1949; JHR archives, which contain work-load questionnaires; correspondence with six other school heads about salary scales and tenure arrangements; information gathered on retirement systems; estimated salary increase figures for the new pay scale (a 50 percent increase was projected), and the final draft of the contract, signed May 18, 1949.

108. See also Anne Holden's notes for minutes of Putney School, Inc., board of directors, Apr. 24 and June 26, 1949.

109. The letter written for Bret Harte is typical. "It is in this that he had been so excellent, the teaching of Ancient and Mediaeval history. He makes these subjects very vivid to the students with his wit, good teaching methods and rich background. He is really a person who has gifts out of the ordinary." The next day, Mrs. H. wrote GBH himself a note, thanking him for offering to let the school rent his house. See also Goodman, letter to SML, and Goodman-CH exchange in JHR archives.

110. CH and Warren Leonard, John and Anne Holden, to SML, personal communications.

111. CH, letter to Ray Rice, 1951, written when she was trying to hire him back.

112. Ray Rice, Gabriel Jackson to SML, personal communications. See also G. Jackson, *A Historian's Quest*, introductory chapter, "The Discovery of a Mission" (New York: Knopf, 1969), p. 9.

113. Union teacher in telephone interview with SML, June 29, 1985.

114. Conversations with former teachers; CH, in recommendation letter for M. Bartlett (director's

file); the other teacher joined the Phillips Exeter Academy faculty the following year. CH, in interview and conversation with SML; alumni recollections. Bill Hinton describes the strike as the most painful episode in his mother's life (quoted by Wallace, "Carmelita Hinton at 82," p. 30). Marisa Lederer has also commented on what she heard of the strike's effect on CH when she arrived in 1949 (interview with M. S. Shaw, May 1985).

115. John Holden, quoted by Wallace, "Carmelita Hinton at 82"; Wallace, ibid., E. Gray to SML; Questionnaires and other recollections from 1952–58 alumni; CDR, MS, pp. 5–6.

116. *Putney Alumni News,* May 1950.

117. CH, in 1981 interview with SML; JHR in first Boston history session ("She doesn't even understand it to this day").

118. Wallace, "Carmelita Hinton at 82," p. 30; Thomas Wendel, letter to SML, June 7, 1985.

119. Stepha Gerassi, in interview with SML, Mar. 11, 1983; Ed and Mabel Gray, in interviews with SML; Joseph Schaaf, conversation with SML, June 26, 1982; Peter Caldwell, letter to SML, Feb. 22, 1985; Barbara Rockwell Henry, in interview with SML, Aug. 1983.

Part IV. Learning Endurance: 1949–1965

1. The concept of density of purpose is Arthur G. Powell's. See A. G. Powell, Eleanor Farrar, and David K. Cohen, *The Shopping Mall High School: Winners and Losers in the Educational Marketplace* (Boston: Houghton Mifflin, 1985).

Chapter 9. The Pioneers Dig In

1. From Antioch booklet "We, THE COMMUNITY" and Antioch College Faculty Manual.

2. CH, penciled comments in "Reorganization" folder.

3. F. Pereira, letter to CH, Nov. 28, 1949; letter from Robert Gannett (Putney's local lawyer) to J. Holden, Aug. 3, 1949; correspondence between Mark Lauter and Gannett, winter 1950. See also CH, letter to Mark Lauter, Nov. 29, 1949, on the parent hecklers.

4. Dexter Strong (headmaster of Pomfret School at this time), letter to CH quoting M. C. McIntosh and describing his similar views, Nov. 29, 1949; idem, conversation with SML, Oct. 1984.

5. CH, in interview with SML; R. Brett, in interview with SML; R. Brett, at memorial service for CH.

6. R. Brett, in interview with SML; also Arms, MS, vol. 2.

7. Corporate Charter of The Putney School and By-Laws, 1950. R. Brett, letter to Sue Mulcahy, Jan. 7, 1980.

8. CH, letter to M. Lauter, Dec. 17, 1949; CH, memo to faculty and staff, Jan. 1959 (referred to in Administrative Council minutes).

9. See J. Caldwell's "Comparison of 1941–42 and 1952–53," report requested by the trustees.

10. J. Arms, letter to M. Coolidge, Aug. 1951. See also an editorial by two work campers in the 1947 *Putney Weeder.*

11. The trustees Executive Committee minutes for Dec. 8, 1956 offer an example of the trustees acting in their advisory capacity.

12. T. Wendel in *Putney Post,* Fall 1981.

13. Marisa Lederer, in interview with Margot Sproul Shaw, May 1985; idem, faculty/staff questionnaire.

14. Many faculty/staff and alumni questionnaires; Ted Dodd, interviews of present faculty, May 1985.

15. Many faculty/staff and alumni questionnaires; interviews of former faculty and staff; Boston area history sessions.

16. Undated article, "What Is a Socialist?" by Jeffrey Campbell in a 1955–56 *Putney Review.* See also Stephen Sachs, tape.

17. Questionnaires from 1940s and '50s alumni; conversations with teachers and alumni.
18. Caldwell, "Comparison of 1941–42 and 1952–53"; comparative staff salary figures gathered from nine boarding schools in 1952 by the Administrative Council (minutes of Administrative Council and trustees' meetings, 1951–56, and school files).

    Charles Brickley, assistant director and academic dean from 1962 to 1985, says that the relatively strong financial position of the staff was a temporary phenomenon. Staff salaries soon lagged behind again.
19. Other sources are George Finckel, interview about Mrs. H.; Wendel in *Putney Post*; Wendel, faculty questionnaire and letter to SML, June 7, 1985; Jeffrey Campbell in *Putney Post*, Spring 1982; men and women teachers' faculty questionnaires and interviews.
20. Treasurer's report to Administrative Council and Board of Trustees, Oct. 23, 1953. CH, reports to board, June 1952, June 1954. See also Doris and MacNiven Conard, in interview with Judy Gregory.
21. Ayer School Survey, 1948–50. The problem was most acute in girls' schools.
22. From introduction to late 1950s questionnaire submitted to eighty students at Hebron Academy and Putney School, part of a research project in democratic values, author unnamed.
23. Up from 2.4 in 1959. Director's report to trustees, June 1956, and June 1960; admissions reports, 1959–61. In 1952, Harvard's President Conant, speaking to the American Association of School Administration proposed an end to the nation's "dual system of education." See also James B. Conant, *Education and Liberty: The Role of Schools in a Modern Democracy* (Cambridge: Harvard University Press, 1953).
24. Trustees' Executive Committee minutes, Dec. 6, 1952; author's recollections.
25. Informal research on parent occupations done by admissions and alumni offices, 1960–65.
26. By 1964, this difference had widened for each of the four schools sampled (Kent and St. Paul's schools and the two Phillips academies, Exeter and Andover). For example, the figures for Putney, versus those for Phillips Exeter Academy, with its $35 million endowment, were

Exeter tuition	$2,100
Exeter real cost	$3,500
Putney tuition	$3,000
Putney real cost	$2,650

    St. Paul's real costs were $4230, its tuition $2100.
27. Alumni office count of occupations made in 1970.
28. Administrative Council minutes, Oct. 25, 1952, Oct. 31, 1953, Sept. 14, 1954. Trustees' Executive Committee minutes, June 19, 1954.
29. Apparent from all council minutes, 1950–65; trustees' minutes, Oct. 26, 1963, Oct. 24, 1964, Oct. 23, 1965, May 21, 1966.
30. R. Brett, in interview with SML; idem, report to trustees, June 20, 1953.

Chapter 10. Looking Outward

1. Peter Gill, in interview with Margot Sproul Shaw; many alumni recollections; CH, Sunday meeting speech to students on Putney Mountain, June 7, 1953.
2. Armstrong, "Privilege and Productivity," pp. 168, 125–26.
3. Alumni figures courtesy of Mary Hamilton (Brearley), Betty Terry (Exeter), and Putney School alumni office; see also C. F. Armstrong, "Privilege and Productivity." Statistical bases for all three schools are not quite complete.
4. CH, report to faculty about Jan. 1954 trip to West Coast.
5. CH, in interview with SML; remarks in several Administrative Council minutes.
6. E. Hamilton, letter to CH, spring 1952. Author's visit to Sheffield Hamilton farm, 1951.
7. Hamilton letter.

8. Ibid; former Little School parents, in conversation with SML.

9. Letters: E. H. Erikson to CH, Nov. 29, 1952; Goodwin Watson (professor at Teachers College) to CH, Dec. 2, 1952; T. E. Dewey to CH, Dec. 6, 1952. See also letter "to whom it may concern" from Benjamin Spock, M.D., May 17, 1948, submitted by A. E. Hamilton.

10. E. Hamilton letter; A. E. Hamilton, letter to CH, Nov. 17, 1952.

11. No reason except Mrs. Hamilton's serious back problems was given for her resignation. Putney teachers whose children attended the Little School in 1953–54 say that Ranger and her assistant teacher ran a good school, even though no parent agreed with every aspect of her philosophy. (SML's conversations with B. Rockwell Henry, Warren Leonard, C. Hinkle, Sept. 1985).

12. C. Brickley does not recall any FBI presence in 1949, but three alumni do.

13. Edward Yeomans, Jr., A Teacher's Odyssey, p. 109; E. Yeomans, letters to SML, Nov. 12, 1983, Aug. 19, 1985.

14. Introduction, "To Live as a Teacher," catalogue of the Putney Graduate School of Teacher Education, second and final version.

15. R. Brett, in interview with SML; SML's recollections of Brett's remarks in trustees' meetings; trustees' minutes, June 16, 1956.

16. CH, in interview with SML; Morris Mitchell, to Administrative Council, Jan. 30 and Nov. 20, 1951; to trustees' Executive Committee, May 11, 1952, Mar. 28, 1953; letter to Carol Crofut, Aug. 10, 1953; letter to CH, Aug. 22, 1952. The low point was five students in 1956–57.

17. The difficulties are shown very clearly in the Administrative Council/trustee review of graduate school after a three-year trial (minutes, 1952–53).

18. Former Putney Graduate School student letters, 1951–53; alumni conversations with SML.

19. Administrative Council minutes, Feb. 13, 1951; former faculty, in interviews with SML; Arms, MS, "1950–51." Also W. Leonard, "Thoughts on a Graduate School," memo to CH and R. Brett, Mar. 23, 1953; folder of Putney teachers' letters evaluating Putney Graduate School, Mar. 1953.

20. Many alumni recollections, especially those of Stephen Sachs and Richard McIntosh.

21. Trustees' minutes, May 18, 1963, May 22, 1964.

22. Stephen Sachs, tape; Morris Mitchell, letter to CH, Aug. 22, 1952, and in Sunday meeting talk, spring 1952.

23. A 1951 survey of 314 Brattleboro adults, selected at random. Lukas led eight younger pollsters in the project.

24. Administrative Council minutes, Oct. 20, 1953, Apr. 20 and 27, 1954.

25. Time, Aug. 9, 1952, quoting "last week's Brattleboro Reformer"; see also Brattleboro Reformer, July 28, 1954; New York Times, July 28, 1954; and letter to New York Times, Aug. 4, 1954, from William Hinton.

26. Boston Globe, July 28, 1954.

27. R. Brett to Executive Committee, July 29–Aug. 5, 1954; Boston Post, Rutland Herald, New York Times, July 28, 1954; letter written by former Putney teacher to CH, early Aug. 1954; R. Brett, letter to CH, Aug. 16, 1954.

28. W. Hinton, letter to R. Brett, Aug. 23, 1954.

29. Questionnaire from 1940s alumnus; Ray Goodlatte, in interview with Sue Mulcahy; Peter Caldwell, letter to SML, Aug. 1, 1985; first Boston area history session; Mark Lauter, in interview with SML. Only four direct printed attacks on Putney School are recorded in the school files; all of these were made in the National Republican, according to a trustee (minutes, Oct. 23, 1954).

30. John Wirth, letter to SML, May 30, 1984; both New York City area history sessions.

31. See Eaton, American Federation of Teachers, pp. 157–91.

32. Tyack, Lowe, and Hansot, Hard Times, p. 155. Dren Geer, address.

33. M. and D. Conard, in interview with J. Gregory.

34. A. Trowbridge, in conversation with SML, Oct. 1985. 1980s Manhattan Country School,

publications, two parents, and a sponsor (Erik H. Erikson) confirm the general facts given. See also CH, letters to A. Trowbridge, May 1, 1973, Apr. 28, 1980.

35. Director's files; also Arms, MS, and Karen Goodlatte, in interview with Sue Mulcahy.

36. Letters in "Successor Business" file.

37. CH, speech to students, 1953.

38. Pamela Daly Vose, *The Masters School: A Retrospective Portrait, 1877–1977* (The Masters School, 1977); conversations with Valeria Knapp, director of the Winsor School from 1951 to 1963, Virginia Dean, of St. Paul's School, and other school administrators active in the 1950s. See also Betty Friedan's popular and useful polemic, *The Feminine Mystique* (New York: W. W. Norton, 1963).

39. CH to trustees, June 1955.

40. From six out of eight faculty members who arrived between 1949 and 1955, interviewed by SML and others; CH, Ed Gray, and Larry Titus, in interviews with SML; alumni questionnaires; conversations with parents; letter to CH from parent and faculty husband, Feb. 8, 1954, in "Successor Business" file.

41. CH, speech to students, 1953; Ray Goodlatte, in interview with Sue Mulcahy; A. Thomas, faculty/staff questionnaire; see also Morris Mitchell, in *Ben Rockwell, 1915–1974*, Memorial to H. Benson Rockwell, ed. Barbara Breasted Whitesides, 1974: "It was generally understood that Ben would like to succeed Carmelita."

42. Letter to CH, Apr. 20, 1954, in "Successor Business" file. See also seniors' comments on good teaching (JHR archives).

43. Comments volunteered by four faculty members and Hugh and Trudy MacDougall; conversations with alumni.

44. Questionnaires from 1953 and 1955 alumni.

45. Described in a poem in honor of CH by Steven Sachs.

46. Clipping folder, undated (context suggests Oct. 1954). In addition to New England papers' stories on CH's retirement, the *New York Times* ran an announcement and the San Francisco *Chronicle* a story.

47. R. Brett, in interview with SML; 1956 letter from CH to Joseph Fineman. John Wirth, letter to SML, Feb. 2, 1986, on influence CH inevitably held with her remaining campus land. C. Brickley says that CH's major influence was exercised in 1969 and 1974, when new heads of Putney School were being chosen.

48. CH, article about her work in the *Putney Post*, Feb. 1959.

49. Alumni recollections of CH at peace demonstrations; Wallace, "Carmelita Hinton at 82"; CH, in interview with SML; author's recollections.

50. Wallace, ibid.; conversations with alumni who had visited CH.

Chapter 11. Turning Points

1. From interviews with R. Hodgdon, CH, and other former faculty and trustees; Jock Glidden, tape. Wesley and October Frost, in interview with SML, Feb. 8, 1986; several faculty and alumni recollections on persistent (though underplayed) theme of Rockwells' privileged background.

2. H. Benson Rockwell (HBR) to trustees, Oct. 22, 1956; William James, *Pragmatism*, Lecture #6 (New York: Longmans, Green, 1907), p. 201.

3. CH, speaking at memorial service for HBR; her exact words are, "He was modest to the point where at times it was a real detriment to him." See also Charles Brickley on CH and Ben Rockwell: "They were so unlike" (from interview with Anne Jafferis, spring 1985).

4. Many recollections of former faculty and students; especially Peggy James, in interview with Ted Dodd, spring 1985.

5. Quotation from HBR, speech in memoriam for Elizabeth Burns, *Putney Post*, June 1969. See

also catalogues, 1955–69; Barbara Rockwell Henry, in interview with SML, Aug. 1984; William Hunt and Peggy James, in interviews with Ted Dodd; interview with Joseph Schaaff; Marisa Lederer, interview and HBR memorial service talk; Allen Shawn, speaking at memorial service for HBR; other faculty and student recollections.

6. Joyce Richardson, speaking at memorial service for HBR.

7. Dexter Strong and C. McIntosh, in conversation with SML; two letters in "Successor Business" file.

8. B. Rockwell Henry, F. Pereira, and CH, in interviews with SML; R. Brett at memorial service for HBR; two alumni (also parents of Putney students) on questionnaire.

9. Ten-page letter to HBR from Reed Harwood, M.D., Oct. 1955; faculty recollections.

10. Article by Patty Parmalee in *Putney Review*, Mar. 10, 1956.

11. The Sight Point farm and Mrs. Hinton's own farm nearby continued to be used by Putney-related groups, most notably for a camp directed by JHR from 1962 to 1984.

12. Ray Goodlatte, "A Salute to Ben on His Departure from Putney," June 1969.

13. Robert Mills, in interview with Laura Heller, Apr. 8, 1985.

14. $24 is a conservative estimate of 1964–65 expenses, the highest for the period under study. It includes $850 paid for equipment, transportation, and referees, one-third of John Caldwell, Jr.'s salary, Caldwell's estimated salaries for other faculty coaches, and facilities maintenance, much of it done by student labor. Precise comparison of Putney athletic expenses for 1964–65 is made with those of Kent School and Phillips Academy, Andover. Of the two, Kent's costs were the higher ($71 per student excluding coaches' salaries and facilities maintenance), Andover's the lower ($65 per student). If Andover's facilities expenses are added, the total comes to $75 per student; $2073 was spent just on adhesive tape in 1964–65 to keep the Andover athlete on the go.

15. R. Mills, in interview with Laura Heller; dozens of other student and teacher recollections.

16. From photocopied collection of HBR's speeches and notes for speeches.

17. Elinor Lander Horwitz, "The Putney Experience," in *McCall's* (1968).

18. B. Rockwell Henry, in interview with SML.

19. Santiago Leon and almost half of other alumni who comment on HBR in questionnaires; interviews with teachers, especially J. Schaaf, Marisa Lederer, W. Hunt.

20. Conversations with alumni, second New York area history session; Marisa Lederer, both at HBR memorial service and in interview; alumni questionnaires, especially Jock Glidden, Santiago Leon, and K. G. Fetka: "So many of us loved Ben."

21. Interviews with teachers; Trudy MacDougall, in interview with SML, Nov. 1981.

22. G. Carow, Midge Brecher, and other teachers, in interviews and conversations.

23. Alumni questionnaires; first and second New York area history sessions.

24. Conversations with former trustees; Administrative Council minutes. "Enrollment problems" were initially the words used to cover the camp's tendency constantly to attract a clientele of 90–120 campers overwhelmingly from the New York area.

25. HBR's concept of a head's responsibility to maintain distance from teachers and staff is confirmed by C. Brickley and other faculty. HBR's self-sacrificing effort is attested to by information from the Boston area history session; alumni questionnaires; interview with Hester and John Caldwell; conversation with Gael Rockwell Minton.

26. From interview with R. Hodgdon and conversation with Rockwell-era trustees and teachers.

27. See the Conards' and other former teachers' comments on HBR's improvements, trustees' and Administrative Council minutes, 1955–56, 1956–57.

28. E. Gray, in interview with SML. C. Brickley writes (to SML, September 1985) that over time, faculty salaries failed to keep up with increases made by other schools. "The NEASC [New England Association of Schools and Colleges] evaluation team called us on it in 1968."

29. M. Leconte, faculty/staff questionnaire.

30. See especially Mac Conard in interview with J. Gregory; Marisa Lederer at HBR memorial

service. The faculty let the faculty manual lapse in 1964 because they no longer needed it, they felt, to guarantee their welfare.

31. See especially Ray and Karen Goodlatte, in interview with Sue Mulcahy, and S. Leon, questionnaire.

32. HBR to trustees, minutes, June 15, 1967.

33. Lovat Cooper-Ellis, in reports to Administrative Council and trustees. The exact increase in first-year college enrollments: 580,000 (29 percent of 18-year-olds) in 1954, 1.2 million (44 percent in 1964.

34. See Conant, *Education and Liberty*, and *The American High School Today* (New York: McGraw-Hill, 1959); Arthur Bestor, *Educational Wastelands: The Retreat from Learning in Our Public Schools* (Chicago: University of Illinois Press, 1953).

35. "International languages" from CH, MS of article in *Progressive Education*, 1944. A sample of the 1961 senior class shows what enrollment in daytime arts courses was like. Over half had taken two years of arts or more, while only seven had taken no arts courses. Seniors' comments also testify to the arts' importance ("Good Teaching" file).

36. R. Spry Campbell, in interview with Elena Dodd. Three alumni remember the same incident. Marya Huseby, Ray Goodlatte, and W. Hunt describe similar conflicts.

37. Caldwell, "Comparison of 1941–42 and 1952–53."

38. Victoria Bryer Robertson, in interview with SML, spring 1982.

39. "Good Teaching" comments and alumni questionnaires pinpoint the "bright spots"; also, R. Mills, "Land Use at Putney," *Putney Post*, Dec. 1963; alumni questionnaires.

40. First Boston area history session. Most years, however, engineering buffs could find some evening activity that interested them—and skilled adult to help make the best of shoestring budgets.

41. Ibid.; alumni questionnaires; curriculum reports.

42. Amy Pudleiner was the teacher who lobbied hardest for the language laboratory equipment. The laboratory was launched in 1962–63.

43. Especially questionnaires from 1958 and 1963 alumni; "Good Teaching" comments on post-strike English teachers.

44. About half of all alumni who mention academics or classroom teachers have a strong opinion on the teaching of writing at Putney, whether positive or negative. This is shown especially from the first New York area history session (source of quotation).

45. Wesley Frost, in interview with SML, about unsupervised neophytes and the excessive informality of teacher evaluations. John Stickler's journal speaks of C. Brickley. Not all 1950s and '60s student comment on history teachers' high expectations is favorable. Hester and John Caldwell, in interview with Laura Heller.

46. See college advisor files, by 1960 thick with records of less well-known colleges visited by both students and advisor; also advisor's reports to HBR and trustees, June 18, 1960, Feb. 5 and Dec. 1, 1962. Arms MS, p. 21; alumni recollections.

47. David Tyack, then assistant freshman dean at Harvard College, in mid-1950s conversation with SML. Records of the in-house study to which Tyack referred are not available, but Dean Whitla, Office of Research and Evaluation, Harvard University, who has also been involved in Harvard College admissions, says that "Putney has always been a special case by any measure" (phone conversation with SML, Nov. 22, 1985). The original synthesis of studies comparing the college careers of private and public school graduates, "Personalities of Public and Private School Days," was written by Charles McArthur. (*Harvard Educational Review* 24 [Fall 1954]). The studies show that "public school students consistently achieve higher college grades than do boys with a private school background" (p. 256). However, in the informal 1950s Harvard study, Putney graduates showed up as one of the few exceptions among private school graduates. Instead, they followed the public school students' pattern (author's recollection).

48. CH. MS for 1944 article in *Progressive Education* and notes for speeches; Arms MS, p. 21;

alumni recollections. See also alumni questionnaires; parents' comments; John Wirth, letter to SML, about student work load.

49. "Good Teaching" comments; Wesley Frost to SML.

Chapter 12. Students: Notes from the Underground

1. Alumnae, in conversation with SML; questionnaires from five male and seven female alumni.
2. Questionnaires from 1950s alumni; HBR, commencement speech, 1961; "Good Teaching" criticisms of teacher favoritism.
3. Student journal; student letter home, Oct. 1955.
4. Wesley Frost, in interview with SML. Questionnaires from 1950s alumni.
5. Jock Glidden, tape, Sept. 1985. See also Steve Sachs, tape.
6. Questionnaires from 1940s and 1960s alumni; Sayre, "Boarding in Heaven"; David Matthes, letter to SML about his brother Ted, Jan. 16, 1984.
7. J. Dewey, "My Pedagogic Creed" (E. L. Kellogg, 1897); first Boston area history session; S. Sachs.
8. Student and faculty recollections of the May 1959, "riot." J. Schaaf, in interview with SML; first New York area history session; Allen Shawn, at HBR memorial service. A 1950s alumnus recalls the power of the Putney *situation*: a community "based on utopian notions—and we were invited to be responsible for it."
9. Questionnaires from 1940s alumni; second New York area history session; W. Leonard, letter to SML, Aug. 1985; conversations with 1950s and '60s alumni.
10. Two years' enrollment statistics show both Putney's contented reliance on old connections and its efforts to reach for new ones (see table). In 1960–61 students came from twenty-four different states and six foreign countries. The geographical distribution was similar in 1964–65.
11. Alumni questionnaire; alumni reminiscences. See also Ed Shore, in interview with A. Jafferis, on Langi's first passage halfway around the world from Tonga to the U.S.
12. R. Small, in interview with SML; CDR, MS; memo by John Holden.
13. The three or four blacks gradually became seventeen by 1968. In 1963, the Putney admissions staff linked itself with the National Scholarship Service and Fund for Negro Students, and in 1965 with ABC (A Better Chance).
14. Questionnaires from 1950s, and '60s alumni; conversations with alumni.
15. Sayre, "Boarding in Heaven"; questionnaires from 1950s and '60s alumni; letter from Philip Hofer to Mrs. V. Knowles, June 3, 1960.
16. First and second New York area history sessions; alumni questionnaires. Material from next two paragraphs from same sources. Wesley and October Frost, in interview with SML, on isolation of some Putney town students; CDR, MS. Contrary views include that of a one-year senior who had taken all the math his suburban high school offered and came to Putney for AP calculus and advanced science, and dozens of similar positive comments (though fewer from 1960s alumni).
17. First and second New York area history sessions; alumni questionnaires; see also Sayre, "Boarding in Heaven"; Arms on "broken homes," MS, "1950–51"; admissions office records available

Analysis of Putney School Student Body

	Alumni Children	(Former) Faculty/ Staff Children	Sibling Pairs	Alumni Siblings	Boys	Girls	Total
1960–61	8	11	28	49	98	88	186
1964–65	14	15	26	45	101	91	192

in 1962; second Boston area history session; and O. Frost, interview; JTK, letter to SML, Dec. 27, 1985.

18. Personal experience, qualified by NAIS *Bulletins*, 1950–65, research in archives of Phillips and Abbot academies, and conversations with teachers, school and college administrators, school physicians, and psychiatric advisors over the years. There is not a single article on counseling in the NAIS *Bulletins* or a single workshop on the topic at NAIS annual conferences between 1953 and 1964. In April 1952, the *Bulletin* reported on a survey of the 265 New England and Middle Atlantic independent boys' college preparatory schools on the subject of "guidance," to which 86 percent had replied. At that time, educational and college admissions guidance was offered by all schools, but fewer than half ever called in a psychologist or psychiatrist. Robert Masland, M.D., of Boston Children's Hospital Adolescent Unit, confirms boarding schools' reluctance to offer adequate counseling and psychiatric referrals through the early 1960s, also attested to in James Heyl, M.D., "Medical Practice in a Boarding School" (1974 MS), "Chapter for a Textbook on Adolescent Medicine." Heyl was school physician at Exeter through the 1950s and '60s. He reports that a highly respected, long-tenured dean of students used to tell teachers in the 1950s that no adult should ever ask a youngster under sixteen about his parents. The respectability of counseling in boarding schools gradually increased as Dana Farnsworth's work in the Harvard Bureau of Study Counsel became known among secondary educators. The advent of the annual Northfield Conferences on counseling in June 1964 finally broke the ice among many resistant educators. Even so, progress has been slow, and counseling dilemmas continue in almost every school.

19. John Coolidge to SML, personal communication, 1985; author's recollections of trustees' meetings, 1958–70. "It's risky" quotation is from author's recollections, and Marisa Lederer, speaking at memorial service for HBR. In 1966, friends of Putney School were still trying to persuade the school to find ready access to psychiatric help (letter from Hans Huessy, M.D., to HBR, Mar. 18, 1966). After 1966, reliable psychiatric help was frequently arranged in Brattleboro.

20. Questionnaire from 1940s alumna.

21. J. Fineman speaking in second Boston area history session. Source of preceding quotations is questionnaires from 1950s and '60s alumni. All material following is taken from Fineman's journal and memorabilia folder.

22. Albert Newlin, letter to his family, Oct. 29, 1953. At least twelve other alumni have mentioned Ives Hendrick's death in alumni questionnaires, letters, and history sessions.

23. *Putney Magazine*, Dec. 1953; Jane Arms's folder on memorial to Ives (poetry books for the library); J. Fineman, letter to his mother, Oct. 28, 1953.

24. Fineman, journal; several discussions recorded in minutes of Administrative Council, winter and spring 1954. See also letter from Dr. Hendricks to Albert Newlin, June 7, 1954.

25. Questionnaire from 1950s alumnus. CH elaborated on this theme in a letter she sent to all Putney parents following the suicide, Nov. 1953.

26. CH, in interview with SML; author's recollections of trustees' meetings, 1965–69; R. Brett, in interview with SML.

27. See especially Alan R. Blackmer, *An Inquiry into Student Unrest in Independent Schools* (Boston: National Association of Independent Schools, 1970), and Peter S. Prescott, *A World of Our Own: Notes on Life and Learning in a Boys' Preparatory School* (New York: Coward-McCann, 1970), especially chapters "Choate Goes to Pot," "Bad Times," and "Dangerous Times."

28. See John Dewey, "The Conception of Freedom" in *How We Think*, p. 256.

29. Teacher recollections; H. and G. Leon, in interview with SML; R. Chave, tape; second Boston area history session.

30. Questionnaires from 1950s and '60s alumni; first New York area history session. Eleven alumnae have volunteered that a few teachers did listen and help. These particularly mention Libby Mills and Marisa Lederer.

31. Second New York area history session; questionnaires from 1960s alumni.
32. Second Boston area history session.
33. Barbara Rockwell Henry, in interview with SML; other teacher recollections.
34. Conversations (1985–86) with Cary Potter, Mrs. William G. Saltonstall, Virginia Dean, trustees of three boys' schools that became coeducational in the 1970s, and others suggest that Putney's direct influence on the development of coeducation was minimal. Most were following the Ivy League colleges' examples in trying to enlarge shrinking applicant pools. However, the teachers and principals consulted say they looked to Putney's methods of carrying out coeducation for reassurance and guidance once the decision had been made.

Faculty and Staff,
Putney School,
1935–1965

Frank Adams, Truck Driver, Receiving Clerk, Kitchen-Diningroom Unit (KDU), 1941–44
Gunilla Akerrin, Dormitory Supervision, 1957–58
Harry Amidon, Kitchen Assistant, 1943–48
Nancy Amidon, House Staff Assistant, 1938–39
Florence Angell, Library, 1942–49
James K. Angell, English, College Requirements, 1942–49
Patrick Archer, In charge of Student Household Jobs, 1953–54
Jenaro Artilles, Spanish, 1947–50
Jane Arms (Kelly), Latin, English, History, 1935–46, 1953–55
Ruth Atwood, House Staff, 1944–46
Katharine Augustinowicz, Secretary, 1949–53
Theodore Augustinowicz, Riding Instructor, 1949–53
Robert Austin, Electrician, 1940–45
Irene Bailey, Cook, 1945–56
Roy Bailey, Chef, 1940–61
Lois Baker, Apprentice Teacher, 1946–47
Hans-Jurg Bally, German, Shop, 1949–50
Fritz P. Bargebuhr, German, Latin, 1948–49
Ernest Barlow, Night Watchman, 1937–40
Helen H. Barnard, American History, English, Geography, 1939–40, 1943–44
Oliver O'Connor Barrett, Sculpture, 1941–42
Eugene Barrows, Night Watchman, 1946–50
Mary Bartlett, Chemistry, Biology, 1948–52
Ralph Becherer, Shop, Crafts, 1953–54
Thelma Becherer, In charge of Housekeeping; Crafts, 1953–54
Charles E. Behr, Youth Hostel, Skiing, Ski tow, School Store, Maintenance, 1935–37
Charles Beveridge, History, 1956–57
Geraldine Biddle, Academic Secretary, 1949–56
Rollins Bishop, Night Watchman, 1950–51
David E. Black, Sculpture, 1950–51
Irene E. Blanchard, Secretary-Bookkeeper, 1947–49
Sally Blood, Secretary, 1948–51
Arthur W. Boatin, History, 1964–65

Dwight Boehm, American History, English, 1942–44
Verna Askey Boehm, Secretary, 1942–44
Patricia Bofricke, Little School, 1956–57
Jack Bolliger, Night Watchman, 1940–42
Lawrence W. Boothby, Physics, Mathematics, General Science, 1949–52
Howard Boyajian, Violin, Viola, 1960–61
Peer Brady, Farmer, 1954–56
Justin Brande, Farmer, 1945–46
Carolyn Bacon Brecher, Dance, 1962–67, 1973–74
John Brecher, Cello, 1962–69
Geoffrey Bret Harte, History, Photography, 1943–49
Charles N. Brickley, History; Assistant Director, 1949–86
Harvey Brigham, Clarinet, 1941–46
Eleanor Brinckerhoff, Office Assistant; In charge of Riding, 1941–42
Cecelia Brinton, Consulting Psychologist, 1940–48
Abigail Brown, English; Magazine, 1949–51
Emilia Bruce, Spanish, 1959–
M. Linn Bruce, Art, Activities, 1959–86
Dorothy Bugbee, Secretary, 1957–58
John Burnett, Heating and Plumbing, 1937–39
A. Clayton Burnham, Farm Manager, 1946–47
Donald Burns, Art, 1946–47
Elizabeth Burns, Head, Little School; Mathematics, 1954–66
Gale Burton, Mathematics, 6th and 7th Grade History, Director of Athletics and Skiing, 1941–42
Richard J. Bushey, Dance, 1960–62
Eugene Butler, Kitchen Assistant, 1943–45
Harris Buxenbaum, Athletics; General Science; Health and Personal Problems, 1946–49
Una Buxenbaum, History, Algebra, 1946–49
Marion Cabell, Office Assistant; Latin, 1937–41
Albert Calvert, Rhythms, Shop, 1937–38
Dorothy B. Caldwell, Secretary, 1952–60
Hester Caldwell, History, 1954–
John Caldwell, Jr., Mathematics; Head of Workjobs and Sports, Assistant to the Director, 1954–
John Caldwell, Business Manager and Treasurer, 1941–58
Jean Campbell (Dyer), Cook, 1944–59
Jeffrey W. Campbell, English; Magazine, 1951–83
Linnie Campbell, Cook, 1947–56
John R. Capper, English, 1965–66
George W. Carey, History, 1953–54
Jean Carey, Store Assistant, 1953–54
Mitchell B. Carey, M.D., School Physician, 1954–56
Phillip Carey, Maintenance Assistant, 1949–50
Carl Carlson, Blacksmith, 1944–55
Jeanette L. Carney, Housekeeper, 1948–49
Jeanne Sarraute Case, French; School Hostess, 1949–66
Charles Celto, Cook, 1937–38
Jean-Marie Chalufour, French, 1941–43, 1948–50
Charlotte Chambers, House Staff, 1940–42
Kimball Chambers, House Staff, 1940–42
Cherie Chao, Store Assistant, 1947–48

Jowett Chao, Chemistry, Geometry, General Science, 1947–48
Mary Chase, Flute, 1944–45
Philip Chase, Boys' Advisor; Summer Camp Leader; Lower School Boarding Department, 1937–42
Russell Chase, Herdsman, 1950–51
Sheila Chase, Herdswoman, 1949–50
Dorothy Churchill, Violin, Viola, Chamber Music, 1945–48
Minnie Wood Clark, Cook, 1935–40
Elizabeth McPherson Clarkson, In charge of Student Household Jobs; Inn Manager, 1940–41
Clayton Coane, Watchman, 1943–44
Faustina Codding, Housekeeper, 1945–46
Guy Codding, Cook, 1944–52
David Cole, Dormitory Head; Sports, 1953–55
Doris E. Conard, History, 1954–59
E. MacNiven Conard, Mathematics, Shop, 1954–59
Paul Cooper, Maintenance Assistant, 1950–52
Pepita Cooper, Spanish, Athletics, 1950–52
Robert H. Corey, History, 1945–48
Roger D. Coulombe, French, 1964–68
Hester Wentworth Crawford, Business Manager, Summer Camp Director, 1936–41
Leta Clews Cromwell, English, 1943–47
John Croston, Cook, 1943–44
David Davenport, Spanish, 1946–47
Hanley Daws, Violin, 1964–65
Ann Day, Secretary, 1947–48
Harold F. Dean, Physics, General Science, Shop, 1943–48
Margaret Dean, Director of Student Household Jobs, 1943–49
Oscar Hugh De Boyedon, Sculpture, 1944–45
Frederic Delzell, Piano, 1937–39
Celina Rotte De Neufville, French, 1935–36
D. C. DeWolfe, School Doctor, 1942–54
Donald Dickinson, Driver, Farm Worker, 1939–42
Dorothy Dickinson, House Staff, 1941–42
Camille Dodd, Secretary, 1953–55
Richard M. Doolen, History, 1959–61
Pauline F. Dort, Assistant Nurse, 1949–56
Herbert Drury, Biology, 1956–58
Leon Dubriske, Cook, 1939–40
Carol Dunbar, Flute, 1957–58
Bertha Dunn, Assistant Inn Manager, 1949–50
Marshall Dyer, Assistant to House Staff, 1949–53
Nancy Earle, Assistant in French, 1944–47
Richard Earle, Director of Athletics, General Science, 1944–47
Gregory Edson, Inn Manager, 1950–52
June Edson, Inn Manager, 1950–52
Lovat Cooper-Ellis, English, College Advisor, 1953–65
John V. Elmendorf, French, Spanish, Mathematics, 1941–43
Mary Elmendorf, Remedial Reading, social service projects, 1941–42
Mary Evans, English, Drama Assistant, Riding Instructor, 1954–57
Valentine Eyre, Russian, Shop, 1950–52
Nathalie J. W. Fallon, Riding, 1940–41

Trudy Feiss, Sculpture, 1960–61
Viola Fenton, Cook, 1937–38
George Finckel, Cello, 1939–50
Marianne Finckel, Piano, 1947–50
Pierre Fischer, Physics and Math-Physics, 1956–58
Françoise Fistick, Potter, 1949–51
Stanley Fistick, Potter, 1949–51
Thomas Flood, Kitchen Staff, 1941–42
Kelsey Flower, French, 1937–41
Angelo Franchini, Ancient and Mediaeval History, 1956–59
Mary Franchini, Reading Skills; Dormitory Head, 1958–59
Roger H. E. Franklin, Physics-Chemistry, Mathematics, 1958–66
Wesley T. Frost, History, 1962–64
Elizabeth Frothingham, Lower School; Book Binding, English, 1937–39
Margaret Gassett, Resident Nurse, 1944–45
Fernando Gerassi, Art, Resident Painter, 1949–53, 1953–68
Stepha Gerassi, Ancient and Mediaeval History, Spanish, Russian, 1949–68, 1976–77
Nancy Gibbs, Secretary-Bookkeeper, 1949–51
Jerre Gibson, Violin, 1962–64
James I. Gilbert, Art, Spanish, 1943–44
Peter Gill, Algebra, Geometry, 1946–48
Theodore Glabach, Farm Manager, 1944–46
Nancy McC. Glendenning, Dormitory Head; Work and Play Programs, 1952–54
Peter C. Goldmark, History, 1962–64
Karen Goodlatte, Library Assistant, Librarian, 1956–82
Raymond S. Goodlatte, English, Admissions, 1951–82
Robert P. Gordy, Drawing, Painting, Graphics, 1963–64
Nancy Grass, Secretary-Bookkeeper, 1949–51
Gideon Grau, Viola, Violin, 1949–50
Charles Gray, Head, Woods Crew, 1939–56
Edwin Gray, Superintendent of Buildings and Grounds; Farm Manager; Painter, 1935–67
Mabel Gray, Dietitian; Head of Housekeeping, 1935–41, 1947–48, 1955–72
Robert H. Gray, In charge of Athletics; Athletics and Work Jobs, 1962–63, 1966–71
Arthur Green, Poultry; Youth Hostel; English, 1935–40
William Green, Mathematics, 1943–45
Anna Rae Greenfield, Head of Kelly House, 1948–49
Richard Gregg, Mathematics, 1944–46
Doris Margaret Grigaut, French, 1940–41
Hubert Grigaut, French, 1939–41
Philip C. Gushee, Drama, 1964–66
Jack Guthrie, English, 1947–49
Georges Guy, History, French, 1949–50
Merton Leggett-Gwilliam, Art, Handicrafts, 1936–39
Eleanor Hamilton, Director, Little School, 1953–54
Genevieve Karr Hamlin, Sculpture (Putney Pottery, 1940s), 1943–44, 1945–47
Margaret Hanford, Flute, 1956–late 1970s
Charles H. Hapgood, Mediaeval and American History, French History and Literature, 1935–36
Anthony Hardy, Mathematics, 1952–53
Lois Harris, Store Manager, 1943–45
Paul Harris, Religious Education, 1943–45

Gerard A. Harrison, In charge of Athletics; Assistant Work Jobs Head; School Trips, 1951–53
Winifred Hartung, Secretary, 1953–54
Ruth Hathaway, R.N., Assistant Nurse, 1940–41
Werner Heider, History, Social Studies, Geography, 1939–44
Erick Heins, Farmer, 1950–51
Alfred E. Heller, English, 1954–56
Dorothy Hemingway, Academic Secretary; 1945–46
Pierre Henrotte, Violin, Orchestra, 1937–39
Bess Hieronymus, Piano, 1945–46
Lena W. Higgins, Cook, 1943–56
Emily Platt Hilburn, Dance; In charge of School Trips, 1953–55
Ray Hilburn, Mathematics, Dance, 1953–55
Bennett D. Hill, History, 1958–59
Sarah W. Hiller, Inn Manager, 1952–56
Cornelia Hinkle, Piano, Folk Dancing, Music, 1939–72
Norwood Hinkle, Music Director, Violin, Orchestra, 1939–72
Carmelita Hinton, Executive Head; Girls' Athletics, 1935–55
William Hinton, Farm Manager; 4-H Club, 1941–44
Ottilie Hirt, Academic Secretary; German, 1935–39
John T. Hitchcock, English, 1948–49
Patricia Hitchcock, In charge of Trips; Photographer; Secretary, 1948–49
Roscoe Hodgdon, Herdsman; Maintenance, 1937–78
Ruth Shattuck Hodgdon, Secretary-Bookkeeper, 1935–86
Irwin Hogenauer, Secretary, 1935–36
Anne Holden, Elementary School; Remedial Reading, Mathematics, 1936–51
Carlton Holden, Heating and Plumbing, 1939–40
John Holden, English, Arithmetic, Athletics, Farming, 1935–42, 1945–52
Stanely Hollis, In charge of Athletics; Work Jobs, 1936–66
Hans Hollstein, German, Horsemanship, 1937–40, 1949–52
Marion Hollstein, History, Latin, Summer Trips, 1950–52
Mary-Stewart Hoopes, Secretary, 1944–47
Claribel Glidden Houser, School Store and Tea Shop, 1940–41
Margrit Rosenstock-Huessy, German, 1935–36
Clyde Hulett, Farmer, Night Watchman, 1935–66
Ruby Hulett, House Staff, 1946–48
J. William Hunt, Drawing, Painting, Graphics, 1964–85
Helen Hurd, English, History, 1937–40
John Huwiler, Violin, Brass, 1950–53
Nan Ibberson, Secretary-Bookkeeper, 1946–47
Mitsue Ito, Inn Cook, 1944–45
Soze Ito, Inn Cook, 1944–45
Gabriel Jackson, English, Spanish, Flute, 1946–48
Adelaide Jahnes, Resident Nurse, 1946–48
Sally Jeffrey, Secretary, 1951–53
Lyda Jewett, Riding Mistress, Farmer, 1941–43
Vivian Johannes, English, Theater, 1937–38, 1947–49
Charlotte Jossman, Latin, Athletics; Academic Program, 1943–45, 1947–54
Elizabeth Jossman, Resident Nurse; Store, 1943–54
Dorothy June, Assistant Potter, 1950–51
Eleanor H. Kamys, Art, 1944–46

Walter J. Kamys, Art, 1944–46
Alan Kaufman, English, 1959–60
E. Doris Keener, Riding Instructor, 1946–47
Charles A. Kelly, Secretary, 1954–55
Jane Arms Kelly, Latin, English, History, 1935–46, 1953–55
Odd Willy Kilde, German, Shop, Soccer, Ski Instructor, 1952–53
Susan Kilde, Housekeeper; In charge of Student Household Jobs; Dining Room, 1952–53
Margaret Kinard, Secretary, 1943–44
John Klimas, Farmer, 1941–42
Barbara Knapp, Riding Instructor, 1956–57
Anthony Kray, Assistant to Edwin Gray, Buildings and Grounds, 1937–42
Margaret B. Laird, R.N., Resident Nurse, 1950–52
Eleanor Lasell, Drama Assistant, 1956–57
John W. Lasell, Jr., Drama, 1954–57
Ion Constantine Laskaris, Drama, English, 1957–63
Judith Laskaris, Library Assistant, 1963–64
Margaret Lawler, Modern and Folk Dancing, 1950–51
Winnie Lawrence, Secretary; School Post Office, 1957–58
Maurice Leconte, French, 1950–61
Patricia Leconte, Evening Activities, English, 1957–61
Felix Lederer, German, Latin, French, 1949–83
Marisa Lederer, Librarian, Italian, German, Admissions, 1949–
Su Jan Lee, History, 1955–56
Walter Lehmann, Wind Instruments, 1949–50
Lilla Leonard, Secretary, 1942–44
Marion Leonard, Elementary School; Alumni Secretary, Librarian, 1939–42, 1951–55
Warren P. Leonard, Mathematics; College Requirements; Assistant Head, 1939–42, 1945–55
Harold Leslie, Violin, 1938–39
Nardus Lessing, Cello, Piano, 1950–61
J. Stephen Lewis, Sculpture, Pottery, Metalry, Dance, 1940–41
James Lewis, Inn Assistant, Store Manager, 1954–56
Molly Lewis, Inn Assistant, 1954–56
Mariolyn Quast Lindstrom, Secretary; Dormitory Head; Modern Dance, 1943–44
Arthur Lithgow, English, Dramatics, 1940–43
Ingeborg Lincoln Lorenz, Store Manager, 1946–47
Polly Lusk, Riding Instructor, 1943–44
John Lynes, Clarinet, Brass, 1939–41, 1947–49
John P. McAuliffe, Cook, 1952–55
Martha McCall, Cello, Piano, 1961–62
Donald P. McCormick, English, 1949–51
Jean Campbell McCormick, Flute, 1949–52
Jean McCoy, Outdoor Staff Assistant, 1955–56
Roger McCoy, Herdsman, 1954–56
Charlotte P. MacDonald, Director's Secretary, 1949–56
Hugh MacDougall, Science, Shop, 1935–42
Ursula Cook MacDougall, English, History, Dramatics, 1935–42
Kay McKearn, Drama, 1937–38
Alice McLaughlin, Flute, 1937–40
Lansing Mallett, Herdsman, 1951–53
Dan Marangiello, Clarinet, Oboe, 1937–39

Donald Marburg, Assistant to Farm Manager, 1937–39
Pearl Marlborough, Assistant to House Staff, 1949–51
Samuel Martineau, Farm Manager, Jan.–Nov. 1947
George Mason, Naturalist, 1956–58
Florence Matthes, Postmistress, Dormitory Rooms Inspector, Assistant at Large, 1951–52
Muriel Mattos, Dance, Athletics, 1948–50
Paul Maxwell, Drama, Dance, 1952–53
Helen Mayberry, Cook, 1937–39
Carol Maynard, Farm Manager, Herdswoman, Horticulturalist, 1935–56
Mildren Mayo, Cook, 1937–40
Ching-Ying Lee Mei, Inn Manager, 1952–53
Georgia-Lee Melvin, Dormitory Head, 1959–60
William F. Melvin, English; In charge of Camping, 1959–67
Sylvia Mendenhall, Drama Assistant, 1948–49
Lee Bruce Menefee, Apprentice Teacher, 1946–49
Rose Miller, Cleaning, 1937–38
Elizabeth Mills, Library Assistant; Weaving, Human Behavior, Alumni Secretary, Dean of Students, 1960–
Robert C. Mills, Biology, Woodland Management, 1958–
Tyree Goodwin Minton, Land Use Coordinator; Biology, 1963–76
David Mintz, Drama Assistant, 1949–53
Aliette Misson, French, 1962–64
Barbara Jaynes Mitchell, Study Trip Director; Admissions Secretary, 1963–64
Morris Mitchell, Head, Teacher Training School, 1949–56
Jacques Montas, French, 1959–60
Maria Montas, Library Assistant, 1959–60
Charles Moore, Latin, Mathematics, 1937–39
Lorraine N. Moore, Piano, 1954–55
Joseph Morill, Night Watchman, 1944–53
Carol Tilden Morris, Sculptor; Mathematics, 1935–37, 1943–44
Daniel Morris, Mathematics, Science, Photography, 1935–43
Esther Kane Morris, Dormitory Head; Office, 1938–50
Thomas Morse, Carpenter, 1947–56
Mara Moser, Spanish, French, German, 1943–48
Louise Moyre, Flute, 1952–55
Ann Carol Mucherino, In charge of Dining Room, 1958–59
Louis J. Mucherino, Riding Instructor, 1957–59
John Nevins, Athletic Assistant, 1939–40
Charlotte Newton, Cook, 1939–40
Joseph Newton, Kitchen Helper, 1939–40
Mertie Nichols, Cook, 1941–42
John Nicholson, Wind Instruments, 1954–56
George Oates, Inn Manager, 1948–50
Margery Oates, Inn Manager, 1948–50
Martha Oberling, French, 1952–54
Ruth Olfene, Riding Instructor, 1947–48
Pierre Oppliger, French, 1943–45
Olga Orthmann, Switchboard Operator, Receptionist, 1956–57
John Otterson, Theater Technician, 1946–47
Monica Owen, English, Camp Director, 1944–45

Ernestine Pannes, Little School, 1958–59
Hilgard Pannes, Little School; Afternoon and Evening Activities, 1958–59
Mary Papielski, House Staff, 1949–63
Emma Parent, Secretary, 1955–56
John Parke, English, History of Art, 1939–40
Penelope Parke, Elementary School; Horsemanship, 1939–40
Dillwyn Parrish, Shop, 1939–40
Marian Parrish, English, Store, 1939–40
Elizabeth Peabody, Assistant in Athletics; Work Jobs, 1943–44
Bertha Pease, House Staff, 1952–55
Winifred Perry, House Staff, 1943–44
James Petrides, History, 1961–62
Norman Pettit, Riding Assistant, 1948–49
Alfred Pfanstiehl, Physics, Photography, Flute, 1945–49
Maria C. Phaneuf, Resident Nurse, 1935–43
Robert H. E. Phipps, Drawing; Painter, 1960–63
Toshiko T. Phipps, Evening Activities, 1962–63
Sophie Piluski, Cook, 1951–52
Sally Pomeran, Folk Dancing, Drama, 1951–54
Marjorie Popp, Bookkeeper, 1952–54
Joseph Post, Business Manager and Treasurer, 1958–
Amy Pudleiner, French, 1960–66
John Pullman, Biology, General Science, 1952–54
Albert Raffanel, French, 1946–49
Horace Reed, In charge of Teacher Training, Putney Graduate School; Biology, 1953–56
Annelotte Remak, Mathematics, Science, 1942–43
Elaine Reneau, Resident Nurse, 1948–49
Ralph Renzelman, Farmer, 1945–46
Kathryn A. Reynolds, Music, Piano, 1960–61
Charles Rice, Drama, Theater Technician, 1953–54
Miriam Rice, Sculpture, 1947–49
Raymond Rice, Art, 1947–49
Helene C. Richards, Secretary, 1942–43
Peter Richardson, Chemistry, Algebra, Athletics, Work Jobs, 1949–52
Elizabeth Riddle, Geometry, Algebra, 1948–49
Fritz Rikko, Piano, Violin, Viola, 1944–45
Herbert Roberts, Farmer, 1943–56
Addis Robinson, Painter, 1937–47
James Robinson, Outdoor Staff Assistant, 1955–56
Barbara Rockwell, In charge of Dormitories; Afternoon and Evening Activities, 1960–64
Henry Benson Rockwell, Admissions Head; History Executive Head, 1952–55, 1955–69
Eric Rogers, Assistant Head; Science, Math; In charge of College Requirements, 1937–40
Janet Rogers, English History, 1937–40
Olivina Root, House Staff Assistant, 1951–52
Julie Rosegrant, Library Assistant, Latin, Academic Secretary, 1942–69
Robert Gardner Rosegrant, Biology, History; Psychological Tests/Measurements; Boys' Advisor, 1942–60
Margrit Rosenstock-Huessy, German, 1935–36
Charlotte V. Sage, Hostess at Inn; House Director, 1935–36
Nathaniel Sage, Co-Director, Business Manager, 1935–36

Friedrich Sandels, Latin, Spanish, 1944–46
Josephine DeVane Sargent, Inn Manager, 1945–48
Dmitri Sazonoff, French, 1944–45
Julia Sazonova, French, Russian, 1944–46
Joseph Schaaf, Music, Violin, Viola, 1953–60, 1972–84
Ewald Schnitzer, History, Literature, Music, 1935–43
Paul Schulz, German, 1956–57
Elka Schumann, Russian, 1962–63
Peter Schumann, Puppetry Evening Activity, 1962–63
Gudrun H. Schutz, Violin, Chamber Music, 1961–62
Virginia Scott, Teacher, Little School, 1953–54
John Shaw, Cook, 1938–39
Olga Shimanovsky, Russian, French, 1947–50
Gunnar Shonbeck, Wind Instruments, 1939–42, 1946–47
Edward A. Shore, Mathematics, Chemistry, Physics, 1954–
Joan Shore, Teacher, Little School, 1954–56
Susan Skerry, R.N., Head Nurse, 1953–56
Dennis H. Small, Storeroom, Post Office, 1946–51
Ruth Small, Cook; In Charge of Dining Room, 1946–51
Edwin S. Smith, History, 1947–49
Laura Smith, Manager of Students' Household Jobs, 1939–40
Lloyd Smith, In charge of Evening Activities Program, 1952–53
Malcolm Smith, Physics, Math-Physics, 1952–56
Margaret Smith, Piano, Trombone, 1956–58
Marion L. Smith, Admissions Secretary, 1947–49
Ruth Smith, House Staff, Head of Work Jobs, 1940–41
Shirley Smith, Poultrywoman, 1943–44
Solomon Smith, History, 1964–67
Bertha Sneck, Resident Nurse, 1943–44
Harry Spaight, Cook, 1947–48
George Spencer, Secretary, 1947–48
Ralph Sprague, Cook, Carpenter, 1937–39
Harold Sproul, Music Director, Orchestra, Choral Group, Cello, 1935–39
Robin Spry, Sculpture, Ceramics, 1951–57, 1958–86
Winston Stanley, Farmer, 1944–45
Margaret Stasik, Housekeeper; In charge of Student Household Jobs, 1954–55
Richard Steele, Shop, 1937–38
Edward Steneck, Inn Staff Assistant, 1952–53
Isabel McL. Stephens, Advisor; In charge of Teacher Training at Graduate School; Mediaeval History, 1952–53
Rockwell Stephens, Public Relations, Admissions Committee, In Charge of Ski Program, 1952–53
Neil C. Stevens, M.D., School Doctor, 1935–46
William Stipe, Art, 1942–43
Charles Stoner, Mathematics, History, 1956–58
Blanche Strange, Secretary, 1945–47
Anna Sumner, House Staff, 1955–56
Tirzah Jane Sweet, Resident Head Nurse, 1946–49
Louis Tavelli, Art, 1954–56
Priscilla Thierry, Violin, 1947–48
Allan M. Thomas, English, 1949–50, 1951–53

Alan G. Thompson, Drama, Work Jobs, 1959–62
John Thompson, Wind Instruments, 1950–67
Sheila Thomson, Office Assistant; General Science, 1941–42
Laurence Titus, Farm Manager, 1948–56
Mary C. Titus, Remedial English, 1948–56
Patricia Towne, Assistant Inn Manager, 1950–51
Mary Lou Treat, Library Assistant, 1955–60
Robert Sherman Treat, In charge of Admissions; History, 1955–64
Edith S. Treuenfels, Mathematics, 1952–54
Beatrice Tyer, Riding Instructor, 1944–45
Elizabeth Ussachevsky, English, 1946–47
Vladimir Ussachevsky, Russian, Piano, 1946–47
Virginia Vitzthum, Academic Secretary, 1945–49
Ann Volkmann, Biology, 1951–55
Laurence Wade, Maintenance Assistant, 1952–54
Darrah Wagner, Little School, Mathematics, 1941–42
Anna Walsh, House Staff, 1944–46
Thomas Walsh, House Staff, 1944–46
Elizabeth Ware, Violin, 1935–36
Joan Strong Warmbrunn, English, 1945–47
Werner Warmbrunn, Chemistry, German, 1944–47
Elizabeth Washburn, Elementary School, 1940–41
Ann Watford, History, 1962–63
Henry Webb, Assistant, Buildings and Grounds; Mathematics, 1935–36
Thomas Wendel, History, 1949–54
Nancy West, Secretary; Spanish; Alumni Director, 1937–57
Addie Wheeler, Cook, 1940–41
Beverley White, English, Drama, 1943–51, 1962–71
Hazel Williams, Housekeeper, Admissions Secretary, 1944–56
Olwen Williams, Pottery, Biology, 1942–49
Flossie Willis, Kitchen Staff, 1941–56
H. Hubert Wilson, History, Student Work Jobs, 1940–42
Muriel Wilson, Office Assistant, 1940–41
John D. Wirth, History, 1959–61
Timothy Wirth, History, 1962–63
Alois Wood, Cook, 1955–56
Elma Wood, House Staff, 1941–43
Sarah Wood, House Staff, 1953–56
Annie V. Woods, R.N., Resident Head Nurse, 1949–50
Magda Woss, French, Spanish, 1939–40
Nancy Yeager, Piano, 1962–65
Edward Yeomans, Educational Advisor, 1935–42

Index